INTERACTIONS WITH
A VIOLENT PAST

INTERACTIONS WITH A VIOLENT PAST

Reading Post-Conflict Landscapes in Cambodia, Laos, and Vietnam

Edited by

Vatthana Pholsena and Oliver Tappe

NUS PRESS
SINGAPORE

INSTITUT DE RECHERCHE SUR L'ASIE DU SUD-EST CONTEMPORAINE
RESEARCH INSTITUTE ON CONTEMPORARY SOUTHEAST ASIA

Published by NUS Press in association with IRASEC

Published by:
NUS Press
National University of Singapore
AS3-01-02, 3 Arts Link
Singapore 117569

Fax: (65) 6774-0652
E-mail: nusbooks@nus.edu.sg
Website: http://www.nus.edu.sg/nuspress

ISBN 978-9971-69-701-3 (Paper)

National Library Board, Singapore Cataloguing-in-Publication Data

Interactions with a violent past: reading post-conflict landscapes in
Cambodia, Laos, and Vietnam / edited by Vatthana Pholsena and Oliver
Tappe. – Singapore: NUS Press, 2013.
p. cm.
ISBN: 978-9971-69-701-3 (pbk.)

1. Indochinese War, 1946–1954 – Vietnam. 2. Indochinese War, 1946–
1954 – Cambodia. 3. Indochinese War, 1946–1954 – Laos. 4. Vietnam War,
1961–1975. I. Vatthana Pholsena. II. Tappe, Oliver.

DS553.1
959 — dc23   OCN823473000

Cover image: Phonsavan, Xieng Khouang Province, Lao PDR, 2010 (Courtesy
of Oliver Tappe)

Printed by: Fabulous Printers

CONTENTS

LIST OF ILLUSTRATIONS

Maps

Tables

Plates

The editors and authors have resolved all copyright issues related to material in this publication. Unless otherwise stated, images are from the authors' personal collections.

ACKNOWLEDGEMENTS

This book originated from a panel on "Haunted Landscapes and Ambiguous Memories: Interactions with the Past in Laos, Vietnam and Cambodia" convened at the 6th EUROSEAS (European Association for South East Asian Studies) Conference in Gothenburg/Sweden in August 2010. The papers by Sina Emde, Susan Hammond, Vatthana Pholsena, Elaine Russell, and Oliver Tappe were presented at the panel. Christina Schwenkel and Krisna Uk, who were unable to make the trip to Gothenburg, stayed onboard for the ensuing production of this volume, which was further enriched by the contributions by Ian Baird and Markus Schlecker. We thank the Max Planck Institute for Social Anthropology (Halle, Germany) and the *Institut d'Asie Orientale* (Lyon Institute of East Asian Studies, CNRS-École normale supérieure de Lyon, France) for their funding of the panel. We are also pleased to acknowledge the support of IRASEC (Research Institute on Contemporary Southeast Asia, Bangkok, Thailand), especially in the final stages of preparing this book for publication.

We are grateful to Pierre Petit and Olivier Ducourtieux for their helpful comments during the panel's discussions, as well as two anonymous referees for their constructive and insightful ideas and suggestions. We very much appreciate Fred Branfman's encouraging messages that gave us an extra motivation to complete this publication. During the preparation of the manuscript, Vatthana Pholsena greatly benefitted from the supportive environment of the Department of Southeast Asian Studies at the National University of Singapore. Oliver Tappe wishes to express his gratitude to the Max Planck Institute for Social Anthropology and its director Chris Hann for their ongoing support to this project. Special thanks also go to cartographer Jutta Turner and to the valiant student assistants, Josefine Brauer and Katharina Ille, of the Max Planck Institute who put together the volume's index. At NUS Press, our gratitude goes to Paul Kratoska for wholeheartedly taking on this publication and Eunice Low for her kind and patient editorial support.

Vatthana Pholsena and Oliver Tappe
Singapore, and Halle, Germany
July 2013

Map 0.1 Field sites referred to by contributors in this volume.

The "American War," Post-Conflict Landscapes, and Violent Memories

Oliver Tappe and Vatthana Pholsena

As soon as the idea of a debt to the dead, to people of flesh and blood to whom something really happened in the past, stops giving documentary research its highest end, history loses its meaning.

— Paul Ricoeur, *Time and Narrative, Vol. III*
(Chicago, IL: University of Chicago Press, 1990), p. 118.

The history of the Second Indochina War (1961–75) — better known as the "Vietnam War" or, in Vietnam, as the "American War" — is a subject of continuous and important scholarship. The politics, diplomacy, and military operations occupy a prominent place in these studies, covering the American and, increasingly, Vietnamese dimensions of the war.[1] Less is known, though, about the impacts of warfare violence upon local societies and populations, including those in Laos and Cambodia, which are being felt to this very day.[2] This significant gap is surprising given that the number of war dead — civilians and soldiers alike — in Laos, Cambodia, and Vietnam during the conflict runs into the millions, including 1.7 million who died at the hands of the Khmer Rouge between 1975 and 1978. Covering localities and events that took place in the three countries, the nine chapters in this volume discuss the manifold legacy of these violent times — the complex aftermath of the war as manifest in the Cambodian, Lao, and Vietnamese scarred landscapes, and their inhabitants' everyday lives.

The Second Indochina War in Historical Perspective

From a Western perspective, the Vietnam War is often narrowed to the American military involvement in South Vietnam between 1965 and 1975 to prevent the collapse of the US-sponsored South Vietnamese government and the communist takeover of Vietnam. However, this Southeast Asian theater of the global Cold War extended beyond both North and South Vietnam, as war spilled over into Laos and Cambodia. The roots of this larger conflict date back to the end of the First Indochina War (1946–54) that marked the final days of the French rule in Southeast Asia and the subsequent independence of the royal governments of Laos and Cambodia confirmed by the Final Declaration of the Geneva Conference in July 1954. The latter also fatefully confirmed the (provisional) partition of Vietnam into a communist zone (ruled by the Democratic Republic of Vietnam; hereafter, DRV) in the north and a non-communist zone in the south (known as the Republic of Vietnam from its creation in 1955 until its fall in 1975). Once Vietnam had been divided at the 17th parallel by the 1954 Geneva Agreements, Laos shared borders with both North and South Vietnam, altogether 1,300 miles of a highly permeable upland frontier. The regional dimension of the Vietnam War was further entrenched by the crucial support of the Việt Minh[3] to the Lao and Cambodian revolutionary movements, as the creation and development of guerrilla bases in the peripheral regions of Cambodia and Laos were largely due to Hanoi's military and financial aid and political guidance since the aftermath of the Second World War (see Goscha 2004, 2010; Engelbert and Goscha 1995). The Vietnamese communists had several reasons for intensifying their efforts to build up military forces and revolutionary bases in neighboring Cambodia and Laos. First, in developing close military and political collaboration with local anti-colonial movements, especially in eastern Laos, the Việt Minh was creating a buffer zone to protect their western flank from attacks from the French troops and to enable their troops to freely intervene in Laos (hence, the invasion by the Việt Minh troops of the two Lao northeastern provinces of Houaphan and Phongsaly in December 1953). Second, the DRV considered it essential that communist movements expand their membership in Laos and Cambodia and train local cadres so they could lead the struggle side-by-side with the Vietnamese, thus carrying out a genuine Indochinese revolution (Vu 2009). At the same time, following the partition of Vietnam, the United States was determined to build a distinctly anti-communist state in Southern Vietnam (and in Laos) as part of what the US administration viewed as a Cold War struggle against communism. Postcolonial civil wars in former French Indochinese countries therefore mirrored the global ideological confrontation, pitting on the one hand communist forces supported by the People's Republic of China and the Soviet Union, and conservative parties backed by the United States and their anti-communist allies in Southeast Asia, such as Thailand and the Philippines, on the other.

The most deadly period of the Second Indochina War began in the mid-1960s during the process of "escalation" as the United States was pouring in aid to support the southern Republic of Vietnam, a regime that appeared to be unable to help itself against an ever more effective communist movement. The insurgent National Front for the Liberation of South Vietnam (the communist organization in the South, referred to as the *Việt Cộng* by the US and the South Vietnamese government) was supplied with men and materials from North Vietnam along the so-called Ho Chi Minh Trail (hereafter, HCMT), in reality a maze of interlocking paths and roads that was set up by the North Vietnamese army to circumvent the Vietnamese Demilitarized Zone (DMZ) dividing North and South Vietnam and which partly ran through eastern Laos.[4] By mid-1964, the Johnson administration (1963–69) was convinced that sustained bombing attacks, directed first against the HCMT in Laos, and then against key targets in North Vietnam, might force the communists to stop supplies flowing into South Vietnam from the North, and thus gave the RVN time to stabilize politically and gradually gain control of the provinces. In March 1965, the US administration initiated Operation Rolling Thunder, its deadly campaign of air strikes against North Vietnam (March 1965–November 1968). In all, Rolling Thunder killed an estimated 52,000 North Vietnamese (Lawrence 2008: 99). A few years earlier, under the Kennedy administration (1961–63), US Air Force aircraft had launched another devastating air campaign, Operation Ranch Hand (whose motto was "Only We Can Prevent Forests") that sprayed about 20 million gallons of herbicide over more than four million acres of South Vietnam (and also partly on the uplands of Laos) between 1962 and 1971 (Young 1991: 82). The spray, including the infamous Agent Orange, is responsible for ongoing environmental damage and human suffering in today's Vietnam (see Chapter 7 by Susan Hammond).

In Laos, the provinces of Xieng Khouang (North-East) and Savannakhet (Central-South) bore most of the brunt of the American bombing raids. In Xieng Khouang, the Plain of Jars (where enough air power could be based to dominate the whole South China and the Mainland of Southeast Asia) turned into the central battlefield of the Lao civil war where Rightist, Neutralists, and Communists fought for the control of this strategically important region. While the Lao communist troops were supported by North Vietnamese soldiers, the USA recruited a "secret army" among a faction of the Hmong ethnic population under the leadership of General Vang Pao, himself a Royal Lao Army officer of Hmong origins.[5] By late 1964, North Vietnamese manpower and supply infiltration through southern Laos showed no signs of losing ground. The US Air Force launched in December of that year air strikes against fixed targets and infiltration routes throughout Laos, which soon expanded in April 1965 to a day-and-night air campaign. The US Air Force initiated a major air campaign in areas being contested by ground forces in northern and north-eastern Laos, as well as along the HCMT in the Lao-Vietnamese border-lands in an attempt to interdict men and material being supplied to the communist insurgency in South Vietnam. A wide variety of munitions were employed, many of which — notably, cluster bomblets — continue to present a threat until the current day (see chapters by Elaine Russell, Christina Schwenkel, and Vatthana Pholsena, this volume).[6] From 1964 to 1973, American planes dropped 2,093,100 tons of ordnance in 580,344 bombing missions in the borderlands of Laos and Vietnam (Khamvongsa and Russell 2009: 289). To escape American bombing, the Lao communist leadership sought refuge in dozens of caves in the mountains of Houaphan province in northeastern Laos, bordering northern Vietnam. Between 1964 and 1973, a cave city emerged in Viengxay district including army quarters, warehouses, and schools — sheltering both soldiers and civilians whose livelihoods were severely affected by the daily bombing raids (see Chapter 2 by Oliver Tappe).

Meanwhile in Vietnam, it was clear by early 1965 that nothing would prevent the collapse of South Vietnam but the direct support of US com-bat troops. The first US combat units landed in Đà Nẵng, a major port city at the Central Coast of Vietnam, in March 1965. By the end of 1965, around 184,300 US servicemen were in South Vietnam, and reached al-most half a million (approximately 475,200) at their peak in 1969 (Young, Fitzgerald, and Grunfeld 2002: 162–3). In the same year, the process of "escalation" reached its heights when those troops moved from a defensive strategy centered on key US bases to all-out "Search-and-Destroy" opera-tions in the more remote border regions. In March 1969, the US Air Force began its secret bombardment of rural Cambodia, aimed at destroying the bases and troops of the People's Army of Vietnam (the North Vietnamese regular army) and the National Front for the Liberation of South Vietnam that utilized the country's eastern border areas as a sanctuary and a storage base for weapons and materials to be transported into South Vietnam.[7] As a result, upland populations living in the Lao-Cambodian-Vietnamese borderlands, who before had little contact with central political powers, were drawn into the international conflict. The war and its aftermath led to considerable socio-cultural transformations and strategies for survival (see chapters by Krisna Uk and Ian Baird).

The communists' victory in 1975 (the Khmer Rouge occupied Phnom Penh on 17 April. Saigon fell two weeks later, and on 2 December, the founding of the Lao People's Democratic Republic was proclaimed in Vientiane) signaled the end of the Second Indochina War, but did not bring about an immediate end to extreme violence. Public disclosure of the Cambodian genocide (1975–78) and the wars that opposed Vietnam against Cambodia and China in late 1978 and early 1979 stunned the world and left socialist movements, especially those in non-Western countries, bewildered.[8] In the interval of a few months, faith in Asian communism and its inspirational model for the anti-imperialist struggle was crushed. In addition to being largely driven by Khmer racist chauvinism, the Khmer Rouge revolution, "neither purely indigenous nor fully imported" as Ben Kiernan (2006: 201) puts it, was a "syncretism" of extensively-borrowed, yet partially followed and locally reinterpreted, foreign revolutionary doctrines. Ultimately, both foreign influences and indigenous components of Khmer Rouge ideology and practice propelled the leaders of the Democratic Kampuchea (April 1975–January 1979) toward their genocidal project which weighs heavily on Khmer collective memory until today (see Chapter 1 by Sina Emde). Under the Khmer Rouge regime, approximately 1.7 million people (one in five) died from malnutrition, overwork, diseases, or were executed by the Khmer Rouge.[9]

Results of war and subsequent socialist revolutions have left visible traces in these countries' human and physical landscapes. The Second and Third Indochina Wars deeply marked both peoples and places, while experiments of orthodox socialism in the aftermath of the conflicts, that is, rural collectivization and population displacement, contributed to the character of the region as a topographic and demographic palimpsest. Today's Lao, Vietnamese and Cambodian landscapes bear inscriptions of competing violent ideologies and their perilous material manifestations. From battlefields and massive bombing to reeducation camps and resettled villages, the past lingers on in the physical, often ruined, environment, but also in precarious objects such as unexploded ordnance (UXO) that are shallowly buried in large areas of contaminated land. These landscapes are a disturbing memento of the tragedy of millions of people. As Mai Lan Gustafsson (2009: xi) observes in the Vietnamese context: "[...] with more than 5 million or 13 percent of the population killed, and with family size at that time averaging six people, it was statistically probable that every family *would* lose someone" (emphasis in the original). A great part of the population in Vietnam has mourned family members killed in the fighting or searched in vain for the remains of loved ones whose bodies were never recovered (see Chapter 3 by Markus Schlecker). It is to these post-conflict landscapes that we turn in this book.

War Landscapes and Lingering Violence

Rather than regarding landscapes as a mere physical reality "out there," geographers, as well as anthropologists, sociologists and historians, have studied landscape as a political, social, and cultural process characterized by the interaction and mutual constitution of human societies and their physical environment (see, for example: Hirsch 1995; Ingold 2000; Miller 2006; Lefebvre 1974). Landscape is a contingent interplay of actuality and potentiality, not limited to a fixed image or immutable representation of an idea as once envisioned by English landscape painters and designers (Williams 1985). Instead, landscape has to be interpreted in its historical, social, and cultural context (Hirsch 1995: 23; Stewart and Strathern 2003). In a similar way, Barbara Bender (1993: 2) argues: "The way in which people — anywhere, everywhere — understand and engage with their worlds will depend upon the specific time and place and historical conditions. It will depend upon their gender, age, class, caste, and on their social and economic situation." This approach to the analysis of landscape as contextual horizon of perception provides a great variety of possible vantage points with regard to human perceptions of their physical environment, examining landscape and humans in their manifold entanglements. The outer appearance of landscapes should not be neglected since the perception of landscapes is a process that takes aspects of aesthetics, memory and materiality into account — all on their own capable to constitute a meaningful environment with which the inhabitants correspond in their daily activities. In short, landscapes are never inert geophysics or timeless artifacts but change in interaction with the people who see and shape them, and whom in turn are affected by them.

The degree of how people perceive themselves as an integral part of the environment might vary considerably from Melanesians who consider themselves as persons as effect of the surrounding world (Strathern 1999) over the ancient Egyptians who extended individual materiality by erecting monumental pyramids (Meskell 2004) to the intensive agriculture that transforms landscapes according to the will of the cultivating subject. What these radical different positions have in common is the constant interaction between people and environment. Landscape in particular has the potential to frame people's sense of place, time and community; as Pamela Stewart and Andrew Strathern (2003: 4) point out: "A place is a socially meaningful and identifiable space to which a historical dimension is attributed. Community refers to sets of people who may identify themselves with a place or places in terms of notions of commonality, shared values or solidarity in particular contexts." The influential French philosopher and sociologist Maurice Halbwachs (1992: 204) argued that group remembrance endured when they had a "double focus — a physical object, a material reality such as a statue, a monument, a place in space, and also a symbol, or something of spiritual significance, something shared by the group that adheres to and is superimposed upon this physical reality." The dense experiential and social qualities of place and landscape therefore not only frame social memory, but they also situate and spatially constitute group remembrance. This complex process manifests itself in a particular way in post-conflict landscapes.

As a physical codification with implications for a community's historical and cultural identity, landscape is a powerful medium and the nexus of past, present and future (see Stewart and Strathern 2003). These entanglements are most dramatic in postwar landscapes from the First World War trenches of Alsace (in northeastern France bordering Germany) to the devastated DMZ region straddling the border between Laos and Vietnam, laden with traumatic memories and present qualms (see Schofield, Johnson, and Beck 2002; Tyner 2010). The violent past manifests itself in various materializations: places "where it happened" dotted with commemorative monuments and museums endorsed with an educational mission; sites where the past haunts the present through the presence of remaining bones in the Cambodian killing fields (see Sina Emde's chapter) or may irrupt unpredictably via the sudden explosion of a "forgotten" bomb in a rice field or at the center of a village (see Christina Schwenkel's and Elaine Russell's chapters). These very material appearances of a past conflict are entangled in one landscape of memory. In other words, post-conflict landscapes have the potential of (forcefully) creating a specific sense of place among the inhabitants not least due to their aggressive materiality — a sense of a landscape as imbued with malevolent agency (see Allerton 2012).

As Daniel Miller (1985: 204–5) notes, war landscapes structure perceptions, "constraining or unleashing ideas and emotions by the people who live within it." Elaine Russell and Christina Schwenkel in this volume make clear that war debris (such as unexploded ordnance or UXO which can be regarded as index of past violent intentionality according to Gell 1998: 17) "[because of its dangerous potency] remains a contested signifier of memory — of past dangers and present uncertainties" (see Schwenkel's chapter). Postwar landscapes and its components — such as battlefields, trenches, bunkers, or war debris — often function as metonymies of past events and histories (Saunders 2002). They can be partially erased by razing or overgrowing — or, on the opposite, set in scene and made visible. As representations of past human conflicts, they embody the contradictions of victory and defeat, heroism and tragedy. These "imperial debris," to use Anne Stoler's (2008) expression, are a constant reminder of the violent past for those who lived through it, triggering memories of warfare through leftover weapons' capacity of injuring and killing.

The opposite is possible too, namely a sense of displacement resulting from the destruction of a place, thereby undermining "any secure sense of abiding place" (Casey 1998: xiii). The victims of forced migration often fill this void with imaginary landscapes in which idealized home and traumatic events intersect. Such ambiguous and often distorted mental landscapes with its inherent conflict of nostalgic and traumatic sentiments demand a special phenomenology that considers articulations and negotiations of shifting imaginaries. Ian Baird provides an account of the forced relocation of a Mon-Khmer speaking ethnic minority community, the Heuny (or Nya Heun), in southern Laos in the late 1990s as the result of the construction of a hydropower dam. The displacement caused not only physical damages (through illness and malnutrition), but also great anxiety and acute feelings of nostalgia among the displaced vis-à-vis their old land. Baird stresses that the Heuny people's attachment to their former place of living cannot be explained solely on the basis of material conditions (access to cultivable land, water and forestry resources), but must also be tied to the spiritual force emanating from "archives of memory" of an ancestral land, conveyed through stories told and retold throughout several generations that ultimately mark a place as "homeland." This forced relocation also contains a hidden script: very few members of the Heuny population joined the communist forces during the Indochina Wars; having been on the "wrong side" during the war, they are careful now not to be labeled as "anti-government" and therefore (reluctantly) conceded to move out of their land.

Contested *Lieux de Mémoire*

Pierre Nora's multiple volumes on the *Lieux de mémoire* (Nora 1984–92) mark a spatial turn in the historical sciences. His ambitious project examined French national sites of memory (including architecture, public festivals, books and monuments) as sites "where memory crystallizes and secretes itself" (Nora 1989: 7) — in other words, where memory is (re-) produced and elicited. According to Nora, we no longer live in nature-made "environments of memory" (*milieux de mémoire*), but instead create self-conscious "sites of memory" (*lieux de mémoire*). Such sites result from the twin processes of "de-ritualization" and secularization of the world: "we must deliberately create archives, maintain anniversaries, organise celebrations ... because such activities no longer occur naturally" (Nora 1989: 12). Landmarks/monuments associated with historical events and linked to activities and processes of collective commemoration are perhaps the best known examples for this perspective on history and memory. As traces of the past (see Ricoeur 1990, 2004) of a given society, such sites are key tools for both historians and anthropologists.

Although Nora was criticized for his strong focus on the (French) nation-state, a questionable holism, and his strict separation between history and memory, he nonetheless inspired numerous studies on material land-scapes and modern memory (see, for example: Winter 2003; François 1996; Rose 2010; Bensoussan 2004; Greene 2002). Objects of research comprise — among others — landmarks as anchors of collective memory, the politics of official commemoration via monuments, and the uncanny affects of relics and ruins on individual memory. Here memories appear as objec-tified or ossified in historical monuments yet maintain a fundamentally in-teractive and dialogical quality (Young 1993). For Nora, memory is always actual, whereas history is only a pale representation of the past (embodied by "dusty" archives). Nora emphasizes the idea of a vivid memory-nation with the *lieux de mémoire* as basic instruments of historical work — "inscriptions" as Paul Ricoeur (2004: 404) calls them. Even if Nora's early enthusiasm of a new history of multiple voices was sidelined in his later works by a critique of state enforced *patrimonialisation*, the concept of *lieux de mémoire* remains a useful analytical tool in post-conflict societies since "the term makes it possible to reassemble the shattered national whole" (Nora 1998: 636). This assessment echoes Bruno Latour's (1996) conception of "assemblages" as complex networks of persons and things. For example, "national" landscapes of memory — landscapes rearranged and reinterpreted in the context of nation-building projects — can be ana-lyzed as assemblages or configurations of a network of various actors in constant interaction, constituting and contesting each other. Yet such sites are often appropriated by the state for official commemorative politics linked to the state-staged national imaginary. Nonetheless, the interplay with local collective memory and individual subjectivities also shapes the meaning of these sites; therefore, the shifting meanings — or the historicity — of sites of memory have to be taken into account as well.

Collective memory implies the idea of a socially constructed and continually reproduced memory — an ongoing project of "reconstructive imagination" (Assmann 1998: 14) aiming at the production of meaning that is unstable and susceptible for ideological/political contention. Which aspects of the past are highlighted often depends on who appropriates a landscape of memory and to what purpose. Official grand narratives of a national past are often standardized accounts that contrast with individual memories and perceptions of certain *lieux de mémoire*. The appropriation of landscape as a medium of memory (and forgetting) appears in various strategies such as naming of special places, physical manipulation, construction of *lieux de mémoire*, and narrative backups of memory associated with certain places. This entails both the creation of meaning and selective forgetting or even repression (Olick 2008). Landscapes appear to be imbued with different layers of memory, as palimpsests that can be deciphered or selectively manipulated, for example by the state seeking to define and control historical meaning. As Oliver Tappe's contribution demonstrates, "eventful" landscapes can become "historical" when the events and persons associated with the place are deliberately commemorated and linked to narratives of national liberation. In the case of Viengxay, the so-called "birthplace of the Lao PDR," the combination of revolutionary commemoration and tourism development created an ambiguous dynamic that turned a few inconspicuous caves in the Lao mountains into a busy center of tourism and commemorative fervor. The fact that the leaders of the Lao revolution spent the "American War" in these caves furthermore gives them an aura of history and heroism. The works of foreign tourism experts on the other hand put more emphasis on the oral memories of the local people so as to give the place more "authenticity" mainly destined for an international audience. Thus, the agenda of this landscape of memory is not coherent; neither is Viengxay a mere stage that reflects state power. As Karen Till (2003: 290) observes, "[…] places of memory and the processes associated with their establishment, demonstrate the complex ways that nationalist imaginations, power relations, and social identities are spatially produced."

Indeed, state narratives of a national past can also coexist with polysemic individual memories and perceptions of certain *lieux de mémoire*. Invoking the national memorial sites of Tuol Sleng and Choeung Ek located in the vicinity of Phnom Penh, Sina Emde alerts us to the emotional importance of memory that can bridge the divide between the state's agenda to legitimize a normative historiography that these two sites serve to convey and the deeply personal memories of the remaining survivors of Tuol Sleng and of the relatives of those tortured and murdered. In particular, through the testimonies the civil parties gave during the investigation of Case 001 (concerning the tortures and mass murders perpetuated on the two sites of Tuol Sleng and Choeung Ek) at the Extraordinary Chambers in the Courts of Cambodia (ECCC) set up in 2006, the tribunal itself became a space of emotional recollections "as the testimonies depict the subjective meanings those national memorial sites hold for the few remaining survivors of Tuol Sleng and the relatives of those tortured and murdered beyond the collective sufferings exhibited and narrated by the Cambodian state," Emde writes. Tuol Sleng and Choeung Ek are places of national commemoration that aim to fuel Cambodian people's collective memory through the sense of sharing the national history of the collective suffering of the victims during the time of the Khmer Rouge. The state cannot achieve this objective alone, however, and acts of personal remembrance, Emde argues, are as important in infusing meaning, that is, a sense of shared place, and adding further legitimacy to the sites and beyond the national narrative.

Sites of memory and their material components are not always easily "readable"; they may convey multiple interpretations and even be reconfigured. Different aspects of memorial material constitute manifold traces of the past that derive their meaningfulness from specific connections or associations with past events, persons, and places. In his chapter, Markus Schlecker shows that material carriers of memory such as the *bia* stones in Vietnam — commemorative stelae that inform of past achievements of meritorious individuals associated with a place — sometimes reemerge from oblivion or are created anew. While in the former case the process of deciphering leads to debates about the significance of a newly discovered stone in Thanh Hà, a rural commune in Northern Vietnam, and its relevance for the place; in the latter case, we witness the purposeful (re)construction of a site of memory, that is, war-martyr *bia*, the villagers' own version of a memorial stone to commemorate exemplary persons who sacrificed their lives during the "Wars of Resistance" (*Kháng Chiến*) against the French and the Americans. Among tribute policies for those who fought and died and for the survivors implemented in Vietnam during the American/Vietnam War, the most important ceremonial innovation by the regime was the creation of an official and secular memorial service for the war dead elaborated upon the public veneration of military heroes in Vietnamese history. Shaun Malarney (2001: 58) has argued that "this new ceremony represented an effort by the state to individually recognize the sacrifice of those who died in battle," and indeed, these ceremonies and the ideas of honor, glorification and nobility of suffering and dying for a "just cause" they conveyed were "compelling" for many Vietnamese. Yet, while the war dead belonged to the pantheon of national heroes from the perspective of the Vietnamese state, the families of those who sacrificed (*hi sinh*) their lives also sought to incorporate them in a different community, made up of kin, both heroic and unheroic (Hue-Tam Ho-Tai 2001: 12). In a similar way, Schlecker shows that war-martyr stelae and the commemorative rituals associated with them are being presently refashioned by local population as they are now included in the ritual care of the ancestral kin group (*dòng họ*). Indeed, engraved on a war martyr *bia* were only those who were descendants of the *dòng họ* in the rural commune of Thanh Hà. These stelae were thus breaking down the state category of war martyrs according to blood ties and locality. The materiality of the *bia* is of special relevance here since it implies durability in time and a "readiness-to-hand" (Heidegger 1962) for both individual and collective memory works.

Inconspicuous, seemingly banal, material landscape can project a variety of images, representations and memories from different vantage points. In her contribution, Vatthana Pholsena studies a road. Road 9 in Savannakhet Province in southern Laos is at once a historical relic — a colonial testimony of French (failed) ambitions in Indochina — a revolutionary icon in today's regime's official memory — as a "strategic route" (*saen yutthasat*) that supported the communist infiltration into Eastern Laos and South Vietnam during the American War in Vietnam — an interdicted space, as remembered by survivors of the US Army bombing, that turned into a road "back to civilization" in times of peace, and finally, as one moves to the "post" era (after the war and beyond the socialist project), a place of unfinished histories entangled in public silence, apparent social amnesia, and private remembrance. To be sure, Road 9 is now a "modern," paved road with hardly any trace of wartime or postwar debris; yet, the past has not been completely erased from the surface, in that one only needs to refocus the historical lens to glimpse "what is dominant but hard to see" (Stoler 2008: 211), that is, the dense historical and political qualities of this landscape and their continual interference into the individuals' subjectivities. What may appear as an unremarkable physical environment to outside observers has retained a still palpable evocation of violence and rift in local residents' perceptions of their past and their present. In a sense, the landscape of Road 9 forms a *milieu de mémoire*, rather than a *lieu de mémoire*, that is, a "natural" environment that is a social space imbued with memory-work conveying differing interpretations of the recent past.

Ruination and Transformation

Yael Navaro-Yashin's discussion of the concept of ruination provides another vantage point for the reading of post-conflict landscapes. Ruination refers to "material remains or artifacts of destruction and violation" as well as "subjectivities and residual affects that linger, like a hangover, in the aftermath of war or violence" (Navaro-Yashin 2009: 5). It includes abject material that ought to be instinctively pushed away, yet at the same time belongs to the physical environment that is hard to avoid (for instance, landmines in flooded Cambodian rice fields). Referring to Latour's engagement with networks of subjects and objects, Navaro-Yashin calls for a relational analysis of ruined, melancholic landscapes; she writes: "An environment of ruins discharges an affect of melancholy. At the same time, those who inhabit this space of ruins feel melancholic: they put the ruins into discourse, symbolize them, interpret them, politicize them, understand them, project their subjective conflicts onto them, remember them, try to forget them, historicize them, and so on" (ibid.: 14–15; see also Gordillo 2011; Schramm 2011). Landscapes ruined by war — or ruined in the minds of dispossessed people as in Baird's case study — produce strong effects that violently bring back tragic events of the past. The Heuyn villagers, in Baird's chapter, continue expressing nostalgic reminiscences of their former lives in their old village settlements (which have been dismantled and are now eaten away by termites). Yet, despite the much deteriorated living conditions, some villagers have gone back, even building shacks in their former village territories and as such enacting small acts of defiance in the face of the government's resettlement plans by reentering a zone of abandonment. Most crucially, as Ann Stoler (2008: 194) reminds us, the term "ruin" serves both as a noun and as a verb; "to ruin" — or "ruination" — is an active, corrosive process "that weighs on the future and shapes the present." Some ruins are neither residues nor relics or (on the opposite) enchanted places, but constitute tenacious traces of a violent past that have shattered people and scarred places. The deformed "Agent Orange Victims," in Susan Hammond's chapter, as ruined bodies, painfully emblematize the violent side of escalating political and ideological struggles of the Cold War and constitute uncanny mementoes of the lasting effects of modern war technology or, to borrow Stoler's (2008: 203) words, "ecologies of remains." Yet, these Agent Orange victims — or "One Significant Ghost" as an American official has labeled them, perhaps to emphasize their haunting, and yet elusive, presence (see Fox 2007) — would have been left outside the public view — by the Vietnamese government itself annoyed by, in their view, an embarrassing war legacy — disregarded by US officials as "Vietnamese government's propaganda" or as Cold War leftovers, had it not been for Vietnamese grassroots efforts, relayed by international activists' awareness and advocacy campaigns, and Vietnamese associations' lawsuits against the chemical companies that manufactured the components of the dioxin known as "Agent Orange." In short, the Agent Orange-affected individuals and Agent Orange-infested landscape in Vietnam remain a contested political ground; they stubbornly continue making claims on the present and the future.

The ambivalences of ruination — in a sense of a process "that 'bring ruin upon,' exerting material and social force in the present" (Stoler 2004: 195) — are exemplified by Schwenkel's discussion of demining and UXO clearance practices in the former DMZ in Quảng Trị Province in central Vietnam. On the one hand, war debris radiates a certain melancholic aura of past destruction, while constituting a lethal threat in the present. On the other hand, because of the impossible task to clear vast areas of land and completely eliminate the risk in an individual's lifetime, hazardous landscapes have become an integral part of their inhabitants' everyday life, and even offer the possibility of economic recovery through the (highly risky but lucrative) informal and transnational trade in war scrap metal carried out by some villagers — who thus constitute a risk society with different modes of perceiving and managing a dangerous environment (Douglas 1992). War remnants thus lie at the nexus between a violent past, potentially prosperous futures, and an uncertain present.[10] Schwenkel shows that the unpredictable nature of explosive remnants of war in this region — that make or destroy landscapes and livelihoods — can be mitigated or, at least, negotiated through risk management and reduction practices. But "cultures of risk" (notions of risk as historically and socially contingent) significantly differ between on the one hand professional, foreign or foreign-trained Vietnamese deminers, and on the other, scrap metal collectors, also commonly referred as "hobby deminers." The use of the term "hobby" clearly denotes the perceived lack of proper training, if not absence of awareness of the dangers inherent to this activity, among local collectors. In their daily search for wartime scrap metal, the latter confront risk, instead of avoiding it. Their risk-taking attitude generates opprobrium in the community because they "appear to violate many of the shared values and notions of risk." Though they may suffer from social stigma, the collectors benefit from risk through their (illegal) trading of UXO in the global market economy; hence, effectively converting risk into a commodity. Yet, adding another twist to an already complex landscape, Schwenkel points out that war debris that are commercialized (scrap metal-cum-war relics) engender much suspicion among western tourists, who consider them as "polluted" due to their perceived association with profit-making calculations and reckless behaviors. Ruins — as abject material — are therefore not just found; they can also be imagined.

It is this possibility of transforming the meaning of war debris that Krisna Uk tackles in her chapter. By drawing on the Jorai experience of the US bombing in Ratanakiri Province in northeast Cambodia, she demonstrates how the ethnic minority villagers' encounter with war-associated objects is reenacted through the reproduction, representation and display of weapon effigies. In a post-conflict context in which people are trying to interpret violence, destruction and defeat as part of their survival strategies, symbolic and material (tactile) appropriation of war-associated objects (such as carving a bombing plane in wood or painting war-inspired themes, like hand grenades, in the crafting and decoration of funerary objects, for instance) can provide a means to control one's traumatic experience and have a powerful therapeutic potential. Uk argues that the meanings conveyed by a tangible object can be subject to new interpretations and positive inversion by war-survivors (especially those endowed with craftsman skills) and their families. Jorai villagers' coping ability is based not only on physical resilience, but also a creative psychological process in which the crafting of warfare objects enables people to harness the objects' intrinsic power for positive purposes, thus turning them into signs of life. Through the acts of making, re-symbolizing, incorporation and display, war-inspired objects have been used for both ritual and everyday purposes so as to become meaningful and aesthetic features of the local landscape. In spite of years of protracted wars, local resourcefulness, not least in the context of the burgeoning tourist industry in Ratanakiri, shows the extent to which the resilience and inventiveness of some post-conflict communities can stretch so as to cope with a physically and spiritually traumatized landscape.

Three decades after the end of the American/Vietnam War and the overthrow of the Khmer Rouge regime, the chapters show that landscapes and peoples in Cambodia, Laos, and Vietnam remain scarred physically, psychologically, and spiritually. Yet, they also uncover instances of (partial) recovery and healing. In recent years, a few ethnic Heuny households have started small coffee plantations in their old homelands where soil is more fertile than in their resettlement areas. NGOs and governmental institutions have begun to engage with scrap metal collectors in Quảng Trị Province in new programs that recognize and make use of their "local" knowledge for the better of society. From 1996 to 2010, some 26,000 hectares of land were cleared of UXO in Laos — though this area represents less than one percent of all land thought to be contaminated with UXO (about eight million hectares). In truth, over the last decade, market forces have played a major role in transforming rural landscapes in these countries. Land concessions (long-term leases of state land to investors) have become a serious and complex issue in Laos and Cambodia. The most widespread, and controversial, aspect of land concessions concerns the lease of vast areas of cultivable land to foreign investors destined to the plantation and exportation of commercial crops (rice, rubber, cassava, etc.). Likewise, the landscape of Quảng Trị Province is being renewed under the impacts of large-scale projects that have involved the construction of new roads, forests, buildings and markets, as well as the development of new plantations. Postwar landscapes overgrown with vegetation or returned to cultivation sometimes "have a prewar innocence about them" (Tatum 1996: 643) evoking deceptive images of a return to normality. But this volume strives to unfold a more complicated story than the all-encompassing narrative of reconstruction and economic prosperity; the reading of post-conflict landscapes requires transcending images and discourses of seemingly unstoppable change lest we forget the enduring effects of warfare violence on human societies and environments.

Notes

1. See the emphasis for a "Vietnamization" of scholarship on the Vietnam War in Miller and Tuong Vu (2009).
2. Scholars of China — Neil J. Diamant, Diana Lary, Stephen MacKinnon, Ezra Vogel, Edward McCord, and others — have begun to study in socio-cultural ways the impact of warfare on 20th-century China (Lary and MacKinnon 2001; Lary 2010). The Vietnam War has its own appalling list of massacres, although fewer studies probing the socio-cultural impacts of these mass

killings have been produced. There are notable exceptions, however, such as Heonik Kwon's thoughtful book (2008) on remembrance and commemorative rituals performed by survivors and descendants of the civilian victims of the Mỹ Lai and Hà Mỹ massacres. See also Fred Branfman's (2010 [1972]) classic documentation of the violent legacy of the US bombing campaigns in Laos, James Tyner's (2010) insightful account of modern military legacies, and Andreas Margara's (2012) recent study of Vietnamese sites of war memory.

3. The League for the Independence of Vietnam (*Việt Nam Độc Lập Đồng minh hội* or Việt Minh), the communist-led patriotic organization, was founded in May 1941.

4. A special group called Military Transportation Group 559 was set up in May 1959 to construct the first North-South Road and to organize the logistics (weapons and supplies) to the South, specifically to Inter-Zone V. In the same month, a North Vietnamese battalion (the 70th) was formed; its task was to transport weapons, ammunition, mail and supplies to South Vietnam through southeastern Laos, as well as to guide the infiltration groups and to help the sick and injured cadres returning to the North (Guan 2002: 35). According to *The Official History of the People's Army of Vietnam, 1954–1975*, "Group 559 transported a total of 165,600 weapons ['artillery pieces, mortars, and anti-aircraft machine guns'] to the battlefields in the South during the 1961–63 period" (Military History Institute of Vietnam, 2002: 115).

5. The CIA decided in early 1960s to take the Hmong people over and use them as the nucleus for the Laotian Special Forces, named after the "Secret Army" or the "Armée clandestine" since the Americans became convinced that the Royal Lao Army would never be an efficient and reliable instrument despite the huge sums of dollars spent on it. In return for support of Hmong aspirations for autonomy, the Americans were able to use the Hmong to strike against the Việt Minh and the Pathet Lao around the Plain of Jars and Ho Chi Minh Trail (Warner 1996; Evans 2002).

6. A recent survey by the National Regulatory Authority (NRA) for the UXO/ Mine Action sector in Laos reveals that more than 50,000 people were hurt or killed by UXO (unexploded ordnances) between 1964 and 2008 (*Vientiane Times*, 6 Feb. 2010).

7. In total, the US Air Force flew 231,000 sorties over Cambodia, dropping 2.75 million tons of munitions between 1965 and 1975. Cambodian Genocide Program, a project of the Genocide Studies Program at Yale University, at http://www.yale.edu/cgp/ [accessed 2 Jan. 2012].

8. On Christmas Day 1978, 12 divisions of the Vietnamese army invaded Cambodia following mounting Khmer Rouge attacks along the Vietnamese border provinces since 1976. By mid-1979, the Vietnamese troops controlled the main populated areas of the country; the Khmer Rouge controlled areas

in the mountains, sparsely uninhabited, of southwest Cambodia and along the Thai border. But although having lost two-thirds of its troops, the Khmer Rouge remained a functioning military force and the Democratic Kampuchea leadership was intact on the Thai border. Vietnam's military intervention of Cambodia undermined China's credibility and prestige (China was the Democratic Kampuchea's main ally). The Chinese "lesson" administered to Vietnam came in the form of a brief "punitive" military invasion which lasted less than a month, between 17 Feb. and 5 Mar. 1979. The "lesson" was rather inconclusive, though, for the Chinese troops' advance made little progress. Nonetheless, the conflicts with the Democratic Kampuchea and China isolated Vietnam — and Laos, its "special" ally — on the international scene.

9. Cambodian Genocide Program, at http://www.yale.edu/cgp/ [accessed 2 Jan. 2012].

10. See Henig (2012) for a related case study from postwar Bosnia.

CHAPTER 1

National Memorial Sites and Personal Remembrance: Remembering the Dead of Tuol Sleng and Choeung Ek at the ECCC in Cambodia

Sina Emde

Not far from the center of the bustling city of Phnom Penh, a place embodies dark memories of Cambodian history: memories of terror, memories of horror, memories of death, and memories of loss. During the time of the Khmer Rouge regime, from April 1975 until January 1979, this place, once built as a high school, was converted into a prison and interrogation center, called S-21, also known as Tuol Sleng. Those who were brought to S-21 were considered enemies of the regime and/or victims of the purges of the Khmer Rouge regime. They were interrogated, tortured and, if then still alive, transported to the killing fields of Choeung Ek where they were brutally executed. More than 12,000 people were killed. Only a dozen were exempted and seven survivors escaped Tuol Sleng when the Vietnamese claimed the city on 7 January 1979 (Chandler 1999: 6; Williams 2004: 237).[1] Those who survived Tuol Sleng still suffer from their experiences while those that lost relatives at the prison are haunted by recurring thoughts about the extreme violence done to their loved ones.

There existed more than 180 so-called security centers and more than 300 documented prison killing sites during the time of the Khmer Rouge regime,[2] but the two sites in Phnom Penh are by far the most prominent ones. This is also due to the fact that they were made national memorial sites after the fall of the Khmer Rouge. Both sites were discovered by the

Vietnamese after they invaded Phnom Penh and the decision to turn these sites into national memorials was also made by the occupying forces. Thus the establishment of these sites is closely linked to state historiography and national narratives of the Vietnamese-backed socialist People's Republic of Kampuchea, the official name of the state of Cambodia from 1979–89. While other mass graves and execution sites were similar in terms of the number of victims killed, it can be assumed that the location of Tuol Sleng and Choeung Ek in and near the capital Phnom Penh played a major role in the decision to turn these sites into memorials.[3]

Both sites were investigative sites of Case 001 of the Extraordinary Chambers in the Courts of Cambodia (ECCC) commonly known as the Khmer Rouge Tribunal. The tribunal was installed in 2006, almost 30 years after the fall of the Khmer Rouge regime. The ECCC is a hybrid tribunal with both national and international elements that tries the "senior responsible leaders and those most responsible"[4] — of Democratic Kampuchea in two cases. Case 001 was against Kaing Guek Eav alias Duch. From 1975 until January 1979, Duch was the commander of the security prison S-2. On 26 July 2010, the ECCC found him guilty of crimes against humanity and grave breaches of the Geneva Conventions of 1949. The tribunal sentenced Duch to 35 years of imprisonment. However, as the time Duch had spent in detention before the trial was taken into account, the time he still will have to spend in prison ended up being only 19 years, too little for many of the victims who participated in the legal proceedings of the ECCC as civil parties.[5]

Yet in this chapter, I do not primarily focus on questions of notions of justice in the tribunal proceedings, as important as they are. I rather look at the tribunal and its investigation sites of Case 001, the security prison S-21, and the related killings fields of Choeung Ek as polyphonic memoryscapes, that is, chronotopic spaces that form and are formed by different practices and forms of remembering and making meaning of the past by different, sometimes very divergent, actors such as the state, civil society and individual persons (see Basu 2007; Cole 2001; Ullberg 2010).

The installation of the ECCC has brought Tuol Sleng and Choeung Ek to new public attention on an international, national, and local level. While there exists a vast body of literature not only on the political history of Cambodia and the history of the Khmer Rouge (see, among others, Chandler 1999, 2008a; Dy 2007; Kiernan 1985, 1996; Vickery 1984), but also on legal debates around the hybrid Khmer Rouge tribunal (Ciorciari 2006; Dyrchs 2008; Form 2009), scholarly work on the memorialization of the KR period in contemporary Cambodia in general and in the context of the tribunal specifically is rather scarce. Within this small emerging body of research, Tuol Sleng and Choeung Ek as national memorial sites are prominent themes (see Hughes 2003, 2005, 2006; Ledgerwood 1997; Williams 2004). Most scholarly work considers Tuol Sleng and Choeung Ek as memorial sites that serve state historiography and commercial interests of the Cambodian government where "memory and memorialization are not performed" (Sion 2011: 19, but see Hughes 2006: 112–26). As recently as 2011, Brigitte Sion stated that:

> It is clear that these government-sponsored memorials serve primarily other purposes — political legitimacy, economic development, and profit making ventures. They are not directed to locals who have a personal connection to memory but to international travelers who feed the global tourism industry and the national economy. To this end, all strategies are acceptable, even if they involve commodifying skulls, capitalizing on human suffering, promoting sites associated with criminals, and ignoring religious traditions. (Sion 2011: 19)

Local remembrance, she argues, takes place in villages and pagodas on religious holidays where "[...] human dignity is respected, mourning rituals have meaning, and the spirits of the murdered can eventually find rest" (ibid.). While there can be no doubt that the government is more interested in political legitimacy and economic development than in mourning the dead,[6] and that indeed most of local commemoration and mourning takes place in villages and pagodas, I will show in this chapter that the testimonies and agency of civil parties and witnesses of Case 001 against Duch at the ECCC and the memorial sites give new meanings to Tuol Sleng and Choeung Ek and personalize national history while at the same time being framed by the political context in which they emerge. I argue that through these processes, the tribunal itself becomes a space of "emotional remembering" (White 2000) as the testimonies depict the subjective meanings those national memorial sites hold for the few remaining survivors of Tuol Sleng and the relatives of those tortured and murdered beyond the collective sufferings exhibited and narrated by the Cambodian state. In this chapter, I ask explicitly about these subjective meanings, and more specifically, how they interact with the collective memories and national histories that are inscribed in these sites and the tribunal itself. My explorations are, as I discuss in more detail below, inspired by Geoffrey White's work (2000, 2004, 2006) that defines practices of remembering as "situated acts in contexts where the past matters" (White 2006: 330) and highlights memorial sites as spaces where personal memories and national histories intertwine.

I base my analysis not only on the video recordings and transcripts of testimonies that civil parties gave at the ECCC but also on observations and interviews I conducted at the memorial sites. However, the investigation of testimonies is pertinent to my argumentation, simply because testimonies are such a central part of the tribunal, and beyond their legal bearing, they constitute a form of witnessing and remembering. As Lawrence L. Langer so aptly highlights: "Testimony is a form of remembering. The faculty of memory functions in the present to recall a personal history vexed by traumas that thwart smooth-flowing chronicles" (Langer 1991: 2–3). Yet testimonies are only one form of remembering the dead evoked by the transitional justice process of the tribunal itself. For the Cambodians involved, they present more an exogenous than a local form of remembering and cannot fully fulfil the need of the civil parties to respect, commemorate and find justice for those who were killed at S-21 and Choeung Ek. I suggest that in order to address these felt shortcomings of the legal process, civil parties and witnesses of Case 001 turn to collective Khmer Buddhist rituals that not only link individual and collective remembrance but address the spiritual side of remembrance that is considered crucial in Khmer thought and belief for mourning and paying respects to the dead. These processes do not only reveal contemporary multiple forms and practices of remembering but display the entanglement of international, national and local ways of making meaning of a violent past in contemporary Cambodia.

In the first part of this chapter, I will introduce the Khmer Rouge period and the structure of the Khmer Rouge Tribunal, including the system of civil parties in court. I then depict the national politics of memory in recent and present Cambodia and ask about individual and collective as well as political meanings of Tuol Sleng and Choeung Ek in the recent history of the country. The third part illustrates the personal meanings these sites hold for the civil parties of Case 001 through the testimonies and interactions of civil parties with the accused Duch in the court room of the ECCC. By drawing on the court proceedings, I also ask about the ways an international tribunal brings collective and individual memories into the public while at the same time falling short of civil parties' expectations. The fourth part turns to rituals performed by survivors and relatives of victims of Tuol Sleng and Choeung Ek as a practice of remembering the dead. I conclude by discussing how these multiple processes at work render the court, Tuol Sleng, and Choeung Ek to interconnected memoryscapes where emotions, personal remembrance, collective memories and state historiography interact through the agency of the actors involved.

From Democratic Kampuchea to the Extraordinary Chambers in the Courts of Cambodia (ECCC)

When the communist Khmer Rouge came to power in April 1975, their victory ended a five-year civil war that had cost at least 300,000 lives in Cambodia.[7] The hope of the Cambodian people that the victory of the Khmer Rouge would finally bring peace and prosperity back to Cambodia was in vain. Instead, the KR launched one of the most radical social and economic revolutions of the 20th century. The state of Democratic Kampuchea, as it was named, was transformed into a communist agrarian state. All cities were evacuated, money was abolished, people were organized into collective labor units in all parts of Cambodia, and communities that were considered potential enemies of the state were dislocated from their homelands into various parts of Cambodia. Monks were defrocked, pagodas (*wat*) made prisons and security centers, and educated and/or urban people were denounced as enemies of the state. The Khmer Rouge categorized the entire Cambodian population into "new people" (*bracheachon thmei*) or "17th April people" (*bracheachon brampi mesa*) and "base people" (*brocheachon mouladthan*) or "old people" (*bracheachon chas*). Base people were peasants residing in those parts of Cambodia that had already been "liberated" and were strongholds of the Khmer Rouge movement during the civil war before 1975. New people were those residing in the cities,[8] those who had undergone formal education, and those who were associated with the former Lon Nol government (Hinton 2005: 9). Often families were separated and children trained to be soldiers and guards. People worked in labor units for long hours and received very little food, often only one or two bowls of watery rice gruel (*babar*) a day.[9] It is estimated that more than 1.6 million people died during the period of Democratic Kampuchea due to torture, execution, starvation and exhaustion (Kiernan 2003).

The Khmer Rouge lost power due to a Vietnamese invasion of the country in December 1978 and January 1979. Returning with the Vietnamese soldiers was the Khmer Salvation front that consisted of former Khmer Rouge who had defected to Vietnam in 1977 and 1978, among them the present Prime Minister Hun Sen. Those returning Cambodians formed the first Vietnamese-backed government of the People's Republic of

Kampuchea that lasted in minor alterations until 1989 (Gottesman 2003). Many of these persons are still in power today, including the Prime Minister. But in some parts of the country, the Khmer Rouge was still active as late as 1998, fighting a guerrilla warfare against the successive Phnom Penh governments. In 1998, a general amnesty declared by the Prime Minister Hun Sen integrated those Khmer Rouge guerrilla forces and their leaders into the Cambodian national state and army. The so-called win-win policy of Hun Sen included the installation of prominent Khmer Rouge leaders into high positions of the Cambodian government.

The Western world, China and Thailand played a major role in keeping the Khmer Rouge movement alive through all those years. Opposing the Vietnamese invasion of Cambodia, they supported the resistance and guerrilla forces along the Thai Border with military and financial aid. They did not recognize the Vietnamese-backed government of the People's Republic of Kampuchea and first gave the Cambodian seat at the United Nations to an exile government consisting of former Khmer Rouge and King Sihanouk before leaving it empty until the United Nations Transitional Authority in Cambodia (UNTAC) period and the official democratic elections of a new government of the Kingdom of Cambodia in 1993 (see Fawthrop and Jarvis 2004). Because of these varying interests of various powers to veil their involvement during and after the cold war, it took more than 20 years to pave the way for an international tribunal to prosecute the senior leaders of the Khmer Rouge. The ECCC was finally officially established in 2006 (ibid.).

The ECCC is located in Phnom Penh, the capital of Cambodia, and may be classified "[...] as a hybrid tribunal because, in its approach to legal substance and procedure, it applies both national and international law" (Form 2009: 905). Due to the application of national law, the ECCC has special provisions for victims' participation to file subsidiary charges as civil parties. However, their legal presentation is not regulated by the ECCC and the provision of legal assistance has been mostly done by a variety of internationally sponsored NGOs who are engaged in outreach and legal assistance programs in the context of the tribunal.[10] Thus civil parties are more than witnesses, they are right-claimers. Case 001 included 91 civil parties' participation of which 22 appeared for testimonies in court. Most of these civil parties had lost relatives at Tuol Sleng and are themselves survivors of the regime. Some are descendants or have returned from exile. Two civil parties, Chum Mey and Bou Meng and one witness, the late Vann Nath,[11] were prisoners in January 1979 and could escape when the Vietnamese troops reached Phnom Penh.

Following the example of other tribunals and truth commissions in post-conflict settings, the proceedings of the court, the testimonies of witnesses and civil parties are archived and thus become historical documents that enter national historiography. In 2011, the ECCC in cooperation with the War Crimes Studies Center at the University of Berkeley and the Hoover Library and Archive, launched the Virtual Tribunal program in order to provide "a lasting legacy for the people of Cambodia that will extend beyond the court's projected termination date of 2013. Working together with the Court, schools, universities, and NGOs, the Virtual Tribunal will be made available to Cambodians at learning centers in schools as well as in provincial information centers and memorials to Khmer Rouge victims".[12] Beyond the documentary records of the trial proceedings and the courtroom videos and transcripts, the Virtual Tribunal aims at including interviews with court personnel and trial participants, media coverage, educational tools and the material produced by Cambodian civil society organizations. All materials should also be archived in hard copy in Phnom Penh.[13] The virtual documentation of the tribunal and the testimonies of civil parties and witnesses render the court a memorial site in the making. The processes at work evoke questions not only about the relationship between private and public, individual and collective memories, but also between history, memory, and emotion.

Individual and Collective Memory, State Historiography and the ECCC

These questions about the dynamics between the individual and the social have been pertinent to interdisciplinary memory studies of the last decades that are trying to overcome longstanding dichotomies of the social sciences such as individual/society or memory/history and other paradigms that separate the realms of the psychological and the social, that is, "personal cognition and emotion from social, political and historical processes" (White 2006: 326). Early works on memory would either focus on individual memory as a field of psychology or on collective memory as a field of sociology and anthropology, in general assuming a clear dichotomy between the two. In psychology, memory refers foremost to the individual's ability to store, retain, and recall information. In contrast, sociology and anthropology have foregrounded the collective and national construction of memory in their works of the last decades. Much of this work is still indebted to Maurice Halbwachs' notions of collective memory as individual memory that is always socially constituted, shared and passed on by the group the individual is embedded in (Halbwachs 1950).

While we are indeed indebted to Halbwachs' insights on memory as collectively constituted, his emphasis on coherence and homogeneity obscures the fact that memory is often contested and discursively constructed by different actors and groups. What can and cannot be remembered or, in other words what is remembered and what is forgotten, what is narrated and what is silenced, is often dominated by state historiographies that serve varying political interests. Official histories, on the other hand, can be supported or contested by individual and collective acts of remembering. Thus, if we indeed assume that through various acts of articulation individual memories enter the collective, but that at the same time the collective frames what is publicly remembered, then we have to place more attention on the processes of how individual and collective memory are mutually constitutive (see Argenti and Schramm 2009; Cole 2001; White 2006).

In a recent article, Geoffrey White alerts us to the polysemic nature of memory that bridges the divide between the individual and the collective. He depicts four crucial aspects of memory that are in dialogue with one another: practice, emotionality, politics, and materiality. The practice of memory relates to "situated acts of memory in contexts where the past matters" (White 2006: 330). In this sense, memory is also chronotopic, linked to time and space (see Assmann 1992: 38–9; Halbwachs 1950; Nora 1989). Memory has a material and temporal side (see Basu 2007; Nora 1989) and remembers and evokes emotions. Yet, all different forms and practices of remembering interact with the politics of memory which refers to questions of power and hegemony in national and collective remembrance. National narratives and state historiography may determine what can be publicly remembered and what must be forgotten and who may be at the margins of the dominant narrative.

In socialist and post-socialist Cambodia, the state has always played a crucial role in the construction of collective memory and public commemoration of the Khmer Rouge (Chandler 2008b). Before the Paris Peace Accords, the Vietnamese-backed government saw it crucial to keep the violence and brutality of Democratic Kampuchea alive in order to legitimize itself as the guarantor for peace in the country. During the People's Republic of Kampuchea, schoolbooks and annual public commemorations as the Day of Tying Anger (*tivea chang kamhaeng*) depicted and remembered the cruelty and brutality of the Khmer Rouge, often in a drastic manner (Chandler 2008b; Hinton 2008). After the Paris Peace Accords and the 1993 elections that brought former allies of the Khmer Rouge back on the national political scene, the period vanished from schoolbooks and was reduced to one paragraph in the history book of Grade 9 (Chandler 2008b: 356). This attempt at national oblivion further strengthened with the general amnesty in 1997 that integrated remaining Khmer Rouge into the Cambodian state and army. It was in 1997 that the Prime Minister Hun Sen announced that it was time "to dig a hole and bury the past" (Chandler 2008b: 356; Fawthrop and Jarvis 2004: 135). But while the government tried to induce collective amnesia, Cambodia reemerged on the international agenda with plans for an international tribunal (Chandler 2008b: 364). It is one of the effects of the ECCC that the history of the Khmer Rouge is reappearing into the Cambodian public education and awareness mostly conducted through programs by internationally sponsored non-governmental organizations. In 2009, the Cambodian NGO DCCAM (Documentation Center of Cambodia) launched a textbook for Grades 9–12 in cooperation with the Cambodian Ministry of Education and started nationwide teacher training. Since 2006, NGOs and the ECCC itself have conducted outreach programs in all parts of Cambodia that informed about the tribunal and initiated new discussions about the KR period (see Sperfeldt 2012).

But despite the different modi of national remembrance over the last 30 years, there are certain interconnected themes that have remained consistent since the fall of the KR regime and, I suggest, frame what can be publicly remembered until today: the avoidance of the blurred boundaries between victim and perpetrator identities by emphasizing the collective suffering and the victimhood of all Cambodians and therefore the Cambodian nation, the embedding of political responsibilities for the atrocities into Cambodian notions of political hierarchy and the focus on the period of Democratic Kampuchea alone in remembering past violence. The ultimate political responsibility for the atrocities of the Khmer Rouge has always been attributed to the leading political figures of Democratic Kampuchea, and discussions of individual and collective responsibilities of all those who were KR cadres have been avoided. Cambodian official memories and state narratives of violence focus only on the period of the state of Democratic Kampuchea from April 1975 until January 1979. The collective metaphor for this period is "three years eight months and twenty days" (*bei chnam brambei khae mphei thnay*) or the Pol Pot Time (*samay a Pot*). By focusing solely on this period of "3 years 8 months and 20 days" the memories of all other forms of violence that occurred in Cambodia from 1970 until 1998 are "forgotten" and the violence of the Khmer Rouge period is decontextualized from the global political conflicts it was embedded in.

The tribunal does not counter these narratives. The ECCC is the result of decades-long, complex negotiations between the United Nations and the Cambodian government who all represent different political interests about what should and what should not be subject to the prosecution of the court (Whitley 2006). As a result of compromises between the diverging political agendas described above, the court also focuses solely on the crimes committed during the official time of existence of the state of Democratic Kampuchea from April 1975 until January 1979, thereby supporting the national narrative described above. Furthermore, by prosecuting only the senior responsible leaders, the tribunal again simplifies the complex shifting ambiguities and subjectivities of victim-perpetrator divisions that have occurred over 30 years of violent conflict in Cambodia.[14] This becomes most evident in Case 001 that deals with the atrocities in the former torture center and prison S-21 and the mass execution site of Choeung Ek. In the next section, I will show how both sites are inseparable from state historiography and coexist in their materiality alongside the different modi of state narratives of the Khmer Rouge past described above. But I also suggest that they have often overlooked emotional and personal sides that are inscribed in their history.

Individual and Collective Memory in Tuol Sleng and Choeung Ek

S-21 was officially opened as the memorial site of the Tuol Sleng Museum of Genocide Crimes in 1980, the mass graves of Choeung Ek opened to the public after the exhumation of the remains of nearly 9,000 victims in the early 1980s (Hughes 2006: 23–6). I argue that, like other places and sites in which the past is produced, Tuol Sleng and Choeung Ek can be seen as iconic mediators, locations for the repeated production of meaning and emotion in remembering the past (White 2006; see also Young 1993). Memorial sites are places "where memory crystallizes and secretes itself" (Nora 1989: 7). They are also places where the collective and the individual, the public and the personal interact (White 2000).

The former prison S-21 site now houses the Tuol Sleng Museum of Genocide Crimes. The compound consists of three buildings: Block A hosts the former prison cells for senior cadres; Block B hosts photos, cloths and artifacts of former prisoners on the ground floor, former individual

Plate 1.1 Block A Tuol Sleng memorial site.

prison cells on the second floor, and exhibitions about Democratic Kampuchea on the upper floor; Block C hosts the paintings of one of the survivors, the late Vann Nath.

The ground floor of Building B hosts thousands of photos of children, women and men imprisoned at Tuol Sleng and killed at the prison or at Choeung Ek. Most of these faces have no names and are thus part of the national history of the collective suffering of the victims during the time of the Khmer Rouge. Despite the fact that Tuol Sleng hosts a huge archive with the "confessions" of those interrogated and tortured, we learn nothing about the individuals imprisoned there, nor why they were brought here. The museum does not address the fact that many of those who were detained and executed were former Khmer Rouge cadres and that those victims embody the shifting boundaries between victims and perpetrators over many years of violent conflict. Instead, the past as a former perpetrator is silenced and the identity as victim emphasized. We do not know their names, their families, where they came from and why they were here. One corner also exhibits a glass box of clothes from former prisoners. The display of suffering focuses on the collective; there is very little of the personal and individual. Many of these persons were killed in Choeung Ek.

The killing fields of Choeung Ek are located 15 kilometers southwest of Phnom Penh in Dang Kao district, but fall within the jurisdiction of the municipal authority of the city. The site was originally a Chinese grave-yard, but from 1977 to the end of 1978, it operated as a killing site and burial ground for thousands of victims of Pol Pot's purges (Chandler 1999: 139–40). Choeung Ek was a national killing site and people who got exe-cuted here came from all different parts of Cambodia. It thus came to stand as a symbol for the Cambodian atrocities and all major commemoration days are usually also performed at Choeung Ek. Today the site has a large glass Memorial Stupa which was built in 1988 and filled with the bones and skulls that were exhumed here in the early 1980s. The stupa embeds the place into Buddhist ontology. Every *wat* in Cambodia has stupas that belong to families who store the ashes of their dead relatives and ancestors within. This highlights the importance of Buddhism even at the memorial sites. Entering the site, one walks through a landscape where signs and bones remind the visitor about the atrocities. Even more than in Tuol Sleng, the dead remain anonymous. We learn no names, no individual stories; we just walk though graves and bones and skulls. In a similar vein to Tuol Sleng, cloths can be seen in the graves and in glass boxes next to them.

It has been pointed out by several authors that both memorial sites were once designed in the period of the socialist People's Republic of Kampuchea as visible evidence for the atrocities committed by the Khmer Rouge and therefore also served to legitimize the Vietnamese invasion in 1979 as liberation of the people of Cambodia. The exhibition of skulls and bones served as "proof" for the atrocities and established the notion of the collective suffering of and the need to renew the nation. Within this narrative, the presence of the Vietnamese in Cambodia during the 1980s was depicted as a necessity for peaceful nation-building (Hughes 2006; Ledgerwood 1997; Williams 2004).

A closer look at Tuol Sleng and Choeung Ek reveals that meanings of these sites have shifted in time and in relation to the politics of memory of the various Cambodian governments described above. In the 1980s, many Cambodians visited Tuol Sleng in the 1980s, albeit partly in state-orchestrated tours (Ledgerwood 1997). More recent works have empha-sized that the sites draw a large number of international tourists while the local interest and significance remain low (Hughes 2006, 2008; Margolin 2007; Sion 2011). Since the tribunal started, the local meaning of Tuol Sleng and Choeung Ek has increased significantly as, again, information

Plate 1.2   Human remains at Choeung Ek memorial site.

tours for Cambodians are organized by the ECCC and NGOs engaged in outreach programs.

David Chandler states that "by October 1980, over three hundred thousand Cambodians and eleven thousand foreigners had passed through the facility" (Chandler 1999: 8). There can be no doubt that many visitors were part of state-organized tours as part of the narrative of liberation and nation-building of the People's Republic of Kampuchea, but the testimonies and interviews I did with civil parties from Case 001 reveal that for Cambodians whose relatives went missing during the KR period, the sites had an individual meaning from the beginning. When word spread in 1980 that the regime had displayed thousands of photographs found in Tuol Sleng, all Cambodians who could afford it went to Tuol Sleng to see if they would recognize their loved ones (see also Chandler 2008b: 361). This was never mentioned in the official histories and documentation of Tuol Sleng, and none of these quests were documented. Even on a personal level, these experiences were not shared widely. A friend of mine, who does not want to be named, remembered in a conversation:

I was only a girl when we went to Tuol Sleng. I think it was 1981. I
still remember the smell, it stank and for the entire time I had my scarf
covering my face, I just could not stand the smell, it still smelled of
blood and urine. We did not find a photo of my father but my mother
she cried the whole time, she never talked about it afterwards. (Personal conversation, 5 January 2010)

It was only after the opening of Cambodia to international visitors
after 1993 that the memorial sites became an international attraction, while
the local meaning for school and public education decreased significantly
due to the political period of oblivion described above. But the sites never
ceased to have a personal meaning for those who lost relatives and loved
ones in these places. Those who had been in exile and returned to Phnom
Penh in the 1990s to look for disappeared relatives also turned to Tuol
Sleng and Choeung Ek. One of those personal experiences was revealed in
the testimony of Martine Lefèvre in the courtroom. Lefèvre was married to
Oun Ket, a Cambodian diplomat who left France for Cambodia in 1977,
following the calls for Cambodians abroad to return to their homeland and
help reconstruction. She never heard from her husband again. In 1980, she
visited the refugee camp Khao I Dang in Thailand and finally learned that
her husband died in Tuol Sleng. In 1991, Lefèvre and her children went to
Cambodia to find out what had happened. In court she remembered:

Two days after we arrived, therefore, on the 18th of July 1991, we
travelled; we go to S-21. And when we arrive in this place, which was
formerly a high school, we are of course completely overtaken by the
horror. And we begin looking through all of the photographs that are
lined up by trying to find Ouk Ket's face, and we do not find him. But
I am able to recognize faces of Cambodians who were known abroad.
All three of us are deeply saddened, of course, but more than that even,
we are very much angered and I have a hard time telling my children to
leave this place because their fists are clenched and they're clenching
their teeth before such a quantity of horror. And then the following
days we go to Choeung Ek. When we arrived there, we are struck by
the mausoleum where all of the skulls are piled up, and we say to ourselves that Ket's skull is among all of these thousands of skulls, and
we look at the pits, which we walk over. There are teeth coming up
through the ground, leg bones, radiuses, pieces of shirts, strings, earth,
were covering the people who were killed there. And we are completely
repulsed. (Testimony Martine Lefèvre, 17.8.2009, Case No. 001/18-07-
2007-ECCC/TC: 25)

Her daughter was deeply traumatized by the visit. Her testimony in court was highly emotional; she depicted how she fell into depression after the visit and even turned suicidal.

Another civil party, Chum Sirath, was a student in France when the Khmer Rouge took power and did not return to Cambodia. After the fall of the regime, he tried to reconstruct the fate of his family. Like Martine Lefèvre, he returned to Cambodia only after the end of the socialist People's Republic of Kampuchea and went to Tuol Sleng to find information about his disappeared brothers.

> Regarding my younger brother, Chum Sinaret, although I have tried my best to do his research, I could not find any more information except the photo that was given to me by my friend who took it from S-21. I went to S-21 in October '93. I saw his name on the list with no dates for the entry and the exit. ... I know Narith died at Tuol Sleng because he died on the 1st of January 1977. At that time I believe Choeung Ek was not yet in existence. (Testimony Chum Sirath 20.8.2009, Case File No. 001/18-07-2007-ECCC/TC: 19 and 43)

These personal experiences have never been officially documented in the memorial sites itself. But through their inclusion in the virtual tribunal and the tribunal recordings, they now interact with the collective memoirs and state historiography of the nation. In his ethnographic explorations of the memorial site of Pearl Harbor, White (2000) demonstrates that sites of commemoration are places where, through the deployment of biographies, storytelling and narrative, personal individual memory, and national history can enter the same discursive space and polyphonic spaces of remembering emerge.[15] I suggest that similar processes are at work at the tribunal where the testimonies interact with state historiography and collective memories narrated at S-21 and Choeung Ek, and new memoryscapes emerge.

But in the narratives above, it also becomes evident that these memoryscapes do not only hold memories. They hold and evoke emotions as well (see Cole 2001; White 1999, 2006). White (2006: 332) highlights the importance of the emotionality of memory next to its practices, politics and materiality: "Acts of memory and sites of memory are inevitably evocative — marked by expressions and ideologies of emotions that convey something about the salience of past events for persons recalling them. ... To the general principle that memory be studied in social contexts, we may add that memory in context will always be to some degree emotional, marked by expressions of affect that signify something about the meaning and force of past events for those doing the remembering."

In agreement with White, I suggest that the testimonies and memories that describe individual experiences at Tuol Sleng and Choeung Ek render the sites and the tribunal itself to emotional memoryscapes where grief, anger and frustration are expressed and evoked. This becomes even more evident in the following section where I discuss the encounters of two civil parties, Bou Meng and Chum Sirath, with the accused in the courtroom.

The Search for the Dead at the Tribunal

The testimonies and encounters with Duch are not only individual memories but quests for the truth about what has happened to loved ones lost. Civil parties who are either themselves survivors or relatives of the dead are still haunted by the question of what really happened at these sites and how and where people died. In a culture where respect and offerings to the dead are crucial for the individual's well-being, the need to present offerings to the dead is essential for peace of mind and closure (Holt 2012; LeVine 2010; van de Put and Eisenbruch 2002).

When the civil parties testified in court and had to confront Duch, many started to ask about the remains of their relatives who disappeared and were known to have been imprisoned and interrogated at Tuol Sleng. In the following, I turn to the encounters of two civil parties with Duch: Bou Meng and Chum Sirath, both whom I interviewed after the trial. Chum Sirath lost two brothers in S-21. Bou Meng is one of the survivors of S-21 but his wife was killed after they were arrested in August 1977. When Chum Sirath recalled his visits to Tuol Sleng, as described above, in search for his dead relatives, he finally turned to Duch and said:

> And what I want to know about my other two brothers and in-law, how long had they stayed in S-21, like in the case of Phung Ton? Was it seven months? Was it ten months? That's what I want to know. I knew that he already knew my brothers ... and if he wanted to apologize, that is his right. And of course, as I said, it's not genuine. I wanted to know the circumstances of the death of my brothers. (Testimony Chum Sirath 20.8.2009, Case File No. 001/18-07-2007-ECCC/TC: 40)

After a lengthy statement by Duch that he could not know the details of all people who disappeared, the president then asked Duch to respond to Chum Sirath:

Could you please respond to his question in relation to the date, exact date, when his brothers-in-law were arrested and executed? So this is his sole purpose, to know the truth of the date, and if you can also shed light on the location where their loved one were executed then it would be grateful to them because they believe that if they can locate where the dead body of their loved one could have been buried, then they can really conduct some kind of religious ceremonies to dedicate or offer some kind of best wishes to them. (ibid. 46)

The wish to know the location of the dead victim for the purpose of conducting a religious ceremony was also expressed by Bou Meng, one of the survivors of the former Khmer Rouge Security prison S-21. Bou Meng was arrested together with his wife and then separated. He survived due to his skills as a painter, but his wife was killed (Vannak 2010). When he testified in court and was confronted with Duch, he asked him the following question:

I really want to ask the accused where was my wife killed. If I know where it is then I would go there in order to pray for her soul, and that I am now being testified before the Extraordinary Chambers in the Court of Cambodia, only the spirit of the earth would know where the soul has gone to or where the dead bodies were buried. So only the spirits of the wind, of the water, of the earth would know. And for those who killed the people, they could tell the truth or they could lie, but only the spirits of the earth, the wind and the water know where my wife died, so that I could pray for her soul. That is all. ... And my question is just to tell me, just to tell me where she was killed or smashed. Then I would go to that location and just to get the soil from that location to pray for her soul because there was not her document at the S-21 Office. I used to have some documents as well, but some of the documents I have I have lost or are missing. (Testimony Bou Meng, Case File N° 001/18-07-2007-ECCC/TC: 86)

The President of the ECCC then addressed Duch and asked him if he could provide information where Bou Meng's wife was killed. Duch answered that he was not sure and continued:

It was beyond my capacity because this work was done by my subordinates, but I would like to presume that your wife might have been killed at Choeung Ek. Meanwhile, to be sure, I would like to ask you to please ask Comrade Huy who may be able to tell you further detail about the fate of your wife. Please accept my highest assurance of my regards and respects towards the soul of your wife. That's all. (ibid.)

Bou Meng then started to cry and covered his face with his hands. The testimonies of the civil parties of the tribunal are filled with these questions and searches for dead relatives. For the civil parties of the Khmer Rouge Tribunal, Tuol Sleng and Choeung Ek are thus not only part of Cambodia's national history but hold the individual memories of those who died there. At the same time, it remains to be seen how far the individual meanings these sites hold for those looking for the remains of the dead will enter the national narrative and will be included in the documentation of the sites. The attempt to obtain individual memories and bring them into the public space in the context of the tribunal as the truth about what happened is seen by the civil parties as bringing justice to the dead and a prerequisite for personal reconciliation. However, as the questions about the fates of their loved ones can never be definitively answered, the tribunal ultimately denies individual recognition and full justice as the following excerpt from an interview with Bou Meng that I conducted together with Nou Va in February 2010 shows.

> I lost my family, my wife in Tuol Sleng. I asked Duch, but he did not release the truth. That is what I think there is no justice. Duch always escapes not to tell the truth, but I told everything in the court, it was true. I was wondering why he said he did not know, he was the prison's chief, he managed the list of prisoners, but now he said he did not know. [...] So, I want him to speak out the fact whether my wife was killed at Choeung Ek, or another place. There are four to five graves that I always come to pray for them. (Interview Bou Meng, 25 February 2010)

In the end, the dead remain in the collective realm of the former prison and mass grave. Civil parties are given no certainty about the location of the dead which leads to anger and frustration. When I asked Bou Meng in another interview about his encounter with Duch, he answered:

> I asked him 'did you arrest my wife name Ma Chhoeun?' And where did you bring her? Then he answered it might have been his guard who took her to be killed at Choeung Ek. Until now my feeling is not fresh and not released. I am still thinking about my wife, we used to be in prison here together. Why now there is only me? (Interview Bou Meng 6 November 2010)

To respect and commemorate the dead, they have no choice but to pay their respects individually and collectively at home, in the pagodas, at the mass graves and in Tuol Sleng. In order to do so, they turn to Buddhist commemorative rituals.

Ritual Commemoration for the Dead

In the following section, I turn to Buddhist commemorative rituals of respect and merit-making. I thereby highlight the importance of often over-looked non-verbal forms and practices of remembrance and coming to terms with a violent past. When it comes to genocide and mass atrocities, the material and narrative forms of memory are often foregrounded (see, for example: Langer 1991; Nora 1989; Young 1993). This may be due to the fact that explorations of the holocaust are still dominant in the study of remembering genocide and mass violence and, therefore, Western forms of remembering dominate the scholarly field. But since anthropology has increasingly turned to memories of violence and suffering during colo-nialism or the slave trade, other, more embodied forms of remembering a violent past, for example, ancestor rituals and sacrifices (Cole 2001; Shaw 2002) and/or spirit possession (Lambek 2002; Stoller 1995), are empha-sized. Only recently has scholarly attention shifted to ritual and performa-tive practices in the context of memorial sites and the sacralization of landscapes of violence (Schramm 2011; White 2004). In the context of Pearl Harbor and Ground Zero, Geoffrey White (2004: 300) highlights rituals as "practices that continually (re)define the (sacred) significance of those spaces through actions that express reverence for those who died (and those who survived)."

Yet I suggest that in Cambodia there is more at stake than sacraliza-tion and reverence for the dead. By turning to Khmer Buddhist rituals, civil parties embed the tribunal proceedings into their own cultural logic and ontology, and by doing so, try to balance the felt shortcomings of the tribunal in terms of justice and consolidation. A range of scholars have emphasized the revival of Buddhism and Buddhist rituals after the Khmer Rouge period as crucial for the reconstruction of community and the re-making of moral orders (Hinton 2008; Holt 2012; Ledgerwood 2008; Kent 2006, 2008, 2009, 2011; Zucker 2006). According to these works, the prac-tice of Buddhism and the performance of Buddhist rituals bring back lost continuity and security after past turmoil and in present uncertain times.

In concert with these arguments, I suggest that Buddhism and Khmer Buddhist ancestor rituals play a crucial role in making sense, remembering and consolidating the deaths of the Pol Pot era. I am making sense of Heonik Kwon's (2006) fascinating study of how mass deaths of the Viet-namese war are memorialized at the sites of two massacres in Central Vietnam. Kwon emphasizes ancestor rituals as central for familial, personal and everyday remembrance as opposed to the state rituals that take place at memorial sites for the "heroes" of battles and massacres.[16] In this sense, he considers local ancestor rituals as an opposition to state politics and national narratives in contemporary Vietnam. Vietnamese ancestor rituals, he argues, move the realm of remembering from the nation to the world of kinship. In contrast to the state that differentiates between heroes and enemies, the world of kinship does not distinguish between victim and perpetrators in their reverence for ancestors. The situation in Cambodia differs in multiple ways. The Cambodian state never made heroes and remembered all the dead of past violence as victims precisely because they wanted to silence debates about their own and other's involvement with leading political figures. Furthermore, Khmer Theravada Buddhist rituals differ from Confucian ancestor rites in Vietnam in several ways (see Holt 2012). But Kwon's emphasis on the transformative and consoling power of rituals for the deaths that occurred also has significance for Cambodia.

Cambodian Buddhism is syncretic, combining classical Theravada Buddhist doctrine (*dhamma*) and animistic as well as Brahman beliefs and practices that stem from pre-Buddhist times (Harris 2005: 49–104). There exists a profound belief in the world of ancestors and spirits and the spiritual world is very real (van de Put and Eisenbruch 2002: 114–7). Karma and reincarnation are central beliefs that guide human behavior. It has been argued that the breakdown of ritual patterns during the time of the Khmer Rouge caused feelings of vulnerability and distress in people the more as spirits "are perceived as forces that can invade the mind and body at any time" (LeVine 2010: 13). Peg LeVine (ibid.: 14) even talks about a "spirit based anxiety" in people: "Fright was the consequence of not being able to appease spirits, maintain obligations to ancestral spirits, or protect oneself and others from possessing, wandering or vengeful spirits."

Thus, like in Vietnam, the many deaths that occurred through violence during the Pol Pot Time are perceived as unnatural and therefore as bad deaths, and since the revival of Buddhism ancestor rituals are important and performed regularly (LeVine 2010). They are at the center of Pchum Ben, the annual festival for the dead that takes place in the tenth month of the Cambodian lunar calendar and at the Khmer New Year (Holt 2012). Two central Buddhist rituals are *bon sakaul* and *sanghadana*. *Bon sakaul* is an invitation of monks to come and recite by those who are conducting the ceremony. The monks receive offerings (*dana*) in the form of money and goods as candles, incense sticks, small towels, tea and drink beverages such as soft drinks. The goods are wrapped as readymade parcels. The participants of the ceremony earn merit (*bon*) which they can dedicate to their ancestors. Sometimes *bon sakaul* is combined with *sanghadana* (food offerings). *Sanghadana* is a food-offering ceremony and is also performed to dedicate merit (*bon*) to one's dead ancestors. Dedicating merit to oneself and to one's dead ancestors is a crucial practice in Khmer Buddhist belief where the accumulation of merit is essential for improving one's karma and being reborn into a better next life (Ledgerwood 2008). Merit can be earned through ordination as a monk, the adherence to the five Buddhist precepts (*sel*), which include the observance of the "holy days" (*thngai sel*) and offerings (*dana*) to the monks and the temple (ibid.: 149). Merit is transferable, that is, the living may perform "rituals and offerings to earn merit and transfer these merit to dead relatives" (Ty 2011: 212). The ceremony is led by monks and *achar* and is a syncretic practice of Buddhist and ancestor rituals. After the participants have prayed to the Buddha and asked for the *sel* (five precepts), rice and food are offered to the monks and to the ancestors. In the rituals that I observed in Takeo province, all rituals involved *sanghadana* where the offerings for the ancestors are collected on a separate plate with a banana leaf and in the end decorated with lit incense. Lit incense is part of all ancestor-dedicated and Buddhist ceremonies. While the food offerings to the monks are taken back to the pagoda, the offerings to the ancestors are thrown outside on the ground near a spirit house or even to the fields.[16] However, all ceremonies that I observed in the capital offered no food but did a *bon sakaul* where they offered wrapped parcels containing candles, incense, towels, condensed milk and drink beverages (see above) to the monks and did not conduct any food offerings at the memorial sites. In all ceremonies, participants ask to donate the merit they gain through the performance of the ceremony to the dead ancestors. *Bon sakaul* and *sanghadana* can be done for dead individuals — that the names of the dead are read before the ceremony is performed, or for collective groups at the pagoda as it happens during Pchum Ben. The rituals can also be conducted at one's home. However, the ceremonies can never be done alone. Monks and *achar* have to be present to conduct the ceremony.

During the annual celebrations of Pchum Ben and on Khmer New Year, rituals for the dead are also performed at Cambodian mass killing sites. The survivors of Tuol Sleng perform *bang sakaul* at the site during Pchum Ben since the opening of the memorial site (Vann Nath 1998: 107; interviews Chum Mey and Bou Meng February 2010). In contrast, several civil parties I talked to mentioned the importance of ceremonies for their relatives who died during the Khmer Rouge time but also said that mostly these rituals are performed locally at the pagoda where the ashes of dead relatives are kept in stupas or the ancestral places in those parts of the country where the ash of family relatives is buried at special places in the village in the ground or even at home.[18]

Chum Sirath who — in addition to the two brothers imprisoned at S-21 — lost 37 family members whose fates he cannot retrace and who disappeared into the many mass graves of the country, also emphasized that he conducts ceremonies for his dead relatives twice a year at Pchum Ben and at Khmer New Year. But sometimes the dead visit his dreams and whenever that occurs, he invites monks to conduct a ceremony at his home (interview Chum Sirath 1 July 2011). Bou Meng told me that every year at Pchum Ben, he tries to go to seven pagodas, to receive the precepts and donate offerings (*dana*) to earn merit for his first wife who was killed in Tuol Sleng or Choeung Ek (interview with Bou Meng November 2010). Yet, there remains a sense of incompleteness precisely because there are no remains of the relatives that disappeared at the usual familial ancestral places. Thus the mass graves and execution sites become symbolic ancestral places both individually and collectively. At a former mass killing site in Takeo province where I also conducted research, people who knew that their loved ones died at that site came and conducted ceremonies, often on special days like Pchum Ben and Khmer New Year.

The interesting aspect is that in the context of the tribunal, these ritual activities also increased at Choeung Ek even if initiated by civil society. Non-governmental organizations that worked in the context of the tribunal encouraged and organized rituals in Choeung Ek. The local NGO Youth for Peace used to perform a *bon sakaul* every time they conducted outreach information tours with study groups to Choeung Ek. The NGO Transcultural Psychological Organization (TPO) organized a *bang sakaul* especially for the civil parties that participated in Case 001. For Bou Meng, the participation in this ceremony at Choeung Ek was an important step to address the incompleteness and frustration he felt after his encounter with Duch. (Interview Bou Meng 5 November 2010)

The day before the Duch verdict, all civil parties gathered in Tuol Sleng and conducted a *bon sakaul*. For the civil parties, it was both a collective and an individual act. Collectively as it was done in the group and performed at a former execution site, individually as people dedicated merits to their loved ones who disappeared. Thus, even though the ritual is performed collectively, it personalizes and spiritualizes these national memorial sites and transcends the purely political and legal realm.

Plate 1.3 *Bang sakaul* at Choeung Ek.

Conclusion

The testimonies and agency of civil parties of Case 001 at the ECCC personalize and emotionalize the state historiography and collective memories of the two national memorial sites of Tuol Sleng and Choeung Ek while at the same time are being framed by the national histories narrated. The civil parties' testimonies give personal voices to the nameless faces and skulls exhibited. But as civil parties' questions about the whereabouts of their loved ones remain unanswered and their demand for a memorial with the names of victims is still under negotiation, it is only through collective rituals and ceremonies that the dead can be respected and remembered and "emotional remembering" (White 2000) can be enacted. These different acts of remembering give new dimensions and new insights not only to the national memorial sites that are so often only seen as state narratives and tourist attractions but also to the ECCC itself. Through their agency of the Civil Parties, the court becomes more than a legal matter. It becomes an emotional memoryscape that reconfigures both the individual and collective memories of the Khmer Rouge period of the Cambodian nation.

According to Paul Basu (2007: 233), memoryscapes are constituted through different "mnemonic worlds" that "articulate with and mediate one another," a process he calls "mnemonic creolisation," invoked by endogenous and exogenous factors. I suggest that this also holds true for the memoryscapes that emerge in the tribunal and at the memorial sites. It is the interplay of the international legal process that initiates the testimonies, the initiative of non-governmental organizations that takes local ritual practices to the national memorial sites and the agency of the Cambodian civil parties that constructs these memoryscapes.

However, that said, the different mnemonic practices do not contest the contemporary collective narrative of a nation of victims that suffered under a few "senior responsible leaders." The existing complexities of blurring and shifting boundaries between victims and perpetrators that become evident in the documents of Tuol Sleng and in some of the testimonies are not fully explored in court. The acceptance of applicants as civil parties to the court declares them victims of Democratic Kampuchea regardless of the question if they or their relatives may have joined the Khmer Rouge themselves at one stage of their lives or even may have been Khmer Rouge cadres. While the civil parties want to know the truth about what happened to their loved ones at Tuol Sleng and Choeung Ek, their narratives give only little insights about the blurred and shifting subjectivities and ambiguities of victims and perpetrators in Democratic Kampuchea that many of those who were detained in Tuol Sleng may embody, and the rituals are performed for the dead as victims of the Khmer Rouge regime.

Notes

1. While seven survivors are known to have escaped Tuol Sleng in 1979, the exact numbers of survivors are not known. Case 001 found other survivors and just recently the Cambodian NGO DCCAM (Documentation Center of Cambodia) has stated that the actual number of survivors was much higher than estimated and may count up to 200 people (Keo 2010).
2. See http://www.dccam.org/Database/Images/KillingFieldsMap975_1979.jpg.
3. Other prison and killing sites such as Kraing Ta Chan in Takeo Province have a similar number of victims, but are not that well-documented and centrally located. Tuol Sleng is well-documented and the Khmer Rouge left an archive behind that allows research into the site. In addition, Tuol Sleng was the only national prison and according to Henri Locard (2011) the biggest one in terms of number of people working there and building size.

4.   This is the definition as written in the law of the ECCC. Article 2 of the law reads: "Extraordinary Chambers shall be established in the existing court structure, namely the trial court and the supreme court to bring to trial senior leaders of Democratic Kampuchea and those who were most responsible for the crimes and serious violations of Cambodian laws related to crimes, international humanitarian law and custom, and international conventions recognized by Cambodia, that were committed during the period from 17 April 1975 to 6 January 1979." (Law on the Establishment of the Extraordinary Chambers, with inclusion of amendments as promulgated on 27 Oct. 2004 (NS/RKM/1004/006), at http://www.eccc.gov.kh/sites/default/files/legal-documents/KR_Law_as_amended_27_Oct_2004_Eng.pdf [accessed 17 July 2011]).

5.   Civil parties and their lawyers appealed that ruling. The interviews of this research were conducted before the appeal judgment of the ECCC of 3 Feb. 2012 sentenced Duch to life in prison. (Summary of Appeal Judgement, Case File 001/18-07-2007/ECCC/SC, Kaing Guek Eav, 3 Feb. 2012, at http://www.eccc.gov.kh/sites/default/files/documents/courtdoc/03022012Summary-Eng.pdf [accessed 12 Nov. 2012]).

6.   The recent official commemoration of the former national "day of hate" (*tivea chong kamhaeng*, lit. day of tying anger) that is now called "day of remembrance" at Choeung Ek on 20 May revealed the state historiography of the Khmer Rouge period almost in an ideal-type fashion. A theater play was performed that reenacted the terror of the Khmer Rouge cadres and ended with the liberation of the Cambodian people by Vietnamese soldiers and the Khmer Salvation front. In the end, pictures of the Prime Minister Hun Sen were paraded.

7.   The estimated number of deaths during Cambodia's civil war from 1970–75 differ widely among scholars and are much less researched than the excess death toll of the Khmer Rouge period. Kiernan (2003) and Heuveline (1998) estimate the number of wartime excess deaths to 300,000.

8.   Peasants who had fled from the rural areas to the cities during the civil war were also considered "new people" (Hinton 2005: 9). Kiernan (2002: 48) estimates the population of Phnom Penh to have counted almost two million in Apr. 1975. Beng Hong Socheat Khmero (2000: 11) states that the capital's population increased from 600,000 in 1969 to 1.5 million in 1975, out of which 800,000 were refugees. Next to Phnom Penh, all major urban centers of Cambodia were evacuated, such as Battambang, Siem Reap, Kampong Cham (Kiernan 2002: 49–51). David Chandler (2008a: 256) estimates that altogether more than two million Cambodians were victims of forced evacuation from the urban areas to the countryside in Apr. 1975.

9.   While all of Cambodia suffered during this period, reports of survivors have shown that conditions were harsher in those areas that were not occupied by Khmer Rouge forces before 1975 and differed for base and new people

(see Kiernan 2002; Vickery 1984). While food was in general very little for people in the cooperatives, some of my interlocutors did eat rice twice a day while the majority reported rice gruel as the food provided. Just as the labor conditions varied in different zones, so did the food provisions. But even when rice was provided, people always would show me that it was rationed to one handful per meal. There were never more than two meals a day.

10. For a detailed exploration of the activities of civil society in the context of the tribunal, see Sperfeldt 2012.

11. Vann Nath, who painted most of the images depicting life at S-21 that are exhibited at Tuol Sleng today and who was a crucial witness in Case 001, died on 5 Sept. 2011 in Phnom Penh.

12. http://socrates.berkeley.edu/~warcrime/virtualtribunal.htm [accessed 31 Oct. 2010].

13. Interview Kris Baleva, In-Country Head of Legal and Content Development of the War Crimes Studies Center, University of California at Berkeley, ECCC Virtual Tribunal, 6 Feb 2010. (http://socrates.berkeley.edu/~warcrime/virtualtribunal.htm [accessed 31 Oct. 2010]).

14. For a more detailed exploration of the politics of memory and the ECCC, see Emde (in preparation).

15. Paul Basu (2007), in exploring memorial sites in post-conflict Sierra Leone, also opposes the common dichotomy between memory and history and talks about memorial sites as memoryscapes where memory and history are co-incident. He asks how in these memoryscapes different "mnemonic worlds" "articulate with and mediate one another" (ibid.: 233). He calls this process "mnemonic creolisation," a process that is invoked by "endogenous as well as exogenous factors" (ibid.). Moreover, places, objects and sites may embody multiple memories of different times, events and epochs that overlap. This process renders sites to palimpsest memoryscapes. He illustrates his example with the Cotton Tree that shadows the National Museum in the capital Freetown. This cotton tree is an important icon of Sierra Leone's slave heritage. "The tree both acts as a witness to the violent uprooting of people from their homeland in the image of the slave market and provides a symbol of sanctuary and protection for the freed slaves on their "return to Africa" (ibid.: 235). But the mnemonic meanings of the cotton tree go back even further. Cotton trees hold a special place in local cosmologies, are considered sacred places and were used as boundary markers. In 2004, Freetown's cotton tree together with a dove became the icon of a new 10,000 Leone note now symbolizing new national unity and peace. Thus, the different interpretations and meanings of the cotton tree overlap and sometimes overwrite each other depending on the history that is chosen to frame it.

16. The importance of rituals for the transformation of bad deaths is also emphasized for post-conflict East Timor by my colleague, Victoria Kumala Sakti (forthcoming). But while in East Timor ritual practices are also related to

negotiations of compensation between victims and perpetrators, such practices of compensation do not exist in Cambodia and the rituals in these two
different societies differ as they are embedded in different religious and cultural logics.

17. I observed a number of these ceremonies in a village in Takeo province
where the offerings for the ancestors were thrown either into the fields or
onto the ground outside the homes where the ceremonies were performed. I
also observed one ceremony at a former mass killing site near this village
and here the offerings were thrown into the mass grave.

18. The practice of keeping the ashes of the deceased differs regionally within
Cambodia. In Takeo province where I worked, special places (*tiet*) existed
in the village where the ashes of the deceased were buried in the soil. This
practice was completely unknown to Machhem, my research assistant who
came from Pursat and had lived in Battambang for many years. In his home
region, ashes were kept at the stupas at the *wat*.

CHAPTER 2

National *Lieu de Mémoire* vs. Multivocal Memories: The Case of Viengxay, Lao PDR

Oliver Tappe

"People had to hide in the forest," said the old, half-blind farmer sitting in front of his family's house in Ban Nakai, Viengxay town.[1] He then pointed to the green hills covered with secondary forest and the occasional swidden rice field. "Many stayed in caves but others had to dig holes and covered them with leaves so that the American bombers could not see them. Our old village was completely destroyed. We could go to the rice fields only under moonshine. The leadership of the party even disapproved of raising colorful ducks and advised us to wear inconspicuous clothes."

Welcome to Viengxay, the so-called "Birthplace of the Lao People's Democratic Republic" (Nivat 2006: 45; see Provincial Tourism Office Houaphan 2007). As a celebrated site of revolutionary history, namely the place where the leaders of the Pathet Lao sought shelter in caves during the US Army's bombing campaigns of the Second Indochina War, Viengxay plays a considerable role in Lao official commemoration politics. This site of memory is presented to visitors as a place of revolutionary solidarity and bravery, of patriotism and sacrifice. A guided tour leads through the caves of the leading figures of the Lao communist revolution such as the late Secretary-General, Kaysone Phomvihane, and "Red Prince" Souphanouvong who stayed there from 1964 until the 1973 ceasefire. Besides heroic stories of the great leaders, the "small fates" of the local population are acknowledged as well. The audio guide reflects voices of survivors of the war, children of the political leaders and ordinary villagers who endured hardships and suffering, and for whom the limestone karst mountains of Viengxay constantly remind them of one of the most violent episodes both in Lao history and their own lives.

A walk through this memorial landscape reveals the ambivalent heritage that imbues the physical environment with meaning: small hidden caves where a household could find cover, rocks bombed out of the mountain faces and scattered around overgrown craters; ruins of former militia compounds and the vast halls of the hospital cave where women gave birth next to dying mutilated soldiers; bomb debris and sometimes even unexploded ordnance which until today threaten the population ... in sum a landscape that represents both shelter and sorrow, both nourishment and death, haunted by traumatic memories of a violent past.

This chapter shall discuss first Viengxay as landscape of war memory by focusing on the interaction of people and their environment, and the influence of official commemoration politics on local collective memory connected to the landscape, on shared images of the past; second, it will focus on the growth of tourism in the former "liberated zone" that creates ambiguous connections between official narratives, multivocal local memories and international views on the broader context of the violent years of the Second Indochina War.

Introduction: Landscapes as Sites of Memory

I consider Viengxay as a key site of memory in the present-day Lao People's Democratic Republic following Pierre Nora's (1989) basic definition of *lieux de mémoire* as sites where memories converge and condense and where people engage (controversially) with their pasts. As deplored by the French historian, such sites are often appropriated by the state for official commemorative politics — linked to state holidays, visited by official delegations and included in a national imaginary (Nora 1998; see Ricoeur 2004: 401–11). Yet the interplay with local collective memory — that is between different intents to remember — continues and will be of particular importance for our analysis. Following Halbwachs' (1950, 1952) insight in the social and cultural constitution and organization of memory, the past is less a given than continually reconstructed and represented (Erll 2008: 7). Collective memory implies the idea of a socially constructed and continually reproduced memory — an ongoing project of "reconstructive imagination" (Assmann 1997: 14) aimed at the production of meaning

which in essence is unstable and susceptible for ideological/political contention. Here the distinction between the local and the national level comes
into play. While local collective remembrance of the past is often directly
linked to the self-ascertainment of a community, on a national level political strategies of legitimization and public relations prevail. However,
these dimensions should not be treated separately since war memory links
individual "small fates" and local history to the overarching grand narrative of national history.

The discursive genesis of this site of memory provides profound
insights in how official narratives of the revolutionary struggle continue to
legitimize the political status quo in Laos. As a national *lieu de mémoire*,
Viengxay is claimed by the Lao People's Revolutionary Party (LPRP),
which at present shapes the meaning of the place as key site of the victorious revolutionary struggle from which the current regime derives its
legitimacy. Simultaneously, the town is promoted as tourism destination
focused on historical entertainment in a beautiful natural environment. In
other words, Viengxay is now a spatial historical document and a potential
economic resource where the interests of the Lao government and the
international development community intersect. The topography of Viengxay
as historical palimpsest comprises various layers to be analyzed both as
media of memory and ideological projection screens, and of course as
components of local life-worlds. The term life-world comprises the sum of
physical surroundings and the everyday experiences of individuals and collectives living together in this environment (Husserl 1970; Merleau-Ponty
1962; Ingold 2000). Therefore, sites of memory must be considered as part
of a larger physical world which constitutes the ground of human experience — prominent landmarks perceived and more or less engaged with
by the local population.

As Vatthana Pholsena and I have pointed out in our Introduction, we
analyze landscape as a cultural process characterized by the interaction and
mutual constitution of people and their physical environment rather than a
mere physical reality "out there." Thus, landscape is a contingent interplay
of actuality and potentiality, not just a fixed image or representation of an
idea. Moreover, landscapes are contested sites of power struggles, in particular if they are shaped and interpreted as state-controlled *lieux de mémoire*
— a hegemonic strategy that encounters resistance by multiple local collective voices or transnational perspectives. Yet, the physical surface of
landscapes should not be neglected since the perception of landscapes is a
manifold process that takes aspects of aesthetics, memory and materiality

into account — all on their own capable to constitute a meaningful environment with which the inhabitants correspond in their daily activities and where visitors are confronted with competing impressions. The negotiations of historical meaning and collective memories are entangled with prospects of development sustained by the prospects of agricultural and tourism development in Viengxay. This makes it a nexus of past, present and future where a bundle of different and at times contesting discourses entertain a complex relation with the physical environment and everyday life-worlds. This intricate interplay between discourses and materiality, affects and iconicity, official historiography and tourism strategies will be explored in the example of Viengxay as a polyvalent, meaningful landscape of memory.

Houaphan Province as Landscape of Violent History and Memory

Even before the irruption of the Indochina Wars, Houaphan regularly turned into a place of chaos and violence. As French travelogues illustrated, marauding bands of multi-ethnic militias ravaged and looted northern Laos in the 1870s. These bands were scattered remnants of the large-scale rebellions that unsettled the Qing dynasty for decades (Kuhn 1970). In Laos, these bands were considered Chinese (Ho) even though upland Tai, Hmong and other ethnic groups sometimes joined the marauders (Culas and Michaud 1997: 224). Yet more often than not, peoples fled from the invading bands either deeper into the forested mountains or — in the case of the Lao who settled in the uplands of Houaphan since the 16th century — to the lowlands. Captain Cupet, member of the Pavie mission, traveled through Houaphan and Xieng Khouang in 1888 and bemoaned the devastations that characterized the landscapes of the northeastern provinces. He mentioned destroyed temples in abandoned villages and suggested a traumatized population: "[The Chinese] raids were renewed almost every year and after a very short time, the majority of the villages had been burned. The inhabitants, hit by incessant requisitioning, obliged to run to the forest every so often to see their huts destroyed when they returned and their fields devastated, abandoned the country little by little" (Cupet 2000 [1900]: 39). The Second Indochina War (1961–75) clearly mirrored this historical situation when the local people fled into the forests and caves of the mountains to seek shelter from the American bombing campaigns.

The chaotic years before the consolidation of French colonial administration changed the demography of the sparsely populated region. Hmong fleeing from the Chinese established villages on the mountain ridges while Tai Deng from Thanh Hoa took over villages and rice fields abandoned by Lao — who partially returned after awhile, creating tensions with the upland Tai groups (Foropon 1927). Further tensions were created by colonial interventions such as taxation policies or the changing administration between Luang Prabang and Thanh Hoa (Gay 1989: 208–10). Messianistic movements occurred among the local population, for example, the Hmong uprising under Chao Fa Pachai (Alleton 1981). The Việt Minh took advantage of local resentments and supported anti-colonial militias. Võ Nguyên Giáp considered war against France as an Indochinese affair, opened up an additional "Lao Front" by establishing joint Lao-Vietnamese forces in Houaphan since 1948 and by backing a young, energetic soldier, Kaysone Phomvihane — son of a Lao mother and a Vietnamese father — who later became the strongman of the Lao People's Revolutionary Party (Goscha 2003: 38–40). Houaphan with its strategic location in the mountainous Lao-Vietnamese border region next to the political and military power centers of Hanoi became a bridgehead of Indochinese revolution. After the First Geneva Agreements of 1954, the remote provinces of Houaphan and Phongsaly were controlled by the communists and considered "liberated zones" (Lao: *khet potpòi*).

When politics of national reconciliation failed and Laos was drawn into civil war between rightists, neutralist, and leftist groups, the leadership of the Neo Lao Hak Xat (the Lao Party communist's official front political organization) fled to Houaphan in 1960 where Kaysone's troops had established full control with support from Hanoi.[2] After a short intermezzo of political negotiations, the civil war escalated in 1963; in particular, Xieng Khouang province became the major battlefield. With the American intervention, the communist leadership retreated from the Plain of Jars and again sheltered in the stronghold of Houaphan's mountains, more precisely in the village of Siang Sü, located only a few kilometers south of Viengxay. When on 17 May 1964 the American bombing of the region started (Ministry of Information and Culture 2000: 915), the limestone karst mountains around the small village Ban Nakai — which later became part of Viengxay — were chosen as a more suitable stronghold than the unprotected plain of Siang Sü. Souvanna Khamdy, today curator of the Kaysone Memorial in Vientiane, recalls how the later politburo member Sali Vongkhamsao sent him to survey the region for suitable bases for the communists to retreat which he finally found in the hundreds of caves in the mountains around the village Ban Nakai (Lao National Tourism Authority 2010: 8–9). Refugees from the heavily bombed provincial capital, Sam

Neua, and other bombed villages followed the revolutionary leaders and their soldiers. A true cave town emerged, named Viengxay, "City of Victory" (then the *nom du guerre* of Kaysone). Since this strategy did not remain secret for long, American bombers attacked the noticeable mountains with full force. The bombing raids were intended to wipe out the communist leadership and the revolutionary troops who were directly supported by North Vietnamese troops. Each night, Vietnamese soldiers filled the craters in the supply routes as they used to do it at the same time along the Ho Chi Minh Trail in Southern Laos (Pholsena 2008; van Staaveren 1993). While Sam Neua was completely razed to the ground, more and more people took refuge in about 200 out of 480 natural caves around Viengxay. With more than 23,000 inhabitants, Viengxay became one of the largest cities in the Lao highlands. Over the years, a viable infrastructure had been constructed within the caves including army quarters, hospitals, schools, factories, and communication networks (Rogers 2005). Yet for most people life was full of dangers and risks, particularly for peasants working in the fields. One of the most frequently told stories from the war is about how the people tended their fields and gardens under moonlight. Both soldiers and civilians suffered from hunger and relied on Vietnamese food supplies. For nine years, the local people had to endure daily bombing campaigns while the communist leadership led its guerrilla war from within the caves. Inside the caves, rooms and corridors had been enlarged with sledgehammers and dynamite and made more comfortable with level floors and concrete walls, ventilation, roofs and drainage (ibid.; Lao National Tourism Authority 2010).

Following the ceasefire in 1973, the leaders left their caves and built houses directly in front of their shelters in case the war erupts again. As provisional capital of the "liberated zone," Viengxay witnessed a profound change since administrative buildings and ministries were built next to newly built roads. The Vietnamese continued their military and technical support. It was not before the takeover of 1975 that the revolutionaries and their entourage returned to Vientiane to proclaim the Lao People's Democratic Republic. However, for the local peasants, hardships and distress continued as the economy was down and agriculture was constrained by ruined fields and unexploded ammunition. Moreover, reeducation camps were established in the region. Senior bureaucrats, members of the Royal Army and even the royal family were taken to Houaphan to attend political "seminars" — a euphemism used for the camps that implied years-long forced labor, malnourishment, illness, and death. Often the camps were misused to settle old scores through denunciation (Stuart-Fox 1997: 172).

Viengxay with more than 400 detainees in 1976 (Khamphanh 2004: 182) became an isolated *khet phiset* ("special zone") and a notorious symbol of remoteness and secrecy.

With the relaxed political climate of the 1990s and the official closure of most of the camps, the Lao government hesitantly opened Viengxay for visitors. With international aid, the site was turned into a promising tourism destination focusing on the violent history of the Second Indochina War and the heroic legacy of the "liberation struggle" of the Lao people. In this process, Viengxay was turned into a showcase and memorial site of the Lao revolution and an arena for self-legitimating strategies of the LPRP. As will be shown in the following sections, the three entangled aspects of Viengxay — site of state commemoration, tourism destination and nexus of different individual war memories — create tensions and ambiguities as well as synergies.

Viengxay, Landscape of Memory — A Topographical Overview

Visitors entering the town of Viengxay are usually surprised by its quiet and picturesque appearance that makes it hard to imagine it as a former arena of war and violence. The oversized roads — reminding of the short career of Viengxay as provisional capital of communist Laos (1973–75) — are lined with gardens and small houses, only now and then interrupted by decrepit and abandoned former administrative buildings displaying a melancholic aura of the faded idea of a socialist resistance capital in the highlands. In contrast, a monument consisting of a peasant, a soldier and a worker celebrates the vision of socialism by the main road. The worker is stepping on a bomb with the letters "USA" — recently repainted — inscribed on it (Plate 2.1). This posture is somewhat ambivalent since it can be interpreted as a sign of victory against the "imperialists" as well as a reference to the explosive legacy of the war lurking to the feet of the people. As Holly High (2007: 70) puts it: "UXO has become part of the very ground livelihoods are built on."

Next to the monument in the town's center, an unremarkable market with a couple of noodle soup stalls is frequented by the occasional tourist group and women from the surrounding villages buying and selling goods. A number of Chinese traders have opened their businesses next to it, including a motorbike store that appears over-dimensioned in this rural area. Yet given the fact that motorbikes are nowadays the most important means of transport in even in the remote mountains, and the large catchment of

Plate 2.1   Revolutionary monument in Viengxay town.

the district capital, the line-up of colorful motorbikes from Chinese production does not surprise. Rather, they stand emblematically for the current
provincial initiatives to make the region attractive for foreign investment
and promote economic development. Next to the market, large ponds dominate the center of the town. They used to be crater landscapes unsuitable
for cultivation and were thus dug out by hundreds of men — forced labor
according to contemporaries — in order to create fish ponds. Halfway to
the Viengxay Caves Visitor Centre, a white "stupa of the unknown soldier"
with a communist star on the top refers to the relationship between Buddhist and socialist ideas in contemporary Laos (Plate 2.2; see Evans 1998;
Tappe 2008). Every now and then, a large concrete plant tub is placed next
to the road inscribed with revolutionary slogans such as "Müang Viengxay
is the birthplace of the Lao People's Democratic Republic," "Müang
Viengxay is a place of solidarity," and "Müang Viengxay is the stronghold
of the revolution."[3] The whole scenery is overshadowed by limestone karst
mountains crisscrossed by the natural cave complexes mentioned above.

The following caves are included in the official tour package: the
office and residence caves of the revolutionary leaders Kaysone Phomvihane

Plate 2.2 "Stupa of the Unknown Soldier" in Viengxay town.

(1920–92), Souphanouvong (1909–95), Nouhak Phoumsavan (1914–2008), Phoumi Vongvichit (1909–94), and Khamtay Siphandone (*1924)[4] whose cave is connected to the Tham Sanglot complex which housed up to 2,000 soldiers and staff (according to the information plate). Inside the caves, only a small amount of crude furniture and other items give a sense of life in this inhospitable and cold environment. Narrow rectangular emergency rooms with oxygen pumps refer to the fear of gas attacks. The cave entrances hide behind huge blast walls that protected the caves from bomb shrapnel and guided missiles. As a photo in Phoumi Vongvichit's autobiography (1987) documents, only provisionary shacks stood outside the cave as temporary resting places. It was not before the ceasefire of 1973 that the party erected concrete houses for the revolutionary leaders — close to the cave entrances in case the bombing restarts (Rogers 2005). Nouhak Phoumsavan's house appears to be in the best condition since Nouhak used to visit Viengxay on a regular basis and other cadres from Vientiane were accommodated there as well.[5] A photo exhibition displaying impressions from the war years occupies one room in Kaysone's house while another small building is reserved for a bust of the late party leader. Visitors leave donations here and light incense in commemoration of the great leader, thereby imitating ritual practice in Buddhist temples.[6]

The impressive Tham Sanglot, the "cave were elephants could pass," was used for theater and dance performances to entertain both soldiers and civilians. Today this large cave with a concrete grandstand is used for large gatherings such as party meetings. In the same complex, the army quarters were established and the so-called artillery cave sheltered the anti-aircraft, now looking across the crater-pocked and overgrown plain of the former airport. Souphanouvong's cave is surrounded by bougainvillea which the Red Prince had ordered from his hometown Luang Prabang. Besides, Souphanouvong dug out a large bomb crater and built a heart-shaped pool instead. The small stupa for his eldest son who died during the war will be explained in more detail below. Recently, the Vietnamese and Chinese embassy caves were included in the tour, and in the future, the vast hospital cave complex (the former "Lao-Cuban Friendship Hospital," located seven kilometers east of Viengxay) will be opened as well, according to the Provincial Tourism Office (personal communication).

The landscape surrounding Viengxay reveals more or less visible traces of a precarious past. Besides smaller caves where lower-ranking revolutionaries, soldiers and civilians resided, or which were used for different purposes such as workshops, factories etc., overgrown relics of concrete foundations indicate the sites of former buildings such as the barracks of Vietnamese engineers that helped to improve the town after the ceasefire. These traces are visible only by locals and well-informed visitors. More conspicuous are the brick basins on the mountain slopes that were used as a water supply for the caves and once linked to them by bamboo tubes. The name of one Hmong village — Ban Kum Chet ("Village Group 7") recalls the former location of a battalion of the People's Army. Further war souvenirs are craters and unexploded cluster bombs that scatter the landscape albeit on a lesser scale than in Xieng Khouang province (see Russell, this volume). While the cases of the cluster bombs are used for various purposes such as planting pots, barbecue cases, and poles for huts, the bombies are collected and sold as scrap metal — even if they are still potentially active. Therefore, the bombs represent ways of appropriation and valorization as well as lethal danger.

The materiality and iconicity of this landscape of violent memory opens it for processes of signification and for struggles of meaning. From the perspective of the state, Viengxay as a national *lieu de mémoire* requires a deliberate shaping of meaning — to make it the unambiguous heroic "birthplace of the Lao PDR" as official accounts would have it. As the following discussion of official commemorative politics will show, certain levels and elements of this landscape are singled out and arranged in a meaningful historical discourse. The official cave tour with its numerous information plates and explanations by the guides fulfills this purpose.

Viengxay as Revolutionary *Lieu de Mémoire*

After the escalation of the Lao civil war and the beginning of the American bombing campaign in 1964, most leftist politicians and their families went to the "liberated zone," more exactly to Houaphan where Kaysone Phomvihane already had established the base of the revolutionary party with North Vietnamese assistance. Many of them did not enter Vientiane again before 1975. In his autobiography, Phoumi Vongvichit (1987: 175) reports how it took him four days in 1964 to bring his family from war-torn Xieng Khouang to Viengxay because they could only travel in the security of the night. While people in Xieng Khouang increasingly had to dig holes in the hills to find shelter, in Viengxay things were prepared for the leading members of the Patriotic Front: "the central committee of the party had drilled caves for us" (ibid.) inside one karst mountain that provided shelter for Phoumi's family. The cave included a garage, a kitchen, a dining room, and bedrooms for all family members who went through the daily bombing raids unscathed thanks to the sheltering rock. Outside the cave, a few simple, provisional shacks, ducked close to the cliffs towering the cave entrance allowed rare moments of fresh air and daylight as one of the photographs illustrates (ibid.: 176). Numerous pictures on information plates in the caves illustrate the life of the revolutionary leaders among soldiers and civilians in the caves.

The cave tour reproduces official historical narratives of the so-called "liberation struggle" (Lao: *kantòsu potpòi*) against foreign oppression. Contemporary historiography as exemplified by the standard history book *Pavatsat lao*[7] tells the story of the valiant "Lao multi-ethnic people" in their centuries-long struggle for independence and unity (Lockhart 2006; Tappe 2008). Wars against Siamese and Burmese "feudalists" and against French and American "imperialists" are key elements within this heroic narrative. According to this teleological history that culminates in the revolution — the "liberation" — of 1975, the historical protagonists of the *kantòsu* are arranged in a genealogy of national ancestors (Lao: *banphabulut*). This official hero pantheon includes heroic kings such as Fa Ngum and Anuvong as well as the revolutionary leaders mentioned above who used to sit at the long table in the politburo cave (Plate 2.3).[8] Viengxay

Plate 2.3 The meeting room of the politburo in Kaysone Phomvihane's cave complex.

fits nicely in the discursive national topography of Laos that represents a specific idea of the Lao nation according to LPRP vision (via narrative, icons and state performances): a multi-ethnic people with a rich cultural heritage that fought for centuries for independence and unity, now united in pursue for socioeconomic development while preserving the culture, in particular the legacy of Buddhist civilization (Tappe 2008, 2011a).

In March 2010, a Buddhist temple was inaugurated in this largely non-Buddhist region. This event became an occasion for celebrating the legacy of the liberation struggle in connection with culture politics and visions of socioeconomic prosperity. On this occasion, a large tour group of 150 persons traveled from the capital Vientiane to the mountains of Houaphan in a commemorative pilgrimage, visited the caves and paid homage to Kaysone with incense and donations. Besides ceremonies at the temple such as almsgiving, political speeches mixed with dancing and singing performances. The dancing performances referred to local cultural "traditions" (Lao: *papheni*) — Lao women dancing with *kaen* flutes, Hmong kids in traditional dress jumping to Thai-style pop music. Between

these acts, an aged veteran of the "struggle" gave a *mò lam* singing performance in which he sang about his war years he spent together with
Kaysone and the other leaders, living in caves and pushing risky military
operations. In a corresponding speech, an official from Vientiane merged
cultural and economic "development" of the district within a general discourse of national construction (Lao: *sang sat*) by emphasizing how Viengxay turned from a crater landscape into a prosperous *müang*. His speech
illustrated the three pillars of contemporary government politics: cultivating
Lao national culture, preserving the legacy of the revolutionary struggle,
and promoting socioeconomic development.

In the foreword to a publication based on 46 interviews with people
who lived in Viengxay during the war — these interviews from 2008
constitute the material for the audio tour as well — the chairman of
the Lao National Tourism Authority, Somphong Mongkhonvilay, states that
"[...] Viengxay was a place of great heroism, ingenuity and solidarity, but
also of great suffering" (Lao National Tourism Authority 2010). Therefore,
Viengxay is considered meaningful because it represents revolutionary
values such as heroism and solidarity but also the hardships of the Lao
people during the war. As a *lieu de mémoire* in Nora's sense, the place
unites official memory discourses of the revolutionary struggle with a
wide range of individual memories of the war which finds its expression
in the cave tour. One crucial keyword here is arguably "solidarity" (Lao:
samakkhi): solidarity between soldiers and peasants, between the communist leadership and "the people," between Laos and Vietnam (in terms of
food supplies, military and technical support by Hanoi; see Lao National
Tourism Authority 2010: 14), and general internationalist solidarity (delegation visits from Cuba, China, etc.; Lao-Cuban friendship hospital). This
emphasis on solidarity ignores the fact that Vietnam and China had their
own agendas in which the support for the Lao communists was a mere by-
product. The comment in the English version of the audio tour states that
during the war the leadership focused "on protecting the people" and that
the armed struggle was a "social revolution" on behalf of the Lao people.
When talking with locals, I frequently encountered this image of close
solidarity between revolutionaries and "the people." In February 2008, a
farmer expressed his gratitude to Kaysone by stressing: "If Kaysone did
not have the idea with the caves, the Lao people would have been wiped
out." Moreover, he repeated Mao's famous phrase that army and people
are like fish and water (Lao: *pa kap nam*) which I have heard from many
interlocutors in Houaphan.

Plate 2.4   Kaysone Phomvihane Memorial.

The focus on the historical role of Kaysone might be a product of the deliberate historiographic and iconographic attempts of the LPRP to present him as the undisputed and decisive leading figure of the "liberation struggle" — thereby ignoring that his dependence of Vietnamese support. His cave is not only the obligatory starting point of every cave tour, but in addition, a huge monument with a five-meter-high statue of the late secretary general was inaugurated in 2010 (Plate 2.4). *The Vientiane Times* (15 December 2009) commented on the occasion of the groundbreaking ceremony: "The event was seen as deeply meaningful in relation to the history and politics of the Party, state and Lao people, especially for the people of the heroic province of Houaphan." With this monument, the party celebrated Kaysone's 90th birthday (13 December 2010), which was the occasion of an almsgiving ceremony with more than 1,000 guests. Again a commemorative caravan from Vientiane was organized to "[...] remember the good deeds and efforts of President Kaysone to seize power from foreign aggressors and lead the nation to liberation in 1975."[9] It is evident that the LPRP keeps the memory of the revolutionary struggle alive and promotes Viengxay as the alpha of the omega Vientiane, linking the "stronghold" in the mountains to the prosperous national center in the

Mekong Basin. This process of signification entails a kind of historical debt relation between the young generation and the forefathers who fought for national "liberation" and allegedly terminated foreign oppression and violence. Kaysone appears to personify this struggle and is glorified officially as national strongman from amidst the Lao people (and not as arm of Hanoi).[10] One young monk gave me the core argument when he pointed out that Viengxay is the most important historical site of Laos because "all revolutionary leaders" (Lao: *banda phu nam pativat*) who fought against "the enemy" (Lao: *sattu*) used to live here.[11]

The caves epitomize the protection of the people by the party as it is propagated in official history books. This image is diffused further by newspapers and TV programs which simultaneously promote Viengxay as destination of educational adventure trips to the place where Lao history found its climax. The years of the war are idealized as time of bravery and solidarity of the "Lao multi-ethnic people" of Houaphan, and directly linked to the existence of a free and prosperous Lao People's Democratic Republic. This heroic image appears as homogenous and without contradictions: the brave Lao people against the imperialists. Yet there are some stains on this idealized image, for example the death of Souphanouvong's eldest son who was allegedly assassinated in 1967 by a Hmong agent working for the CIA (yet other versions of this incident suggest internal quarrels within the Pathet Lao). However, this episode is often mentioned as example of revolutionary self-sacrifice. As one former soldier told me in March 2010, Souphanouvong's son refused to stay in the caves or be sent to Hanoi like other children of the leaders. Instead he sought direct confrontation with the enemy. Finally, his recklessness made him an easy target for the opponents. In the audio tour, Souphanouvong's daughter Nyotkaeomany speaks about this traumatic event for the family and fosters the image of the "red prince" as revolutionary leader who endured hardships and sacrifices for his people instead of living an easy life in the palace. A photo in the Souphanouvong Memorial in Vientiane shows him doing garden work in Viengxay, one of his favorite pastimes according to various accounts that refer to it as marker of his modest lifestyle and proximity to the everyday life of the commoners.[12] The vivid description and original voices of the audio tour bring the past — and purposeful images of the past — to life. These voices are key elements of Viengxay as site of memory since they tell the visitor directly about the past and have a clear pedagogical function by making history more imminent and entertaining, not only for students' excursions and party delegations but for private tourists as well. The post-conflict landscape of Viengxay reveals various dimensions and links to official historical discourses as well as family memories.

For domestic tourism, the site appears as the place where everything began and everything happened, a site for self-ascertainment, patriotism and pride. Caravan tours reenact the arduous trip from the cities at the Mekong to the remote mountains of Houaphan. Most Lao visitors have heard stories of Viengxay from relatives who lived in the liberated zone and are anxious to see the famous place where the revolutionary leaders and the people fought side by side. Yet, some are surprised about the low living standards and almost refuse to believe that life within caves was possible. Furthermore, for some younger visitors Viengxay seems to be also a place for recreation and party.[13] The *lieu de mémoire* Viengxay does not only imply the reconfiguration of revolutionary memory but also images of rural authenticity, simplicity, and hard life.

As mentioned, the narratives of the caves tour are informed by certain indebtedness toward the generation that sacrificed their lives for the "liberation." The configuration of the cave tour implies a morality that demands a "correct" historical memory on behalf of the valiant people. In this sense, the increased activities of state commemoration create both a historical debt to the revolutionary leaders — a highly questionable ideological meaning — and an idea of local pride that is promoted by phrases such as *müang vilason* ("heroic town," as stated in a speech during the temple inauguration). The reconfiguration of war memories during the cave tour entails national recognition for the local people and their plight during the war and a view of history beyond socialist textbooks. Visitors from the capital usually know about the "birthplace of the Lao PDR" and show respect toward the elder generation that carried the yoke of "the struggle." Shared memories — either direct memories or memories mediated by books or guides — link the heroic and traumatic aspects of the war, resulting in manifold images of the past that are particularly dramatized in tourism-related encounters as shown below.

It seems as if there had occurred an unusual collaboration between an authoritarian regime and the international development community — through the promotion of tourism projects in rural areas[14] — in creating a truly national *lieu de mémoire* functioning as legitimizing device for the "victors of history" and their teleological narrative of the "liberation struggle." Then again this runs counter to Nora's original vision of *lieux de mémoire* as multivocal sites concerned with the idea of a dynamic, living memory-nation. The landscape of Viengxay is appropriated by state commemoration and thus endangered of being solidified and monumentalized, even though small voices are included in accordance with Western ideas of oral history directed against hegemonic master narratives. Indeed, we witness dynamic interactions between national and local memory discourses, where the small voices with their will to remember on the one hand claim historical agency while simultaneously affirming the grand narrative of the Lao "liberation struggle." If Viengxay exemplifies this idea of a site of memory, a materialized cultural configuration — including encroachments by state-orchestrated commemoration — the pure "historical" counterpart might be the linear, rigid, and simplifying narrative of the *Pavatsat lao*. However, these elements do not exist in pure form but intersect and constitute each other. Viengxay reproduces the official historiographical myth of the multi-ethnic liberation struggle while simultaneously allowing polyphony of various perspectives on the past to be nourished by interacting individual and collective memories. Yet in general, Viengxay as memorial site fulfills the preconditions as suggested by Pierre Nora: 1) the material aspect through the stone of the caves and the rocks, through monuments and documents; 2) the symbolic aspect through imaginations of a heroic revolutionary past; and 3) the functional aspect through state rituals and tourism business. As will be discussed in the next section, the field of tourism provides insights into how the materiality of landscape constitutes the ground for interactions with the past which can be characterized by either fascination and entertainment or bewilderment.

War Memory and Tourism

The former cave city of Viengxay is a relative latecomer on the touristic map of Laos. Its remoteness and purposeful isolation left the site shrouded in secrecy for many years before it was opened for visitors in the 1990s. After the revolution of 1975, many reeducation camps were established in the region — violent places were members of the royal family, the former government or other political prisoners were held captive for months and years, some of them until their death. Today, the "stunning and beautiful landscape"[15] glosses over past sorrows and invites foreign and domestic tourists alike to attend organized tours through the various cave complexes of Viengxay, first of all the residence and office caves of the prominent leaders of the Lao revolution. As mentioned earlier, landscapes can be seen as an iconic environment that is constantly shaped and negotiated. While their material and affective powers undoubtedly have an impact on the local population, outside forces can influence and alter the perception of the landscapes: new ways of seeing the landscape, selective foci and points of view, and changing discursive regimes transform the relationship between people and landscape. As indicated above, the exploitation of landscapes for ideological or economical purpose has a strong impact on how people perceive their surroundings. In the case of Viengxay, both aspects meet in the domain of tourism. In particular, the cave tours have been established to provide income for the region and simultaneously propagate the official narrative of the heroic Lao "liberation struggle."

Within the broader framework of poverty alleviation and the quest for alternatives to opium cultivation, tourism was identified as an alternative for poor provinces such as Houaphan.[16] Among tourism experts, the caves of Viengxay were identified as one of the most promising destinations in the remote Northeast of Laos (Rogers 2005). Although Houaphan enjoyed a tenfold increase of tourists between 2003 and 2010, the province ranks only 14 from 16 provinces in Laos with a meager 22,116 international visitors from a total of 2.5 million, almost 90% of which came from Asia and the Pacific (Lao National Tourism Authority 2011: 6). Domestic tourists constitute the bulk of visitors in Houaphan, though.

The United Nations World Tourism Organization (UNWTO) and the Netherlands Development Organisation (SNV) cooperated with Deakin University to elaborate a heritage interpretation and management plan in 2006. One aspect of promoting sustainable tourism in the region was to "create employment opportunities for local people, boost income levels and contribute to improving livelihoods in the area."[17] Thanks to this international cooperation, a professional tourism infrastructure has been established around the Viengxay Caves Visitor Centre. Local guides, most of them Hmong, received English-language training and the necessary knowhow to deal with expectations and sensitivities of tourists.[18] The interaction between locals and tourists led to new perspectives and perceptions of the war years in Laos. In comparison to the notorious tourist hotspots in Vietnam, such as the Cù Chi tunnels where the factor of entertainment is prioritized at the expense of historical correctness, the educational aspect in Viengxay is well-received by foreign visitors.[19] Only rarely are popular images of the Vietnam War reproduced; music by The Doors was played in one instance within the audio tour. The vivid audio tour is mainly characterized by historical information, original statements of survivors, and impressive sound effects such as the din of B-52 planes and detonating bombs. In addition, information plates display historical photos that give an impression of everyday life inside the caves. In particular, pictures of underground schools and factories demonstrate how consequently the idea of a cave city had been put forward during the war.

The backside of this ambitious project was that the tours had to reproduce official narratives of the Second Indochina War.[20] The foreign advisors had to accept the low priority the authorities gave to critical historical discourse for being able to carry through the envisaged projects dedicated to rural development and heritage protection.[21] The history of the reeducation camps has to remain a taboo and is until today not included into the topography of Viengxay as official *lieu de mémoire*. The camps are referred to by the guides only in passing as political seminars where members of the *ancien régime* just had to endure some ideological education and communal work and returned to Vientiane as "proper socialists." Details of brutality and suffering in the camps are left aside. Instead, the guides demonstrate local pride, a sense of place as inhabitants of a "heroic landscape" where the people took the main burden of the liberation struggle. Here, it has to be distinguished between domestic and international tourism since both types of visitors have different understandings and perceptions of the landscape and the corresponding historical narratives.

When I visited Viengxay the first time in 2008, for two weeks I met only a few busloads of Lao civil servants or students, mixed with the occasional Western backpacker. Things have changed considerably: there are not only more buses and organized caravans from major Lao cities, but also private cars doing the adventurous trip to the "stronghold" where history took place as now marketed in the Lao cities for the new educated and rich urban middle class. In contrast, the number of international tourists has not increased much and the *falang* (Lao: "Western foreigner") are sometimes surprised when faced with the larger groups of Lao visitors which have to be guided with megaphones due to the group size. They mostly leave the audio guides to the Western tourists since the Lao "don't need much historical explanation" as the head of the tourism office pointed out in 2010. They just want "to see" the caves. Domestic tourists seem to be less interested in firsthand accounts of the war — many of them grew up with war-related stories from the elders — than in the experience of "being there."[22] Personal memories are linked with the historical arena where "it actually happened," thereby creating discursive entanglements that recall Nora's idea of living memory.

The "authentic" voices of eyewitnesses interviewed for the audio guide evoke immediate interest and even compassion by foreign visitors — or "deep respect for this people" as one young American backpacker put it. He and other foreign tourists I interviewed in 2010 were fascinated by the extreme living conditions that prevailed in Viengxay during the war. Damp caves lit by smoky oil lanterns, the devastating destruction of

Plate 2.5   Entrance of Faydang Lobliayao's cave.

rice harvests, hurried cooking at 5 a.m. before the daily bombing started: such powerful images are conjured up by the massive materiality of the caves together with the original voices of the audio guide.[23] On the one hand, the tourists feel a bond to the local people and their plight during a sideshow of a global conflict. On the other hand, the cave tour provides education about the Second Indochina War and the American involvement in Laos, the "secret war" that Western tourists are not always aware of. Interestingly, the cave tour fosters a latent anti-Americanism that is widespread among alternative travelers.[24] Other *falang* are just ashamed about the asymmetric conflict between a highly technicized power and a small peasant society, thereby ignoring the wider geopolitical context of the Second Indochina War. Moreover, they praise the kindness and hospitality of the local people that "suffered so much" (Swiss tourist, 2010).

As Michael Herzfeld (1996) observes, tourism is a site of cultural intimacy due to its often ambivalent and embarrassing encounters between different cultural identities. Not only are Western tourists (or urban Lao visitors) culturally different from local peasants which causes problems of communication. Perhaps even more crucial is the different knowledge about and perceptions of the regional past. Consequently, travelers with historical half-knowledge taken from guidebooks confront the local Hmong guides — who consider themselves as Lao patriots — with offensive statements such as "You are suppressed by the government, aren't you?" (Dutch tourist, 2008). Other reasons for embarrassment are produced by ambiguous historical episodes such as the death of Souphanouvong's son at the hands of a CIA Hmong agent which might be embarrassing for the "patriotic" Hmong. Yet another version of this story would be even more embarrassing for the LPRP because it suggests a quarrel among party cadres. Such stories spoil the nice image of the monolithic people against imperialists as it is presented for the international audience.

The cave tour allows visitors to enter a dialogue with events and persons from the past. Viengxay emerges from obscurity as a living and lived landscape embodying multiple meaningful memories. However, these memories are selected and controlled by the LPRP and its hegemonic history discourse. Moreover, tendencies of shaping a coherent heterotopia of the war for tourist consumption influence the various interactions with the landscape. Despite these present transformations, Viengxay is far from being fully appropriated by revolution or tourism and still exudes a multivocality of contrasting memories.

Multivocal Memories of Viengxay

The merit of the audio guide of the cave tour is the inclusion of different personal memories of the traumatic war period. One particularly dramatic narrative informs about a bomb hitting a cave, thereby causing a fire that killed people and destroyed Buddha images.[25] Other memories are inherently ambivalent since they tell of both fear and happiness. Hansana Sisane, son of revolutionary veteran Sisana Sisane, recalls these occasional "joyful moments" in his account of his childhood in the caves and other times of danger and fear (Lao National Tourism Authority 2010: 36). Following Schwenkel's (2006) discussion of Vietnamese war memories, Viengxay can be considered a new social space for memory work. As will be shown, state efforts to maintain historical hegemony and standardized narratives of the past contrast with a polyphony of different memories and perspectives. Yet the oral history project for the audio tour appears to support official narratives of the heroic "liberation struggle." Indeed, in combination with the massive materiality of the caves, the personal memories give an imminent and emotive experience of the war and evoke sympathies for the people in the caves. Lao visitors are reminded of how their ancestors suffered for national independence and unity in a more efficient way than in dull history books like the official *Pavatsat lao*. Original voices are exploited to stress revolutionary values such as bravery, solidarity, perseverance, patriotism, self-sacrifice. Ironically, the historical discourse is simultaneously enriched and mainstreamed here.

However, many other accounts of the war years lack the heroic glorification of official narratives and are occupied with the loss of friends and relatives and the hardships of everyday life. The half-blind man quoted above is only one example of the majority of peasants and foragers who were confronted with a radical transformation of the landscape that used to be the base of their livelihoods. Suddenly, access to the fields was restricted by daily bombing with cluster bombs and napalm. At the same time, the landscape provided shelter through caves and holes people dug out in dense forest. Ironically, it was the domain of the spirits, caves and jungle — where usually no Lao would dare to spend the night — which was now the key to survival while the rice fields turned to ambivalent places of nurture and lethal danger. These contradictions haunt the memory of the witnesses and refer to the disruptions of security and subsistence during the war years. The fact that these disruptions entailed displacement and migration contributes to the general feeling of a world turned upside down. The aggressive soundscape of war is still strikingly present as most elderly people accompany their accounts with sound of bombs, artillery and airplanes — acoustic memories laden with affects of fear and loss. Today, each UXO incident haunts the population with disturbing images of the past. The official "heroic landscape" contrasts with the small fates of a population overrun by the effects of global Cold War politics and is until today suffering its aftermath.

Seeing the Lao tourists strolling relaxingly through the caves and enjoying a barbecue afterward — for example, at Nouhak's old house if it is an official delegation — one is tempted to think that Navaro-Yashin's "hangover"[26] of the violent past is about to fade away. This estimation might be valid at least for the cave landscape which is "tamed" by efforts of tourism development and turned into a tangible *lieu de mémoire* of revolutionary commemoration. However, the people who remember the war are still haunted by the affects of fear and helplessness instilled by the American planes. In my interviews, onomatopoetic references to the bombing campaigns often replaced words — imagine an elderly woman looking at you intensely under her traditional Tai headscarf and shouting a series of voluminous "boom" sounds. She shares her resounding memories by repeating the soundscape of the war which creates an uncanny layer on the now idyllic scenery of Viengxay and its pleasant surroundings. Here, direct memories are mediated by sensual experiences, unlike the following generations who link their more rational accounts of hardships and poverty to their own difficult start in life as people of upland "poor districts."[27]

Memories of extreme poverty and family tragedies during and in the aftermath the war add another dimension to Viengxay as a site of memory. Even if corresponding with positive images of community and solidarity in times of crisis, the melancholy evoked by memories of trouble and loss pervade the stories I collected in Viengxay. The head of the Viengxay Caves Tourism Office — whose story is also included in the audio tour (Lao National Tourism Authority 2010: 27) — told me how the war violently entered his life. When he was about nine or ten years old, a 500-kg bomb hit his family's house, killed his grandfather and injured many other relatives. His father had to bury the corpse in a hurry since everybody was afraid of more attacks. This story is exemplary of how the young generation in the Lao uplands was confronted with the war and then often became easy targets for communist recruitment attempts for the fight against the "aggressors" (see Pholsena 2006). They associate with the landscape a sense of loss, feeling a "spatial melancholia" (Navaro-Yashin 2009: 16) which emanates from the very ground they stand.

Another perception is the nostalgia implicit in organized caravan tours "back to the caves." They not only focus on a time of violence and sorrow but also on group solidarity that was crucial for the "liberation." These tours appear as rituals of community (see Connerton 1989) and stress the idea of the patriotic and heroic "Lao multi-ethnic people." In many conversations, local people stressed that ethnic (and class) difference did not matter then, that the whole ethnically heterogeneous people of Houaphan — the "land of heroes" (Vongsingh 2006) — fought together for national liberation. This view is of course one-sided and leaves out, for example, the pressure on the Christian inhabitants of the region (Weldon 1999). Yet it fosters local pride and a sense of coming to terms with the violent past through the idea that the sacrifices were not in vain and had instead created the foundation for future prosperity. The narrative of "from crater to *müang*" as told during the festivities for the temple inauguration reflects the hopes of the local population for a participation in national development.

During a walk with a 30-year-old local Hmong in the surroundings of Viengxay (January 2010), I could sense the various discursive and phenomenological aspects of this memorial landscape. Around 1990, many households from his village in Xieng Kho District were resettled to Ban Phou Say which at present constitutes the largest Hmong quarter of Viengxay town. Gardens and upland rice fields constitute the base of local livelihoods while the forests still provide important resources for consumption and trade — yet my informant remembered when hazardous UXO contaminated this important source. UXO forms a link between local livelihoods and the history of the war. In passing, he referred to overgrown craters and aisles between the rocks which allowed hidden manoeuvring by Lao and Vietnamese soldiers. He explicitly referred to the latter as important allies in the war and respected them — like many of my local interlocutors did[28] — for the alleged selfless contribution to the Lao liberation struggle. Hidden within a cassava plantation, inconspicuous remnants of old Vietnamese barracks almost evaded my gaze. These belonged to a compound for Vietnamese technicians who moved to Viengxay after the ceasefire to reconstruct the resistance capital of the Pathet Lao. The Hmong admitted that neither the successful struggle nor the modest reconstruction of Houaphan would have been possible without Vietnamese aid.[29] Comments like this contribute to the impression that at least parts of the Lao population still feel historically indebted toward Vietnam — while many critical voices remain skeptical about the ongoing Vietnamese influence in Laos and often complain about the arrogant attitude the Vietnamese hold toward the Lao. Besides referring to the role of the Vietnamese in the war, my informant also stressed the contribution of the Hmong people to the revolution. He took me to the cave of Faydang Lobliayao who led the pro-communist faction of the Hmong during the civil war (Plate 2.5). This cave was not part of the official cave tours and only recently integrated with the tourist infrastructure through inclusion in trekking tours. Considering themselves as Lao patriots despite their relative marginality, the Hmong of Viengxay emphasize their contribution for the revolutionary struggle in particular toward a Western audience that often only knows about the "Vang Pao Hmong" as he called the historical adversaries of Faydang. Starting from a discussion of upland cultivation, we were suddenly contemplating the intricacies of the Lao civil war and the cultural complexity of the country. This walk allowed me to participate in local perceptions of the landscape and its history, in the discourses and affects it evokes. Glorification of the past interacts with memories of hard times and results in a profound sense of place.

The landscape appears as a benevolent source of nourishment and as a dangerous place where lingering legacies of the past manifest themselves as active explosives. Everyday interaction with the landscape works mainly through agriculture and regular walks to fields and forests for hunting and gathering food. UXO poses a latent threat by which the landscape continuously recalls the war as aggressive materiality and index of past intentionality (Gell 1998: 17). The landscape is thus contaminated not only by violent memories but also by physical hazards. Even though not a direct witness of war, my informant's sense of the place indicated at how knowledge of the landscape was essential for survival under harsh conditions during the American bombing campaigns. In contrast to this immediate interaction with the environment, the top-down perspective of the American pilots implies a completely different perception of Houaphan's landscape: facing the endless green topography of forested mountains, the pilots appeared to do warfare against a landscape instead of people.

Questions about the camps were smiled away by my informant. In general, the prisons and reeducation camps that mushroomed in the region after the revolution remain a taboo in contemporary Laos. It is indeed difficult for foreigners to raise this issue in conversations and one usually gets only meager information. The dark side of the camps can be explored in some published life histories (see, for example: Bounsang 2006; Khamphanh 2004; Nakhonkham 2003). Former RLG official Bounsang Khamkeo (2006: 247–9) mentions public projects in Viengxay which depended on forced labor by camp inmates.[30] These memories tell of the brute force of a paranoid regime; of humiliation, violence and death from maltreatment, illness and malnourishment. This is the "other" landscape and "dissonant heritage" (Tunbridge and Ashworth 1996) of Houaphan: not the caves of heroism and solidarity, but the barb-wired fields of hatred and violence. Perhaps the most traumatic episode for many Lao exiles is the imprisonment of the Royal family in the former "Hotel No. 1" — today the Thavixay Hotel apparently oblivious of its ambiguous history — followed by the fatal deportation into a reeducation camp (Evans 2009).[31]

Euphemistically called "production units,"[32] the compounds were labor camps where most detainees died from malnutrition and mistreatment. The innocent statement, "By the late 1970s, the caves were emptied and the quiet life of the countryside returned,"[33] and the suggestion of Viengxay as "World Peace Site" (Suntikul *et al.* 2009: 160), must feel like slaps in the face for former camp victims and their families. Since the LPRP was responsible for the establishment of the inhuman camp system, a clear distancing from this policy by the present leadership would be required to deal with this traumatic episode of recent Lao history. While it is still ignored by the official cave tour, visitors sometimes hear rumours about which of the derelict building and caves were used as prisons after the revolution.[34] Like the camps-turned-villages in Vatthana Pholsena's case study (this volume), the materiality of former camp sites probably reveals nothing about the suffering that took place here. In the future, they might be turned into commemorative sites where people burn incense for the deceased or perhaps allow even cathartic experiences in cases of actual localizations or reburials of the victims (Verdery 1999).

The different perceptions of Viengxay as landscape of memory by various individuals and collectives epitomize the multivocality of memory discourses linked to certain places and spaces characterized by an iconic openness that even hegemonic historiography can only partially reduce. Perhaps even the opposite is true, namely that this multivocality — plus official strategies to deliberately shape the meaning of the place — entails an excessive imposition of meaning (Augé 1995) that adds "text" to the palimpsest rather than erasing it.

Conclusion

The different landscapes of Houaphan — from "land of heroes" to land of lingering violence — are not exclusive. Since they are constituted by heterogeneous and contradictory perceptions, they form aspects or layers of the physical landscape. The Lao government tries to level this diversity and stresses the heroic and revolutionary aspects of Viengxay, thereby producing absences and ambiguities. The official cave tour creates a specific spatial configuration that only partially overlaps with the agricultural landscape as relevant for many local peasants. The appropriation of the landscape by the LPRP as a clearly shaped revolutionary topography did not fully erase other meaningful layers. Moreover, some "wounds" of the landscape are already "healing": craters are filled with soil or used as fish ponds, UXO is being cleared and removed. The idea of Viengxay as a bomb-crater-turned-healthy-and-lively-town suggests the healing of both topographical and social wounds. The perception of this post-conflict landscape is deeply entangled with the contemporary development discourse and with hopes for a better future. Reading Viengxay as a historical palimpsest (Huyssen 2003) reveals these complex and contradictory entanglements as converging layers of an ambiguous past comprising revolutionary heterotopia, precarious life-worlds and partially erased traces of violence.

The preparation of Viengxay as a national *lieu de mémoire* is the latest step of appropriation of history by the LPRP that had been only partially achieved through publications such as the *Pavatsat lao* which is read — if at all — only by Lao citizens. Now the Lao government is able to present its idea of the righteous "liberation struggle" to a larger audience including Asian and Western foreigners. The mainstream American image of the just war of the "free world" against Communism appears pale and overtly simplified in comparison — even though the Lao version is not the most complex one as well. However, the struggle of the "Lao multi-ethnic people" for independence and unity seems to be more legitimate concerning the hardships the local population, who did not know much about the Cold War conflict, had to endure. Contrary to American pop-cultural images of "evil Communists," the revolutionary leadership appears sympathetic to foreign visitors with respect to the propagated image of selfless patriots sharing the plight of the common people. Therefore, the cave tour is a clear attempt of claiming legitimacy for the revolutionary cause and a quest for historical credibility that is fostered by the support of international development organizations.

Furthermore, the cave tours create historical meaning and make sense of the heavy toll the local population had to pay during and after the war. Individual suffering is collectivized and rationalized through a coherent narrative of a historical mission aimed at national liberation from foreign oppression. Necessary sacrifices are recognized, and instead of being relegated to some dry statistics, they take centerstage within a landscape of memory prepared both for state commemoration and tourist consumption. What for many witnesses of the "secret war" must have been an incomprehensible violent chaos is now shaped as a soteriological grand narrative of a finally victorious struggle between good and evil. Accordingly, the revolution of 1975 is legitimized in retrospect as well. With the narrative of the struggle promoted in this way, it will entail more links to individual memories insofar that the latter are sometimes shaped according to the former model.[35] Thus even traumatic memories of loss and sorrow can be linked to the heroic history of the "people" and turned into a positive meaningful light. As discussed above, many accounts of the war stress the violent impact of the Cold War on local livelihoods as well as the idea of having participated in an important historical era.

Reading the landscape of Viengxay as a memorial palimpsest, one cannot fail to notice the weak traces of erased meanings. In particular, the time between 1975 and 1986 remains obscure and is seldom referred to. The rare cases where people mentioned this time focused largely on a rough idea of general poverty — yet without clarifying all reasons that might be taken into consideration. While it makes some sense to blame the war for the the ruined landscape and the precarious livelihoods of the rural population, the failure of orthodox socialism is usually not acknowledged. The memories of the local population are clear enough not to romanticize the "quiet" postwar years. Instead, hardships such as hunger and the hazard of UXO, are emphasized — while the suffering of the prisoners in the reeducation camps usually remains untold.

As a *lieu de mémoire*, the caves of Viengxay provide a functional and impressive materiality. They represent the nexus of a network linking past and present, destruction and development, Lao peasants and the Pentagon, local livelihoods and international tourism. In combination with craters and cluster bombs, the caves are icons of the "secret war," perhaps the most violent episode in Lao history. The landscape produces ambivalent affects that oscillate between sorrow and pride, between melancholy and hope. Moreover, it is the target of memory politics controlled by the ruling Lao People's Revolutionary Party whose self-image depends largely on the glorification of the liberation struggle. Viengxay provides the material base for the hegemonial discourse of the state as well as for individual self-ascertainment and hopes. It remains to be seen which implications the transformation of the landscape for touristic consumption will have for the local population — if there will be more contested views of the past, memory struggles, a stronger affirmation of belonging, or haunting images of the violent past entangled with economic interest and entertainment. Commemorative practices such as official delegations paying homage at Kaysone's cave and listening to heroic stories of the "struggle" foster the "national" meaning of the place and create a certain revolutionary nostalgia.

When one asks — following Michael Herzfeld (1991) — who decides on the history of a place, the answer in the case of Viengxay must be: the Lao People's Revolutionary Party in cooperation with Western heritage and tourism experts, even if this project of historiography remains largely state-centered. While this cooperation goes beyond one-sided revolutionary historiography and grants more room to multivocal local perspectives, the voices of the victims of the camp system still remain excluded. To talk about social amnesia would be too strong a statement since the decade of orthodox socialism is rather silenced than forgotten. Ambivalent places such as the former "Hotel No. 1" might be sites of negotiating the historical meaning of Viengxay/Houaphan in the future. The increasing popularity of the region as a destination for both domestic and international tourism will heighten the awareness of the ambiguities of this memorial landscape with its inherent violent legacies — and will lead to further dissection of this monumental palimpsest. The stains on the glorious image of the "birthplace of the Lao PDR" are evident but until now lack the potential to undermine the official discourse on Viengxay as one of the key national *lieux de mémoire* in contemporary Laos.

Notes

1. Interview in Viengxay, 8 Mar. 2010. This chapter is based on three fieldtrips to Viengxay between 2008 and 2011. Parts of it have been presented at the 6th EUROSEAS Conference in Gothenburg/Sweden (2010) and at the 3rd International Conference on Lao Studies in Khon Kaen/Thailand (2010). I would like to thank all participants for their interest and critical feedback. Special thanks go to the staff of the Houaphan Provincial Tourism Office and the Viengxay Caves Visitor Centre for their kind support and hospitality.

2. According to the Geneva Accords of 1954, the Communist-controlled provinces of Houaphan and Phongsaly were to be integrated into the Lao kingdom along with their armed forces. When rightist groups pushed the Neo Lao Hak Xat out of the first coalition government in 1959, Communist troops refused integration and started armed resistance (Evans 2002: 110–5; Tappe 2010).

3. Lao: *müang viengxay pen ban koet khòng sathalanalat pasathipatai pasason lao, müang viengxay pen bòn taohom khuam samakkhi, müang viengxay pen müang thi man khòng kanpativat.*

4. These five names form the well-known line-up of the revolutionary struggle and are considered the most important Lao national heroes of the 20th century in official discourse (Tappe 2008).

5. The local people emphasized that even in his old age, Nouhak was eager to visit the old stronghold. This contradicts the witty assessment of Colin Cotterill (2006: 97), writer of the humorous Dr. Siri novels: "Once the old cave dwellers' houses were complete and all the documents and personal belongings moved into them, there had been no reason, none at all, for the senior cadres to go back into the caves. Such a visit would have been no more likely than the Count of Monte Christo popping back to the Château d'If to reminiscence over the happy times he'd spent there." Rather, the intensive years of battle, fear, and feelings of closeness and solidarity must have created affects that turned into nostalgia during the years of bureaucratic everyday life in Vientiane.

6. Kaysone appears as venerated ancestor and thus ironically linked to a spirit world which used to be rejected by socialist orthodoxy.

7. "History of Laos," Ministry of Information and Culture 2000.

8. While Fa Ngum and Anouvong are considered as heroic, patriotic kings of a glorious past, the first politburo (Kaysone Phomvihane, Nouhak Phoumsavan, Souphanouvong, Phoumi Vongvichit, Poun Siphaseut, Khamtay Siphandone, Sisomphone Lovanxay) consists of 20th-century national heroes (Grabowsky and Tappe 2011).

9. *Vientiane Times*, 21 Dec. 2010.

10. However, the oversized concrete monument for Kaysone provoked some critical comments. A young salesman told me in June 2011 that the construction of the monument had swallowed too much financial resources that could be put to better use in this poor region, and that some people had to renounce their land for only a small compensation.

11. He connected to the discourse of the old generation of "preachers of the revolution" (Ladwig 2009) such as Luang Vichit who died in 2010 at the age of 85 and who spent 15 years with the revolutionaries in the liberated zone.

12. An eyewitness account of Souphanouvong's life in Viengxay states: "While Prince Souphanouvong was in Viengsay, the war was raging and bombs were launched ceaselessly, but he still had the courage to get out of his cave to take care of his garden, to grow and water vegetables. He was wearing the clothes of a simple peasant [...]" (Khambay 1989: 137). Souphanouvong's willingness to reject a royal lifestyle and to share the plight of the locals is exemplified by numerous photos in museums and books which show him working in his cave office or among the peasants in the rice fields (Tappe 2011a).

13. See Schwenkel (2006: 18) for the "new antimemory functions and meanings" of Vietnamese war sites.

14. Pioneering projects of community-based tourism in Luang Namtha Province focused on eco-trekking and homestays in ethnic minority villages (Lyttleton and Allcock 2002; Neudorfer 2007). The tourism initiatives in Viengxay — and related projects in Xieng Khouang — combine these approaches with historical education on the Second Indochina War (see below).

15. Information plate, Viengxay Caves Visitor Centre.

16. Laos belongs to the so-called Least Developed Countries (LDC). More than 50 international NGOs working in projects related to poverty reduction in rural Laos and important donor organizations such as the Asian Development Bank give financial aid, for instance, in pro-poor and sustainable tourism projects (Suntikul *et al.* 2009: 158; Tappe 2011b). As one of the 47 districts that are considered "poor" by the Lao government, Viengxay district is among the target regions for rural development. Since 2006, the United Nations World Tourism Organization has been supporting projects in the region, with the Dutch development organization SNV being the main implementing agency.

17. *Vientiane Times*, 25 Nov. 2009.

18. I am indebted to Rik Ponne (Lao National Tourism Authority, Vientiane) for sharing his knowledge about the history and organization of the Viengxay Caves tourism project.

19. For Vietnamese war tourism, see Schwenkel 2009 and Alneng 2002.

20. The tone of the information plates is far more moderate than the labels in museums such as the Lao National Museum and the Lao People's Army History Museum which are characterized by verbal attacks against the "American imperialists and their lackeys" (see Tappe 2011a). For example, one plate at the tourism office states: "In these caves the Pathet Lao established a 'hidden city' of government ministries, housing, offices, shops, schools, hospitals and military barracks. From here the future leaders of the Lao PDR directed their political, military and ideological campaign. The caves and surrounding area supported a population of around 20,000 people during nine years of ferocious air bombardement that destroyed the landscape."

21. Rik Ponne, personal communication, 2010.

22. According to the head of the Viengxay Caves Visitor Centre in Mar. 2010. He explained to me the logistics of guiding 150 visitors from Vientiane through the caves who came to Viengxay on the occasion of the temple inauguration.

23. Lao National Tourism Authority, 2010; see as well the official Viengxay website of the LNTA, at http://www.visit-viengxay.com [accessed 1 Nov. 2012].

24. In discussions, travelers often make a connection between Laos and Iraq and Afghanistan — a (self-) critical anti-war discourse that is shared by the Lao to a much lesser extent.

25. http://www.visit-viengxay.com/viengxay-the-past-voices.html [accessed 1 Nov. 2012].

26. Navaro-Yashin (2009: 5) refers to "ruination" as "[...] subjectivities and residual affects that linger, like a hangover, in the aftermath of war or violence."

27. In 1997–98, the incidence of poverty in Houaphan was estimated at 75% (Rigg 2005: 75). At present, all districts except Sam Neua are officially declared "poor district" (Messerli *et al.* 2008: 17).

28. For example, elderly people remember how the Vietnamese refilled the bomb craters on the strategically important Road 6 (linking Sam Neua with the Vietnamese border) every night. American intelligence from 1969 acknowledged the good condition of this road despite daily bombing, at http://www.foia.ucia.gov/docs/DOC_0000835644/DOC_0000835644.pdf [accessed 1 Nov. 2012].

29. The role of the Vietnamese is reduced to mere advisors and "volunteers" in Lao historiography in order to cultivate image of truly "national" Lao revolution.

30. Khamphanh Thammakhanty (2004: 173) presents a day's schedule from a prison camp in Et District that included about 11 hours of hard physical labor.

31. Khamphanh Thammakhanty (2004: 265) reports that the royal family had been wrapped in blankets and buried without any religious rites in a mass grave.

32. According to an American intelligence report from 1992, at http://www.foia.cia. gov/docs/DOC_0000215613/DOC_0000215613.pdf [accessed 1 Nov. 2012].

33. Comment of the Voices of Viengxay Project, at http://www.visit-viengxay. com/viengxay-the-past-1973-1975.html [accessed 1 Nov. 2012].

34. Sparse reports about prisoners — including the royal family and American POW — held captive in Viengxay can be found in declassified CIA sources, at http://www.virtual.vietnam.ttu.edu/cgi-bin/starfetch.exe?jzXm7@63yDFYD 2X0mWCCF0eNVaePFbd9UvFs@p.O80HGAdG54ZG0iiz8pCsVYmqU0Qq6w Hc.JR753CGFBEb@GkSuVf4gFKTIJ1YThGQCbec/3671408012.pdf [accessed 1 Nov. 2012].

35. For parallels between hegemonic narratives of the war and individual narratives, see Pholsena 2006.

CHAPTER 3

War-Martyr *Bia*: Commemoration and *Perdurability* in Rural Vietnam

Markus Schlecker

Every human person records, reflects on, and must try to understand clearly the ancestral line and consanguinity, so as to consciously attend to the ancestral line, the stream of blood of the ancestral kin group, to keep this stream of blood scarlet forever and ever. That is the moral principle of human beings toward their ancestral lines, their ancestors, their families. 'When drinking water, be conscious of its source.'

— From a preface to a genealogical record book
of an ancestral kin group in Thanh Hà commune.

Introduction

In a recent contribution to a collection of essays on Southeast Asian ideas of power, Catherine Allerton (2012) describes Indonesian villagers' idea of land as possessing agency ("the energy of the land"), which according to her informants had killed a visiting engineer after he had announced the opening of their native land for commercial exploitation. What her discussion gradually works out is an intertwining of spatial concepts of human and ancestral belonging to land. During fieldwork in Thanh Hà (2006–07), a commune in rural Northern Vietnam, I came across very similar expressions of local soil being angry, fierce and mischievous that caused harm. Unlike Allerton, I consider this not direct expressions of an agency of land; rather, as euphemisms to talk about angry and harmful ancestral spirits that were known to dwell below the earth.

When we speak of landscape, we tend to think of this in contrast to nature as that which human minds and hands purposively alter to serve specific needs or please certain aesthetic senses (Hirsch and O'Hanlon 1995). In Vietnam, attentiveness has always been directed at the creation of physical markers that transform soil into a meaningful land or landscape. Halls, altars, shrines, temples, pagodas, graves, and even plain dwellings are such markers. They record previous human existences and at the same time assert that, as ancestors and other divinities, they continue to be present and hold sway over the locality. Physical markers make possible ritual encounters and thereby ensure a vital relatedness between past, present, and future generations *through land*.

One especially significant class of physical markers of land are commemorative stelae (*bia*). They are an important component of religious and sacred sites in Vietnam and inform visitors of the past heroic and meritorious achievements of persons associated with the place. Commemorative stelae are considered historically significant for two reasons. First, the custom of stelae harks back to ancient times and in this sense an aura of a long and dignified tradition surrounds them as a class of objects. One of the best-known *bia* are the stelae-carrying stone turtles inside Hanoi's Confucian temple of literature *Văn Miếu*, built between the 11th and 14th centuries. Engraved on these *bia* are the names of successful candidates for offices in the feudal administration. Second, commemorative stelae are usually made of stone and their solid materiality, by resisting decay, inspires a general sense of respect toward them, as objects with their own long history. Social upheaval and natural disasters may have led to the disappearance of different stelae, but every now and then they turn up again as if to assert their authority.

This was also the case in Thanh Hà, a rural commune belonging to Hải Phòng's impoverished coastal district Tiên Lãng in Northern Vietnam.[1] Roadworks for the installation of the commune's first sewage system had turned up a stone slab. Its rectangular shape and rounded edges on one side suggested that it had to be a stela of sorts. Villagers had soon gathered around the discovery and everyone offered ideas as to its origin and significance. It was then decided by a few elderly men that it should be immediately carried to the nearby pagoda and left there until its identity could be established.

The sudden presence of the stone in the pagoda's courtyard was not entirely welcomed by the village's Buddhist followers. Speculations were triggered by two outsiders, visiting elderly women from a nearby commune, who pointed out the stone's peculiar green shading.[2] They questioned that it was even a *bia*. For the two women, the color indicated the presence of a goblin (*yêu tinh*) who had come to reside inside the stone. Soon, the pagoda's elderly women grew very concerned that in the guise of a dignified ancient stela, a malicious power had been brought to their sacred place, akin to a Trojan horse. Fellow male Buddhist followers were called and urged to remove the stone from the pagoda's premises swiftly.

The brief vignette from Thanh Hà illustrates that commemorative stones build an intersection of several important themes. The women's anxiety about the stone being potentially harmful is instructive insofar as it was clearly triggered by its unknown origin, purpose, and history. Its shape, on the other hand, suggested that it had once informed its reader of past meritorious deeds. Clearly, there was a general sense of hope among villagers that the stone retrieved might add further prestige to their village. Third, the stone shared with other commemorative stelae the positive quality of being very solid and lasting, appreciated not only by villagers. Wandering ghosts, the souls of deceased persons whose passage to the other world had been obstructed, were known to seek refuge in solid places, such as a tree, a small out-door shrine, or stones, seemingly to compensate for their lack of stability.

Ritual Revival and War-Martyr Stelae in Thanh Hà

Commemorative stelae are not only being discovered in contemporary Vietnam. New ones are being made. Some of these merely replace older ones that were destroyed or had disappeared. Often this happens as part of larger reconstructions of pagodas, temples, and shrines. Others are specifically made to record donations, especially within the context of such reconstructions. The donor's name, place of residence, and the donated sum are carefully engraved. These donation stelae, while their uses hark back to ancient times, were possibly the most common variant of all newly fashioned commemorative stelae in Thanh Hà commune.

Another one were *bia hậu* or *bia mua hậu*, which listed deceased persons without heirs who could perform ancestor worship. By paying a one-time sum, families could give the soul of a deceased childless relative into the ritual care of the ancestral kin group (*dòng họ*) where the name was engraved into the *bia mua hậu* and from then on included in regular prayers. *Dòng họ* groups, in other words, were at first taking over the task of family ancestor veneration, since a kin group only commemorates ancestors from the fifth generation backwards.[3]

The revival of village customs and reconstructions of ritual sites has been documented by several anthropologists (Kleinen 1999; Endres 2000;

Malarney 2002; Truong Huyen Chi 2001), as has been the post-reform flourishing of spiritual cults and mediums whose following transcend local communities (Taylor 2004; Endres 2008; Pham Quynh Phuong 2009). What has received somewhat less attention are the revival of local patrilineal ancestral kin groups, so-called *dòng họ*.[4]

In Thanh Hà, *dòng họ* groups had clearly become active since the inception of the economic reforms (*đổi mới*) in 1986, which initiated a full-scale shift from a centrally planned to a market economy within the unchanged political framework of a one-Party state. The changes involved a certain disentanglement of state and Party organs, the abolition of the rationing system, a long-term leasing of farming land to families, the transformation state-run cooperatives from employers to service providers, and the opening to foreign investment. One memorable comment by a villager was, "Our *dòng họ* is more actively meeting than [my hamlet's] Party cell!" Their dignitaries, frequently old revolutionary or military heroes and retired cadres, set up various committees headed by a chairperson and vice-chairperson. One man compared the ancestral-cult committee to a "board of managing directors." A basic contrast was, however, noticeable between those kin groups that gathered frequently and had reinstated their ritual practices and those that were either in a process of dissolution or a state of slumber. In the most populous of Thanh Hà's four village communities (*làng*), 20 *dòng họ* groups had their main place of worship, though only eight, possibly up to 12 of them, were in a process of reviving their gatherings and expanding their activities.

Amidst this revival of annual or even semi-annual gatherings to venerate common patrilineal ancestors with a growing number of attendants, *dòng họ* groups also explored ways to enhance their prestige and influence. Ritual dancers from the local temple, who usually performed for village festivals, were invited to perform sacrificial worship at a *dòng họ* gathering. The highest-ranking dignitaries started to wear traditional *áo dài* style ritual tunics and circular headgear (*khăn đống*), as had been the case before the revolutionary changes in the 1940s. Ancestral altars, halls, and graves were rebuilt and enhanced in an effort to outdo other *dòng họ* groups. The deeply entrenched ritual competitiveness among villagers over local prestige had been a main target of the socialist anti-lavishness policies, which by and large the Party leadership had kept in place after the economic reforms. It was noted by central and local authorities that since the economic reforms, ritual competitiveness in local communities was on the rise again. Not infrequently, local cadres were themselves taking part in the conspicuous consumption of precious resources, such as hosting lavish funeral banquets.

Most of the constructions had been done only since 1999 when *dòng họ* groups started to receive larger donations from well-to-do urban-dwelling members and overseas Vietnamese. These contributions were then recorded on separate donation stelae, typically located at the entrance of the ancestral hall.[5] The issue of donations pinpointed what was most vital for a *dòng họ group*: its scope. Patrilineal ancestral lines were eagerly traced back to increase the size of the *dòng họ* beyond Thanh Hà and to include as members heroic figures and more recent dignitaries, such as decorated revolutionary fighters and war martyrs. Elderly men designed large genealogical charts by hand or enrolled computer-skilled relatives to print impressively looking pedigrees.

To add further substance to their prestigious membership, *dòng họ* groups planned or had already fashioned another form of stelae, what they called war-martyr *bia*. The ritual competitiveness clearly built an important background to the recent trend among *dòng họ* to fashion war-martyr stelae. What is remarkable about these stelae is that they conjoined two potentially antagonistic domains: the Party State's cult of war martyrdom, as part of its wider sphere of historical truth and political instruction, and the non-state domain of ancestral worship, which celebrated the significance of particularistic kin ties, common patrilineal descent and common substance — the *họ*. Engraved on a war martyr *bia* were only those who were descendants of the *dòng họ*.[6] These stelae were thus breaking down the state category of war martyrs.

Perdurability

In the present chapter, I use the term *perdurability* to emphasize and explore the materiality of commemorative stelae as solid, lasting objects in conjunction with their renewed significance in Thanh Hà for the commemoration of war martyrs.[7] By deploying this term, I wish to capture a widespread appreciation among Vietnamese of manifestations of what I argue is a metaphysical quality, that of non-transience. In its pure state, it is imagined to reside as an immaterial quality in the spiritual realm of *âm*. *Âm* is the sphere of all sacred beings, ancestral spirits and other divinities. *Perdurability* refers to the materializations of non-transience as it enters the human sphere of mortality, transience and imperfection, known as *dương*. *Âm* and *dương* correspond to the Chinese cosmological terms *yin* and *yang*.

Perdurability is thus recognized and appreciated in its manifestation in things and events in the human world. The ethically highest-ranking

Plate 3.1 Ancient stela with *chữ nôm* inscriptions. Today situated on a village temple's premises, but claimed to have been ancestral kin group stela.

instance of its manifestation is the ancestral gift of life. Vietnamese imagine the ancestral life-giving act in terms of a meritorious deed (*công*) which entails a moral indebtedness (*ơn*) on the part of the recipient. The human person is construed in terms of this conjoining of non-transience, the divine soul (*hồn*) with the perishable substances of human "flesh and intestines" and the worldly life forces or energies (*via*).[8] The materiality of a particular grave and the terracotta sarcophagus inside, for instance, are judged and appreciated in terms of their ability to resist decay, their *perdurability*. This is because, more significantly, they safeguard the *perdurability* of the bones, which I argue occupy an intermediary position between the highly perishable bodily substances and *via* and the non-perishable *hồn* (Schlecker n.d.).

Perdurability denotes a unity of two basic dimensions: a material lastingness and the idea of a continuous relatedness. The most obvious case of this moral conceptualization is the idea of the *họ*, which I translate as *ancestral relatedness*. People reckon their kin relations to one another through common patrilineal descent. Descent, referred to as the "flow of *họ*" (*dòng họ*), is conceptualized as a unity of a common substance and relatedness through time.[9] The idea of a continuous relatedness pertains most significantly to the moral concept of an enduring link between merit (*công*) and indebtedness (*ơn*). This idea, I argue, is just as integral to the significance of a stela as is its solid materiality, its ability to persist through time.

The socioeconomic reforms of the country, which had begun in the late 1980s, entailed a disintegrative process for many rural communities, which in turn undermined the valued and desired manifestation of *perdurability*. In the past, the pre-reform household registration system, in conjunction with the all-pervasive rationing and state-employment systems, had prevented most people from migrating to cities. For Thanh Hà villagers, the disintegrative process in the reform era manifested itself primarily in the form of outward migration and a decoupling of state rewards from wartime achievements. Both were recognized as fatal for the community and it seemed that recent efforts to revive the local ritual life, especially among the village elders, constituted efforts to counteract this trend.

Thanh Hà Commune: Depopulation and the Waning of War-Martyr Allowances

Villagers recognized a pervasive disintegrative process affecting their commune through two chief changes: ever more local residents moved away to urban and industrialized semi-urban places, often they did so for good. Second, the commune's outstanding wartime achievements were becoming decoupled from state support as the generation of war-martyr spouses and veterans was dwindling. The first change affected especially the materiality of inhabited spaces and of the very bodies of those now absent, those who had previously contributed to the livelihood of the commune. The second change undermined especially the moral concept of a continuous relatedness, of an unceasing dedication to those who had given away their lives in war.

Rural communes in Northern Vietnam experience dramatic depopulation in the present era of economic reforms when urbanized centers hold the promise of much more profitable work. Thanh Hà's isolated location meant that this trend was here especially pronounced. Three rivers geographically isolate its coastal district, Tiên Lãng. Much of the traffic to and from Thanh Hà travels on timeworn rusty ferries. Villagers often explained to me their economic plight with reference to the isolated location. They spoke of being "cut off," Thanh Hà being a "river islet," and of living at the end of the district road. Many eagerly awaited announcements of any plans to build a seafood processing plant.

Visitors to the commune would soon notice the general absence of men and women in their 20s and 30s. There were also noticeably few families with young children. A good number of houses stood deserted in the commune with windows and doors shut by wooden boards. When I first accumulated basic biographical data on the local population of the most populous hamlet, known as Hamlet 7,[10] the term *cắt khẩu* would often be read out, which meant that a family had formally deregistered from Thanh Hà. Roughly, one in three families had at least one member residing in an urban center or working abroad as a guest laborer. These villagers support their elderly parents and young children who have stayed in Thanh Hà.

Michael DiGregorio (2007) has argued plausibly that the ritual revival in his fieldsite — a Northern Vietnamese village of steel recyclers — is to be understood as a response to the "dissolution of locality," as an outcome of labor migration. "The reconstruction of ritual space has become emblematic of an effort by the older generation to create this community and the claims on wealth, time and energy it entails" (ibid.: 464). My observations of commemorative practices in Thanh Hà concur with DiGregorio's account. Yet I want to explore the idea that for villagers in Thanh Hà, the threat was as much about dissolution of space, epitomized by boarded up houses, as it was about an actual loss of bodies. Depopulation meant that ever fewer people, especially the younger generation, would contribute to the livelihood of the village communities through productive work and offspring, but also through their continued ritual veneration of ancestors and local war dead.

The second major dimension of Thanh Hà's disintegration in the reform era was that state commemoration of wartime achievements was becoming decoupled from actual state allowances. Many Thanh Hà families depended critically on these allowances.[11] In addition, the commemoration of war martyr built for villagers the only remaining bond between their geographically marginal commune and the centers of power in Hanoi and Hải Phòng city. A widespread concern that the commune's wartime sacrifices for the country were becoming insignificant meant that Thanh Hà was becoming ever further marginalized within the country.

Thanh Hà commune was said to be wealthier than all other communes in Tiên Lãng due to its large number of *War-Martyr Families*, an earlier state support scheme.[12] According to record books in the commune's *Office for Labour, Invalids and Social Affairs*, over 18% of families had registered. War-martyr families, along with war-afflicted individuals (veterans, sick soldiers, Agent Orange victims), received monthly allowances, which constituted a considerable item in a peasant family's monthly budget. In most cases, it was the aging mother or father, who lived with a son and his family, and who thus contributed to the family's overall budget.

But this advantage over neighboring communes was on the wane. The younger brother of a war martyr put this most succinctly:

> ... many [from] here died [in the war] and that's why here a lot of people receive payments; ... and all the [other] communes along the main road are badly off; ... but in a few years, all the old people will have died and then no more payments will be made; all of the old people are very old already, all of them are 60, 70, 80 years old, they will all soon die; in just over ten years, no more payments will be distributed by the state.

The limitation of war-martyr allowances to the remaining lifespan of one or two, often elderly, individuals was widely perceived in Thanh Hà as building a tension with the Party State's commemorative slogans: "The Country of [our] Ancestors will always remember [your] Services" (*tổ quốc ghi công*) and "Forever Remembering Our Indebtedness" (*đời đời nhớ ơn*). Benoît de Tréglodé (2001) and Shaun Malarney (1996; 2002: 172ff; 2007) have detailed the ways in which the communist leadership fashioned a state cult of worshipping exemplary persons who had accrued merit during the revolutionary struggle and Wars of Resistance. The cult was not built from scratch, but elaborated on existing concepts and ritual practices, in particular the custom of recounting heroic tales to educate people about moral conduct. For both authors, state socialist worship of exemplary persons was to instil a sense of unity among survivors and subsequent generations. Collective emulation of exemplary persons, often rendered an accrual of merit (*công*), was to help build the new society.

For Thanh Hà residents, the dwindling generation of recipients of war-martyr allowances heralded a more general reorientation of the Party State away from a rewarding, ideological, state to a post-ideological welfare provider.[13] It is highly indicative that the more recent *Poverty Household* support scheme is not related to any meritorious achievement, but rather formally acknowledges the economic deprivation of households, irrespective of whether this is self-induced or not. In part, it reflects the growing impact of advisory bodies of foreign governmental and non-governmental organizations. Most importantly for us here is that the *Poverty Household* scheme signals the transformation of the Party State, which once laid great stress on the demonstration of meritorious service and loyalty as the precondition for dispensing support and other privileges.

The commune had received the highly prestigious 1st- and 2nd-Class Orders of Resistance from the national government. Every public event in Thanh Hà was suffused by references to the Wars of Resistance and the People's Army, including elementary-school festivals, kin-group death-day commemorations, and village festivals. Local government cadres repeatedly spoke of Thanh Hà as having a "revolutionary tradition" (*truyền thống cách mạng*).Yet as war-related rewarding state support gave way to undiscriminatory poverty reduction programs, such laudatory speeches struck villagers as empty and fatigued gestures.

War-Martyr Stelae as a Ritual Appropriation

Both of these major changes, an increasing depopulation and the decoupling of state support from wartime sacrifices, prompted villagers to ritually appropriate the commemoration of the war dead. One especially noteworthy case was an annual commemoration of a raid on Thanh Hà by the French army in 1948 to quell the local anti-colonial resistance. The commemoration was organized by members of the lay Buddhists of the largest village community in Thanh Hà on their own initiative.[14]

Another, somewhat less conspicuous, ritual appropriation of wartime commemoration concerned war-martyr stelae that listed members of an ancestral kin group, those who had been formally recognized by the government as war martyrs. This meant that the Party State's broad category of war martyrs was being broken down according to blood ties and locality. Precisely the deep-seated preference for particularistic ties based on ideas of common descent and common region had become targets of the revolutionary crackdown on feudalist customs and institutions and were still throughout the pre-reform era, at least formally, discouraged.

War-martyr stelae were clearly also another instance of efforts to add further prestige — to honor (*tôn vinh*) — to one's kin group, tacitly vying with other such groups under the watchful eyes of the deputy chairman for *Cultural Affairs*.[15] Yet, I argue that the ritual fervor was more acutely driven by the above processes of depopulation and decoupling of state support from wartime achievements. Ancestral relatedness was seen by many elderly villagers as a way to counteract depopulation by holding regular gatherings that brought together villagers from afar. And as genealogical charts were redrafted and expanded, the scope of such gatherings could increase. At the same time, solid forms were clearly desired so as to enhance *perdurability*, the unity of a material lastingness and a continuous relatedness between villagers and meritorious ancestors.

Two elderly villagers from the wealthy Lương kin group of Hamlet 7, Mr. Huân and Mr. Khê, explained the large genealogical chart of their *dòng họ* and expressed the moral force exerted by the *họ* on people to gather in their native place.

> Huân: Officially, this man's branch is the main branch, but this man went into exile. [And after he] went abroad ... [he] gave birth to many children, who adopted the foreign language. [They do] not [speak] Vietnamese anymore.
>
> Khê: [But] when he comes back, [others] have to acknowledge that this man acts in the capacity of the head [of the ancestral line].
>
> H.:   His roots are here. That's right. He may work as a director or a medical doctor [over there], but he still carries the name of his ancestral line. [Some come back] after five generations, [they] come back to affirm their ancestral line, sometimes even seven generations. They go abroad and then come back.
>
> K.:   He married over there. But he had to come back to his native land and affirm [his relatedness to] parents and grandparents. For however many generations, one still has to come back to reaffirm [one's relatedness].

H.: That is, over here, one has to carry the ancestral-line name of one's father ... the father had become naturalized [over there], [but] the children are Vietnamese. ... After seven or eight years of war, he still did not come back...

K.: That's the way it is. It keeps being handed down from this generation onto the next generation; it's still like that ...

H.: [Pointing at the ancestral chart:] That is, from this one [founding ancestor] to that one [down] there are 11 generations. Each born [by the previous generation], [all the way] down. For instance, this man here. [Pointing at an ancestor high up in the chart] He lived in Huế. In feudal times, he went there to fulfil his duty, resisting the foreign aggressors, resisting the Chinese feudal clique who had come to fight us. So after that, he was conferred a title in the temple or pagoda [there]. They inscribed his name there, a kind of endowment from the emperor ...

K.: ... he became a general by resisting the enemy, was given a royal decree. This was inscribed into a stela in the shrine at the end of our village.

H.: And now, we transfer this all to a new *bia* [of the Lương ancestral-kin group]: who in our ancestral line, in which generation, has taken part in the resistance against foreign aggressors.

K.: The stela has to be made from stone. [It will be made] this year.

H.: Engraved in stone!

K.: This year, because [before that] we did not have the money. This year, we began a collection campaign. All the men support and contribute money to make this stone stela.
[...]

H.: Whether abroad or in this country, for the death-day commemoration, one comes back. All have to come back. Every year, they also worship and make offerings.

The way in which Huân and Khê repeatedly stress here the moral force of the *họ*, ancestral relatedness, that it supersedes the significance of economically superior urban centers and places abroad, exemplifies well a widely shared mode of reasoning among villagers. The moral force outlasted Thanh Hà natives' migration histories and occupational changes. The making of a war-martyr stela indicates an effort to create tangible form ("Engraved in stone!") for this moral force, to enhance *perdurability*.

The significance of the *bia*'s lasting materiality was expressed by Huân and Khê in conjunction with their effort to extend their kin group's relatedness through time. Remarkably, the war-martyr stelae, most of them still in the planning and money-pooling phase, were to include ancestors from feudal times whose meritorious service to the country long preceded the actual category of "war martyrs" (*liệt sĩ*).[16] This was an effort to extend the lines of descent of meritorious persons far beyond the temporal frame of the state's cult of war martyrdom.[17] Thanh Hà villagers, in other words, both limited the veneration of war martyrs to selected individuals, members of one's own kin group, and expanded membership beyond official frame of Era of the Wars of Resistance.

We recall the opening story, where the elderly women grew concerned that the mysterious stone, discovered during construction work, was possibly housing a goblin. Its unknown origin, history, and purpose had clearly triggered this unease. Here, in contrast, villagers were actively bestowing a history on their stelae. By engraving a long list of dignified ancestors, kin groups charged the solid materiality of these commemorative stones with a venerable temporal continuity, thus contributing toward the *perdurability* of the stela.

Concluding Remarks

Vietnamese appreciate the manifestation of *perdurability* in a solid stone stela. I have argued above that this appreciation centers most significantly on the enduring relationship between the provider of a meritorious service (*công*) and the grateful recipient who has become indebted (*ơn*) in this manner. The subject of memory has here less to do with European preoccupations with the problem of representation (Terdiman 1993). It is rather an ethically charged understanding. Here, memory is a moral stance, an acknowledgment of one's indebtedness and commemoration of the appropriate action.

Many villagers experienced the reform era as one in which the Party State moved its attention away from the achievements of their family members and fellow villagers in the Wars of Resistance and their enduring of hardship throughout the pre-reform times. The shift from a rewarding ideological pre-reform state to a pragmatic welfare state since the reforms has entailed that communes' wartime prestige is clearly moving off the agenda and becoming decoupled from material rewards. Mass organizations, revived in the 1990s, were considered ineffectual performances that only covered up the growing distanciation of the leadership from rural concerns. The transformation of state-run agricultural cooperatives into mere service providers had resulted in great income disparities among families, which also triggered demands for a greater appreciation of past wartime services by family members.

Local appreciation of *perdurability* in ritual objects, sites and events has become heightened against this background. War martyr stelae illustrate well the ritual appropriation of war-time commemorative forms whereby the commemoration of past merit is selectively caught in the fall, so to speak. While the Party State had fashioned a cult of war martyrdom that was to convey a sense of a national unity and supersede the role of particularistic ties, regional loyalties, and patrilineal descent, war martyr stelae reverse this program. Heroic ancestors who had fought against Chinese invaders in feudal times were being tied to war martyrs from the French and US-American wars. In another sense, this move paralleled the construction of a national history under the Communist Party, which also foregrounded continuities between revolutionary heroes and military leaders from feudalist times (Pelley 2002).

The increasing depopulation in Thanh Hà meant that ever fewer, especially younger villagers could ensure the commemoration of past merit as ritual performers and narrators of local stories of the past. The loss of an appreciative and materially rewarding attention by the Party State has prompted villagers to step up efforts and enhance *perdurability* in ritual contexts. The desire for *perdurability* is not limited to *bia*. It can be found in a range of ritual contexts, especially the construction of gravesites (Schlecker n.d.). Common to these activities are efforts to achieve a material lastingness of ritual objects so as to ensure a temporal continuity of the existential bond of merit and indebtedness between ancestral souls and human beings.

The ritual fervor among Thanh Hà's *dòng họ* groups is exemplary of wider trends in Vietnam today where authorities have recently taken up a more conciliatory approach to these groups. Through personal conversations, I learned of activities in another province where the local government had begun to award government certificates for *cultured* conduct to such *dòng họ* groups, unthinkable until recently. Once considered a main obstacle to a successful transition toward a modern socialist nation, *dòng họ* groups were now formally acknowledged in Thanh Hà's village regulations as viable entities that helped to maintain social order and provided support to members in need. Many of these groups had set up specific hardship funds. Therefore, rather than consider the activities surrounding war-martyr stelae as simply opposed to the Party state, both its central and regional manifestations, it seems more appropriate to consider this as part of a process whereby the leadership is gradually shedding its role as an ideological educator of the masses and local non-state groups stepping in to help people orientate themselves in often volatile and destitute circumstances.

The legacy of wartime sacrifices and its commemoration are central to this trend. With regard to soldiers who died violent deaths, the fashioning of war-martyr stelae is a deliberate attempt undertaken by local kin groups to extract, as it were, individual war martyrs from the state domain of historiography and war-time commemoration. War-martyr stelae can therefore be considered part of a wider trend to reclaim the significance of land as the medium for relatedness between those above and below it, against official representations of land.

Notes

1. The following discussion builds on 12 months of fieldwork, which investigated broadly social support with a special focus on kin relations and death rituals. In addition to the main methods of informal conversations with inhabitants and observations, basic biographical and socioeconomic data were collected on all families in Hamlet 7, the most populous hamlet with about 1,000 inhabitants and 350 households. Two-hour interviews were conducted with over 150 households in Hamlet 7 and additional data on remaining households compiled. The focus on Hamlet 7 and its village Đông Úc was balanced with a participation in all major commune events in Thanh Hà.

2. One of the women was said to have extra-sensory or psychic skills and to run a private shrine in her own village.

3. Alternatively, a family could ask the local pagoda to perform worship for the childless relative where equally a one-time sum was paid and the name was then engraved into a *bia mua hậu*. The practice of paying a one-time sum for this service explains why this action contains the word *mua* (to buy).

4. Discussions of ancestral kin groups in the reform era have usually appeared as part of more encompassing accounts of cultural change and continuity (for example, Kleinen 1999; Luong Van Hy 1992; Jellema 2007). As part of a linguistic study, Luong Van Hy (1990) explored ideological structural dimensions of the Vietnamese kinship system. Previously, I focussed on the significance of kin metaphors of shared substance and actual kin relations for imaginations of the social in the reform era (Schlecker 2005).

5. Many *dòng họ* in Thanh Hà, however still lacked a hall of their own. In these cases, the large ancestral altar was housed in the private house of the head of cult. Several *dòng họ* had also become active in non-ritual domains. Some had set up their own stipend funds to encourage their members' children to study hard and reward them financially. This move was to a considerable extent part of a recent rapprochement between government and *dòng họ* groups, also reflected in passages of the current village regulations, drafted

by Party members, which acknowledged the contribution of *dòng họ* groups toward the good "cultured conduct" of villagers.

6. Membership in a *dòng họ* group is determined by patrilineal descent rules, excluding all affines. Women, even after marriage, belong to their father's *dòng họ*, but only men are registered as ritual actors, referred to as *đinh*. Currently, female members are often admitted, but clearly assume a marginal position. It was recognized among Thanh Hà villagers that the past had brought about changes and that nowadays, women were not as strictly ex-cluded from ritual affairs as had been the case in the feudalist past. For some elderly villagers, the participation of women in traditionally male ritual affairs indicated the empty, mock character of contemporary performances.

7. My use of the term *perdurability* owes to anthropological adaptations of Peircian semiotics (see especially Metz and Parmentier 1985; Parmentier 1987; Munn 1992; Daniel 1996, Keane 1997). Different representational orders regiment a reading of signs in ways, where the manifestation of *perdurability* may or may not be recognized and appreciated. A modernist knowledge order, as it is driven by the Party State, discourages people to ima-gine a unity of a material lastingness and the idea of a continuous relatedness.

8. While my discussion here of these concepts of death, the human person, and afterlife derive mostly from my own fieldwork in Thanh Hà and previously in Hanoi, additional valuable sources were Chanh Cong Phan (1993) and Kwon (2006, 2008).

9. The "flow of *họ*" includes female siblings and excludes all affines. By cus-tom, *dòng họ* gatherings are strictly male business, whose members are in this context referred to as *đinh* or, when counted, as *suất đinh*. In the current times, female members are often admitted, but clearly assume a marginal position.

10. The term *làng* had never been an administrative unit but, in the words of John Kleinen, denoted "a physical cluster of dwellings and at the same time a rural commune with a certain social cohesion, which does not exclude conflict ... *làng* is the socio-cultural denominator of an administrative unit" (Kleinen 1999: 7). Up until the Revolution, the term *xã* had denoted such clusters of dwellings as administrative units. The interim revolutionary government then chose the term *xã* to designate its new commune units, usually comprising several *làng* communities, replacing and often subdividing the pre-revolutionary administrative units of cantons (*tổng*). The *làng* com-munities were then formally subdivided into smaller units, first called *xóm* (neighborhoods), then during coop times (late 1950s–late 1970s) renamed and partly restructured as *đội* (brigades); after the inception of the reforms in the 1990s, they were renamed as *thôn* (hamlets; often also translated as village). In present-day Vietnam, a speaker often seamlessly shifts between the terms *thôn*, *làng*, and sometimes *xóm*, while referring to the same socio-spatial entity. The main focus of the present study, Đông Úc is one of Thanh Hà

commune's four *làng* communities and consists of seven of Thanh Hà's
13 *thôn* or hamlets.

11. Most of families in Thanh Hà depended on the unprofitable rice cultivation,
    but typically augmented their income with work as hired laborers, side-line
    businesses, breeding poultry, pigs, fish, and shrimp, part-time work in a
    shoe factory or industrial park near Hải Phòng. The all-pervasive poverty is
    endemic to the whole coastal district Tiên Lãng, which in turn is the poorest
    in the province of Hải Phòng. Over 15% of Thanh Hà's families had regis-
    tered with the "*Poverty Household*" state-benefit scheme to be exempted
    from various fees, receive free medical care, and to obtain loans from the
    Bank for Agricultural and Rural Development for a much lower interest rate.
    Villagers estimated that around 70 to 80 percent of the population had taken
    out such loans.

12. According to the official guidelines for war-martyr allowances, recipients are
    either both parents, the spouse, or the person formally recognized as having
    raised and supported the war martyr as a child. For one war martyr, the
    allowance was about 355.000 VND a month (ca. 18 EUR, as of 2007), for
    two it was 600.000 VND (ca. 30 EUR). Where the war martyr had been
    posthumously recognized as such after 1 Oct. 2005, the recipient received a
    one-time lump-sum of about 7 million VND. If the war martyr had already
    children, they also receive about 355.000 VND a month during the whole
    time they are registered at an educational facility until they reach the age of
    18. These amounts may not seem like much, but when set against the average
    income in Thanh Hà, one realizes that they are not insubstantial. According
    to my own semi-structured survey of 300 households, which took into ac-
    count informal sources of income, a family who depends entirely on agri-
    culture, earns often as little as somewhere around 200.000 to 300.000 VND
    a month, for the whole family. For inhabitants of Thanh Hà, this kind of
    income was comparable to a state salary. It was thought to be not terribly
    much, but it was stable, a quality much appreciated by those who struggled
    with unpredictable harvests and fluctuating market prices for agricultural
    produce.

13. The post-revolutionary and pre-reform Subsidy State (mid-1960s to late
    1980s) under general secretary Le Duan bore resemblances with John Ken-
    neth Galbraith's (1983) concept "compensatory power." This mode of power
    seeks to gain submission by offering affirmative rewards. Much of state prac-
    tices during that time centered around the judging of actions and the dispen-
    sion of graded rewards and privileges. The emergent Welfare State with its
    corporatist mechanism and co-optation strategies, on the other hand, comes
    close to what Galbraith called "conditioned power." Rather than offering
    reward, submission is sought through persuasion that the interests represented
    by the corporate organizations is in every one's interest. This mode of power
    is closely related to the growth of large organizations. In Galbraith's work,

the focus lied on large corporate businesses in a capitalist order. Yet still it appears plausible that mass organizations and state bureaucracies in Vietnam deploy a very similar mode of power that seeks to condition belief. Co-opting and enrolling people into Vietnam's re-animated mass organizations is a mode of persuasion that their interests are heard. Yet clearly in Vietnam, the power to condition is still very limited (see especially Jeong 1997).

14. Clearly, one major impetus for this event was that one of the victims was the village pagoda's monk whom the French had tortured and killed. Significantly, this was done parallel to the decennial commemoration of the same event by the local government and various smaller annually occurring speeches. Yet while the state commemoration foregrounded a joyous and proud sense of victory, despite the eventual defeat of Thanh Hà, the Buddhists sombrely recalled the violent and untimely deaths of the victims. A Buddhist monk, together with different worship priests, performed prayers for the salvation of their souls at the pagoda. Ritual dancers from the local temple were invited to perform sacrificial worship to ensure the well-being of the village community. The local government representatives had been invited and were respectfully acknowledged in the speeches, but it was clear that they perceived the situation as highly ambivalent. The cadres kept a visible distance to the performance and waited inside a small room of the pagoda.

15. A commune in Northern Vietnam is governed by the People's Committee (*uỷ ban nhân dân*), which is headed by a chairman and two deputy chairmen. In Apr. 2004, decree 107/2004/ND-CP by the central government determined that commune level People's Committees were to divide responsibilities between two deputy chairmen, one responsible for economic and fiscal problems, the other for cultural and social affairs. The deputy chairman for cultural affairs determines whether ritual activities, including the construction of grave sites and ancestral halls, conform to laws and regulations. In practical terms, he or she keeps a close eye on the population's *cultured* conduct, including quarrels, lavishness, gambling. In this, the deputy chairman is assisted by local residents in the villages and hamlets who are either part-time employees of his office or members of the watchdog *Fatherland Front* organization.

16. The war martyr category was according to Benoît de Tréglodé (2001; cit. by Malarney 2007) already fashioned in 1925, long before the national uprising in 1945.

17. This point is also supported by Malarney's (2007) account of the connection between the commemoration of war martyrs and the ancient custom of venerating what he called *exemplary dead*.

CHAPTER 4

Laos — Living with Unexploded Ordnance: Past Memories and Present Realities[1]

Elaine Russell

The Long Shadow of War

The 1959–73 civil war in Laos, which became part of the wider Second Indochina War, killed, injured and displaced hundreds of thousands of civilians.[2] The US military conducted massive bombing campaigns during the last nine years of the conflict, dropping over 2.1 million tons of ordnance (US Senate Congressional Record 1975: 14,266). This left Laos the most heavily bombed country per capita in history. Today the shadow of war continues to intrude into the daily lives of the Lao people in former war zones and imposes a heavy burden on the entire country. Remnants of war — the visible scars of bombing on the landscape and remaining buildings along with massive contamination from unexploded ordnance (UXO) — provide constant reminders of the past while continuing to threaten the physical, psychological and economic well-being of the people (see Khamvongsa and Russell 2009; Prokosch 1995; Tyner 2010; Henig 2012). Many older Lao have vivid memories of horrific events, hardships and the loss of loved ones during the war. After US bombing in northeastern and southeastern Laos intensified significantly in 1968, civilian survivors began arriving to refugee camps in Vientiane. Soon journalists reported the refugees' experiences.[3] Additional stories have been documented over the years by writers and filmmakers.[4] While some accounts are difficult to verify, the overwhelming preponderance of evidence reveals a common thread of truth. All the survivors tell of terrible suffering and are haunted by violent memories, emblematic of what Navaro-Yashin (2009: 5) calls ruination — the "subjectivities and residual affects that linger, like a hangover, in the aftermath of war or violence."

Younger generations of Lao may not remember the war, but it still shapes the course of their lives today. In a country where 70 percent of the population relies primarily on subsistence farming, with some households supplementing their income through trade, commercial crops and other economic activities, it is estimated that half of the arable land and one-third of the total country is contaminated with UXO.[5] The *National Survey of UXO Victims and Accidents Phase 1*, published by the National Regulatory Agency for UXO/Mine Action in the Lao PDR (hereafter: NRA) in 2009, reported that at least 30,000 civilians have been killed and 20,000 injured by UXO accidents since the bombing began in 1964; 20,000 of these casualties occurred after the bombing ended in 1973 — a continuation of the original violent intentionality (Gell 1998: 17) in times of peace. Remnants of war challenge the Lao people's everyday livelihoods as well as cultural beliefs. People have been forced to adapt to the grim reality of their situation, struggling to go on in very difficult conditions. It is ironic that UXO, which killed or injured an average of 300 people a year from 1990–2008 (NRA 2009; casualties have steadily declined since 2008), also provides many rural villagers with a source of income from work in the UXO clearance sector or through the collection and sale of scrap metal from the war (see also Schwenkel's contribution, this volume). This chapter will recount the events leading to the mass bombardment of Laos and discuss the violent legacy of the Second Indochina War, namely the ongoing threat by UXO. As a kind of violent, decentralized *lieu de mémoire* (Nora 1989), it haunts and shapes the everyday lives of the rural population of contemporary Laos.

A Brief History

External Intervention and Civil War in Laos

The First Indochina War (1946–54) entailed a sharp internal division in both the Lao and Vietnamese societies. While parts of the political elites in both countries aligned themselves with French colonial rule, the communist movement under the guidance of Ho Chi Minh took up armed struggle against colonialism. With support from the Việt Minh, Lao communist forces were established in the aftermath of the Second World War. By 1953, Lao and Vietnamese revolutionary troops had control of Phongsaly and Houaphan provinces, which border southwest China and northwestern Vietnam respectively. The Việt Minh defeated the French at Điện Biên Phủ, a remote valley in northwestern Vietnam near the Lao border, on 7 May 1954, effectively ending the war and French rule in Southeast Asia.

During 1953–54, world powers met in Geneva, Switzerland, to negotiate a series of agreements to end the First Indochina War. The treaty temporarily divided Vietnam into two parts along the 17th parallel: the Democratic Republic of Vietnam in the north and the State of Vietnam (replaced by the Republic of Vietnam in 1955) in the south. It called for elections to be held to form a new government unifying the north and south, but the south refused to participate. The stalemate led to a growing insurgency and the formation in 1960 of the National Liberation Front (NLF), which carried out guerilla operation in the south. This eventually turned into a full civil war between the north and south, and continued to spill over into Laos where a network of supply routes for the insurgents was established — the so-called "Ho Chi Minh Trail" (see Introduction and Pholsena's chapter, this volume).

As part of the Geneva Agreements, *The Agreement on the Cessation of Hostilities in Laos* was signed on 20 July 1954. Laos was declared a sovereign, neutral nation, and foreign forces were required to withdraw from the country with the exception of a small French force to train the Royal Lao Army (Stuart-Fox 1997: 85–7). The North Vietnamese forces never fully withdrew and continued to train Lao communist troops (Conboy 1995: 13). At the same time, American and French military advisors continued to work in the country with the Royal Lao Army. The Geneva Agreement called for the Royal Lao Government to reconcile with the Pathet Lao — the name under which the Lao communist movement was known internationally — by integrating Pathet Lao troops into the Royal Lao Army, reintegrating Phongsaly and Houaphan provinces with the rest of the country and holding elections to establish a new coalition government. However, these goals were undermined as Laos became embroiled in the growing ideological struggle of the global Cold War. Conservative, or Rightist leaders, who opposed the formation of a coalition government with the Pathet Lao, gained support from the American government. At the same time, Communist leaders and some Neutralist (those non-aligned with Rightists or Communists but desiring reconciliation and cooperation between all political groups) were supported by China and North Vietnam. The ongoing interference and manipulation by outside countries led to further political radicalization in the 1960s.

The American government under President Eisenhower's administration (1953–61) was determined to stop communism from taking hold in Southeast Asia, believing in the Domino Theory, that is, if one country came under the Communist rule, then the surrounding countries would follow in a domino effect. Initially, the greatest concern was over the situation in Laos. The Program Evaluation Office (PEO) was created within the US Embassy in Vientiane in 1955 to funnel money to the Royal Lao Army and Government. From 1955–58, the US government gave $120 million to Laos in an attempt to strengthen the Royal Lao Army and Rightist leaders within the government. About 85 percent of the funds went to the army, while other payments went to government ministers and influential Lao. The flow of US money to support Rightist leaders led to corruption and became a major political issue (Evans 2002: 93–104; Rust 2012).

Despite American efforts to block a coalition government with the Communists, Prime Minister Souvanna Phouma reached an agreement with the Pathet Lao in 1957 and formed a provisional coalition government (Stuart-Fox 1997: 96–7). Elections were held in 1958. US efforts to influence voters were unsuccessful as the Pathet Lao gained a strong footing in the newly elected coalition government. The US undermined the success of the coalition by creating a financial crisis. Aid payments were withheld and America insisted on a devaluation of the Lao currency. Prime Minister Souvanna Phouma was unable to maintain leadership and resigned after only eight months. Another government was formed by Phouy Xananikon, a conservative leader with US backing. He immediately opposed the Communists and did not include any Pathet Lao leaders in his cabinet (ibid.: 102–4). The Royal Lao Army and defense ministry came under the direction of General Phoumi Nosavan, who stepped up repression of Pathet Lao members and eventually arrested several key leaders (Tappe 2010). Meanwhile, the DRV had shifted their political struggle into an armed struggle against South Vietnam and strengthened their efforts to control the Lao-Vietnamese border regions and build up Lao guerillas to facilitate the infiltration of South Vietnam with soldiers and supplies via the Ho Chi Minh Trail. Internal strife in Laos escalated after Phoumi Nosavan staged a military coup in December 1959, followed by rigged elections in April 1960 in which Phoumi's rightist Committee for the Defence of National Interests (CDNI) prevailed.

Captain Kong Le, a Neutralist in the Royal Lao Army who was upset by American interference in Lao politics, led his troops in a counter coup in August 1960 — which provoked another Rightist coup backed by the

US four months later. As a result, Captain Kong Le and some of the Neutralist forces joined the Communist Pathet Lao to fight the Royal Lao Government. The civil war had effectively begun (Evans 2002: 105–17).

World leaders gathered once again in Geneva in May 1961 to nego- tiate an end to the conflict in Laos. After further meetings, the participants signed the 1962 Geneva Agreement on Laos. Once more, the nation was declared a sovereign neutral country, and foreign military troops and inter- vention were prohibited. The US hoped that the new agreements would halt the use of the Ho Chi Minh Trail and reduce the growing insurgent threat in South Vietnam (Evans 2002: 123–5). But the agreements had little effect on the Lao civil war or the continued use and expansion of the North Vietnamese supply routes as the civil war in Vietnam continued to grow.

The US "Secret War" in Laos

While the US had supplied military funding, arms and training to the Royal Lao Army since the mid-1950s, the Central Intelligence Agency (CIA) greatly expanded covert and illegal operations in Laos beginning in 1960. The US wanted to stop Pathet Lao insurgents (assisted by the North Vietnamese Army) in their fight to unseat the Royal Lao Government and establish a communist Lao state and stem the flow of North Vietnamese arms and support to the communist insurgents in South Vietnam (ibid.: 130–40). Both covert US operations and North Vietnamese military acti- vities in Laos were in direct violation of the 1962 Geneva Agreements. From 1960–70, three separate US presidential administrations (Kennedy, Johnson and Nixon) kept the US role in Laos a secret from the US Con- gress and American people. Later, these covert operations became known as the US "secret war" in Laos.

The American military and CIA advisors felt the Royal Lao Army was ill-suited to fight a guerilla war against the Pathet Lao and North Viet- namese Army in the rugged mountains of north and southeastern Laos. Instead, the CIA recruited, trained and armed a surrogate counterinsurgency force from ethnic hill groups.[6] The mostly Hmong, Mien and Khmu forces were led by Vang Pao, a Hmong officer in the Royal Lao Army. Vang Pao and a group of Hmong fighters had fought with the French against the Việt Minh in the First Indochina War.

The CIA built a secret airstrip at Long Chieng, a remote, narrow valley midway between Vientiane and the Plain of Jars in Xieng Khouang Province. The airstrip served as the operating base for the Special Forces. In addition, a series of dirt airstrips were established on mountaintops around the Pathet Lao-held areas where single engine aircraft could deliver Special Forces and supplies. The CIA reregistered US military and commercial planes with two civilian airlines. The stated purpose was to fly humanitarian missions to deliver food and medicine to Lao villagers caught in the warzone. In truth, the airlines were owned by the CIA and most of the pilots were US military personnel who were reclassified as civilians (Conboy 1995: 63–4). The planes were used to deliver troops and arms.

The communist Lao movement, headquartered in Houaphan Province (see Tappe's chapter), was assisted by the North Vietnamese Army. They controlled several regions of eastern Laos, although boundaries were not straightforward and shifted as the war progressed. The Plain of Jars in Xieng Khouang Province, bordering Houaphan Province, became a major battleground throughout the war. For years, the Pathet Lao and North Vietnamese Army fought the US-funded Special Forces and sometimes the Royal Lao Army for control of this region.

In June 1964, Pathet Lao and North Vietnamese forces shot down a US reconnaissance plane and a short while later a fighter jet over northern Laos (Haney 1972: 268). The US used these incidents to argue their case for bombing Pathet Lao and North Vietnamese positions in northern Laos. The Lao prime minister gave his approval. The bombing was extended in December 1964 to a second campaign, which became the larger of the two, aimed at leveling out the Ho Chi Minh Trail in southeastern Laos (Van Staaveren 1993). The bombing campaigns continued throughout the rest of the war.

The Scale of the Bombings

US military records reveal that America dropped over 2.1 million tons of ordnance in 580,000 bombing missions on Laos from 1964–73. This is more ordnance than the US dropped during all of the Second World War in Europe and the Pacific. It was the equivalent of a planeload of bombs dropped every eight minutes, 24 hours a day, for nine years.

For the first time, the US used large numbers of cluster bombs. Cluster bomb casings were dropped from planes and opened mid-air to release anywhere from 100–700 small bomblets the size of a soup can or orange. More than 270 million bomblets, including 19 different designs, were dropped on Laos (Hizney 2006: 15–25; see as well Parsch 2012 and Prokosch 1995: 81–125). It is estimated that 30 percent, or close to 80 million bomblets, did not detonate (Khamvongsa and Russell 2009: 293). Cluster bomblets are similar to landmines, only they have more deadly

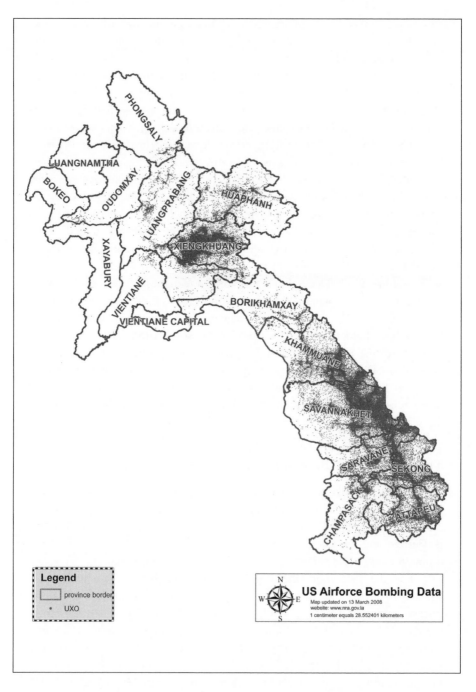

Map 4.1 US Military Strike Data (Source: Lao PDR National Regulatory Authority).

Plate 4.1   Cluster bomb casing and bomblets.

consequences. Some sprayed shrapnel up to 150 yards, while others spread ball bearings or nails.

The heaviest bombing took place in the southeast along the Ho Chi Minh Trail where about 1,720,000 tons of ordnance was dropped. US military records indicate 380,000 tons of ordnance was dropped on northern Laos, primarily in Xieng Khouang and Houaphan provinces (US Senate Congressional Record 1975: 14266). The bombings targeted not only military troops and facilities, but also civilian villages, fields and livestock. After President Johnson (1963–1969) ordered a halt to bombing missions over North Vietnam in 1968, the bombing campaigns over northern and southeastern Laos escalated dramatically. In 1967, close to 128,000 tons of ordnance was dropped on Laos. The following year, this amount almost doubled then increased nearly fourfold in 1969 to 515,000 tons. The bombings in 1970 and 1971 continued at the dramatic rates of 453,000 tons and 437,500 tons, respectively (ibid.). The bombs fell day and night. The town of Xieng Khouang, former capital of Xieng Khouang Province, was completely leveled in 1969.

Plate 4.2 Drawing from *Voices from the Plain of Jars*.

My village stood on the edge of the road from Xieng Khouang to the Plain of Jars. There were rice fields next to the road. The first time the airplanes bombed the road but didn't bomb my village. At that time my life was filled with pleasure and happiness. With great happiness because the mountains and forests were beautiful through nature: land, water and climate suitable for we rice farmers. And there were many homes together in our one village. But that dream did not last long. Because the airplanes came bombing my rice field until the bomb craters made farming impossible. And the village was hit and burned. And some relatives who were working in their fields without shelter came running out to the road to return to the village, but the airplanes saw and shot them — killing the farmers in a heart-rending manner. We heard their screams, but we couldn't go to help them. When the airplanes left we went to look but they had already died.

— 1970 account of a civilian bombing survivor from
Xieng Khouang in Branfman 2010 [1972].

The Secret War Revealed

After the bombing campaigns intensified, large numbers of civilian survivors started arriving to refugee camps located near Vientiane. Their stories began to reach the outside world over the next few years. Up until this time, the US had denied bombing northern Laos, and the inaccessibility of war zones had made it impossible for journalists to verify. Although the Nixon administration (1969–74) finally admitted to the bombings in 1970, it denied that civilians had been targeted. Survivors refuted this claim.

Two young American men, Fred Branfman and Walter Haney, who were teaching English in Laos at the time, collected the refugees' stories and presented the information in testimony before the US Congress.[7] Fred Branfman (2010 [1972]) published survivors' drawings and accounts of the bombings in his book, *Voices from the Plain of Jars: Life under an Air War*. Walt Haney (1972) wrote a chapter about the US secret war in Laos, which was published in the Gravel Edition of the *Pentagon Papers*.

The following quote is from a report written by George Chapelier (quoted in Haney 1972: 276), a United Nations advisor in Laos, after interviewing dozens of refugees from the Plain of Jars in 1970:

> By 1968, the intensity of the bombings was such that no organized life was possible in the villages. The villagers moved to the outskirts and then deeper and deeper into the forest as the bombing reached its peak in 1969, when jet planes came daily and destroyed all stationary structures; nothing was left standing. The villagers lived in trenches and holes or in caves, and they only farmed at night. All informants, without exception, had his village completely destroyed. In the last phase, bombings were aimed at the systematic destruction of the material basis of the civilian society.

The End of War

The US government signed the Paris Agreement with the North Vietnamese in January 1973, agreeing to cease military operations and withdraw from Indochina. The Royal Lao Government and Pathet Lao followed by signing a ceasefire, the Vientiane Agreement, in February 1973. However, the protocol implementing the ceasefire was not completed until September of that year (Evans 2002: 166–9). The two sides formed a new coalition government.

By December 1975, the Communists had taken control of the country and government, establishing the Lao People's Democratic Republic. Families were torn apart as some members decided to flee the country while others remained behind. Approximately 300,000 people, close to ten percent of the population, left Laos over the next few years (ibid.). Many ended up in refugee camps in Thailand and eventually resettled in other countries, primarily France, the US, and Australia.

The Lao who returned to their villages in the former war zones found their houses destroyed and their fields, which had once yielded rice and vegetables, filled with UXO — everything from large bombs and cluster bomblets to mortars, landmines, rockets and hand grenades. Over 186 types of ordnance from the war have been found.[8] People soon discovered that danger lurked everywhere — buried in the dirt under houses, in school-yards, rice paddies, orchards and stream beds, even nestled in the branches of trees. Cluster bomblets and other ordnance lay in wait for a farmer throwing a hoe into his field or staking his water buffalo to the ground, a teenager cutting down bamboo or a child picking up a small metal object that looked like a toy.

Today people still remember how many were killed right after the war, before they understood the danger from UXO buried in the land. In the village of Ban Nong Boua, located near the former Ho Chi Minh Trail, Mr Kee, the village headman, described the situation in an interview with Sean Sutton of the not-for-profit humanitarian demining organization Mines Advisory Group (MAG 2011b):

> So many people were killed in the bombing during the war. The vil-lagers could not stay. They lived in caves and in the forest. Every house in the village was destroyed — everything was gone. After the war we tried to start again and many were killed farming because of the UXO. When we farmed we would fill buckets up with bombs and bury them in the bomb craters. We thought it was scrap — we didn't know they were dangerous. Then people started to die. That's how we found out. We found out the hard way. I found a bombie[9] and threw it into a crater but it blew up in the air. I was lucky because I was behind a termite's nest so I wasn't hurt.

Legacies of War — Almost 40 Years Later

The legacies of war continue to haunt the nearly 6.6 million people living in Laos today. Unexploded cluster bomblets and other ordnance have been found in all 17 provinces of the country and in one-quarter of over 10,500 villages (Handicap International 1997). For many in Laos, the war lives on.

The Human Toll

The NRA survey on UXO victims, published in 2009, covered 95 percent of the villages in Laos and documented at least 30,000 deaths and 20,000 injuries to civilians from UXO accidents (1964–2008). Close to 20,000 of these casualties, including 8,000 deaths, occurred from 1974–2008, or after the war had ended and the bombing stopped in late 1973. Cluster bomblets caused 13.2 percent of UXO accidents from 1964–2007, but this increased to 29 percent during the period 1999–2008 (NRA 2009).

The first six years following the end of war brought 1,500 casualties annually as families returned to their land unaware of the overwhelming presence of UXO. Casualties slowly declined over time as people became more cautious in handling the ordnance and remained at about 300 per year from 1990–2008. From 2008–October 2012, another 683 UXO casualties were reported. Significantly, the number of casualties has fallen steadily from 298 in 2008 to 117 in 2009 and 2010, 99 in 2011 and 44 through October 2012. Children and teenagers, primarily boys, are particularly at risk, making up 43.5 percent of casualties from 2008–2012 (NRA 2009, 2011a/b, 2012; Government of Lao PDR 2012a; IRIN 2011). Eastern Savannakhet Province, primarily the districts of Vilabuly, Phine, Sepon, and Nong, which were traversed by the Ho Chi Minh Trail, experienced the highest number of casualties in the country with 25 percent of the total. Xieng Khouang Province, the focus of the northern bombing campaign, had the second highest number with 12 percent of total casualties (NRA 2010a).

The Lao PDR government is putting a UXO/Mine Accident and Victim Reporting System in place to keep an accurate record of accidents and casualties as well as a Survivor Tracking System that will track data on the needs of UXO survivors (Government of Lao PDR 2012b: 2). However, these systems have been slow to become operational and provide data to the public. But statistics can be numbing, only numbers and percentages. They do not begin to describe the ways in which the presence of UXO has permanently changed people's lives. Hundreds of children have been orphaned. Families have been left without a father or mother to work in the rice fields, care for the children or run the household. Helpless parents mourn the loss of their children.

Of the 20,000 UXO accident survivors (1964–2008), the majority were left seriously disabled and 13,835 lost anywhere from one to four limbs (NRA 2009: 46). Many survivors have been blinded. These injuries dramatically changed the victims' lives. Aea Lee, a farmer from Xieng Khouang Province, struck a cluster bomblet while working in his field in November 2008. He lost the lower half of both his legs. Now, he and his family must adjust to a new reality as he may no longer be able to farm his rice fields.[10]

People with disabilities can face discrimination and isolation in the Lao culture because of the way Buddhist or animist beliefs are sometimes interpreted. In some cases, disability may be viewed as being caused by bad karma or the presence of evil spirits. While families support and care for disabled relatives, other villagers may avoid them. Disabled children sometimes are not allowed to continue in school, and adults may find it difficult to find someone to marry.[11]

In August 2008, Legacies of War[12] members visited the Lao Disabled Women's Development Association. My colleagues and I met Bouma who was learning to spin thread and weave fabric on a wooden loom. Near the end of the war when she was ten years old, she helped clear a road. A US jet dropped a bomb as the group worked. Her foot was hit and badly damaged, making it difficult for her to walk. She said her family had cared for her, but she felt isolated in her village. She began to cry as she told us no one would ever marry her. She would never have a family.

Attitudes are slowly improving with the help of organizations that provide services to the disabled and educate the public, such as the Lao Disabled People's Association, Handicap International, the Lao Disabled Women's Development Association, World Education/Consortium and the Cooperative Orthotic and Prosthetic Enterprise (COPE).

The consequences of UXO contamination cause profound impacts on society. When a parent dies or is disabled, children often drop out of school to help support the family. If a husband is killed or disabled, women must assume the role as head of the household and work to support the family. The presence of UXO has led women into non-traditional jobs, such as demining work. MAG first hired women to work on their clearance teams in 1997 and formed the first all-female team in 2007 (Mines Advisory Group 2011b). The Lao PDR government demining program, UXO Lao, followed suit in 2008. John Dingley, the United Nation's (UN) senior technical adviser to UXO Lao, pointed out, "These are good jobs, and we want to create as many opportunities as possible for women in post-conflict settings" (IRIN 2011).

Economic Impacts

Beyond the terrible human costs, the presence of UXO has severely hindered efforts to bring Laos out of poverty and meet the United Nations Development Program's (UNDP) Millennium Development Goals (MDGs) for the Least Developed Countries of the world. Although Laos has experienced healthy economic growth over the past ten years and made progress in other measures of development, it ranked 138 out of 187 countries on the UNDP human development index in 2011 (UNDP 2011). The Lao PDR government struggles to provide people with basic needs, including

Plate 4.3 All-female demining team in Khammouane Province, Laos (Photo courtesy of the Humpty Dumpty Institute).

food security, healthcare, education and infrastructure — a safe water supply, sanitation, roads and electricity. The following sections briefly discuss areas of the economy affected by UXO.

Agriculture

In 2007, the World Bank identified 9.2 percent of total land area in Laos as arable land, that is, land suitable for intensive agriculture with seasonal and permanent crops and permanent pasture. It is estimated that half of this land is contaminated with UXO. It becomes more and more difficult for farmers to find enough land to grow an adequate amount of food given population growth, expansion of commercial and plantation crops for export, urbanization, government relocations of villages to accommodate projects such as hydroelectric dams and other competing land uses. In many places, farmers must risk planting crops in contaminated fields in order to feed their families.

Poverty

In 2008, 34.7 percent of the people in Laos lived below the national poverty line (Messerli *et al.* 2008: 132). Food security for subsistence farmers in many rural areas is a constant challenge. A 2007 UN World Food Program (WFP 2011) study on food security found 50 percent of children under the age of five in rural Laos to be malnourished. Poverty is caused by many factors, including the inaccessibility of remote mountainous regions, low productivity levels of agricultural land and a lack of public services. The presence of UXO only exacerbates the problems. UXO has been found in 41 of the 46 poorest districts.

Healthcare

Healthcare facilities in Laos are woefully inadequate for the needs of the Lao population. UXO casualties further strain an already overburdened system. Victims often must travel anywhere from half an hour to several hours to reach one of the 800 Health Centers or to a larger district hospital, none of which are equipped to handle the severity of traumatic UXO injuries. It can take an additional four hours or longer to reach one of the nine regional hospitals with better facilities. Many victims die or lose limbs because treatment is delayed or inadequate (see Table 4.1).

Table 4.1 Travel Time to Medical Facilities.

Accessibility Class	Percentage of villages	Percentage of population	Cumulative percentage of population
0 to 0.5 h	61.5	74.6	74.6
0.5 to 1 h	11.9	9.2	83.8
1 to 2 h	9.8	6.6	90.4
2 to 4 h	9.6	5.6	96.0
4 to 7 h	5.3	3.0	9.0
More than 7 h	2.2	1.0	100.0

Source: Messerli *et al.* 2008: 70.

On 4 November 2010, Legacies of War members visited a village in eastern Savannakhet Province. I spoke with the parents of a ten-year-old boy who had died two weeks earlier. The boy had found a cluster bomblet in the forest and not knowing what it was, threw it to the ground. He sustained severe head injuries from flying shrapnel while two other boys were slightly injured. The parents managed to find a ride to the clinic in Sepon a little over an hour away. The staff at the clinic said they were unable to help the young boy given the nature of his injuries. The hospital in the city of Savannakhet, with more skilled staff and better equipment, was a five-hour drive away. The parents took the boy home where he died that night.

Healthcare costs, including the cost of transportation to reach health-care facilities, are borne primarily by patients. Foreign donors provide contributions for specific healthcare programs in some districts, while the Lao PDR government spends only 1.5 to two percent of the government budget on healthcare.[13] In 2007, only 3.8 percent of the Lao population was covered by some form of public or private health insurance.[14] Families of UXO victims often do not have enough money to cover the cost of healthcare. Many must spend what little cash they have available and often are forced to sell livestock and other assets and/or borrow money. A 2004 survey of 289 child UXO survivors found that only 27 percent of families were able to cover healthcare costs, 47 percent used their own money supplemented by selling assets or borrowing money and 26 percent relied solely on selling assets or borrowing money (Bertrand 2004: 29). In some situations, a lack of cash means survivors do not receive any treatment at all.[15]

The Health Equity Fund is a pilot project that began in 2004 to provide funding for the poor. By 2009, the program had expanded to 31 districts and provided healthcare funding to 128,227 people.[16] Funding for the program comes from the government and foreign donors and is administered largely by the Swiss Red Cross. There are plans to expand the program throughout Laos to ultimately cover close to two million individuals. The needs for physical and psychosocial rehabilitation, economic rehabilitation and vocation training for UXO victims far outstrip available services. These services are provided primarily by not-for-profit organizations.

Infrastructure

Many rural areas with UXO contamination lack basic infrastructure. Before these projects can be built, the land must first be cleared of ordnance, which substantially adds to project costs. An analysis of projects funded by the Asia Development Bank and World Bank in Laos found that an additional $20 million was spent for UXO clearance in order to build the projects, which included roads, clinics, school, water pipelines, irrigation structures, power lines and dams. The study also found that UXO clearance costs for a power project to provide 33,000 households in rural northern Laos with electricity increased total costs by five percent (UNDP 2007).

Coping with a Violent Landscape

Landscapes in former war zones are filled with remnants of war that evoke painful memories and pose a constant threat to people's physical and

Plate 4.4 Bombed Buddhist temple in former Xieng Khouang capital.

psychological well-being (see Introduction, this volume). The following short case studies illustrate the many ways a violent landscape intrudes into people's daily lives, and presents stories of individuals and how they have responded to this reality.

Scars on the Landscape

The massive number of large bombs that exploded in Laos during the war left vast areas pockmarked with giant craters, many of which are still evident today. Early on, farmers used these craters to dispose of UXO, while today many uncontaminated craters serve as fishing ponds. Other reminders of the war are found at historic sites such as Tham Piu cave (discussed below), a preserved portion of the former Ho Chi Minh Trail near Sepon, and the bombed-out Buddhist temple and French hospital in the former provincial capital of Xieng Khouang. At many sites, people have built altars to light incense and pray for those who died.

Plate 4.5 Warning about UXO at Plain of Jars Site One.

Tourism with a Warning

The Plain of Jars in Xieng Khouang Province is named for the large stone jars scattered throughout the valley, some of which stand six to eight feet tall. In 1998, the Lao government and UNESCO began a multi-year phased program to safeguard and develop the Plain of Jars. Archaeologists think the jars may date from 500 BC to 800 CE and possibly were used as funeral urns (UNESCO 1998). But even here, the war left its mark. At the entrance to the Plain of Jars Site One, a popular tourist destination, signs warn visitors to walk within the white markers and not wander off the path where unexploded bombs remain. Numerous bomb craters are found among the jars with signs indicating when the bombs were dropped. There are also caves where villagers lived during the war.

The MAG office in the center of Phonesavan, Xieng Khouang Province maintains a small exhibit to educate tourists and other visitors on UXO and the organization's demining work in the region. COPE also has a visitor center at their facilities in Vientiane with a powerful exhibit that includes personal stories, videos, photographs, art pieces and other displays on the impacts of UXO and the challenges faced by the disabled.

The Constant Threat

The psychological strain of living in a dangerous, unstable landscape wears on people as they go about their daily lives. Many farmers must clear and plant their land to grow food for their families never knowing when they might strike a cluster bomblet or other ordnance. Mothers often insist on walking their children to school for fear they will be hurt by UXO along the way. Other parents simply keep their children at home. In some regions, UXO Lao and not-for-profit organizations, such as World Education/ Consortium and Handicap International, teach children and adults about the dangers of UXO, how to avoid it and what to do if they find it. A pilot program, implemented by the Swiss Red Cross, trains villagers in the basics of emergency trauma care for UXO injuries. Handicap International is considering a similar program.

Income from the UXO Sector

While the presence of UXO provides a major barrier to economic development in many areas, the formal UXO clearance sector also creates jobs. UXO Lao employs over 1,000 people for demining and risk education (UXO Lao 2010). Private demining companies and not-for-profit organizations working on demining, risk education and victim assistance hire hundreds of Lao workers (see as well Schwenkel's chapter in this volume for demining practices in Vietnam).

In addition to formal UXO clearance programs, an informal sector has developed over the years as locals find innovative ways to reuse bomb materials or sell them. Cluster bomb casings are turned into house supports, fence posts and planter boxes; pineapple-shaped cluster bomblets are defused and used as cooking stoves or oil lamps; and metals are made into tools, pots and dishes. Explosives are sometimes extracted from live ordnance and sold. In recent years, poverty has driven villagers to search for bomb fragments, and sometimes UXO, to sell to foundries for extra cash. A building boom in Vietnam and Laos has increased demand for scrap metal to make rebar for supports in brick buildings. The metals from exploded and unexploded ordnance provide high-quality materials available for a relatively low price. This potential of transformation reflects the

Plate 4.6 Exhibit of cluster bomblets falling at the COPE visitor center Vientiane.

Plate 4.7　Bomb casings used for a fence (Photo courtesy of the Humpty Dumpty Institute).

ambivalence of war debris, which has both malevolent and beneficial capacities (see Henig 2012; Saunders 2002).

Informal collection activities can be risky as inexperienced collectors find live munitions and attempt to collect, transport or defuse them. Despite risk education and government laws that make it illegal for individuals to tamper with or take UXO, the practice goes on. People are desperate for the additional income. While in Xieng Khouang Province in 2008, I observed individuals and entire families scouring hillsides with inexpensive metal detectors that can be purchased in Vietnam for as little as $10. A couple drove past on their tractor carrying a large bomb casing. And at the local foundry, there were huge piles of live munitions that had been brought in by local farmers.

To substantially reduce the practice of illegal UXO collection, economic alternatives must be found. MAG identified 86,000 pieces of live munitions in the Xieng Khouang foundry in 2009. The organization has suggested it might be better to legalize collection and train local farmers to safely handle the UXO (Legacies of War 2009). However, this is a controversial proposal. Interference with UXO, including collection, has caused 6.68 percent of all UXO accidents through 2008 (NRA 2009).

Plate 4.8 Live ordnance brought to the Xieng Khouang foundry over three months in 2008 (Photo courtesy of Boon Vong).

Lives Changed Forever

Almost every family in Laos has a story to tell of how the war and its aftermath affected their lives. The ways in which people cope with living in a violent landscape vary widely. The following individual accounts present a range of reactions and responses.

Lae — Keeper of Tham Piu Cave

Tham Piu cave is a huge limestone cave located in the mountains of Xieng Khouang Province just northeast of Muang Kham village and about two hours from the provincial capital of Phonesavan. Legacies of War members visited Tham Piu cave on 24 August 2008, and met a local villager named Lae, who maintains a small museum and serves as guide for visitors to the cave. At the time of the bombing, he was not in the area, but his whole family died in the cave. The leaflet from the museum states that Tham Piu cave served as a home for a large number of civilian families who were forced to move there once US bombing made it impossible to remain in their villages. On 24 November 1968, two US fighter jets targeted bombs

Plate 4.9   Lae 2008 (Photo courtesy of Boon Vong).

Plate 4.10   Tham Piu Cave (Photo courtesy of Boon Vong).

directly into the mouth of the cave. The explosions killed 374 people. Most people were incinerated by the explosion, some were buried alive by falling dirt and rocks, while others, trapped inside, died slowly of starvation. When the cave was finally opened, corpses were found holding one another, children clinging to adults.

The cave has become an important Buddhist shrine for local residents and a tourist stop for foreign visitors. Near the parking lot and the museum at the base of the mountain is a memorial with a statue of man carrying a dead child. Partway up the paved path and stairs to the cave is a white shrine. Local visitors and tourists often light incense and candles and leave flowers here in remembrance of the individuals who died in the cave after the fatal American air strike. In honor of those killed, 24 November is a "day of remembrance" in the Lao PDR.

Lae works to keep the history of the war alive. To this day, he is very angry with the Americans. "Why would they kill all these innocent people?" he asked. He wants the world to know what happened at Tham Piu. Lae is bitter that some people try to refute the story of the Tham Piu massacre, saying the cave was used as a base for North Vietnamese and Pathet Lao troops. He insists this is not true. "Go look for yourself," he kept repeating.

Manophet — Building a Future for the Young

In August 2008, Manophet took Legacies of War members on a tour of the UXO Lao offices in Phonesavan, to a UXO clearance site and to the local foundry in Xieng Khouang Province. During our time together, he told us the story of his life; a life defined by war and its consequences.

Manophet was a year old in 1971 when a US bombing raid destroyed his family's village on the Plain of Jars. That night, his parents grabbed their seven children from the burning house, but in the chaos and confusion they became separated. Manophet, his mother and two siblings eventually reached a limestone cave in the mountains. They lived in the cave with three other families for the remainder of the war as bombs fell around them. It was a constant struggle to find food, and several people in the small group died from starvation and illness. Somehow the rest survived, malnourished and weak.

When the war was over, Manophet's family was reunited. His father and three siblings had spent the intervening years in a refugee camp near Vientiane. The night of the 1971 bombing, Manophet's 12-year-old brother had been wounded by shrapnel. His father and uncle left him in a cave as

Plate 4.11 Manophet 2008 (Photo courtesy of Boon Vong).

they went to find help, but he was gone when they returned. They assumed he had died.

After the war, when Manophet was 12 years old, he and several friends found a small metal ball and began kicking it around. He walked away for a minute then heard the explosion. Five of his friends died from the shrapnel of a cluster bomblet, or bombie as the Lao call them. As a young man, he and his brother were injured by shrapnel when another bombie exploded near them. Over his lifetime, he knew hundreds of people who were killed or injured by bombies and other UXO.

During the 1990s, Laos opened up to Western countries and allowed more visitors. A Hmong family from the US visited Xieng Khouang in 1994 and brought a picture to Manophet's parents of their missing child, now an adult. Another Hmong family had found him the night of the bombing and had taken him with them as they walked across the mountains to safety. Eventually, they crossed the Mekong River to a refugee camp in Thailand. Although Manophet's family was ethnic Lao, the Hmong family adopted the brother Moua and took him with them when they resettled in the US. Moua finished school and is a medical interpreter in Minneapolis, Minnesota.

Plate 4.12 Bounmy and Thoummy 2008.

Moua wrote to his family and in 1997 received permission to visit them for ten days in Vientiane. It was an emotional reunion. To show his gratitude to the Hmong family who raised his brother, Manophet adopted three orphaned Hmong boys and raised them along with his own son.

Manophet taught himself English and worked as a tourist guide then a translator for UXO Lao. He also taught children about the dangers of bombies and other UXO through a program that is part of the school curriculum. At night, he ran a private English school for young people of all ethnic backgrounds from villages in Xieng Khouang Province. He wanted the next generation to have more opportunities in their lives, a brighter future. Manophet was diagnosed with heart problems in 2008 and died of an aneurism in May 2010 at the age of 41. The provincial hospital in Xieng Khouang was unable to treat his condition. By the time he was flown by helicopter to the hospital in Vientiane, it was too late.

Thoummy and Bounmy — Cluster Bomb Ban Advocates

I first met Thoummy and Bounmy in August 2008 at a meeting of Legacies of War and the not-for-profit World Education in Phonesavan, Xieng

Khouang Province. Both young men, born long after the war in Laos had ended, were injured in UXO accidents. At the time of the interview, they were volunteers with World Education, helping victims of UXO accidents to adapt to their injuries. Both were shy and uncertain as they told us their stories.

When Thoummy was eight years old, he hit a cluster bomblet while digging up bamboo shoots with a spade. The explosion left him unconscious. He was taken first to a district clinic then to the regional hospital due to the severity of his injuries. He woke the following day to find he had lost his left hand. It took him several months to recover physically, but much longer to accept the change to his life.

The same year, Bounmy hit a cluster bomblet while digging a fishing pond for his family. He was 16 years old. He was rushed to the nearest medical facility. They were able to save his life, but he lost the lower half of his left arm.

I had a chance to see Thoummy and Bounmy again in November 2010 in Vientiane at the First Meeting of the State Parties to the Convention on Cluster Munitions (CCM — discussed below). They had both finished school and were working as project assistants for the UXO Survivor Assistance Program at World Education. They were also active in Ban Advocates, a group of UXO survivors who advocate on behalf of the treaty to ban cluster munitions. Thoummy gave a moving speech at the opening ceremonies of the CCM meeting, describing the difficulties of those who have been disabled by UXO and advocating that all countries ban these terrible weapons. I learned Thoummy had recently married. Thoummy and Bounmy have blossomed into confident young men, demonstrating that UXO injuries and disabilities need not hold anyone back from a full and productive life.

Moving Forward and Finding Hope

Progress in the UXO Sector

Almost four decades after the end of war, UXO remains a critical issue in Laos. The sheer magnitude of the problem, with UXO contaminating one-third of the land, makes it infeasible to eradicate all UXO from the country. It is not cost effective to clear remote, mountainous regions with little or no population. However, it is possible to eradicate UXO from the most populated regions, including areas in and around villages, agricultural lands and land designated for public and private development projects. This goal is achievable with adequate funding. Yet, only modest progress has been made to date due in part to a slow start in dealing with the problem and the lack of sustained funding to carry out the work.

UXO Clearance

For the first 20 years after the war, Lao villagers had to cope with the overwhelming presence of UXO without any government help or outside humanitarian demining assistance. Before villagers understood the deadly nature of UXO, they often picked up cluster bomblets and other ordnance with their hands and placed them into bomb craters or along fence rows. They tilled their fields, dug irrigation canals and planted gardens on land that had become lethal. It was only after many people died or were injured that villagers learned to be more cautious. And yet, there was little choice but to remove the UXO and plant their fields.

The war left terrible devastation and an economy in shambles, which meant funding for UXO clearance was not available. The Lao PDR began returning to a market-based economy in the late 1980s and accepting assistance from industrialized countries (Laos received a large amount of financial and material aid from the Soviet Union and Vietnam from 1975 up until 1990 when the Communist government in the Soviet Union ended and Russian aid to Laos ceased).

In 1994, the Mennonite Central Committee and MAG sponsored a pilot UXO clearance project in Xieng Khouang Province. When MAG staff arrived in the province, they were shocked to find that villagers accepted the hundreds of UXO deaths and injuries that occurred each year as unavoidable. They thought it was just something they had to live with.[17]

The Lao government asked the UNDP to create a UXO Trust Fund in 1995 to manage contributions from donor countries for clearance activities, and established UXO Lao, a national demining program in 1996. The NRA was created in 2004 and began coordinating the UXO sector in 2006, while UXO Lao continued demining work in the field. The NRA managed some foreign donations while other countries, such as the US, funded UXO sector not-for-profit organizations directly. As of 2011, there were five international not-for-profits assisting UXO Lao in humanitarian demining and eight commercial companies clearing UXO for development projects in addition to the government's UXO Lao teams (NRA 2011). In recent years, the Lao Army has done some demining work under contract to foreign entities who are investing in commercial agricultural projects.

However, this work has not been carried out under NRA standards, and most of the acreage cleared has not been reported.

UXO Lao works in the ten most contaminated provinces. Area Clearance Teams clear large tracts of land for release back into agricultural use by local farmers, while Roving Clearance Teams respond to reports of UXO found by local villagers, traveling to these sites to defuse and remove or destroy the ordnance in place.

From 1996 to September 2012, close to 32,000 hectares of land were cleared of UXO. However, this represents less than one percent of all land thought to be contaminated (one-third of the country or 7.9 million hectares) and only 16 percent of the possible 200,000 hectares of high-priority agricultural lands identified by the NRA in the *The Safe Path Forward* reports (discussed below). Over 1.3 million pieces of UXO were destroyed during the same period, including 571,929 cluster bomblets out of an estimated 80 million total and an unknown number of other types of UXO, which are contaminating the land (Government of Laos 2012b). Clearance activities have become more efficient in recent years with better equipment and additional staff training and experience. Charlie Stonecipher of the US State Department Office of Weapons Removal and Abatement (WRA) called the UXO clearance sector operations in Laos the gold standard in the field.[18]

Funding the UXO Sector

Funding for the humanitarian UXO sector (as opposed to land cleared for private commercial ventures) in Laos comes almost entirely through donations from foreign countries and international organizations. The Lao PDR government contributes less than one percent of expenditures to the UXO sector, primarily by providing administrative overhead and making small contributions to victim assistance.[19] Over the period 1996–2009, 21 countries and the UNDP contributed a total of $119 million for UXO clearance, risk education and victim assistance. Table 4.2 summarizes UXO sector expenditures for 2006–09. Expenditures for clearance operations by not-for-profit organizations were $46.5 million, while for-profit organization expenditures were $23.2 million.

Contributions to the humanitarian UXO sector averaged $12 million annually from 2006–09. But in recent years, donations have increased significantly in order to help Laos meet the treaty obligations of the CCM. In 2010, individual foreign countries and the European Union provided close to $15.6 million in donations and approximately $15.9 million was donated

Table 4.2 UXO Sector Expenditures.

Summary	Expenditure (US$)				
	2006	*2007*	*2008*	*2009*	*total*
Clearance Operations	15,787,828	16,669,358	19,558,129	17,674,133	69,689,448
UXO/Mine Risk Education	175,159	–	–	94,280	269,439
Victim Assistance	2,336,843	874,300	1,078,702	841,382	5,131,227
NRA	578,762	830,827	1,199,205	1,076,951	3,685,745
Overall Total UXO Sector Expenditure	18,878,592	18,374,485	21,836,036	19,686,746	78,775,859
Average per annum (four years)					19,693,965
Percent Distribution					
Clearance Operations	83.63	90.72	89.57	89.78	88.47
UXO/Mine Risk Education	0.93	–	–	0.48	0.34
Victim Assistance	12.38	4.76	4.94	4.27	6.51
NRA	3.07	4.52	5.49	5.47	4.68
Overall Total UXO Sector Expenditure	100.00	100.00	100.00	100.00	100.00

Source: Table prepared by Michael Boddington primarily from NRA Annual Reports and 2009 information from MAG).

in 2011. Donations in 2012 shot up to almost $34 million with significant contributions from Japan (see Annex 1).[20]

US funding for the UXO sector in Laos began in 1995 with money from the USAID Leahy War Victims Fund and $80,000 from the WRA. From 1996–2012, the WRA contributed close to $47 million for humanitarian demining, risk education and victim assistance, and the Leahy War Victims Fund contributed about $10 million for victim assistance and general healthcare programs,[21] an average of $3.2 million annually. In contrast, from 1964–73, the US spent on average $2.7 million per day bombing Laos — or $985.5 million a year for a total of $10 billion over nine years (1964–73 dollars).[22]

The US Congress held the first ever hearing on the impact of UXO in Laos in April 2010, helping to educate members of Congress on the issue. And in recent years, Congress increased funding for the UXO sector in Laos substantially to $5.1 million in 2010, $5 million in 2011, and $9 million in 2012.[23] Legacies of War has recommended that Congress consider funding the UXO sector at a minimum of $10 million a year for the next ten years. This would allow humanitarian demining groups to adequately plan their work and operate effectively, that is, retain trained staff and purchase equipment. If funding levels vary substantially year to year, it is very difficult. A consistent, reliable funding stream is essential to successfully clearing priority lands and meeting the treaty obligations of the CCM.

In July 2012, US Secretary of State Hillary Rodham Clinton made a brief but historic visit to the Lao PDR, becoming the first US Secretary of State to visit the country in 57 years. While in the country, she had the opportunity to visit COPE and meet a 19-year-old man who recently lost his forearms and sight in a cluster bomblet accident. The State Department is considering a regional approach for funding the clearance of UXO in Laos, Cambodia and Vietnam and may recommend that Congress provide sustained, long-term funding.

Victim Assistance

In 2010, there were four Lao and 13 international not-for-profit organizations as well as six Lao PDR government programs and four United Nations agencies providing victim assistance in the UXO sector (Government of Laos 2010). However, the needs are vast and resources extremely limited as most providers serve a small population in only one or two districts. Victim assistance work includes data collection, medical care, physical rehabilitation, psychosocial rehabilitation, economic rehabilitation/vocational training and advocacy services.

COPE is a local not-for-profit organization in Laos that provides orthotic/prosthetic devices and rehabilitation services, including physiotherapy and occupational therapy. Located in Vientiane, they work in partnership with the Lao National Rehabilitation Centre (NRC) and provincial rehabilitation centers. About 50 percent of the people COPE fits with prosthetics are victims of UXO accidents.[24] COPE has developed innovative designs for wheelchairs and prosthetics to meet the needs of farmers and villagers living in rural areas of Laos.

Over the four year period 2006–09, victim assistance expenditures in Laos totaled just over $5.1 million. The NRA estimates that $27.4 million is needed over the next five years to provide basic services and meet obligations under the CCM. The largest needs are for village-level trauma response followed by economic rehabilitation (NRA 2010b).

Focusing Attention on the Problem

The Safe Path Forward 2003–2013 and The Safe Path Forward II

The Lao PDR government adopted *The Safe Path Forward 2003–2013* in 2003 and began implementation in 2006. This document outlined a ten-year national strategic plan for clearing UXO from high-priority lands, primarily agricultural lands and other public areas, such as villages, schools, and infrastructure facilities. Clear definitions of what constitutes contaminated lands (for instance, the concentration of UXO, proximity to population, and other factors) still need to be developed, and the government needs to conduct a comprehensive technical survey to identify and prioritize contaminated lands appropriate for clearance. While there are plans to carry out these tasks in cooperation with local districts, work has not yet begun.

On 22 June 2012, the Lao PRD government adopted the *National Strategic Plan for the UXO Sector in the Lao People's Democratic Republic 2011–2020, "The Safe Path Forward II"* (NRA 2012). This document presents a more comprehensive look at the UXO sector and what is needed to comply with the provisions of the CCM. The document sets out goals, strategic objectives and major actions to update the clearance strategy and needs for risk education and victim assistance.

The *Safe Path Forward II* sites a 2008 sector evaluation as providing useful insights into the amount of land that may require UXO clearance. This study was conducted in the 47 poorest districts of the Lao PDR and found at least 500,000 hectares of contaminated land. Of this amount, 200,000 hectares may be appropriate for clearance and release back into agricultural use (NRA 2012: 2). This study also identified approximately 20 percent of upland rice fields for possible clearance, while the remaining 80 percent might be released through technical surveys. Clearing these lands would take at least 16 years at 2008 funding levels, or with increased funding this could be accomplished in ten years. However, these are not official targets and represent only one evaluation based on existing data, pending a detailed field survey.

The solution of the UXO problem is an integral part of the implementation of the Millennium Development Goals (MDG). In 2010, the Lao government worked with the UNDP to adopt a ninth MDG initiative consistent with the strategy in *The Safe Path Forward II* and commitments under the CCM. Resolving the UXO problem is seen as essential to bringing the country out of poverty and ending its status as a Least Developed Country by 2020.[25]

The Convention on Cluster Munitions

The CCM[26] is an international treaty to ban the manufacture, use, sale, trade and stockpiling of cluster munitions. Other provisions in the agreement commit the State Parties to destroy existing stockpiles, clear cluster munitions from affected countries and provide victim assistance. The treaty entered into force on 1 August 2010, and the First Meeting of the State Parties to the CCM took place in Vientiane, Laos from 9–12 November 2010. Delegates to this convention adopted the 2010 Vientiane Declaration and the Vientiane Action Plan, detailing provisions for implementing the treaty.[27] Two additional meeting of the State Parties were held in Beirut, Lebanon on 12–16 September 2011, and Oslo, Norway on 11–14 September 2012.

By 10 October 2012, the CCM had been signed by 111 countries, including most European countries, Canada, Australia, New Zealand, Japan and countries in Africa, the Middle East and Central and South America. Of the Signatory States to the CCM, 77 countries had ratified the treaty to become State Parties. A number of countries have already destroyed their stockpiles of cluster munitions at considerable cost. However, other countries who manufacture and/or use cluster munitions have remained outside the process, including the United States, Russia, China, India, Syria and Israel.

As the country with the greatest contamination of cluster bombs in the world and over half of all cluster bomb deaths and injuries worldwide, the Lao PDR took a lead in the treaty process and was one of the first nations to sign and ratify the CCM. The Lao government saw the treaty as an opportunity to focus world attention on the UXO problem in Laos and to attract additional funding for humanitarian demining, risk education and victim assistance. The Lao PDR goals for meeting treaty requirements, which reflect the difficulty of totally eradicating UXO from the country, are defined in the *Safe Path Forward II* and the ninth MDG. The NRA developed a concept paper for implementing the treaty requirements (NRA 2011b).

The key to meeting treaty obligation lies in obtaining adequate funding on a sustained basis, given that the humanitarian UXO sector in Laos is almost entirely dependent on donations from foreign countries and organizations.

Conclusion

The aftermath of the second Indochina War, with nine years of massive US bombing, has haunted Laos for nearly four decades. Since the first US bombs fell in 1964 to the present day, over 50,000 civilians in Laos have fallen victim to accidents from unexploded munitions. In addition to the human toll, remnants of war evoke painful memories for many survivors and exacerbate daunting economic challenges. Living amid the threat of UXO has been a grim reality in the daily lives of far too many people for far too long. Despite risk education programs in schools and villages, men, women and children in up to one-third of the country cannot escape the constant danger. Ironically, at the same time, the UXO sector has become a part of rural economies, providing jobs and income. The people of Laos have learned to cope, transform and innovate while living in a violent environment.

UXO can be considered as a *lieu de mémoire* according to Pierre Nora (1989). Due to its aggressive materiality, it is a constant and at times relentless reminder of the violent past haunting the present livelihoods of the people of contemporary Laos. Moreover, UXO carries a symbolic meaning as being emblematic for civilian victims in (post)war contexts. As an impetus for peace-time political interaction and even as an economic resource, UXO also implies a functional dimension. Yet, there is a consensus that these decentralized and dangerous sites of memory, which constantly evoke past violence, have to be eliminated as soon as possible.

Now there is renewed hope for major progress in eradicating the problem by focusing on reducing casualties and clearing agricultural lands in rural districts where the poorest people struggle to grow enough food and support their families. The significant reduction in UXO casualties since 2008 indicates that UXO clearance and risk education programs are making progress in preventing accidents and saving lives. However, it is not clear if other factors may be at work as well, such as fewer people searching for scrap metal after metal prices declined in the recent economic downturn. But the reduction in casualties is encouraging as the UXO sector looks for increased support for its work.

The Lao PDR, parties to the CCM and other international donors, especially the US, must continue funding work to remediate this terrible legacy and allow the people of Laos to live safely on the land once more.

Annex I International donor activities, 2012

Who	When	How much	1 Year equiv in USD	For what	Source(s)
European Union	1 Oct. 2012	€1.3mil between Oct. '12 and Aug. '15	$568,360	UNDP, UXO Lao, and NRA projects. The funds will be used to support the National Regulatory Authority's policymaking, UXO sector coordination and regulatory work, as well as the UXO Lao operation in Attapeu province, which includes clearance, roving tasks, surveys, land release, risk education and training.	*Vientiane Times* (http://www. vientianetimes.org.la/FreeContent/ FreeConten_EU.htm)
Japan	Aug. 2012	$2.2mil over three years	$733,333	Japan Mine Action Service, for clearance in Pakxong district in Champasak province and Laongam district in Saravan province.	http://laovoices.com/japanese-expands-uxo-clearance-in-the-south/ http://www.nra.gov.la/resources/ Newsfeed%20-%20newsfeed%20page/ JMAS%20MOU.pdf
Japan	July 2012	$1.3mil	$1.3mil	Two new unexploded ordnance (UXO) clearance projects in Champasak and Attapeu provinces.	http://laovoices.com/japan-boosts-uxo-clearance-efforts-in-laos/ http://www.la.emb-japan.go.jp/ japans_oda_to_laos/the_grant_ assistance_scheme_for_japanese_ ngos/2012/shomei240720.html

Annex I continued

Who	When	How much	1 Year equiv in USD	For what	Source(s)
New Zealand	June 2012	$1.89mil	$1.89mil	UXO Trust Fund, for UXO Lao.	http://www.undplao.org/newsroom/NZ_UXOLao_signing%20ceremony_12June_2012.php
European Union	June 2012	€4mil	$5,246,400	National Strategic Plan for Unexploded Ordnance (UXO).	http://laovoices.com/eu-funds-uxo-climate-change-projects/
Japan	May 2012	$11.2mil	$11.2mil	For Japanese-made vehicles, computers, and equipment.	http://laovoices.com/japan-backs-uxo-clearance-human-resource-development/
Norway	May 2012	$15mil over 5 years (2012–16)	$3mil	Clearance run by Norwegian People's Aid (NPA) Laos is set to begin in Saravan, Xekong and Attapeu provinces.	http://laovoices.com/norwegian-uxo-survey-gets-underway-in-southern-laos/
Australia	April 2012	A$1mil	$1,036,800	UXO Trust Fund, for UXO Lao (in addition to A$5 mil since 2009, and A$24 mil since 1996).	http://www.undplao.org/newsroom/2012/Press_Release_AusAID_UNDP_Signing_FINAL.pdf
United States	June 2012	$9mil	$9mil	Clearance, victim assistance, and mine risk education.	http://laovoices.com/us-donates-additional-us9-million-for-uxo-clearance/
Total:			$33,974,893		

Notes

1. I would like to thank Mike Boddington, an expert in Disability and Rehabilitation at the National Science Council within the Prime Minister's Office, Laos PDR, for reviewing this chapter and providing information on the unexploded ordnance (UXO) sector. I'm also grateful to Channapha Khamvongsa, Executive Director of Legacies of War, for her review and access to the organization's materials and photographs. I appreciate the help of Vivi Saensathit for translating Lao passages and sharing her recollections of war sites visited in Laos. Thank you to Boon Vong for his personal notes and photographs. I am indebted to Fred Branfman and Walter Haney for their important work collecting the stories of bombing victims during the war and bringing the truth to light. I am grateful to UXO Lao for taking me to clearance sites to see fieldwork in progress. My thanks also go to the staff members of the not-for-profit agencies working in the UXO sector in Laos for their important insights on the affects of UXO on the Lao people. Finally, I deeply appreciate the many individuals in Laos who shared their personal memories of the war, loss of loved ones and experiences as survivors of UXO accidents. *Kop Chai.*

2. Verified data on the total number of civilian casualties during the Lao civil war are not available. Substantial casualties and displacement were described by survivors who fled to the refugee camps near Vientiane during the war and later to the camps in Thailand after the war. It is estimated that 20 percent of the Hmong population died during the war and close to 300,000 people, or 10 percent of the total population, fled Laos by 1980 after the Communist takeover in 1975. See Evans 2002: 150, 178. Also, the 2009 National Regulatory Authority (NRA)'s *National Survey of UXO Victims and Accidents Phase 1* reported that from 1964–2008 over 50,000 civilians were killed or injured by unexploded ordnance (UXO) alone.

3. For example, Don Riseborough, "Laos Agony on the Plain of Jars," *The Sydney Morning Herald*, 15 Feb. 1970; Jack Anderson, "Gentle People in War," *Herald Journal*, 11 Apr. 1971; Seymour Hersh, "How We Ran the Secret War in Laos," *New York Times*, 29 Oct. 1972; see also Fred Branfman's Blog *Laos Automated War Archive* on early articles, at http://fredbranfman. wordpress.com/laos-automated-war-archive/

4. See Khamvongsa and Russell 2009; Pholsena 2010; as well as documentaries: Silberman 2002; Eberle 2007; Kuras 2008; and Mordaunt 2008.

5. While comprehensive technical surveys of UXO contamination are not available, the official estimations on UXO contamination are based on US military strike data and a Handicap International Belgium 1996–97 partial survey (see Handicap International 1997, 2007).

6. Thai paramilitary forces, organized and trained by the CIA in Thailand, joined the effort to train the insurgent troops (Conboy 1995).

7.   See Walt Haney's (1971, 1972) papers on the Legacies of War website, at http://www.legaciesofwar.org/resources/walt-haney-papers/

8.   Campaign to Ban Landmines/Cluster Munition Coalition, *Landmine Monitor Report 2009*, at http://www.the-monitor.org/lm/2009/countries/pdf/lao_pdr.pdf, p. 3.

9.   The word "'bombie," used in the Lao PDR to describe cluster bomblets, has been in use since the time of the second Indochina War. While it is not documented exactly where it originated, it most likely comes from the French word "*bombe*" in combination with the Vietnamese word for ball bearing "*bi*." Cluster bomblets have soft metal shells in which hard steel ball bearings are embedded. At the time of the Vietnamese conflict 1964–73, French was the dominant foreign language in the region, and cluster bomblets were in use over Vietnam. Personal correspondence with Mike Boddington, an expert in Disability and Rehabilitation at the National Science Council within the Prime Minister's Office, Lao PDR and formerly a consultant to the NRA Victim Assistance Office, 17 Apr. 2011, Vientiane, Laos.

10. Personal communication with Barbara Lewis of World Education in Laos, 14 Dec. 2008.

11. Comments from staff members of the Lao Disabled People's Association, World Education and Handicap International in meetings with Legacies of War members in Vientiane, Aug. 2008.

12. Legacies of War (www.legaciesofwar.org) is a US-based nongovernmental organization focused on raising awareness about the history and aftermath of the US bombings in Laos and advocating for increased US funding and support to the UXO sector in Laos.

13. Personal correspondence with Mike Boddington, 11 Jan. 2011.

14. Ibid.

15. The accident that killed the 10-year-old boy (discussed above) also left a piece of shrapnel lodged in the thigh of a 12-year-old boy who was nearby. The boy was also taken to the medical clinic in Sepon, but his parents did not have enough money to pay the doctors to operate to remove the shrapnel. They returned home with only a bandage on his leg. When Legacies visited the village two weeks later, the wound had become infected. Legacies members took the boy to the Savannakhet hospital to remove the shrapnel, but without that intervention, he could have become very ill.

16. Personal correspondence with Mike Boddington, 11 Jan. 2011.

17. From an interview with Lou McGraff of MAG in Jack Silberman, *Bombies* (Bullfrog Films, 2002).

18. Personal correspondence with Mike Boddington, 19 Apr. 2011.

19. Ibid.

20. NRA (2011a) and Legacies of War, Table of International donor activity, see Annex I.

21. Legacies of War *Master Fact Sheet*, 30 May 2012 (not published). Data from the US State Department Office of Weapons Removal and Abatement's reports *To Walk the Earth in Safety*, and based on conversations with WRA staff Charlie Stonecipher.

22. Calculated by Titus Peachy of Mennonite Central Committee using US bombing data and costs per bombing mission contained in the *US Senate Congressional Record*, 14 May 1975.

23. Legacies of War *Master Fact Sheet*.

24. Personal communication with Joe Pereira of COPE (18 Sept. 2008).

25. The ninth MDG includes three targets: 1) Ensure the complete clearance of UXO from priority/high value agricultural land by 2020; 2) Reduce substantially the number of casualties as a result of UXO incidents; and 3) Ensure the medical and rehabilitation needs of all UXO survivors are met in line with treaty obligations under the Convention on Cluster Munitions (see http://www.la.undp.org/content/lao_pdr/en/home/mdgoverview.html).

26. For more information, see Convention on Cluster Munitions, at http://www.clusterconvention.org/; and the Cluster Munition Coalition, at http://www.stopclustermunitions.org/

27. "Vientiane Meeting Yields Concrete Action Plan for Cluster Bomb Disposal," *Vientiane Times*, 15 Nov. 2010.

CHAPTER 5

War Debris in Postwar Society: Managing Risk and Uncertainty in the DMZ

Christina Schwenkel

On 1 August 2009, the frontpage headlines of the popular *Tiền Phong* [*Vanguard*] newspaper captured the attention of its readers with a rhetorical question and mocking observation: "Only after another three hundred years will Vietnam be clean of bombs and mines?" The accompanying color photograph showed a young Vietnamese soldier protected only by his green camouflage uniform and army-issued hard hat, carefully removing unexploded ordnance (UXO) from a contaminated site. Between 2004 and 2008 alone, the article reported, a joint Vietnamese-US clearance project had disposed of more than 24,000 explosives from 1,300 hectares of land (Kiều Oanh 2009).[1] Given the extensive use of bombs, mines and other explosives by the United States during the war, at this speed, the article determined, it would take 300 years to clear the remaining contaminated 6.6 million hectares (ibid. 2009). On the same day, the English-language daily, *Việt Nam News*, published the results of a US-funded study on the number of people killed (437) and wounded (489) by UXO in Vietnam over the past five years. Hazardous war debris, the article pointed out, remains a great risk to the population and a "serious obstacle to development" in rural areas,[2] particularly in the province of Quảng Trị, which is reported to have the highest density of explosive remnants of war (ERW) in the entire country.[3]

One week later, the newspaper released a glowing report about the rapid economic development of Quảng Trị, celebrating its "East-West

Economic Corridor" as the center of the region's commercial and international trading activities.[4] Accompanying the text, an image of large transport trucks importing goods across the Laos-Vietnam border gate at Lao Bảo suggested economic mobility and transnational interconnectivity. New economic zones, nonstate enterprises, locally-owned businesses, and an emerging service sector appeared to have transformed this war-ravaged landscape into a flourishing zone of industrial and agricultural production, commerce and trade.[5] Moreover, the commodification of former US military bases and war sites along the infamous Highway 9, packaged and sold to international visitors as the "DMZ tour," has likewise reconfigured the economic and memorial landscape of Quảng Trị (Schwenkel 2009). Yet for all the new opportunities and signs of a long-awaited recovery, citizens continue to face substantial hardships and challenges stemming from the war with the United States. In the summer of 2009, an exhibit on Highway 9 at the Vietnam Museum of Ethnology in Hanoi also reminded its viewers of Quảng Trị's intrinsic duality — the promise of progress beside the specter of disaster.[6] In this chapter, I examine the strategies used to manage the risks and uncertainties associated with the enduring and potentially explosive legacies of war debris in Quảng Trị in both formal and informal UXO clearance activities, focusing on the divergent and at times overlapping ways in which risk is assessed, regulated, confronted, and mitigated.

The concept of "risk" as an analytical tool to understand modernity and contemporary political economy has long occupied scholars in the humanities and social sciences. As Anthony Giddens argued in *Modernity and Self-Identity*, "Modernity is a risk culture ... [T]he concept of risk becomes fundamental to the way both lay actors and technical specialists organize the social world" (Giddens 1991: 3).[7] In the field of anthropology, Mary Douglas (1990, 1992) took this claim even further, arguing that risk cultures — in the plural[8] — are defined by shared constructs of danger and threat that reinforce moral boundaries and regulate social conduct. Notions of risk, scholars continued to show, have never been stable or historically fixed, but are culturally contingent, fluid, and subject to debate.[9] Moreover, in an age of unprecedented global capitalism, risk and uncertainty cannot be understood as simply negative or potentially destructive forces that require intervention and control. As Caitlin Zaloom has argued in her work on the "productive life" of risk, risk-taking has been actively embraced and cultivated in the marketplace and on the trading floor where "risk reaps reward" and signifies "exemplary acts of productivity" by rationally calculating economic actors (Zaloom 2004: 365). Active engagement with risk, in other words, is fundamental to the growth of a neoliberal economy and its governance strategies that identify risk and risk management as key to regulation, control, and development. Contemporary risk cultures, according to Nikolas Rose, are "characterized by uncertainty, plurality and anxiety, and [are] thus continually open to the construction of new problems and the marketing of new solutions" (Rose 1999: 160).

In this chapter, I approach demining and UXO clearance practices in the former DMZ through the analytical lens of risk perception and risk management. I am interested in the emerging tensions between strategies of risk aversion and confrontation in the formal and informal sectors of ERW disposal; that is, in the field of professional demining and in the scrap metal industry. As Douglas and Wildavsky (1983) pointed out long ago, social and political dissent over what is considered hazardous and how to reduce risk are common in every culture and society. Gaps between expert opinion and public perception of danger have engendered new institutions, alliances, and forms of knowledge to mitigate risk and regulate "risky activity" (Beck 1992: 4; Douglas 1992: 11). Here, I explore how such differences played out on the ground in the region in and around the former DMZ as impoverished residents, many of whom served in the military of the former Republic of Vietnam, attempted to rebuild their lives and communities in the still hazardous landscapes of Quảng Trị. Because of its dangerous potency, war debris remains a powerful signifier of past trauma and present uncertainty. And yet for some it may also offer the possibility of economic productivity, though not without substantial risk. As "imperial debris" (Stoler 2008) that continues to linger on the landscape and inflict new casualties on local communities almost four decades after the US military exited the war, ERW are ambiguous, abject matter out of place that surface unexpectedly and behave unpredictably. As such, they are imbued with the power to make or destroy postwar lives and livelihoods.[10]

The first part of the chapter examines the specific strategies and interventions used in Quảng Trị to reduce the threat of risk associated with remaining explosive remnants of war. During my research, these interventions were fundamentally transnational; that is, they integrated the knowledge, technologies, resources, and expertise of actors and institutions, both in and beyond Vietnam. They were also multi-sector, representing collaborations between private industry, government agencies, and nongovernmental organizations. The case study provided here focuses on a joint US-Vietnamese UXO clearance mission on the edge of the former DMZ. It highlights the transmission of a particular set of risk knowledge and risk-mitigation practices from foreign, professional deminers and clearance technicians to Vietnamese deminers-in-training. Risk management and reduction, however, was not without its consequences, and local populations were subjected to a range of new hazards and uncertainties as land was made safe for cultivation and re-habitation. Moreover, the elimination of risk through UXO clearance inadvertently enabled the state to implement new governance strategies and policies of market-based development.

The second part of the chapter examines the complex and often ambivalent responses to risk by scrap metal collectors who confront danger and negotiate unpredictability in their daily economic activities. Dominant risk knowledge and management strategies associated with hazardous war debris, while potentially effective in reducing the number of casualties and deaths, produced a set of norms and proscriptions that governed behavior and gave shape to a moral community that identified risk avoidance as rational and ethical. Scrap metal collectors, on the other hand, as unofficial deminers in the informal economy, appeared to transgress these institutionalized norms by seeking out and engaging risk. However, as I show below, these economic actors adopted their own forms of risk management that at times overlapped with official discourse and practices. Moreover, their perilous economic activities intersected with another set of risk knowledges — that of the global market, where risk-taking itself, in its many forms, is normative capitalist practice. Using the example of collectors at the former Khe Sanh marine base who sell unearthed war relics to international tourists, the last section highlights the fraught encounter between disparate risk cultures — one that stresses avoidance and another that requires its engagement — and the ethical boundaries that are rigidly drawn between purity and contamination. The chapter concludes with an analysis of the intersections between risk aversion and confrontation, and the new alliances that have started to form among the diverse actors and stakeholders who are actively involved in the removal of hazardous debris from the landscape of the former DMZ.

Managing Risk through Removal of Explosive Remnants of War

In recent years, a new addition can be found on the landscape of Quảng Trị: large colorful billboards that warn children to avoid unearthed UXO and caution farmers not to cultivate land in areas known to be heavily mined and not yet cleared. Designed in an artistic style reminiscent of state agitation posters seen throughout the country, the billboards are the result of a risk education campaign meant to inform local communities about the dangers of encountering and handling war debris.[11] Located directly south of the 17th parallel that temporarily divided Vietnam between 1954 and 1975 owing to the Geneva Accords of 1954, Quảng Trị was the most bombed and mined area in the country.[12] Butting up against the demilitarized zone, the province was heavily occupied by US troops and military bases during the war, and it became the site of many long and protracted battles as US forces and their allies strove to halt the southward movement of troops from the People's Army of Vietnam (PAVN). It is estimated that more than 83 percent of the province remains contaminated with ERW.[13] This situation has presented great risks and hardships for populations in the area — citizens, including children, are regularly maimed or killed by explosives[14] — as well as unexpected opportunities and alliances. The broad implementation of risk reduction strategies has facilitated new partnerships between international organizations, local government institutions, and the National Army in the fields of victim assistance, information management and UXO clearance. And from these collaborations, a new occupation and area of expertise has emerged: that of the internationally-trained and certified, professional Vietnamese deminer.

Demining work in Quảng Trị is by no means a recent activity. Immediately after the end of the war, the Vietnamese military sent a group of technicians to begin the long and arduous process of clearing the landscape of mines and unexploded ordnance. Casualty rates were reportedly high, and formal training minimal, although many Vietnamese who participated in the war had experience with defusing ERW.[15] When international organizations arrived in Quảng Trị in the 1990s, the transfer of knowledge, skills, standards, and practices from foreign experts to young Vietnamese recruits was identified as essential to effective, long-term risk elimination and livelihood improvement. One operation I visited in 2000, managed by former US military personnel working for a private contractor in cooperation with a US NGO, offered Vietnamese recruits six weeks of intensive, comprehensive training designed to meet the "quality assurance" and safety standards of the "international demining community." Training units, run by US instructors, typically comprised 25 male soldiers between the ages of 18 and 20. To advance in the program, it was required that recruits pass all examinations with a minimum of 80 percent, and with only one chance at retesting. Many failed. Those who went on to become internationally-certified deminers would "lead good lives in the Vietnamese military," one US trainer declared. The top-down transfer of expert knowledge, technologies, and best practices was intended to lay the groundwork for future risk self-management and self-efficacy. As one onsite trainer explained: "This is a turnover system; we're giving them high-quality training and state-of-the-art equipment to continue to use after we're gone. And I'll leave knowing they won't have any accidents or problems because I taught them the best way [to demine] that I could."

It goes without saying that professional demining is a high-risk occupation. And while there is a particular prestige in Vietnam attached to national and humanitarian service that rebuilds the country and improves the lives of vulnerable populations, US trainers felt they had to make the risks worthwhile by providing incentives. To do this, they focused on improving the social benefits and cultural capital they saw their young trainees, most of whom came from impoverished backgrounds, as needing and desiring:

> We've given our guys a better lifestyle. We've commandeered better quarters for them — with beds, fans, and televisions. So they have a nice place to live. We take really good care of them — make sure they have good food and water ... Their whole standard of living has come up dramatically and you can see it in the way they walk and carry themselves. They're very proud to be in this unit and they work very hard to be here.

Self-assurance and the development of what the professional miners called "team spirit" were considered critical to the success and morale of the training unit, and would later serve as an effective tool of risk management during disposal operations. At the individual level, this was cultivated through the establishment of joking relationships and the use of English nicknames and phrases with Vietnamese trainees. "Here!" a Vietnamese technician called "Dunk" by his American colleagues said as he handed me a rare, one-*đồng* coin from 1983. "Small change!" he laughed in English.[16] Group activities, on the other hand, were carried out to build trust, loyalty, and camaraderie between the recruits and also between the recruits and their trainers: "We also do fun things like take them to the beach and buy them food and beer. If someone has a birthday, we throw a party. Next week our unit is playing in a football tournament against another demining unit. If our guys lose, they'll be working on Saturday (laughs)." Fostering high morale and a joint sense of purpose through off-base leisure activities thus served as a form of risk and danger management when working "on the grid" (section of land to be cleared).

In order to reduce risk and improve safety, explosive ordnance disposal is, out of necessity, collective and highly interdependent work. During my visit to the "5–14 grid" on a former US marine base, technicians worked in two-man teams for brief, but intense, 30-minute shifts on a 25-square-meter plot, supported by a team of safety and quality assurance (QA) specialists who accompanied the mobile command post. The work was slow and laborious, and required deep concentration. Each move had to be meticulously executed, as one small error could prove fatal for team members. Technicians gently probed the earth with a long, thin detector inserted at a slight angle into the ground, up to 30 centimeters if clearing for agriculture or reforestation.[17] If resistance was encountered at any point while probing, an excavation was immediately carried out. An onsite UXO technician explained to me the procedure:

> To do this you start approximately ten centimeters before your point, excavate down ten centimeters, and then slowly begin to probe until you excavate [the ordnance]. You can imagine probing only three centimeters — about one inch — at a time: probe, find something, excavate; probe, find something, excavate. Imagine how long it takes to do that ... One of the smallest land mines is an M-14, which is larger than one inch. So no matter how it's placed in the ground, if you're probing every inch, there's not a chance to miss it.

Indeed, over a two-week period prior to my arrival, the team had excavated two hand grenades, eight 37-mm anti-aircraft shells, one 82-mm and one 81-mm mortar bomb. After removal and identification, technicians were required to perform a visual examination to assess the perceived risk involved in moving a device to an "s-h-o" (safe holding area). There, it would await weekly relocation to a secure demolition pit where collected explosives were detonated en masse each Friday. If risk was deemed too high, preparations for evacuation of the immediate area would begin and disposal was carried out in the place of discovery.

Though the clearance of ERW greatly reduced the threat of traumatic accidents, it also posed a new set of risks and uncertainties for affected populations. Demining can be highly disruptive to local economic activities and damaging to recovering landscapes. During the war, the extensive use of bombs and chemical defoliants in the region left much of the landscape devastated and deforested (see Susan Hammond's chapter). Over the past several decades, natural regrowth and recultivation have slowly transformed this wounded landscape into productive fields, farmlands, and forests. The removal of UXO hazards, however, often required the selective re-deforestation and clearance of land, and the temporary resettlement of local residents. This secondary destruction was seen as unavoidable and provisional. As one US technician pointed out: "It's a necessary evil to devastate the area we are working in. We cannot search the ground if we have plants on it, so we have to cut them down. Which is worse: cutting a tree or leaving a land mine?" The destruction of crops in impoverished communities was a strong concern expressed by both local citizens and clearance technicians, and demining units attempted to mediate these secondary risks by minimizing the economic and environmental impact of their work. In one example provided by the technician quoted above:

> There was a pineapple plantation about six by six meters. And the guys [deminers] went in to search and dig up the anomalies, the metal signatures. But the owner didn't want them digging up his pineapple fields because the fruit was about so big [indicates size] and close to being harvested. So we decided to cordon off that area, wait until the harvest in another month or two, and then resume our search. That made the owner happy. We're not going anywhere for the next few months so we can wait. This is a poor community and the owner has a valid concern. This is his food crop and he doesn't want it dug up by our guys. So we're able to work with the locals that way and we've received tremendous support from them on account of it.

Likewise, the destruction of reforested land also proceeded carefully and selectively according to a set of risk reduction strategies that aimed to preserve the landscape to the extent that it was possible. UXO clearance teams required at least one meter of space between trees to access their root systems and the surrounding soil. Consequently, in densely forested areas, only the selective cutting of trees was deemed necessary. This also provided the advantage of shaded working conditions for deminers who frequently labored under the scorching sun in high temperatures. Carrying metal detectors, brush clearing equipment and basic excavation tools, such as a hoe and a trowel, clearance technicians combed sites, carefully listening for signals of detection. If positive, they mitigated risk by digging to the side of the object and advancing at an angle to avoid direct pressure and possible detonation. In the aftermath of clearance, recultivation and/or reforestation was typically carried out locally (by farmers themselves), at times with the assistance of US-based "peace trips" that brought volunteers to Quảng Trị, including US veterans of the war and their families, to assist in replanting cleared land. These gestures of reconciliation and renewal signaled the symbolic end to cycles of violence and destruction through the collective rebuilding of landscapes and livelihoods.[18]

The preparation of land for new housing required a more invasive and rigorous clearance strategy. Contrary to the removal of ERW from farmland, in areas of new construction, a "deep search" of up to three meters underground was necessary. This also necessitated the displacement of residents, particularly as urban expansion and infrastructure development — such as new roads, markets, and industry — prompted the growth of communities and the establishment of new settlements. There is no shortage of work for UXO technicians in Quảng Trị; for the province to "progress" economically, for officials to carry out plans to build industrial parks and beach resorts, the scope of clearance activities must likewise keep pace. At times, such operations inadvertently fed into state modes of governance that aspire to "modernize" the population and the built environment. During a trip in 2000 to Đông Hà, the capital town of Quảng Trị, a resettlement project in an outlying district had been prioritized for UXO clearance by local authorities. 25 makeshift homes were slated to be "reorganized" (removed from the landscape) due to their provisional, haphazard construction and placement on the landscape. After clearance (of both the structures and the buried explosives), permanent housing for 100 families would be built in accordance with a model of rational and orderly land use planning. While serving the needs of local communities through the reduction of immediate danger and risk, ERW removal in this example also emerged as a technology of power "imbued with aspirations for the shaping of conduct in the hope of producing certain desired effects" and outcomes (Rose 1999: 52).

Confronting Risk in Scrap Metal Collection

Despite the rigorous monitoring and evaluation of official UXO clearance sites, including a "quality control check" performed by three different quality assurance technicians at the end of each operation, errors do occur. "With the rough terrains and all, explosives can be overlooked," one technician acknowledged during my visit. However, as long as bombs and mines are situated deep in the ground, he maintained, they should not pose an immediate threat — unless dug up and handled. "Even a bombie on top of the land is safe as long as it is left alone. Touch and movement could potentially detonate a device." Risk education campaigns, therefore, explicitly warn local populations, especially children, not to approach, touch, or attempt to move any suspected ordnance, and to report sightings promptly to local authorities. For the most part, these campaigns have been effective in spreading their safety messages. According to a 2008 study conducted by the Technology Centre for Bomb and Mine Disposal (BOMICEN) in cooperation with the Vietnam Veterans of America Foundation (VVAF),

97.8 percent of the communes surveyed in Quảng Trị had distributed educational materials about UXO risk to residents or had organized awareness activities, primarily through schools, community meetings, traveling entertainment troupes, posters, public address systems, and local media (BOMICEN and VVAF 2009: 84). In a Project Renew study conducted with the Departments of Foreign Affairs and Health, 93 percent of respondents reported having been exposed to mine education information, primarily through television (Project Renew 2006: 51). And while accident rates on the whole have progressively decreased over the years,[19] UXO contamination remains a serious hazard, especially for one group whose accident rate has conversely increased: scrap metal collectors.

After the end of US bombardment of Southeast Asia, a vigorous trade in war scrap metal emerged in the informal economies of Vietnam, Laos and Cambodia.[20] With the expansion of a global market economy, this trade became increasingly transborder and transnational. Scrap metal from Vietnam travels to Laos, China and beyond; while metal detectors are often imported from abroad. After economic reform policies were launched in Vietnam in 1986, the industry grew significantly. According to a 2008 study, 40 percent of current scrap metal collectors in the adjoining provinces of Quảng Bình, Quảng Trị and Thừa Thiên-Huế joined the trade between 1988 and 1998, when the price of metal began to increase and new equipment — namely, metal detectors — arrived on the scene. Approximately 50 percent of current collectors began their work after 1998 when the average price paid per kilogram more than doubled (Norwegian People's Aid and Project Renew 2008: 46). The price has since continued to rise, and in 2010, a collector could earn up to US $5 per day (Ngo 2010). As the trade expanded and attracted new and younger collectors, accident rates likewise increased, particularly among ethnic minority communities where in some cases they doubled (Project Renew 2006: 22). Today in Quảng Trị, scrap metal collection has now surpassed farming to become the province's most hazardous occupation. During my last trip to Quảng Trị in July 2010, collectors — young and old alike — were still easy to spot at work in the hills that run adjacent to the repaved and widened East-West Corridor. Such sights differed little from those of my previous visits. As I recorded in my fieldnotes in 2004: "At one point we drove around the bend to find a pair of large tractors parked on a plot of freshly overturned soil next to two young boys with metal detectors and earphones, heads down, eyes intently focused on the ground, slowly making their way across the mounds of red dirt."

It comes as no surprise that scrap metal collectors, and their risk-taking activities, are largely motivated by financial need. As Michael DiGregorio has argued in his work on the recycling industry in Hanoi, "The informal sector [of junk scavenging and selling] has thus become, at once, an innovative, adaptive and efficient economic sector, and a refuge of the poor" (DiGregorio 1995). In Quảng Trị, poor households are often at an additional socioeconomic disadvantage given that many of them were on the "wrong" side of the war. This is articulated most clearly in the film *Living in Fear* (*Sống trong Sợ hãi*, 2005), directed by Bùi Thạc Chuyên, that follows the postwar life of a southern Vietnamese soldier who has little choice but to provide for his family by collecting scrap metal from minefields. Today, the average scrap metal collector in Quảng Trị is male, 34 years old, with a mean monthly income from other work of US$50. They typically invest around US$20 into a metal detector, often imported from China, and collect an average of 16 kilograms of metal per day of work, which they then sell to a local dealer (Norwegian People's Aid and Project Renew 2008: 50–4).[21] Like the scavengers in Hanoi, scrap metal collecting and selling in Quảng Trị "typically draw on a rural labor force, appear as small-scale owner-operated enterprises, [and] are often characterized by hierarchical and dependent economic relationships" (DiGregorio 1995), in this case, between collector and dealer. Moreover, they also "carry a high degree of social opprobrium" (DiGregorio 1995). This is not only because of the legal ambiguity of their work — although scrap metal collection, including from bomb fragments, is not illegal per se, the unearthing, dismantling, and selling of UXO is. Rather, the stigma attached to scrap metal collectors has more to do with the risky nature of their work. Collectors appear to violate many of the shared values and ethical principles of risk that Mary Douglas saw as regulating conduct in the normative "risk culture" of a community.[22] Collectors confront risk rather than avoid it. They turn a hazard into a potential (Zaloom 2004: 366). They profit from risk, and in the process they commodify it. As such, in Douglas' terms, scrap metal collection becomes a form of social pollution that signifies a breakdown of the social and moral order.

Collectors are not the only segment of the population engaged in conduct considered to be high risk. Despite extensive mine risk education, children are still frequently the victims of UXO accidents. Between 2000 and 2005, playing with landmines accounted for 11 percent of all accidents in Quảng Trị, 64 percent of which involved children between nine and 11 years (Project Renew 2006: 28).[23] While these victims had access to risk information, they were not always able to apply it. Unexploded ordnance can be difficult to identify and certain types of explosives may be mistaken for rocks or other natural debris, one NGO representative explained as we drove by the house of a family whose four-year-old son tragically died when his older brother innocently threw a small "stone" at him. Adults may also engage in risky behavior to protect their families and property. For example, they may dispose of UXO themselves by throwing unearthed explosives into adjacent ponds, which serve as a temporary safe holding area until demining units can remove them. The difference here, however, lies with intentionality. The child who mistook a grenade for a rock did not intend to throw an explosive at his brother, while the adult who tossed the explosive into the pond, albeit with great personal danger, intended to eliminate risk from the immediate environment. The scrap metal collector, on the other hand, challenges normative practices of avoidance through intentional engagement with risk, despite awareness of the dangers involved in such acts.[24] As such, when accidents do occur, there tends to be moral ambivalence about their state of victimhood. In the words of a Vietnamese representative of Clear Path International (CPI), a landmine survivor support organization:

> CPI and MAG [Mines Advisory Group] condemn the dangerous economic pursuit of reclaiming wartime ordnance for resale as scrap metal, but some financially marginal Vietnamese families cannot resist the instant cash they can earn from their freelance activities. Although survivors such as Mr Nam [a now-disabled collector] aren't considered 'innocent' victims of unexploded ordnance accidents, their family members are. (Tran 2009)

Among the international demining community in Quảng Trị, scrap metal collectors are commonly referred to as "hobby" deminers,[25] a term that suggests a layperson involved in a *voluntary* activity done for recreation, rather than need. The following dialogue between the author, an NGO administrator, and an international demining technician reveals the particular social world that hobby deminers are thought to occupy and move through, one that is at odds with the moral, cultural, and technological order of their trained recruits.

> NGO: Christina saw three men on the side of the road with their detectors this morning, and one guy was hammering away. Sounds to me like hobby demining.

DT: If it was close to here, it could be our guys setting out the gridlines and hammering in a stake.

CS: This was on the way to Trường Sơn National Cemetery.

DT: No, definitely not our guys. Must have been hobby demining.

CS: What's that?

DT: Those are guys with homemade detectors who don't have the training, and yes they lose people. They typically dig out the ordnance, remove the explosives to sell on the black market, and then sell the scrap metal to a dealer. It's a dangerous job.

Several insights can be gleaned from this brief exchange. First, in contrast to Vietnamese *professional* deminers who receive quality training by certified specialists, use high-tech, state-of-the-art equipment, and adhere to international safety standards and procedures, *hobby* deminers are thought to possess insufficient knowledge and inferior technology, and do not follow any standardized risk management practices. Their high accident and fatality rates, compared with the "zero percent rate" of professionals, further suggest a lack of safety awareness and adherence. Second, scrap metal collectors are not considered good moral citizens like their counterparts. Their illicit, profit-driven, self-serving activities in the underground economy conflict with the self-sacrificing work of deminers in the service of national defense and nation-building. In short, while the internationally-trained deminer works to protect and maintain the risk boundaries of the community, the scrap metal collector seems to defy them, paradoxically increasing the very threat (to self, family, and wider community) that the former strives to eliminate.

Mary Douglas' work on purity and danger (1966) is useful for understanding the social stigma attached to the risky behavior of scrap metal collectors and their trade in UXO. As abject matter out of place, explosive remnants of war are an enduring form of "pollution"; legally ambiguous, disruptive, and dangerous, they are the cause and the consequence of political, economic, moral, and social disorder. The picture of "hobby deminers" as reckless and naïve, and participating in an illegal trade, however, is far from complete. Collectors, too, have their own set of risk management strategies that they use to mitigate threat and maneuver safely in the hills. They are risk takers and makers, who set their own normative boundaries of a risk community (Lash 2000: 61). For example, experienced collectors tend to be well-versed in the different types of UXO and their perceived levels of risk, which in turn influences their collection practices. Cluster munitions are considered the most dangerous devices and tend to be left

alone, according to a study in Quảng Bình, Quảng Trị and Thừa Thiên-
Huế. 85 percent of those surveyed claim they do not touch or pick up
ERW they believe to be hazardous; while close to 10 percent claim they
report unsafe UXO to local authorities.[26] These negotiations with risk suggest that some collectors can be thought of as rational, rather than irrespon-
sible, economic actors whose trade in risk is likewise based on particular
calculations of probability.

Collectors have a different relationship to dominant notions of risk
in Quảng Trị, one that is largely mediated by the vagaries of the market.
As Caitlin Zaloom has argued, "Risk-taking actors and marketplaces are
fundamental to contemporary economies." (Zaloom 2004: 383). In capitalism, the lure of profit encourages and necessitates risk, and the possibility of gain may override the prospect of loss. Thus, despite the risks
involved, scrap metal from the war offers collectors a chance to participate
in, and potentially benefit from, a global economy that has otherwise left
them behind. The new roads, economic zones, and trade centers have
offered their families few financial opportunities to get ahead. As Richard
Moyes (2004) has shown in his work on post-conflict Cambodia, scrap
metal collection is fundamentally a global trade that "links impoverished
rural communities to international markets" and resources.[27] However, as
the following case study of a collector at Khe Sanh marine base shows, it
is precisely this link to and encounter with the global market that makes
scavenging and trading further suspect.

Recycled "Base Waste": Risk and Contamination in the DMZ

Quảng Trị province is well-known in US public history for its protracted
battles during the war and its strategic military bases. Positioned along
Highway 9, just south of the DMZ, many US military installations were
within firing range of northern artillery and subjected to regular attack
from enemy forces. Bases including Camp Caroll, Khe Sanh, and Cồn Tiên
were consequently dubbed "machines for killing Marines" on account of
the heavy casualties suffered.[28] Highway 9 thus remains a deeply meaningful, almost sacred landscape in American memory of the war, and a priority
destination for returning US veterans (Schwenkel 2009). As the number of
tourists traveling to Vietnam rose steadily in the 1990s, local authorities
embarked upon transforming the ruins of the region into a popular "DMZ
tour." Tourism to remote districts served to expand the scope of international trade in scrap metal far beyond neighboring Laos and China. As
the DMZ became a landscape of commodified war memories, collectors

began to sell a new product — "base waste" or objects left behind by US forces — to new consumers: international tourists eager to participate in the war tourism industry.[29]

Nestled among coffee trees in a new economic zone close to the Lao Bảo border crossing, Khe Sanh Combat Base is a highly anticipated stop on the tour.[30] As the site of one of the most decisive and debatable battles in US history of the war, it was also the most well-known in American popular memory. As Stanley Karnow pointed out, the protracted two-month battle and siege of Khe Sanh by enemy forces in 1968 was "daily fare for American television viewers" (Karnow 1983: 552). Over a period of nine weeks, more than 75,000 tons of bombs were dropped on enemy troops, "the deadliest deluge of firepower ever unloaded on a tactical target in the history of warfare" (Karnow 1983: 553).[31] In the 1990s, little remained of the original base, except for traces of the original airstrip, scattered rounds of spent ammunition, and rusted scrap metal from US aircraft. "Don't wander off the path," tour guides warned groups of European and American visitors in the early years of the tour, pointing to the threat of lurking land-mines and the need to comply with a particular code of "risk avoidance" conduct when touring the area.

In fall of 1999, a western tourist in Huế, where the 12-hour DMZ tour began, offered me the following advice: "Do not go to Khe Sanh. It's not worth it. It's just a piece of flat, red land. Nothing is left except for some kids selling fake war relics." This quote is significant for several reasons. First is the idea that former US bases, including Khe Sanh are largely empty of historical signifiers. That is, there are no visible signs of the war left to keep the past alive and tangible in the present. As land-scapes have healed — now fertile with pepper, rubber, and coffee — the certainty of the past is much less clear. Artifacts of war thus serve as mnemonic devices that bridge the gap between then and now. As David Lowenthal has argued, "Memory and history both derive and gain empha-sis from physical remains. Tangible survivals provide a vivid immediacy that helps to assure us there really was a past" (Lowenthal 1985: xxiii). But these survivals, as the tourist in Huế expressed, engender much suspi-cion about origin and authenticity, and the life history they are assumed to possess. Most importantly, the tourist's word of caution reveals the ambi-valent relationship that exists between consumer and vendor, between the international tourist and the scrap metal collector who converts past trauma (the soldier's biography) and present risk (the process of scavenging) into a market commodity.

Each day when tour buses pulled in to Khe Sanh, a small group of vendors hurriedly approached visitors and followed them as they explored the grounds of the former marine base. In the wooden boxes they carried, collectors displayed exhumed "base waste" left behind by US troops, including razors, forks, spoons, coins, bullet casings, medals, pins, lighters, compasses, and dog tags. One young couple I first met in 1998 had been selling base waste to tourists since the mid-1990s.[32] Scrap metal collection and resale at Khe Sanh was their primary means of economic survival and they continued this trade for another decade, even with the decline in supply and demand.[33] Armed with a metal detector and a simple tool to excavate objects, the husband scavenged the hills of Hướng Hóa District around Khe Sanh, sometimes in the company of other collectors. Like professional demining, collective scavenging was an important strategy to reduce the strong probability of risk.

Though the market was tightly controlled — not just anyone could show up at Khe Sanh and peddle souvenirs — there was the potential to earn higher profits by selling scrap-metal-cum-war-relics to tourists, rather than to dealers. This is because the meaning and value attached to the objects differed considerably. Relics from the base were not scrap metal whose value could be calculated according to substance and weight. For example, in 1998 I purchased a PAVN medal from the couple for 10,000 đồng (US$0.70). At that time, a collector would need to scavenge around five kilograms of metal to earn that amount, and yet my purchase did not even weigh 100 grams. Much of what the collectors exhumed and sold at Khe Sanh would be of little worth if traded individually with the dealers; the scales of measure in the recycled metal industry ("mass" and "bulk") necessitated the loss of individual form and meaning. To be profitable, scrap metal needs to be accumulated, not individuated. Consequently, when trading with a dealer, the specific life history of an object is irrelevant, and subsequently, so is the question of its authenticity (Appadurai 1986).

In the tourism industry, however, it is precisely this history that endowed an object with power and value, transforming "scrap" into a fetish, a commodity, a meaningful souvenir. Like trench art,[34] the war relic served to mediate between the living and the dead, transmitting sentiment from the past into the present. If the aura of this history was lacking or somehow unconvincing — the fork was too polished or the razor too sharp — the object was disconnected from its presumed biography and labeled "a fake." The vendors were aware of the importance of this visual economy of authenticity — more value was attached to the rusted and misshapen

Plate 5.1 War scrap metal collector, Khe Sanh, 2004 (Photo courtesy of Christina Schwenkel).

dog tag than the polished fork, for example. They were also acutely aware of the ambivalent feelings that international tourists had for their commodities. The relics were desired and yet despised. Tourists were enchanted by them, but also repulsed. They liked to look, but did not often buy. "*Không bán nhiều!*" [Not much sold!], one vendor lamented in 2004 after a tour bus drove away.

Elsewhere, I have referred to re-commodified objects that US soldiers disposed of or unintentionally left behind as "souvenirs of death," (Schwenkel 2009: 87) borrowing from the work of Susan Stewart (1993). As an abject object infused with affective power and potency,[35] the "souvenir of death" at Khe Sanh was considered by many tourists to be polluted and taboo. Its abjection placed it firmly outside the moral and symbolic order of "proper" collection and consumption practices (Kristeva 1982). For Mary Douglas (1966), pollution occupies a liminal and highly ambiguous social position as both dangerous and powerful, attracting and repelling. However, it was not the suggestion of a violent past and the implied fate of the soldier who once possessed the object that made it impure and abject. Indeed, it was precisely the artifact's connection to trauma and death that lured the viewer to gaze in the first place ("Keep walking," a father urged his young son who paused to look in 2000). As the work of social theorists has long shown, there is no shortage of interest in, or western cultural taboo against, the commodification and consumption of trauma and suffering.[36]

What then made the war relic contaminated? At Khe Sanh, tourists were not merely uneasy with the aura of death that haunted the landscape and imbued the unearthed objects. In their wider travels, many had avidly sought out the violent histories and legacies of war; trauma tourism in Cambodia, Laos and Vietnam remains a key attraction. Rather than death, the source of contamination was linked to unorthodox practices of risk and their entanglements with the market. These were not accidental souvenirs; the collectors actively broke with normative, risk-aversion conduct to excavate and sell the relics, turning risk into commodity and profit. Commodification, of both risk and its found object, tainted the encounter between vendor and consumer. On tours, foreigners expressed their discomfort with paying for the scavenged souvenirs; many considered the trade, and by extension the vendors, to be unscrupulous. The relics were thought of as intimate objects used in daily ritual activities (eating, shaving, etc.); they had unknown but assumed individual biographies. To engage in risk-driven market exchange, and to further encourage the industry, would be to defile this history and contaminate memory. In the highly moral risk economy that the tourists subscribed to, relics were pure and untainted if found fortuitously rather than purchased intentionally, and thus productive of profit. Consequently, there was no condemnation of a self-proclaimed "war buff" when he disregarded the risks to wander off the airstrip, pick up a shattered marine helmet, and excitedly declare, "I'm taking this with me!"

Conclusion: Intersecting Risk Cultures in Quảng Trị

> After more than forty years, only now returning to Tà Cơn. Youth volunteers from Đồng Trạch commune, Bố Trạch district, Quảng Bình province who worked and fought to build the Trường Sơn road [Ho Chi Minh Trail] have now come back to visit. No more enemies, just historical vestiges. Changed scenery, different sights than forty years ago. Proud that the Fatherland swept the nation clean of enemies. Rebuilt landscapes; new economic zones rising from lands once occupied by the US military. A mix of emotions — both joy and sadness: So long heroic martyrs who sacrificed your lives for the nation on this very soil.
>
> — 14 April 2010 entry in Impression Book at Khe Sanh Museum

How does a landscape "heal"? Can wounded landscapes fully recover from the destructive forces of a violent war? New roads, homes, forests, buildings and markets suggest that regeneration and renewal are well underway in Quảng Trị, yet freshly-dug holes in the hills along Highway 9 tell a more complicated story. Like the comments in the Impression Book at Khe Sanh, these new wounds also remind us to think more critically about celebrated narratives of growth, to consider what lies behind or literally beneath the rebuilt landscapes (UXO, base waste, corporeal remains), the changing scenery, and the economic prosperity.

There is no uniform way that people rebuild their lives and landscapes in the aftermath of war. As this chapter has shown, new business and professional opportunities emerged in postwar Quảng Trị as a consequence of lingering, hazardous, imperial debris that has also claimed the lives of thousands of residents. Deminers, scrap metal collectors, international trainers, NGO officers, tour guides, tourists — all have contributed in unique ways to reshaping postwar economic, social and memorial landscapes that continue to pose a threat to the public. As demonstrated above, these groups of actors maneuvered within very different, if not competing, moral economies of risk, at times intersecting and other times colliding. Yet risk not only revealed itself to be a purely destructive force, its productivity should also be noted: new alliances, subjectivities, and sociospatial relations all point to the "productive life of risk" (Zaloom 2004) at work in Quảng Trị.

In recent years, there have been notable efforts to encourage more productive collaborations between the different groups involved in clearing the landscape of war debris — namely, between "professional" and "hobby" deminers. NGO and governmental institutions have begun to reach out to scrap metal collectors to involve them in programs that recognize and make use of their localized knowledge for the betterment of society. Experienced scrap metal collectors, for example, have significant knowledge of munitions and of Quảng Trị's geography and history, perhaps more so than young recruits and international specialists. Recruitment of trainees from the families of UXO victims is another humanitarian gesture meant to integrate stigmatized community members into the formal (and thus "legitimate") economy. Though in their infancy, such programs can play an active role in providing a stable and safer employment for scrap metal collectors, while reducing the negative connotations attached to their trade. At the same time, such programs may also lead to new forms of regulation of the industry that might allow for less rigid moral boundaries around emerging cultures of risk and their risk management strategies.

Notes

1. The field of UXO detection and removal has been remarkably transnational since the founding of the Technology Centre for Bomb and Mine Disposal (BOMICEN) in 1996 under the Ministry of National Defense. International cooperation with humanitarian and governmental organizations, as well as global corporations from Germany, Norway, England, Australia, China and the United States have contributed new technologies, risk assessment strategies, and knowledge practices to national demining efforts, which have also served to strengthen bilateral relations, particularly in the case of the United States where such cooperation has been key to the process of reconciliation.

2. "War Ordnance Kills 437 in Central Việt Nam in Last Five Years," *Việt Nam News*, 1 Aug. 2009, p. 3.

3. See, for example, BOMICEN and VVAF (2009); and Project Renew (2006).

4. "Quảng Trị to Enhance Use of East-West Economic Corridor," *Việt Nam News*, 8 Aug. 2009, p. 2.

5. In the last ten years, for example, the Lao Bảo special economic-commercial zone [Khu Kinh tế Thương mại Đặc biệt Lao Bảo] has attracted 41 projects with a total capital investment of more than 3.1 trillion Vietnamese đồng (US$187 million), contributing approximately 30% of the provincial budget (Dương Vương Lợi 2010). State-established new economic zones focus on the agricultural production of cash crops that include coffee, rubber and cassava. Lao Bảo is also the busiest international border crossing with Laos.

6. Images and objects from the exhibit, "Highway 9: Opportunities and Challenges" (Đường 9: Cơ hội và Thách thức), which ran from June to Oct. 2009, can be viewed online at http://www.vme.org.vn/exhibitions_special_details. asp?ID=61

7. Like Giddens, Ulrich Beck (1992), who coined the term "risk society," also sought to produce a globally applicable theory of risk that could best capture the essence of capitalist modernity in western societies.

8. See also Lash (2000).

9. Caplan (2000); Lash (2000); Boholm (2001).

10. The term "matter out of place" was originally coined by Mary Douglas (1966) in her classic text, *Purity and Danger: An Analysis of the Concepts of Pollution and Taboo*.

11. Interview with Development & Public Affairs Officer, Project RENEW, Đông Hà town, Quảng Trị, July 2009.

12. The administrative borders of Quảng Trị have since shifted. Before 1975, Quảng Trị was the northernmost province of the Republic of Vietnam. After the war, its expanded to incorporate areas of Quảng Bình (the southernmost province in former "North Vietnam") into its administrative jurisdiction.

13. In a survey conducted by BOMICEN and VVAF of six heavily impacted provinces, Quảng Trị had the highest percentage of contaminated bomb and

mine areas (83.8%), followed by Quảng Ngãi at 52.7% (BOMICEN and VVAF 2009: 40).

14. To again cite the BOMICEN and VVAF study, Quảng Trị had the highest number of landmine and UXO victims in the six surveyed provinces, with 361 accidents — 158 of which resulted in death — between 2003 and 2008 (BOMICEN and VVAF 2009: 53). An earlier study conducted by Project Renew with the Departments of Foreign Affairs and Health in Quảng Trị provides more detailed statistics on landmine casualties in relation to gender, age, occupation, education and ethnicity (Project Renew 2006: 16–21).

15. For example, members of the "suicide unit" (*đội tự tử*) were responsible for such work. After their defusal, bombs were typically pried open and the explosives removed to be recycled and used in self-made weapons. Such skill and labor also played a central role in guerrilla combat strategies in southern Vietnam, as the photographer Dương Thanh Phong documented in the book, *The Documentary Album of Cu Chi 1960–1975, Album no. 2* (Khu di tích lịch sử địa đạo Củ Chi 2002).

16. The smallest currency on the market at that time of my visit was a 200-đồng note.

17. This is based on estimates that farmers typically till less than a third of a meter of land during cultivation.

18. For more on these projects as healing practices, see Schwenkel (2009: 38–45).

19. The total numbers of victims per year decreased from 214 in 1990 to 134 in 1995 to 57 in 2001 and 49 in 2005 (Project Renew *et al.* 2006: 61–2).

20. On Vietnam, see Norwegian People's Aid and Project Renew 2008; on Laos, see Geneva International Center for Humanitarian Demining 2005; on Cambodia see Moyes 2004 for Handicap International, Belgium, Mines Advisory Group (MAG) and Norwegian People's Aid.

21. Poorer collectors may make their own homemade detectors.

22. Douglas (1990, 1992)

23. Between 1975 and 2008, 31% of all UXO fatalities in the province were children.

24. According to Norwegian People's Aid and Project Renew, 93.76% of collectors have been exposed to mine risk education (Norwegian People's Aid and Project Renew 2008: 55).

25. For example, see Patt (2000) and Bensinger (2003).

26. Norwegian People's Aid and Project Renew (2008), pp. 59, 99. See also Geneva (2005), pp. 31–2 for similar findings in Laos.

27. Cited in Geneva (2005: 12–3).

28. "Border Recessional: The Return of Con Thien," *Time*, 19 July 1971, at http://www.time.com/time/magazine/article/0,9171,905360-1,00.html [accessed 14 Feb. 2013].

29. On this industry in southern Vietnam, see Schwenkel (2006) and Alneng (2002).

30.	In Vietnamese memory, Khe Sanh is referred to as Sân bay Tà Cơn, or Tà Cơn airport. Thus, while international tourists visit "Khe Sanh," domestic tourists go to "Sân bay Tà Cơn."

31.	Karnow reports a death rate of less than 500 for US troops and more than 10,000 PAVN forces (ibid.). Though active in the battle, the number of ARVN combatants killed in action at Khe Sanh is not provided.

32.	When we first met in 1998, I took their picture at the couple's request; in return, they presented me with a gift: an old French coin found on the premises, a tribute to the layered histories of empire-building along Highway 9, a former colonial road that linked Annam with Laos. The following year, I returned with the photograph, and an article on the vendors published in the *Los Angeles Times* (Lamb 1999). Through the irony of their market activity — the commodification of imperial debris under late socialism — they had achieved international notoriety.

33.	"Base waste" is of course exhaustible. As of 2010, the husband was still selling war relics at Khe Sanh, though he had incorporated into his display mass-produced souvenirs sold across the country, such as Chinese-made Zippo lighters meant to mimic originals from the war. The wife had passed away after a brief illness.

34.	See Saunders (2003).

35.	See also Krisna Uk's chapter in this volume.

36.	See Feldman (2005); Sontag (2003); Boltanski (1999); Kleinman and Klenman (1997).

CHAPTER 6

A Social Reading of a Post-Conflict Landscape: Route 9 in Southern Laos

Vatthana Pholsena

Introduction

The road that is the focus of this article — Route 9[1] — is one of Laos' most important national highways, as well as being a key component of the East-West Economic Corridor, linking the city of Mawlamyine in Southeastern Burma with the port of Đà Nẵng in Central Vietnam (Quảng Trị Province) via Northeast Thailand and Southern-Central Laos (Savannakhet Province).[2] Route 9 runs for 324 kilometers across Quảng Trị and Savannakhet Provinces to the Thai border. Because of its strategic alignment and economic potential, the completion of the up-grading of Route 9 in the first half of the 2000s was duly fêted in Laos' national newspapers. In fact, the restoration was closer to a revival: at the end of the Vietnam War, the road was in ruins, a war-ravaged landscape. Just a few years before turning into a conduit to "modernity" at the dawn of the 21st century, Route 9 was known among military planners and local inhabitants as the "death road" (Vietnam Museum of Ethnology 2009: 41).

As initially laid out, the covert route between North and South Vietnam that came to be called the Ho Chi Minh Trail[3] followed the eastern slope of the Trường Sơn mountain range, crossing Route 9 just south of the demilitarized zone in South Vietnam. However, the route had to be changed early in 1960 after a stack of weapons left behind by North Vietnamese infiltrators on the Trail was discovered and reported to the ARVN (Army of the Republic of [South] Vietnam) (Prados 1998: 15). The 559th

Transportation Group (the North Vietnamese logistics unit in charge of building the Trail and carrying supplies across the DMZ demarcation line) reacted to the consequent intensification of patrolling by shifting the main infiltration route in early 1961 to the *western* side of the Trường Sơn mountain range. This new route ran through the panhandle of southern Laos via the vicinity of Sepon (also spelled Tchepone), in eastern Savannakhet Province on Route 9, an area that soon became a strategic center and logistics base area for the North Vietnamese Army and one of the most important nodes on the relocated Trail. In parallel, from 1964 onward, Washington's first priority was to assist the military effort in the southern Republic of Vietnam. The US Air Force subsequently launched in mid-1964 its first air strikes against fixed targets and infiltration routes (particularly the Ho Chi Minh Trail) throughout Laos, which soon expanded in April 1965 to a day-and-night offensive air campaign in southeastern Laos in an attempt to stop supplies flowing into South Vietnam from the North. As the US bombing of the Trail grew in intensity, it led inevitably to a widening of the war into central and southern Laos.[4]

Today, Route 9 runs through open, flat lands filled with rice-fields and vegetation, rising toward the Trường Sơn mountains as one gets nearer the Vietnamese border. Physical remnants of war, on or around the road, have all but disappeared (except for commemorative sites in Phine and Sepon Districts and in Ban Dong on Route 9, which I will discuss later). Sepon villagers are no longer confronted with a landscape in ruins on Route 9; the road is no longer scattered with wartime remnants — unexploded ordnance (UXO) and bomb casings, cracks and craters. But the absence of damage does not equate to an absence of memory. In Sepon District, where I conducted fieldwork between 2006 and 2012, Route 9 projects ambivalent images. To villagers in this impoverished rural area, the two-lane paved road both constitutes and represents economic development, but is also a place of darker times, of memories of violence and rift. In post-socialist Laos (and other developing countries), road construction is a top priority for state economic planners as part of the effort to lift the rural population out of "backwardness" (both material and cultural) by integrating them with the modern, market-based economy. In general, the rural population in Sepon District has welcomed the arrival of a paved road running through or near their villages; they share with the country's economic and political elites the view that roads symbolize — and can bring about — "progress" and "modernity." Yet, to some local residents, Route 9 has come to embody over several decades different, sometimes contradictory, connotations that more often than not are expressed in statements whose meaning is left implicit. Thus, there exists a salient contrast between today's physical landscape around Route 9 and the villagers' historical memory of the road. Several anthropologists and historians have stressed the importance of symbolic meanings and socio-psychological dimensions of roads in studying social impacts of roads among local communities (Colombijn 2002; Flower 2004; Rosman 1996; Thomas 2002; Nishizaki 2008; Weber 1976). By looking at different meanings attached to Route 9 during the war and its aftermath, I would like to open a window into people's experiences of past conflicts and their postwar memories.

This chapter consists of two parts. The first part describes the origins of the road during the pre-colonial and French colonial periods, then shows the strategic meanings that were attached to Road 9 during the "American war" in Vietnam, Laos and Cambodia (1961–75). In the second part, I discuss the socio-psychological dimensions of the road in the postwar official and, especially, private memories. In a landscape where there are few "vehicles of memory" such as museums, battleground sites, or commemorative monuments, I take an approach that focuses more on the experience of the war and the private (postwar) memories of events among Sepon villagers that lived through the Vietnam War and its aftermath. In other words, I am interested in exploring social — rather than cultural — representations of the war. Much as remembering is an individual act, as Halbwachs showed, each person is a member at various times of one, or several, social groups whose experiences and memories of past events are not identical to other groups (Halbwachs 1992: 53). To put it differently, we should not assume that memory expressions in the private sphere coalesce into a single collective, albeit unofficial, memory. In the second half of the chapter, I take into account the "multiform social experience of the war" (Lagrou 2000: 3) by looking at different social groups that coexist along Route 9 in Sepon District — war veterans, bystanders, former reeducation camp detainees — and interrogate how their divergent experiences of the conflict and its aftermath shape their postwar memories.

The choice of this methodology has also been prompted by the context of postwar Laos where a process of democratic transition has not taken place (unlike in former communist regimes in Eastern and Central Europe) and official representations of the past (and the war) leave little room for alternative voices in the public sphere. Thus, the Cold War-cum-civil war in Laos, pitting the Royal Lao Government against the Pathet Lao (as the Lao communist movement was widely known) and its immediate postwar consequences (purges and reeducation camps) have been silenced in the public memory. I therefore concur with Alon Confino when he argues in his study of memory in postwar West Germany that "since some views about Nazism could not be made public, we should look for their expression in social practices and representations where they were not directly discernible but fairly unexpected. These kinds of sources, practices, and representations may ultimately reveal more about attitudes and beliefs" (Confino 2000: 100). Silences in the public sphere should not be translated too quickly into acts of forgetting — rather, they should also be considered in relation to memory expressions in everyday life and the private sphere.

Route 9: From an Instrument of Empire to a Cold War Front Line

A Road to El Dorado

French colonial planners initially believed that the Mekong River would serve as the natural pathway for France's penetration into the hinterlands of the Indochinese Peninsula.[5] Despite their energetic efforts and dedication, the early attempts and repeated failures by French explorers to overcome the rapids in southern Laos and northeastern Cambodia gradually dissipated any hopes of building a commercial artery linking southern Laos with Annam and Cochinchina (present-day central and southern Vietnam, respectively) via the Mekong River's tributaries.[6] Soon, these explorations were replaced by equally enduring enterprises to "discover" land routes that would physically connect the coastal region of Central Vietnam to the Mekong valley on the other side of the Annamite Chain. The colonial ventures eventually led in 1912 to the construction of a road — a segment of today's Route 9 — from Đông Hà in Quảng Trị Province, running through Savannakhet Province, to the left bank of the Mekong River, though it was not until 1930 that an all-weather road would be completed.

In truth, the path through the *Ai Lao* mountain pass[7] in the Annamite Chain — that is, the "ancestor" of *La Route Coloniale* No. 9 — "discovered" in 1877 by Jules Harmand, one of the pioneering explorers of the French Indochinese space, had long been known to the hill populations and the ethnic Việt.[8] A major study undertaken by Lê Quý Đôn, a high-ranking mandarin under the Trịnh rule, entitled *Phủ biên Tạp lục* and written in 1776, takes the form of a compilation of miscellaneous records on the peripheral lands of Thuận Hóa and Quảng Nam.[9] This document provides invaluable information on the ethnic Việt's penetration and nascent colonization of the hinterlands of Central Vietnam, including the region of Khê Sanh-Ai Lao, at least one century before the arrival of the French.[10] The construction of a military post and the administrative organization of the area denote the establishment of a bureaucratic presence of the Việt Empire in these recently annexed highland provinces, though efforts to implement effective control bore little fruit (Lemire 1894: 14–6). Beyond the military and political aspects, hill peoples and lowland ethnic Việt are shown to be interacting daily on the ground; Lê Quý Đôn thus notes patterns of exchanges involving upland agricultural and forest products (rice, chickens, buffaloes, bamboo shoots, textiles, etc.), on the one hand, and lowland items (salt, dried fish, *nước mắm*, iron and copper objects, silver jewelry, etc.), on the other.[11] The mandarin also mentions trade roads linking the coastal region in Central Vietnam with the Mekong plains, traversing the present-day northeastern province of Thailand, and also extending all the way to Vientiane (Li 2002: 121–2).

In late 19th-century France, a road network that had earlier facilitated the diffusion of state power to a limited extent was enormously expanded, for the first time creating something approaching national unity and a high degree of political and economic integration (Weber 1976: 195–220). This instrumental approach to communications was shared by colonial administrators in Indochina who used roads (and railways) as technologies of empire (Del Testa 2001: 28). The French colonial project to create a unified geographical space on political, economic and commercial levels (chiefly at the expense of trade with Siam) (Goscha 2012), and the disappointments brought about by the Mekong's indomitable nature, explain France's determination to conceive and proceed with the construction of roads between their Lao and Vietnamese colonies. Every male aged between 18 and 45 in these territories was forced to serve as *corvée* labor annually, the work generally involving the construction of colonial infrastructure (mostly roads, bridges, and railways).[12] In Sepon, the few men still alive who participated in the *corvée* to build sections of Route 9 certainly remembered it. "We were forced to work as *coolies* [in French] on a 15-day shift and then the French would select another batch of men from the village. We even had to bring our own food," one old man recalled. Though those colonial roads and paths aimed to serve as conduits for the diffusion of colonial power, commercial opportunities and fruitful investments in the country were to remain part of the myth of a Lao "El Dorado": the country neither met its own administration's expenses nor benefited France. Although the road was for some a site of memories of the colonial past, for most people I spoke with the road more often evoked recollections of the "American

War" and its aftermath.[13] Accordingly, I turned my attention away from
the period of the road's construction and toward its wartime and post-
conflict significance.

A Cold War Front Line

Laos became engulfed in the turmoil of the Cold War in Asia in the early
1960s when its internal politics became internationalized. Elusive aspirations to a neutral position were crushed by the rivalry among Lao political
factions that were heavily sponsored by foreign allies: on the one hand,
the Pathet Lao was backed by the Democratic Republic of Vietnam (DRV)
and the Communist Bloc (headed in Asia by China); on the other hand,
the United States and its allies in Southeast Asia, notably Thailand, threw
their weight behind anti-communist Lao groups. The degree of external
pressure on the civil war in Laos was such that a resolution of the conflict
progressively eluded its political leaders, in spite of their attempts to form
coalition governments (in 1957–58, and again, in 1962–63). In mid-1961,
the North Vietnamese-Pathet Lao forces captured the districts of Sepon,
Phine, and Phalane in the east of Savannakhet Province and gained control
of Route 9 in these areas. The road embodied on the ground the Cold
War-induced Lao civil war: to the west of Muang Phalane on Route 9 lay
the "US-controlled puppet/enemy zone" (*khet sattu*), while the eastern region formed the "liberated zone" (*khet potpoï/khet issala*), as villagers in
Sepon recalled the divided territories. Key locations on Route 9 constituted
the shifting front line. "We conducted our missions in the rear zone (*neo
lang*), spying (*seup lap*) and mobilizing (*ladom*) in the enemy districts of
Atsaphanthong and Atsaphorn [situated to the west of Muang Phalane].
We entered villages at night and explained to their inhabitants the revolutionary system (*labob pativat*) as opposed to what was the Vientiane
regime," a former Pathet Lao agent, who lives in Ban Thakhong (located
about five kilometers east of Sepon town), recollected in words still reflecting wartime mental boundaries.

Members of families often remained separated for the duration of the
war, unable to travel either eastward or westward, living on either side of
what may be called an "internal border." "I left for Savannakhet town in
1959 with my younger sister. Road No. 9 was blocked in 1960 and we
could no longer go back to our village, not until 1977 after the Liberation,"
an elderly woman from Ban Natheuy in Vilabuly district located to the
northwest of Sepon district remembered. Some — such as soldiers and

personnel of the Royal Lao Army and Government, as well as petty traders (most of whom were Vietnamese and Chinese migrants) — never returned, having fled upon the advance of the communist troops. "When Thakhong [where a small French-supported RLA post was set up] fell in 1960, my father [a former Kuomintang soldier] fled to Savannakhet. He left alone without his wife and children. He didn't come back after the war," recounted a woman who still lived in Ban Thakhong. To combatants and civilians alike, the space enveloping Route 9 figured as a fractured landscape, the road having lost its primary function — as a technology of mobility and communication — and turned instead into something approaching the metaphor of an "iron curtain."

To villagers who stayed in "the front zone" (*neo naa*), Route 9 was transformed into a field of violence, a road "to flee and to hide from" (*lee phay*) when US bombing raids picked up in the mid-1960s. As the US interdiction campaign intensified, villagers dwelling in the vicinity of the road were forced to abandon villages, houses, rice fields and cattle, and flee to the nearest mountain slopes or caves where their "refugee lives in the forest" (*sivit ophanyob yu paa*) began and were to last for a decade. These predominantly lowland wet rice farmers switched entirely to upland shifting cultivation — an ancient farming technique characterized by the clearing and burning of a plot in the forest, which is then farmed for a year or two before moving on to another location. This form of agriculture to a great extent saved the villagers' lives by providing a more flexible and mobile technique of rice cultivation (in contrast to sedentary paddy field cultivation), which helped people flee the bombing. Their constant and deepest fear was to be spotted by US planes that regularly flew over the mountain areas. They shed their pre-war clothing and dressed themselves instead with pieces of clothing collected and recycled from sandbags left by the "enemy" in abandoned military campsites, Vietnamese military uniforms (obtained through bartering) and even American parachutes. In a villager's words, they gradually turned into some "un-human figures" (*bor khü khon*). More than 30 years have passed since the end of the conflict, and the old men and women of Sepon may not remember dates and locations exactly; on the other hand, they vividly recall the glaring lights of the planes "that wheeled like a cloud of insects" and an overwhelming sense of dispossession: "we were no longer human beings," declared one elder. "During the "struggle against the French" (*samay tor tan falang*), we hid for a few days in the forest, then could return to the village. We could light a fire. But during the "American War" (*samay songkharm amelica*), we stayed for years in the forest, living in darkness (*yu baep müt*). We'd become like animals (*khü sat*)" (Pholsena 2010: 276). To local residents, the region of Route 9 became an interdicted place, from which they were expelled, literally and figuratively, to the outer confines of civilization over that decade of bombing.

The bombing finally stopped in 1973 following the ceasefire signed between the Neo Lao Hak Xat (the political organization of the Lao communist movement) and the Royal Lao Government in February of that year. The period of transition before complete takeover by the NLHX lasted less than two years. Unlike the revolutions in South Vietnam and Cambodia, the final step in the conquest of power by the Lao communists involved relatively little violence. A coalition government was formed on April 5, 1974. The NLHX gradually built up its influence in urban areas, attracting the support of students and some members of the elite, as well as to some extent that of a population weary of war and unhappy with the rising cost of living (mainly due to the embargo imposed by neighboring Thailand on the import of consumer goods and oil). The Communists also benefitted from the weakening of the right-wing camp, which was deprived of Washington's finances and military aid and undermined by its own internal divisions. Anti-American and anti-capitalist protests intensified in Vientiane, Thakhek, Savannakhet, and Pakse. The entry of the Khmer Rouge and North Vietnamese troops into Phnom Penh and Saigon on 17 and 30 April 1975 respectively, hastened the end of the regime. In May of that year, the NLHX called for an open insurrection throughout the country. On 26 August, troops of the Lao People's Army entered Vientiane and the major provincial cities, including Savannakhet.[14] A revolutionary cadre recalled walking with his companions on the Trail from the Vietnamese border, stopping first in "Muang Phine" (where the Lao communist headquarters was then located) for a few days to "prepare the take-over of Savannakhet town" before marching on to the provincial capital along the track of Route 9. "We were instructed on how to talk, behave, eat properly … and even how to use toilets! We'd been living in the forest and had no clue about urban life. We were countrymen (*khon baan nork*), entering the city (*khaw müang*)," the war veteran explained. During those historic days and weeks, the road reverted — briefly — to its role of connecting urban and rural areas, and (more significantly) blurred the dyadic relation of "core" and "periphery" by bringing the "peasant" revolution to town. But to villagers who gradually came down from the mountains and out of the caves after the ceasefire, Route 9 looked like anything but a "victory road," as discussed in the next section.

Route 9: An Ambivalent Site

The Official Memory

The repairing of the road in the immediate postwar period involved the participation not only of soldiers from Vietnam's People's Army (see Christina Schwenkel's chapter), but also hundreds of prisoners from the defunct Royal Lao Army who had to contend with the hazard of UXO in addition to the hardships of imprisonment (topics to which I shall shortly return). An estimated 20,000 Vientiane-side military personnel, police officers and civil servants involved with the "old regime" (*labob kaw*) were sent to "reeducation camps" (euphemistically translated from *sun samana* in Lao, which can be translated literally as "seminar centers") set up in remote areas throughout the country after 1975.[15] Several of these camps were established along Route 9 and in the uplands nearer the Vietnamese border (see map below). In fact, the eastern section of Route 9 is scattered with villages that were former sites of reeducation camps, including Ban Setthamouak, Ban Phonmouang, Ban Kheng Khan (on Route 28A) and Ban Dong. 30 years later, little evidence remains of the brutality of the war on Route 9 and the painful reconstruction process that followed, except for the presence of scrap metal (becoming increasingly scarce due to villagers collecting and selling it), bomb craters too large to be filled up and government/international agency posters that warn residents of unexploded munitions (see below).

The task of reading post-conflict landscape "text" is even more challenging in post-conflict countries where wars subsided only recently or the rule of the victors prevent any reconciliatory representations of the past (Steinberg and Taylor 2003). In the East of Savannakhet Province, the landscape of Route 9 is dotted with a few war monuments and postwar infrastructure (mainly bridges) that stand as reminders of the "socialist friendship" era when the country was in a dire economic situation and received the help of other communist states (the former Soviet Union, Hungary, Czechoslovakia, Poland, Bulgaria, Romania, and Vietnam) (Vietnam Museum of Ethnology 2009: 44). Three sites on Route 9 can be read as officially-sanctioned *lieux de mémoire*, "sites of memory," through which are channeled representations of the past in a freeze-frame to capture a particular historical moment in collective memory (Nora 1989). Two of them are located in the district towns of Phine and Sepon, and the third is situated in Ban Dong, some 15 kilometers from the Lao-Vietnamese border. The monument in Muang Phine is composed of a wide horizontal fresco carved in stone, in front of which has been erected a statue of

Plate 6.1 "You should not allow your children to go and collect scrap metal or to use metal detectors," warns this poster in Sepon District, Lao PDR.

Plate 6.2 War memorial in Phine District.

two soldiers (one supposedly Vietnamese, the other Lao), both carrying a Kalashnikov rifle and one holding the Lao flag. More interestingly, the fresco shows combatants and civilians (husbands and wives, mothers and children) united in the "anti-imperialist struggle," conveying "narratives of suffering, sacrifice, indebtedness, and citizenship" (Schwenkel 2009: 108). This monument is a memorial through which the Lao state is able to

Plate 6.3 War memorial in Sepon District.

display its gratitude and appreciation for those who suffered for the "just cause." However, this "memoryscape"[16] overlooks the reality of the conflict as a civil war in Laos, as only the victors' account is being displayed.

The monument's distinctive socialist iconographic style and the vivid scenes represented on the stone wall sharply contrast with the bland "victory" site (*anusavaly*) in Sepon town, furthermore obscured by unkempt vegetation, at the center of which stands a derelict Buddhist stupa, overlooking Route 9. An explanation for the more flamboyant commemorative monument in the district town of Phine may be related to the location of the revolutionary headquarters in that area during the war.

The third and last commemoration site is located by Route 9 in Ban Dong. The old settlement of Ban Dong (*Ban Dong Kaw*) is better known among historians of the Vietnam War as the site of one of the most fiercely fought battles of the Second Indochina War. Between 8 February and 25 March 1971, the armed forces of the Republic of Vietnam (South Vietnam) launched an offensive campaign in the border area straddling Savannakhet and Quảng Trị Provinces with the objective of disrupting the Ho Chi Minh Trail. The limited offensive campaign aimed to attack westward from Khe Sanh (Quảng Trị Province) along Route 9, seize the storage depots and destroy the supplies stockpiled around Sepon, and withdraw back to South Vietnam. The campaign, famously known as Operation Lam Sơn 719, was a disaster for the ARVN and led to much bloodshed on both sides. In this ferocious battle, some 45 percent of the 17,000-man invasion forces were killed, wounded, or left missing in action, while North Vietnamese casualties totalled an estimated 13,000 (Nalty 2005: 151). On the communist side, the battle is today included in the pantheon of renowned victories over "the imperialists and their puppets" by the "revolutionary armed forces" (*Pathet Lao Daily* 2005: 47). To this end, an exhibition center (*horng vangsadeng*) was built on Road 9 in the large area where reeducation camps and dormitories for prisoners used to be located in the New Ban Dong (*Ban Dong Mai*). The new village was set up along Road 9 after 1975, and about one kilometer from the old settlement located further from the road (Mithouna 2001: 88). According to the main entrance's inscription, the site specifically aims to celebrate "the Lao-Vietnamese common battlefield in the region of Road 9."

I first visited the site in October 2008 (having passed through it on numerous occasions in previous years). The building of the exhibition center was still at an early stage, though battlefield remains (supposedly from Operation Lam Sơn 719) had already been moved to the area surrounded by high fences. Lying on unkempt grass in corners of the field were bomb casings, artillery pieces, anti-aircraft guns, vehicle and plane wreckage, including that of a tank, and various unidentifiable pieces of scrap metal (see pictures below). They looked less like (soon-to-be) museum exhibits than abandoned remnants. In any case, the villagers did not need these objects to remember wartime years: large bomb craters had become an integral part of the natural landscape of the Old Ban Dong village.

When I returned to the area in February 2010, the construction of the exhibition center was finished. But the interiors of the edifice remained empty and the wartime wreckage was still lying in the same spot. The caretaker told me that nobody knew when the center would be open to the public: "the building is still empty. I heard that there were plans to bring some exhibits from the countryside and Vietnam." Then the man turned to his neighbor and chuckled: "Well, if there's anything left to collect around here!" The construction of housing for war veterans to be located behind the center — where labor camps used to be, according to the caretaker — had not begun. The head of the Provincial Department of Information and Culture in Savannakhet, who oversaw the exhibition center project, lamented that "there was not enough money to finish the project"[17] even though the commemoration site has had the attention of the authorities at the highest level: the Lao PDR's President and Party Secretary-General, Choummaly Sayasone, visited the place twice to check on the progress being made. He "arrived by helicopter and stayed maybe half an hour," recalled the caretaker. I most recently visited Ban Dong in June 2012. The exhibition center was by then open, and I was able to wander inside the building this time. A huge painting depicting a battlefield (presumably, the famous Operation Lam Sơn 719) covered the entire wall facing the entrance door. The (few) exhibits (mainly, bomb and rocket remains) were laid out in a circular fashion, along with black-and-white pictures of battles fought in the area of Route 9 during the Second Indochina Conflict. In the last exhibition room, a large map of the Ho Chi Minh Trail straddling the borders of Vietnam, Laos, and Cambodia was hung on the wall, its legend written in three languages: Vietnamese, Lao, and English. Outside the center, a new larger than life sculpture of two soldiers, one Vietnamese and the other Lao, was standing in front of the edifice. The day I was there, an excavator was removing wartime wreckage to create an open space in front of the musem building; as a staff member of the memorial site explained to me, "everything has to be ready for the official inauguration on December 12, 2012." The New Ban Dong exhibition center was indeed officially opened on that day in the presence of top-ranking Party officials from Laos and Vietnam to finally fulfill its dual role as the medium of public memory of a triumphant victory on the one hand, and vector of official amnesia of the more recent ambivalent past on the other. In the next and final part of the chapter, I would like to elucidate the more subtle traces of the war and its aftermath in Sepon in its inhabitants' every day, private memories.

"A Beautiful Road"

Today Route 9 runs out from Savannakhet Province's capital at the city's largest market and bus depot. The two-lane paved road connects the provincial capital with a few small district towns along its length, transporting local travelers, traders, villagers, and students alike on minibuses and *songthaew*[18] that leave the bustling market each hour. Passengers ranging further afield may take the international bus that departs once a day for

Plate 6.4   Exhibition center, Ban Dong, June 2012.

Quảng Trị Province in Central Vietnam or any one of a number of buses across the bridge that spans the Mekong River, linking Savannakhet with Mukdahan in northeastern Thailand. When one travels through Savannakhet Province's former conflict zones, it is hard to match the present-day scenery with this graphic description of the road in the aftermath of the fighting: "Route 9 was like a cemetery. The bodies of dead enemy soldiers, damaged tanks, cannons and military vehicles were scattered along the road. Unexploded land mines and bombs continued to create carnage long after the battles had ended" (Vietnam Museum of Ethnology 2009: 41). It took exactly 30 years for the road to revert to its status of "motor of modernity." Those inhabitants in Sepon old enough to remember had been keeping close track of the road's rehabilitation process.

> 'In 1983, Route 9 was a dirt road, in terrible condition, with holes and cracks. In some places, you even had to bend to go through; otherwise your face would get scratched by brushwood,' recalled a customs officer at the border check-point in Densavanh on the Lao-Vietnamese border. 'It'd take 3 days and 3 nights to reach Savannakhet town from the [Lao-Vietnamese] border: one night in Sepon village, a second night in Setthamouak, and a third night in Seno or Donghen. In 1985,

the Vietnamese [soldiers] came to help repairing the road, after that
the travelling time came down from three nights to one night only. In
1994, it was possible to cover the distance in one day, from 6 am to
6 pm. In 2005, we had the road as it is today: 4 hours by bus or less
than 2 hours by car.'

The precise account of this man who was born in Sepon district and
fought in the Pathet Lao army during the war resembles the discourse of
government plans for economic development in that it portrays the renovation of the road as a crucial factor in the recovery of the district. In
post-socialist Laos, one of the resonant symbols of "modernity" as opposed
to "backwardness" is the existence of paved roads linking villagers to
markets, and thus to economic "progress." The completion of the up-
grading of a 71-kilometer section of the road in late 2002 prompted this
buoyant comment in the English-language national newspaper, the *Vientiane
Times*: "Road 9 is an important national road linking Road 13 South to
Vietnam. It is considered by the Government as a strategic route for the
overall socioeconomic development of the country and more specifically
for the people and ethnic groups who will use this road to access, trade
and transport their products to the urban markets."[19] Laos lies in the center
of the Greater Mekong Sub-region (better known as the GMS), an area
that has received substantial investment from the Asian Development Bank
(ADB) and other institutions with the aim of further integrating the GMS
member states' economies.[20] The planned road grid in the GMS is expected
to place Laos at the center of the regional transport network and thus to
propel the country out of its geographic and economic isolation — one of
the chief causes (in the view of political and economic decision-makers)
of its structural vulnerability — and Route 9 plays a key role in reaching
this objective.

Nevertheless, I argue that to villagers of Sepon, these ideologically
loaded terms such as "progress," "civilization" and "development" have not
been simply passed down by outside authorities, but in large part have
been shaped by villagers' very own wartime experiences. Unlike plans
and reports authored by state agents and international aid agency experts
insisting on the road as an example of modern advancement, villagers
made it clear that they also situated their narration of the road restoration
process in a historical timetable that followed their own recovery from the
war. "After the war, the road was nothing like it is today. It was an area
covered by forest and vegetation, it was a dangerous road. To those who
weren't living here it is very hard to imagine that," a woman in her late

Plate 6.5 Road 9 in Sepon District, September 2008.

60s from the village of Nabor in Sepon district told me. "We never thought that we'd survive and live long enough to see Route 9 becoming a beautiful road," elderly villagers would often repeat in my casual conversations with them. For some local residents, the road's significance goes beyond the tangible benefits it brings in the form of economic benefits to encompass its nonmaterial, social-psychological dimension (Nishizaki 2008: 434). I would argue that these rural survivors saw the revival of the road as a metaphorical process that has lifted them out of war-born rift and violence and back to a civilized state. But their linear and positive narrative of the road rehabilitation may also perform as a means of putting their memories of a more recent and troubling past behind them.

A Field of Unfinished Histories[21]

The history of labor camps in post-1975 Laos has yet to be written. What we know about them mainly comes from a few oral and written testimonies (published and unpublished) by former detainees who either managed to escape or were freed after years of imprisonment.[22] Grant Evans, the noted anthropologist on Laos, made one of the rare comments on Lao reeducation camps in recent years in his review of the memoirs by Nakhonkham Bouphanouvong (Bouphanouvong 2003). He wrote in vivid terms: "The camps were designed to terrorise both those outside and those inside into submitting to the will of the new regime. Arbitrary justice was of its essence. Those who survived the experience were deeply scarred by it. Some committed suicide in the prisons, some returned home broken and withdrawn."[23] Those who wrote or spoke about their experiences in labor camps did so in their country of exile, in France, Australia or the United States. These testimonies are undoubtedly partial; they aim after all to denounce the "totalitarian" character of the present regime. They therefore do not pretend to be objective, which does not necessarily mean that their accounts ought to be dismissed. Those memoirs should be reviewed critically, but it is hard to refute that these detainees' rights had been severely violated. These prisoners were sentenced to forced labor, though in fact they were condemned to "nothing," as Todorov argued in regard to detainees in communist camps in Eastern Europe, since there had been no judgment or legal punishment (Todorov 1995: 121).

After the communist victory, the Eastern section of Route 9 (including the districts of Phine, Vilabuly and Sepon) was converted into an exclusionary site of exceptional state rule. The presence of the labor camps amid the war-contaminated landscape condemned the region of Route 9 to remain for many years a place at the margins where the new regime could wield its "justice" upon the defeated. Prisoners were assigned to conduct repairs on Route 9 in an UXO-infested landscape. Accidental explosions occurred, injuring and killing detainees (Mithouna 2001: 147). In the then deeply hostile atmosphere charged by the scars of civil war and Cold War ideology, these deaths were considered by guards and commanders of the camps as just retribution for those "who served the Americans" (Mithouna 2001: 148). War vestiges in Sepon were thus not merely inert residue; deadly remains such as UXO also operated as instruments of punishment, though more often than not they mutilated and killed indiscriminately, prisoners and local villagers alike.

Once designated as the "cradle of the revolution," places such as Sepon, Lako, Pha-Bang or Ban Dong (see Map 6.1) were selected because of their remoteness and difficulty of access so as to prevent (although not entirely successfully) detainees from escaping to Savannakhet town or across the Mekong to Thailand. There existed several types of reeducation camps (governed with varying degrees of severity), to which assigned were different categories of military personnel, policemen and government employees according to their rank and political importance. Thus, the highest-ranking officers were sent to more remote camps characterized by harsher conditions, situated in Houaphan province in the North (see Oliver Tappe's contribution, this volume) or in the Eastern uplands in the South (including those set up in Lako and Pha-Bang in Sepon district). On the other hand, prisoners of lesser rank detained in camps such as Ban Phonmouang seemed to have received (relatively) less harsh treatment, being assigned to work in sawmills instead of on the highly hazardous rehabilitation of Road 9 or to perform hard physical labor in the more remote uplands.[24] I would like to turn now in the final section to the landscape wherein people live, "the world as it is known to those who dwell therein, who inhabit its places and journey along the paths connecting them" (Ingold 1993: 156).

Today Route 9 in the east is a (relatively) smooth paved road with hardly any trace of wartime or postwar remnants; yet, the past has not been completely erased from the surface, in that one only needs to refocus the historical lens to glimpse "what is dominant but hard to see" (Stoler 2008: 211). As Steinberg and Taylor point out in their study of postwar Guatemala's landscape, "often, [rural survivors'] remembering is an inconspicuous, everyday act [...] These are intangible, yet palpable, memories of the mind, memories that have not left an obvious, permanent mark on

La Route n° 9

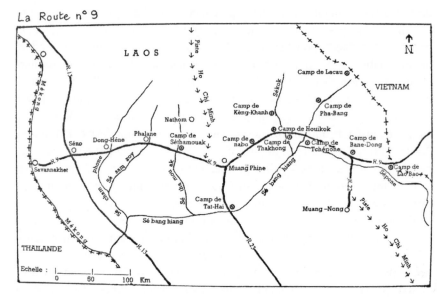

Map 6.1 Reeducation camps on Route 9 between the late 1970s and the mid-1980s (Source: Mithouna 2001: 7).

> I have taken the map from the published memoirs of a former prisoner
> who was detained in various reeducation camps along Road 9 until the
> mid-1980s (Mithouna 2001). This simple map indicates the location of
> these camps along the road; but, I argue, it is precisely its plainness and
> neatness which make it visually striking. This is a representation of a
> space through a politically-charged lens that prompts one to imagine
> oneself on an (arguably sinister) journey between two black dots —
> camps — on that central line that is Road 9.

the visible landscape — at least to the outside observer" (Steinberg and
Taylor 2003: 453). Local residents did not say much about the history of
the reeducation camps in their area, but not because they were unaware
of it: locations of reeducation camps and identities of former *samana*
detainees who settled in the district were hardly a secret. (For example,
Ban Setthamouak in Muang Phine is known by the local inhabitants as
Ban Samana, as it first emerged as a reeducation camp and is still today
populated by former detainees who never returned to their home province
or district). Some families even temporarily hosted prisoners when the
latter first arrived in the area as reeducation camps were yet to be built
(by the detainees themselves). But individuals and families, who used to
live on the opposite sides of the invisible, yet conspicuous, longitudinal

border that cut through the country during the civil war, have now to live together in close proximity.

Stanley Cohen suggests that whole societies may choose to forget uncomfortable knowledge and turn it into "open secrets" which are known by all, and knowingly not known (Cohen 2001: 138). He introduces the term "social amnesia," which refers to "the mode of forgetting by which a whole society separates itself from its discreditable past record. This might happen at an organized, official, and conscious level — the deliberate cover up, the rewriting of history — or through the type of cultural slippage that occurs when information disappears" (Cohen 1995: 13). As shown above, the "rewriting of history" is being taken care of by war monuments erected on Route 9, with the same partial version of events — that of the victors — being narrated in the available official accounts of the war and revolution. The "cultural slippage," by contrast, is more the result of conscious actions by individuals that have chosen the path of forgetting about unsettling events. But we need to further interrogate this will to forget lest we limit ourselves to a moral explanation — translated either into acts of atonement or guilty repression of a troubling past — of a collective attitude; to use the words of Confino, "the notion of repression as an explanatory device tends to obscure rather than reveal human motivations where silence and expression coexisted in ambiguous, multiple ways" (Confino 2004: 95). In line with Jay Winter's elegant observation, we refuse "the commonplace view that silence is the space of forgetting and speech the realm of remembrance" (Winter 2010: 4).

I initially assumed that the reason why residents in Sepon did not talk about reeducation camps (at least spontaneously) was due to the sensitive nature of the issue. Yet, the topic of the *samana* camps was not taboo (I was introduced to former detainees by local residents without any request on my part). Only later on did it occur to me that it was partly because detainees and villagers, most of whom were bystanders at that time, had few exchanges during the conflict. During a casual conversation, a woman I often talked with in the evening recalled that her only contacts with *samana* prisoners occurred when some of them stopped by her house and asked for some water: "They were on their way to the camps, I think," she vaguely remembered. Todorov suggested with regard to inhabitants who lived near communist camps in Eastern Europe that "it was much more prudent to mind one's own business: you [were] less likely to be contaminated by the plague if you [steered] clear of its victims" (Todorov 1995: 125). This was confirmed by a conversation I had with a former detainee's wife, who recalled that "any villagers who were seen talking to prisoners were called upon by the authorities." In the immediate postwar context in Laos, as the regime strove for survival,[25] it was hardly surprising that the population, returning to their devastated villages and contaminated lands, would have stood by their leaders and considered that these prisoners who fought on the "Vientiane side" deserved their "sentence."

It was evident that "amnesia" was a device used in official narratives of national memory. Private memories, based on everyday communication and informal situations, revealed more about attitudes and values. In Ban Thakhong, I met a woman who enlisted as a Pathet Lao agent and worked as a guard in a labor camp for women in Muang Phine in the 1980s. "There were about a hundred of them," she recalled as we were chatting on her veranda. "They were prostitutes (*mae chang*) [at the time of the war] from Savanh [Savannakhet town] who had to be reeducated [she used the ideologically loaded term, *datsang*, which can be translated literally as '(re)adjust and (re)build']." She then mentioned that "these women pulled a plough, like buffaloes, when they worked in the rice field. It wasn't a punishment, just to teach them. Anyway, there were several on each plough, so it wasn't really forced labor." These detainees would leave the camp after over a year: "the girls had learnt their lessons and didn't misbehave again." The former communist agent's experiences of the war and its aftermath have shaped and crystallized her postwar memories into a moral attitude, legitimized further by the state's narratives of indebtedness and citizenship (see above).

I turn now to members of a distinctive social group who live in the vicinity of Route 9 — former reeducation camp prisoners — and explore how their experiences of the war and its aftermath, but also the official memory of the conflict, shape their postwar private memories. The places represented on the map above are now villages that are indistinguishable from any other, at least to outside observers and first-time visitors (shacks and barracks that used to shelter detainees have long since disappeared). Until my first visit to Ban Phonmouang, located on Route 9 some 40 kilometers from the Lao-Vietnamese border, I did not know that this "new" village (it was created after 1975) used to be the site of a labor camp. Without scratching too hard at the surface, however, it soon became apparent in my conversations with its inhabitants that several of the residents were "Vientiane-side" (*fay Vientiane*) soldiers from "the North" (the provinces of Luang Prabang, Oudomxay, Luang Namtha, Sainyabuly), who got sent to *samana* camps in Sepon and, after their release, never returned to their home provinces. It was not uncommon for former prisoners to stay in places where they had been detained, especially northerners who had completely lost contact with their relatives (who on their part might have fled to Thailand or a Western country) during their imprisonment and therefore had no one, and most often no land and no work as well, awaiting them in their village or district of origin. Some of them (re)married and started a new life, like the elderly man — a former RLA fighter and a native from Phongsaly (the northernmost province of Laos) — I met at the market in Sepon town where he and his wife (who was from Pakse, the provincial capital of the neighboring southern province, Champasak) run a small café-restaurant. The man barely mentioned his years fighting for the RLA, but said that he spent several years in Ban Phonmouang, first as a *samana* prisoner, then as a worker at a state-owned sawmill after completing his "sentence." By then, he was earning some kind of salary ("200–300 kip a month, which was enough for a couple, but not to raise a family!") and receiving 10 kilograms of rice each month. At this point in our conversation, the man used the distinctive phraseology that I heard wartime communist agents and revolutionary fighters utter time and again: "We lived with the support of the State, with the State (*yu nam lat*)." The man's identification with a regime that had him punished for having served "the enemy" was remarkable, and yet, had a certain predictability under the current political circumstances: by stressing *overtly* his political allegiance, the former detainee showed his identity as a "reeducated" man. We should be constantly aware of the pitfalls of "psychologising interpretation" of postwar memory and history (Lagrou 2000: 17); but at the same time, it is important to understand why an individual would express sentiments and memories that differ in part with his experience of the war and its aftermath. In other words, the point is not to "guess" the reason(s) for an individual's particular remembrance — or his "psychology" — but to explore the relations between changing cultural, political and social settings and people's memories and mental views of the world they live in.

I wondered afterward whether, had our conversation taken place in his house (or in a more private setting), the former prisoner would have expressed other memories that may have been silenced in the public — *social* — space of his café located in the center of the district's market. Winter has defined silence as "a socially constructed space in which and about which subjects and words normally used in everyday life are not spoken" (Winter 2010: 4). This "circle of silence" is socially enforced by groups of people who have internalized at some point in time norms and codes that dictate what is sayable and what is unsayable. In Sepon District, I would argue that the contours of the social space of silence — the distinction between the spoken and the unspoken — were determined by those who happened to be on the winning side of history, including war veterans, bystanders, and former reeducation camp guards. If a candid discussion on *samana* camps could not take place in a public space, then the focus should shift to exploring the private sphere. The opportunity arose one afternoon when after finishing an interview with a war veteran in Ban Thakhong, the villager, who was my guide in Sepon, pointed out a house at the base of the embankment of Route 9: "the husband used to be a *samana* detainee," she told me. "If you want, I can introduce you to him and his wife." I hesitated to reply for a few seconds, uncertain about her motive; however, I quickly sensed that her suggestion was casual and friendly. Only later on did I understand that, in her view, meeting former *samana* prisoners was not a sensitive issue (to the contrary of what I initially thought): these individuals no longer represented any threat, having been confined to the losing side of history. We went back the following morning. The couple's wooden house on tilts was modest and hidden from the main road at the bottom of a slope. As she usually did, my guide let me conduct the interview alone and returned a couple of hours later. That tacit arrangement suited us both well.

After some rapid introduction, the former prisoner, a man now in his 60s, readily began the narration of his post-1975 life. He was born in Sainyabuly Province in North-Western Laos. He joined the RLA in 1960. Following the communist victory in 1975, he was first sent to a reeducation camp in Nam Bac in Luang Namtha Province (Northern Laos), where he and the other prisoners were assigned to work on upland rice fields ("But we never ate the rice we grew and never knew where it was sent to," the informant noted). In 1978, he and other detainees were transferred to the South in Sepon District. They took a boat to Luang Prabang, and then were flown to Savannakhet town. From there, they traveled on Route 9 "by night because they [their guards] feared that we could remember the way back and be tempted to escape." The man remembered that it was raining on the night they reached their final destination in October 1978. He evoked the "hardship of the first few years" when he and his fellow prisoners had "to start everything from scratch." In the beginning, they made their own huts (*tup*) that could shelter one or two persons. The prisoners had been sent to work in the saw mill. When the site became operational, they were able to cut wooden planks and build "bigger and more durable accommodation." Rice was supplied "by the State"; for the rest — other food staples — they "got by." After some time, the detainees made a request to move to a village site located near a stream that had earlier been abandoned by their inhabitants, "some Lao Theung,"[26] following a devastating epidemic. Vangboun village since then had been known as cursed and inhabited by malevolent spirits. "But the *phi* (spirits) were powerless against Vientiane soldiers," his wife interjected for the first time in our conversation. She had just come back from some errands and sat with us on the house veranda. I initially was unsure whether she was being ironical in making this remark, and then realized by the grave look on her face that she was not. She could not explain why exactly "Vientiane soldiers" were immune to the spirits' malicious actions; in any case, the authorities agreed to the prisoners' request and after some time wives and children of some detainees joined them.

The man's slow return to a more normal life began from the mid-1980s after he got married in 1982 (with his present wife, a villager of Chinese and Phuthai descent from Ban Thakhong) and was released from the camp. Thanks to some savings, they bought a buffalo ("a good investment") and gradually acquired some livestock and a plot of rice field in Ban Thakhong. They do not have children of their own and have adopted a child from a "Lao Theung family." The couple's recollection at times took unexpected turns. "We were often told by detainees from Setthamouak that we were very lucky to have been sent further east," the husband said without further explaining. As recollections of my encounter with former prisoners from that village some years earlier quickly ran through my mind, I understood what he implied: he and his companions were "fortunate" for not being assigned the task of clearing Route 9 of unexploded ordnance, which maimed and killed a number of *samana* detainees in Setthamouak. On the other hand, his wife's recollections were less restrained. After some 45 minutes of conversation, she appeared to relax and became more animated. In the first few months of their arrival, she told me, the higher-ranking military personnel were sent to live with local families, including hers, in groups of three to four people. Some households (like that of their current neighbors across the road, she claimed in an accusatory tone) "did not give the prisoners anything to eat. They ignored them as if they were dogs!" She added that the prisoners "were not allowed to gather in groups of more than five people" and "each had to sleep in his own corner of the house so that they could not plot together any escape plans." Her husband meanwhile was nodding quietly in agreement with his wife. Camps were moved further east nearer the Lao-Vietnamese border, she further recollected; nonetheless, lots of prisoners escaped and "those who were caught were executed." While widespread amnesia defines the official memory in regard to the civil war and its immediate aftermath, unofficial sentiments in the private sphere reflect a more complex picture of postwar remembrances, many of which remain muted. I do not interpret the former prisoner's incomplete recollection as a conscious action of selective memory; rather, I argue that his narration is a balancing act between reconstituting a meaningful life (reflected in a narrative of struggle, in which he eventually prevailed to become a farmer and an ordinary citizen in Ban Thakhong) and remembering darker experiences of his past (which also formed part of his social identity).

Conclusion

This chapter reflects on certain of the civil war's legacies in Laos by means of a social reading of the landscape of Route 9. Residents of Sepon, one of the district towns on Route 9, welcome the potential for economic advancement the road represents and the higher mobility it offers. Nonetheless, to older residents, the cause for celebrating the restoration of the road in the early 2000s went beyond the renovation of an important piece of national infrastructure: they metaphorically see the revival of the road as a route back to civilization. Civilization here is defined in fundamental terms, that is, as a state of affairs counterpoised to the violence and savagery that residents experienced during the war (from bombing and land battles) as well as in its aftermath (from unexploded ordnance and "counter-revolutionary" attacks). Civilization in a more "advanced" sense is also being restored, in the form of the road's ancient importance as a trading route. Therefore, for local residents, the road's significance goes beyond the tangible benefits it brings in the form of access to services. For these people, the restoration of Route 9 represents a source of healing, with travel and trade resumed, craters filled in, and lingering memories of violence slowly dwindling.

The conversion of Route 9 into a paved road and the clearance of war debris have not translated into a complete erasure of the past, however. The post-conflict landscape through which the road runs is dotted with mnemonic sites that reflect a partial version of the past (the public sites of war commemoration in Phine and Sepon districts), as well as invisible traces — indiscernible legacies of former reeducation camps — that embody unofficial remembrances of the war and its consequences yet to be reconciled. Social amnesia — a conscious action to overlook an unsettling past — may define the state's narratives of national memory, but in the private sphere expressions of unofficial sentiments reveal more about the complex negotiations between forgetting and remembering. The choice of resorting to moral concerns to explain individual actions runs the risk of obscuring human motivations: silences should not be translated readily into acts of contrition or sentiments of shame or guilt. Some villagers in Sepon District who lived through and survived the war and its aftermath seldom evoked memories of detainees or reeducation camps because they were indifferent to, or were little aware of, the detainees' conditions of imprisonment at that time — and remain so until today. Others spoke casually of these places and their prisoners. Some former detainees who never left the location of their captivity chose to express memories that emphasize their postwar recovery of a normal life, though others found in their memories and experience elements to reveal in the intimacy of the private sphere a more ambiguous past. The lack of democratization and the absence of a public space for Lao citizens to freely debate their country's past further contribute to maintaining this arbitrary yet pregnant dividing line from the political center down to the village level between those who feel they have the right to speak about the violent past and those who are denied this privilege.

Notes

1. Route 9 is also commonly called Road No. 9 or Highway No. 9.
2. "Economic corridors" are a key element of the Asian Development Bank's strategy of regional development and Laos is traversed by three of these: the Northern Economic Corridor (linking Northern Thailand with Southwest China via Northwest Laos), the North-East Corridor (linking Northern Vietnam with North-East Thailand via Vientiane and North-Eastern Laos), and the East-West Economic Corridor (linking Eastern Burma with the port of Đà Nẵng in Central Vietnam via Northeast Thailand and Savannakhet Province, Southern-Central Laos). Laos lies in the center of the Greater Mekong Subregion (GMS), an area that has received substantial investment from the ADB and others with the aim of further integrating the GMS member states' economies. The GMS includes Burma, Cambodia, Laos, Thailand and Vietnam, as well as two southern Chinese provinces, Yunnan and Guangxi.
3. The HCMT was, in reality, a maze of interlocking dirt roads that were gradually and partially upgraded to cobbled roads so that North Vietnamese trucks could move in an almost uninterrupted flow all year round.
4. From 1964 to 1973, American planes dropped 2,093,100 tons of ordnance in 580,344 bombing missions, which approximately equated to a bombing every eight minutes, 24 hours a day, for nine years. According to these statistics, Laos is the most heavily bombed country per capita in the world.

Attacks on the Trail intensified from 1968 onward; whereas 52,120 missions were carried out in 1967, this figure almost trebled in 1969, amounting to a total of 148,069 sorties flown in that year. The bombing finally halted in 1973. Bombs still continue maiming and killing scores of people in today's Laos, however. At the end of the war, it was estimated that 78 million unexploded cluster bomblets had been left in the country's rural areas. All figures are quoted from the very informative article by Channapha Khamvongsa and Elaine Russell (2009). A recent survey by the National Regulatory Authority (NRA) for the UXO/Mine Action sector in Laos reveals that more than 50,000 people were hurt or killed by UXO (unexploded ordnance) between 1964 and 2008, *Vientiane Times*, 06/02/10.

5. The political term *l'Indochine française* was formerly adopted in France in 1887. French Indochina was composed of five entities: Laos, Cambodia, Tonkin, Annam and Cochinchina (the last three composing present-day Vietnam), governed by diverse regimes of control and administration: directly-administered entities or colonies (Cochinchina, Central and Southern Laos) and indirectly-administered territories or protectorates (Tonkin, Luang Prabang, Cambodia, Annam).

6. For accounts of the French Mekong expeditions in the second half of the 19th century, see, for example, Francis Garnier 1985 (1873) and Milton Osborne (2000 [1975]).

7. Where the border town of Lao Bảo in Quang Trị province is now located.

8. This road through the Ai-Lao mountain pass was mentioned by Charles Lemire in his travel diary during his exploration of the region in Aug. and Sept. 1892. The French colonial officer also described another road located to the north of the "Route Coloniale N. 9" that was laid out by the Kinh before the arrival of the French, which he referred as the "Route Mandarine," traversing Central Vietnam and Southern Laos all the way to the Mekong River (Lemire 1894: 33).

9. In present-day Central Vietnam.

10. According to Li Tana, it is "[t]he single most important account of the border region written on eighteenth-century Đàng Trong, a miscellaneous account of the border region written by the high Trịnh official, Lê Quý Đôn" (Li 2002: 17).

11. On the "salt roads" connecting the uplands and the plains, and their inhabitants, in Indochina, see also Jean Le Pichon (1938: 364) and Tran Duc Sang (2004: 71–87).

12. Personal interviews with villagers in the districts of Sepon, Phine and Vilabuly, in June 2005 and Mar. 2006.

13. *Corvée* road works were among other deeply unpopular demands (such as heavy taxes) imposed by the French administration upon the rural population in colonial Laos, especially in the highlands. In consequence, French rule had to face several insurrections led by upland groups. There were a series

of revolts beginning in 1896, reaching a peak between 1910 and 1916, and finally dying out in the 1930s, all of which expressed resistance to the French administration. These rebellions remained politically inconsequential until a unifying cause, that is, communist-led anti-colonial struggle during the First Indochina War (1946–54), succeeded in gathering their remaining participants into one larger movement.

14. The coalition government resigned on 28 Nov. A few days later, on 2 Dec. 1975, the founding of the Lao People's Democratic Republic (*Sathalanalat Pasathipataï Pasason Lao*) was proclaimed.

15. See reports by MacAlister Brown and Joseph J. Zasloff in *Asian Survey* between 1975 and 1979. Other sources give a higher number of prisoners, up to 50,000 (Viliam 2009).

16. To use Schwenkel's expression (2009: 107).

17. Personal interview on 29 Apr. 2010, Savannakhet Capital.

18. Pick-up vehicles with two parallel benches in the back for passengers.

19. *Vientiane Times*, 20–23 Dec. 2002.

20. The GMS include Burma, Cambodia, Laos, Thailand and Vietnam, as well two southern Chinese provinces, Yunnan and Guangxi.

21. This subheading was inspired by the following reflection by Confino: "Some trips, to use a metaphor from the world of traveling, actually have a final stop. Historical understanding, a trip of unexpected consequences if ever I knew one, is not one of them" (Confino 2000: 93)

22. The few memoirs that have been published include Mithouna (2001); Nakhonkham (2003); and Bounsang (2006).

23. Grant Evans, "Book Review: Lao Gulags," *Bangkok Post*, 13 Sept. 2003.

24. Personal interviews with former detainees in Oct. 2008 and Feb. 2010 in Ban Thakhong, Ban Nabor, Ban Phonmouang, and Sepon town.

25. The state's new prime minister and strongman, Kaysone Phomvihane, escaped at least one assassination attempt in 1976; rural areas were hit by severe drought in 1976, then severe flooding in 1977 and 1978; counter-revolutionary guerillas were still rife in some areas in the northern and the southeastern regions until as late as the late 1980s.

26. Popular Lao term that broadly refers to Mon-Khmer-speaking populations living in the country.

CHAPTER 7

Redefining Agent Orange, Mitigating Its Impacts

Susan Hammond

In the documentary film *A Story from the Corner of the Park* by Vietnamese director Trần Văn Thủy, we are taken down a narrow alley in Hanoi, to the small home of a three-generational family. The film unfolds to tell the story of how this family is affected by Agent Orange from a war long over. When the film came out in 1996, there was very little attention to Agent Orange's impact in Vietnam; few Vietnamese and even fewer Americans knew that there were an estimated three million Vietnamese with illnesses associated with exposure to Agent Orange, including at least 150,000 children born with severe multiple birth defects believed to be caused by their parents' or grandparents' exposure.[1] The Vietnamese government was in the process of normalizing the country's relations with the United States and there was little support for those who brought attention to the "wounds of the war" during this sensitive time in US-Vietnam relations. Ten years later, those victims of Agent Orange, an herbicide used during the war in Vietnam that was contaminated with dioxin, have their photos displayed in exhibits throughout the country, their stories told in the Vietnamese and foreign press, and their fate discussed in high-level meetings between the US and Vietnam.

But why now, three and a half decades after the end of the war, has the fate of those affected by Agent Orange become a *cause célèbre* in Vietnam? Is it simply because the United States and Vietnam have reached a point in their relationship that the painful aspects of the war can now be brought to light? If so why is there intense focus by the media, by government officials, by individual Vietnamese on those affected by Agent Orange and not as much focus on the victims of the other legacy of the war —

Unexploded Ordnance? Why has there been increased international attention on the "Agent Orange Victims"?[2] How much of this hesitance by the United States to confront this "significant ghost" of the war in Vietnam, as former US Ambassador to Vietnam Raymond Burghardt referred to Agent Orange, is based on the inability of the many in the United States to put the Vietnam War behind them?[3] More fundamentally, what is an "Agent Orange Victim" and how have the lives of those born today been altered by a chemical whose use ended more than 40 years ago?

After recounting the reluctance of both American and Vietnamese governments to confront the issue of "Agent Orange Victims" until very recently, I briefly review the history of the use of Agent Orange and other herbicides during the American-Vietnam War. The wartime damage to the environment of the defoliants, and the ongoing environmental dangers of the residual "dioxin hotspots" around former US military bases, as I explain in the following sections, is becoming more understood and in various stages of being mitigated (Hatfield 2009). I, nonetheless, argue that the physical, psychological, social, and economic damage caused by the use of Agent Orange have long been controversial and will take much longer to address. Due to improper manufacturing, the herbicide has become a defining symbol of the ongoing damages of the war inflicted upon the human and ecological landscapes in Vietnam. I discuss in the final part of the article the political impacts of Agent Orange as it plays out in Vietnam, in the United States, and internationally, which are complex and tend to lead to polemics that have hindered progress on finding a solution to the "Agent Orange issue." However, Agent Orange must be understood and redefined in order for the real work to begin to mitigate its ongoing health and environmental impacts.

Misinterpreting Agent Orange or Denial?

American visitors to Vietnam often note how surprised they were to find that the Vietnamese have "forgotten the war," that they have "forgiven" the United States, and that they hold no "hatred or ill-will" for Americans. On the surface, these statement are correct. More than 75 percent of the population of Vietnam is under 40 with no personal recollection of the American war. For most Vietnamese, the United States is first of all a country, not a war. However, it is simplistic to say that the war has been "forgotten." For those families who lost loved ones during the war or after to one of its ongoing legacies, there is a daily reminder when they make offerings to their family altars. The Vietnamese who fought on the side of the Americans including those who left Vietnam as refugees have their own memories about the war.

As for "forgiving the United States," on the surface this is also true. For those who were alive during the war, most will say that they never blamed the "Americans" for the war but blamed the US government at that time. They point out that it is Vietnam tradition to make peace with their enemies after the war is over. However, for many in the US, Vietnam is considered first a war and second, a country. Unfortunately for Vietnam, it has taken the United States a lot longer to make peace, for 20 years after the war, the United States imposed a trade and diplomatic embargo on Vietnam, hindered postwar reconstruction efforts and blocked most humanitarian assistance. Even today, relations with Vietnam for many, including some US congressional officials and State Department staff, are often hindered by the "Vietnam Experience" and all that entails. While Vietnam and the Vietnamese people may have been able to "put the war behind them," in many respects the United States and its people have not, and this inability to come to terms with Vietnam hinders its ability to address the ongoing legacies of that war.

This is most vividly seen when dealing with the issue of Agent Orange. For many years, the US government was wary of dealing with Agent Orange, hoping that it would not gain momentum in Vietnam. In 2005, while visiting the US Embassy in Hanoi with an American delegation, our delegation was told by the Public Affairs officer that he was "tired" of hearing about Agent Orange and that it was just "propaganda being encouraged by the Vietnamese government."[4] It was not until the past few years that one could have a constructive conversation with US Embassy officials in Vietnam about Agent Orange. The Embassy would eventually go as far as to acknowledge that this issue was hindering US-Vietnam relations or at the very least admit that it was "an irritant."[5]

It has become clear to me over time that some in the US government have vastly misunderstood what Agent Orange meant to the Vietnamese people and government. As a result, they took a very defensive position and either refused to talk about it or called Agent Orange a "propaganda campaign"[6] by the Vietnamese government to gain the war reparations that the Vietnamese signed off on years ago.[7] Many did not understand that the focus on the Agent Orange's impacts began at the grassroots and had been met with considerable resistance by the Vietnamese government who was trying to move forward with the United States and did not want to raise this unpleasant business of Agent Orange. Nor did the Vietnamese government want to give the wrong impression to the world that Vietnam was a large toxic waste site just as it was beginning to export its rice, fish and other agricultural products. When calling for "Justice" for Agent Orange Victims became more widespread, the United States could not believe it was not government-led (government sanctioned perhaps, but not driven by the leadership that was divided on the issue).

What the US Embassy missed was that advocating for addressing the legacy of Agent Orange in Vietnam followed a similar path as advocacy for this issue in the United States. Former Northern Vietnam Army soldiers frustrated by the lack of the Vietnamese government's response to the illnesses they and their families faced, which they believed were associated with exposure to toxic herbicides in the South, began to speak out and request assistance for those affected by Agent Orange (Nguyễn Đôn Tú 1997). They were backed by a group of doctors and scientists, such as Lê Cao Đài, Phan Thị Phi Phi, Nguyễn Thị Ngọc Toàn, Nguyễn Thị Ngọc Phượng, Võ Quý and others who had spent the war years in the regions sprayed by herbicides and had since been conducting research on the ongoing impacts of Agent Orange (Westing 1984; Lê Cao Đài 2000). By having unimpeachable "revolutionary backgrounds," these early activists were able to get the Vietnamese government to pay attention to continuing impacts of Agent Orange.[8]

Why Agent Orange?

The most widely used herbicide sprayed by the US Air Force in "Operation Ranch Hand" during the Vietnam War was nicknamed Agent Orange after the orange stripe around the barrel identifying the contents as a 50-50 mixture of two herbicides, 2,4-Dichlorphenoxyacetic acid (2,4-D) and 2,4,5-Trichlorophenoxyacetic acid (2,4,5-T). If those two chemical components were the only contents in the 55-gallon barrels of Agent Orange, this aspect of the war in Vietnam would have remained a footnote in most history books. When speaking about Agent Orange today, we would be referring to the historical environmental damage or destruction of more than five million acres of the landscape in Vietnam, to the ongoing degradation of the sprayed areas that have not since been restored or re-purposed. Or possibly to refer to how this damaged landscape has altered the livelihood and spiritual life of populations that were so closely tied to the upland forests (Maitre 2006). These impacts were significant enough at the time of the war for the term "ecocide" to be coined in 1970 to describe them (Zierler 2011: 15–9).

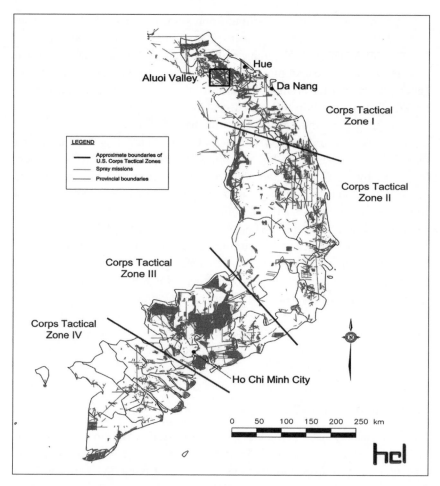

Plate 7.1   Spray map of all herbicides used during the war in Vietnam, April 2000 (Sources: Hatfield Consultants and US Department of Army).

If the barrels only contained 2,4-D and 2,4,5-T, the average Vietna-mese and the average American would have no reference point for the term "Agent Orange." There would likely be little memory in Vietnam or in the US of the actual spraying of the more than 20 million gallons of herbicides, other than by those who carried out the spraying or by the estimated 4.8 million Vietnamese civilians who lived directly under the spray runs (Stellman *et al.* 2003: 685).[9] Others, particularly those who lived in the mountainous regions, may recall the spray planes that pur-posely targeted 500,000 acres of their cropland in an effort to deny the "enemy" food. Lê Cao Đài vividly recalls the spraying in the central highlands in his memoir:

> Day before yesterday [24 July 1967], while some of us were on our way to the hospital's farming plots, we crossed a hilltop just as enemy planes were spraying defoliants. This was some time between seven and eight o'clock in the morning. Three C-130 planes flew in a triangle formation very high above.[10] Then, as they approached us, they turned into a line formation and seemed to hover above the treetops, causing the leaves to shake. We had only enough time to hide behind tree trunks. Then we saw something like a patch of mist spreading over the forest.
>
> We covered ourselves with our ponchos and held handkerchiefs over our faces as we waited for the chemicals to settle. Then, we continued hiking to our fields. There, our workers were calling to each other to cut off all the young cassava tops. Those who had lived in the battlefields for many years say that only by doing so can we save the manioc roots underneath; otherwise, some days later, the chemicals will defoliate the cassava, and the underground manioc will turn bitter and become inedible.
>
> By the time I returned to the hospital some days later, I could hardly recognize the path I had taken a few days before. The once luxuriant, green forest stood denuded; dead, yellow leaves lay all about the ground; the bare branches looked like gaunt hands reaching into the sky (Lê Cao Đài 2004: 149–50).

However, due to improper manufacturing of the herbicide 2,4,5-T, Agent Orange has become a symbol of the ongoing health and environmental consequence of war, as evidence that wars do not end when the bombs and bullets stop and not only impact the generation who fought or lived through the war but also potentially the succeeding generations. This has ensured that Agent Orange stays in the memory and physical landscape of hundreds of thousands of US veterans and their families and millions of Vietnamese and their families. Potentially, Agent Orange will continue to have an impact on the people on both sides of the Pacific for generations to come.

"Agent Orange" Defined

Usually when speaking of Agent Orange and its impacts, we are actually talking about dioxin. During the manufacturing of the 2,4,5-T component of Agent Orange, 2,3,7,8-Tetrachlorodibenzodioxin (TCDD), or "dioxin," was also produced as a contaminant when the temperature used to induce the chemical reaction was too high. The manufacturers were aware that they could have prevented, or at the very least reduced, the amount of dioxin produced by lowering the temperature of the chemical reaction used to produce 2,4,5-T to below 100 degrees Celsius. Alternatively, they could have filtered the 2,4,5-T after production to remove the dioxin contaminant (Sohn 1957; Trapp 1965). As the herbicide program escalated in 1968 and 1969, the manufacturers of 2,4,5-T increased their output to meet the demands of the US Department of Defense; as a result the amount of this unnecessary and unwanted contaminant varied from manufacturer to manufacturer and batch to batch depending on what measures were taken by the chemical companies to reduce the dioxin contaminant.[11]

Since the Vietnam War, TCDD has been found to be the most toxic of the persistent organic pollutants. The US National Toxicology Program (NTP) and the International Agency for the Research on Cancer list TCDD as a known human carcinogen, and in animal studies, it has been found to cause reproductive and developmental damage (Institute of Medicine 2009). It is not possible to know for sure exactly how much dioxin was distributed throughout Vietnam during the war. However, by using data from the testing of the remaining barrels of Agent Orange stored at Gulfport, Mississippi and Johnston Island after the herbicide program ended, Stellman *et al.* estimated that anywhere from 221 to 366 kilograms of dioxin was in the more than 15 million gallons (57 million liters) of dioxin-contaminated herbicides sprayed, stored and spilled throughout southern Vietnam (Stellman *et al.* 2003: 684). It is important to note the dioxin is rarely measured in kilograms; the more common measurement is in parts per million (ppm), per billion (ppb) or per trillion (ppt). To put this into perspective, one ppt is the equivalent of one-twentieth of a drop of water in an Olympic-sized swimming pool.

Nonetheless, it is much more common to hear the term "Agent Orange" to describe the ongoing environmental and health effects of the herbicides than the term "dioxin." Diane Fox notes that Agent Orange has come to have many different meanings including: the 50:50 mixture of 2,4-D and 2,4,5-T; a generic term for all the herbicides used during the war; chemical warfare; a disease or condition, that is, "dying from Agent Orange" or a synonym for a birth defect; and it has been called a diversion, whereas one assumes every illness and birth defect is caused by Agent Orange so the real underlying causes are ignored (Fox 2007: 7–17).

It is due in part to these various meanings of "Agent Orange" that it has become so political, so controversial and so misunderstood. As a result,

Plate 7.2 C-123 planes spraying herbicides over southern Vietnam, 1968 (Photo courtesy of the US Air Force).

it has taken the better part of the past 37 years since the end of the war to finally reach a point where the American and Vietnamese governments can dialogue about Agent Orange in order to find common ground instead of talking past each other or placing blame.

Agent Orange's Impacts Then and Now

During the first several years of the war, the biggest concern about the use of Agent Orange and the other herbicides was focused on the damage to the ecosystem. Within two to three weeks of spraying, the leaves would drop from the trees which would remain bare until the next rainy season. About ten percent of the trees sprayed died from a single spray run. Multiple sprayings resulted in increased mortality for the trees. Extensive logging off of the defoliated trees also contributed to the destruction of 20 percent of the forest lands in southern Vietnam that may have regenerated if simply sprayed by herbicides. A minimum of 20 million cubic meters of timber was destroyed, though estimates range as high as 75 million if you take into consideration the additional impact of plows, bombing, napalm strikes and harvesting of defoliated trees (Westing 1984: 11; Westing 2002: 3).

Even today, the damage from the herbicides used during the war persists in the form of ecologically degraded landscapes in some parts of Vietnam. The prewar forests that existed in the upland forests before the spraying took hundreds of years to reach an ecologically-balanced mixture of large numbers of species of flora and fauna. Natural regeneration would take centuries to reproduce those landscapes. In addition, in some of the sprayed areas, soil erosion and landslides have sharply lowered soil nutrient levels and altered the topographical features of the landscape (Dwernychuk 2010).

The US military had assured its soldiers, its allies and the local Vietnamese population that the herbicides were not harmful to humans or animals, even dropping leaflets before some spray runs stating that the

Plate 7.3   A defoliated hillside and subsequent erosion in A Lưới Valley, 1993 (Source: Hatfield Consultants).

Plate 7.4 MACV pamphlet panel, 1968.[12]

herbicides were harmless. The herbicides were handled without protective gear, American soldiers recall reusing the Agent Orange barrels for BBQs and showers. There is little evidence to show that the US military knew that the herbicides they were using were harmful to humans or animals (Young 2009: 40–1). While the chemical companies and some advocates have insisted that the American government was aware of the dioxin contamination, the part of the military making the decision on where and how the herbicides would be used did not likely know that they contained dioxin and that this dioxin was toxic. The soldiers on the ground certainly did not know (Agent Orange Litigation 2006).

However, a 1969 study found that the 2,4,5-T component was teratogenic (fetus deforming) on laboratory rats (Courtney 1970: 866). Subsequent analysis of 2,4,5-T found that it was contaminated by TCDD. In April 1970, the US government restricted the use of 2,4,5-T in the United States and as well as in Vietnam. By the end of Operation Ranch Hand in January 1971, the damage to the landscape of Vietnam was already done. Testing in 1971 by three scientists from Harvard University found that the fish from the Đồng Nai and Saigon Rivers and the Cần Giờ coastal waters had elevated levels of dioxin ranging from 18–814 ppt (Baughman 1973: 31). Tests of human breast milk revealed levels of dioxin as high as 1,850 ppt, leaving no doubt the dioxin had entered into the food chain and into Vietnamese population. What was little understood at the time was that the dioxin contamination from the herbicides would continue to cause harm for decades to come.

A Lưới Valley: A Living Museum of Agent Orange

The A Lưới Valley (formerly Shau Valley) in Thừa Thiên-Huế Province in central Vietnam is microcosm of the herbicidal war in Vietnam. The valley is 40 kilometers long and three kilometers wide and is bordered to the west by Laos. The steep mountains surrounding the valley were covered with triple canopy forest, the type that Operation Ranch Hand was aimed to eliminate. 224 spray missions were flown in the valley, which was also heavily bombed, during the war (Hatfield 1998).[13] The Vietnam Forest Inventory and Planning Institute estimates that prior to the war, forests covered over 80 percent of the land area; after the war this was reduced to 50 percent.[14] When one visits the valley today, one can still see areas of that remain barren of trees, although now many of the hillsides are covered with Acacia and Eucalyptus plantations, in part to stop further erosion and degradation of the soil, and in part to provide an income to the valley inhabitants.

For most of the war, the valley was under the control of the North Vietnamese Army. However, for a short period of time, the area housed three Special Forces bases: A Lưới in the north was operational from May through December 1965; Tà Bạt in the center of the valley from March 1963 until March 1964; and the A So base (formerly known as Shau base) in the southern end of the valley was operational from 1963 until 1966 (Hatfield 2000: 1). The valley was mainly inhabited by ethnic minorities, namely, the Ta Oy (Tà Ôi), Katu and Pa Co (Pa Kô), who prior to the American war, lived in the steep mountain terrain. The older residents of the valley vividly recall the planes coming over and the "mist that would settle on the crops" and how the crops would die a few days later. They talk about how they had to move down from their ancestral home in the hills to find food after their crops were destroyed by the herbicides, to find shelter after their homes were torched and to find safety so as not to be mistaken as the "enemy" by the US army and ARVN forces.[15] The hill people who for generations practiced shifting cultivation leading a mobile life, whose spiritual lives were tied to the forests, were now forced to till land in the valley floor, where there was a scarcity of water during the dry season, with poor-quality soil pock-marked with bomb craters and littered with unexploded ordnance.

The Center for Research and for Actions Against Trauma and Exclusion (CEDRATE) provide further examples of how the herbicides have had ongoing psychological, spiritual, cultural and economic impacts among those who lived in A Lưới District.

> Before the war, there were forest genies and 'fortune tellers' [shamans]. But with dioxin poisonous substance, all trees have been destroyed. So the genies had to move to farther places. In the past, all ailments were caused by forest genies and ghosts. 'Shamans' know whether those illnesses are caused by forest, stream or earth genies ... If the disease is caused by the forest Genie, the shaman will go to forests to pray and gather leaves to organize a ceremony for treatment of the disease ... If all those ways of treatment are not effective, they would say that the disease is not caused by Gods, but dioxin.
>
> — Elder in A Ngo Village, A Lưới
> (Doray and de la Garza 2006: 32–3).

The herbicides not only destroyed the forests that had provided a livelihood and traditional medicines but also were home for the various spirits that were vital to the animistic beliefs of the many ethnic minority people of this region (Doray and de la Garza 2006; Maitre 2006).

In the mid-1990s, Hatfield Consultants chose the A Lưới Valley for their research on the levels of residual dioxin that remained in the soil.[16] As the area was far removed from any industrial site and under no intensive agricultural practices, any TCDD found in the valley could be traced back to the American War. Hatfield found that where herbicides were sprayed by airplanes, the levels of dioxin ranged from no detectable levels to slightly elevated levels, especially below the soil surface. It is believed that some of the dioxin that remained on the surface after spraying during the war would have broken down in the hot tropical sun. The dioxin that remained would have been washed away after years of heavy rain and soil erosion. The good news of their research was that for vast majority of the area of southern Vietnam, where there was aerial spraying of herbicides, there is no present-day threat from the dioxin (Dwernychuk 2006: 3).

However, Hatfield found that the more significant concern lay within and around the former US bases where the herbicides were stored. At the

A So base, in operation for three years, Hatfield researchers found levels of dioxin up to 897.85 pg/g (ppt). Even the Tà Bạt and A Lưới Special Forces bases, which were in operation for less than a year, had elevated levels of TCDD ranging from 4.3 pg/g to 35 pg/g.[17] Hatfield also found that fish and ducks feeding in the contaminated area had high levels of dioxin in their fatty tissues. Moreover, the population that lived on the former base, even those who did not live in the area during the war, also had elevated levels of dioxin in their blood and breast milk. This proved beyond a doubt that the TCDD from Agent Orange was still found in pockets of the land in southern Vietnam, particularly around former military bases, and that the dioxin was continuing to enter the food chain, causing a health threat to a generation born long after the end of the war. Some remains of the war are neither residue nor relics, but constitute tenacious traces of a violent past that continue to inflict damages upon the ecological and human environment in Vietnam.

In 1991, Mr. Ngan and his wife, both Pa Co, moved from Hồng Thủy Commune in the north of A Lưới District to the former A So base (now Đông Sơn Commune), which at the time was promoted by the government as a new economic zone.

> I was able to save some money and start a fish farm, but I did not know that the land was contaminated with dioxin. My wife has been pregnant 13 times but most of the pregnancies only lasted two or three months. One of my daughters was born with birth defects; she died when she was two. My eldest daughter went up to the 11th grade but she was not able to go to school every day because of her terrible headaches, she also had to have an operation on her head. One of my daughters is almost blind and cannot move easily. My wife also has some health problems. I have had problems with my legs, for two years I was not able to walk, I had treatment and physical therapy and I can now walk again but it is still very painful, I cannot walk more than a few kilometers. I think that I am affected by dioxin because I never had these health problems when I lived in Hồng Thủy commune. I think maybe it is because of the dioxin poison because it is not just me, but my children as well.[18]

Mr. Ngan and his family lived on the former A So base from 1991 until 2000 when he and the other families living in this area were relocated to a new village one kilometer away. The perimeter of the contaminated section of the base was fenced off. Mr. Ngan is now raising vegetables and fruit trees in his garden but he says it is very difficult because his wife and children cannot help him.

Plate 7.5   A cow grazing outside the perimeter of the dioxin hotspot at the former A So base, 2010 (Photo courtesy of the War Legacies Project).

Hotspot Theory

Following their research in A Lưới, Hatfield posited that there might be other such "dioxin hotspots" throughout southern Vietnam; former military bases were of particular concern, especially bases where Operation Ranch Hand was located or there had been repeated perimeter spraying. Since the mid-1990s, Hatfield has surveyed former US military installations in southern Vietnam and has identified at least 28 potential "dioxin hotspots." Additional testing in the past five years done by Hatfield and Vietnam's Committee 33[19] at Đà Nẵng, Phù Cát and Biên Hòa bases, all of which were Operation Ranch Hand hubs, have found that parts of the bases are highly contaminated with TCDD and in need of remediation (Hatfield *et al.* 2009).

At the Đà Nẵng airbase, Hatfield found up to 365,000 ppt TCDD on the site where the barrels were loaded onto planes — 365 times the international acceptable standard for dioxin contamination in industrial locations. Walking in this sector, one can still detect a strong chlorine smell

Plate 7.6   The former herbicide storage site at the Đà Nẵng airbase, 2010 (Photo courtesy of the War Legacies Project).

from the phenols (solvents) in the herbicides, reminiscent of garden weed-killer. One can also see the blackened soil caused by the oxidized chlorine molecules in the herbicides where no grass or shrubs can grow. Of parti-cular concern are those hotspots where the TCDD is contaminating the food of local residents. A short walk away from the former herbicide loading area on the Đà Nẵng airbase is Sen Lake where the dioxin-contaminated sediment is the feeding grounds of fish that were found to have up to 400 times the acceptable level of dioxin, with the average being about three times the acceptable level of TCDD. Local residents who had consumed the fish in the lake have the highest levels of TCDD in the blood of any of the other residents Hatfield tested in Đà Nẵng. One 45-year-old man, who used to fish and consume his catch in the contaminated pond, had 1340 pg/g TCDD in his blood — approximately 200 times the level found in the blood of those living in industrialized nations and more than 400 times the level found in the blood of those living in the north of Vietnam (Hatfield *et al.* 2009: xiv). The lake is now blocked with a tall concrete wall prohibiting local residents from fishing in the lake (Hatfield *et al.*

2009: xi). Agent Orange-infested areas in these "dioxin hotspots" are not only legacies of war, but these landscapes containing toxic debris exert ongoing ruination of people's lives "as a corrosive process that weights on the future and shapes the present" (Stoler 2008: 194); I discuss in the next sections the uncertain fate of "Agent Orange Victims."

Who is an "Agent Orange Victim"?

The vast majority of those in Vietnam who are believed to be affected by Agent Orange are those who were directly exposed to the herbicides or were exposed at the dioxin hotspots and now have cancers and other illnesses that have been found to be associated with dioxin. However, children with birth defects and other disabilities that are believed to be associated with their parents' or grandparents' exposure to Agent Orange have received the most attention in Vietnam and around the world. In recent years, these Agent Orange victims have been the subject of at least a half a dozen international documentary films. They have been photographed by renowned documentary photographers, frequently written about in foreign and domestic newspapers and the subject of several books, including a compilation of Vietnamese fictional short stories published in the US (Waugh and Lien 2010).[20] In world history, "Agent Orange victims" as ruined bodies painfully emblematize a violent intervention in the name of freedom and security as part of escalating ideological struggles of the Cold War in Asia. When the issue of Agent Orange is raised in Western and Vietnamese media, it is the image of those children with severe birth defects, often unable to talk, who are lying prone on a bed in a poor rural village in need of round-the-clock care, which comes to the minds of most people. The child labeled as "Agent Orange victim" faces the greatest medical and educational challenges yet whose needs are not yet being met. They are the children whom Trần Văn Thủy notes "are pitiful beyond human endurance; they might create revulsion if we simply let our movie camera capture the naked reality" (Trần Văn Thủy 2004).

The majority of people with disabilities in Vietnam, including those believed to be affected by Agent Orange, live in rural areas of the country. Mr. Đồng (40 years old) and his wife Thủy (39 years old) live in Thiên Châu Commune, Thiên Phước District, Quảng Nam Pronvince on a small plot of land about five kilometers down a very narrow road that crosses a river bed that is impassable during parts of the rainy season. This area was heavily sprayed by herbicides during the war, not only to defoliate the forests but also for crop destruction. Đồng and Thủy who grew up in

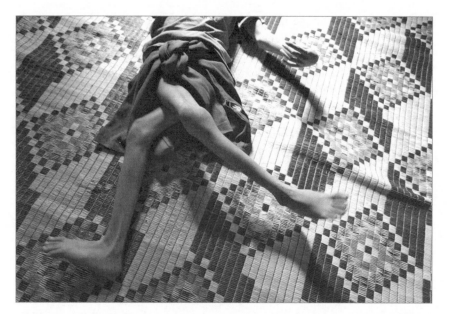

Plate 7.7   Child in Đồng Nai Province with an unnamed condition that causes paralysis that is typical of what the Red Cross believes is caused by exposure to Agent Orange, 2010 (Photo courtesy of Trần Thanh Sang for War Legacies Project).

this region have had seven children — five born with some level of birth defect. Đồng earns less than US$40 a month raising rice and vegetables on his farm. His wife cannot help as she must be home with her two sons aged 25 and 18 who are completely paralyzed with a condition that appears to be similar to cerebral palsy but has not been diagnosed as the boys have never been to a doctor. They must be spoonfed, bathed, their toilet needs cared for, and frequently moved to avoid bed sores. Another son who had the same condition died when he was 23.

Thủy is also home with her 11-year-old daughter, Kim Hướng, who has arrhythmia and Down's syndrome. Kim Hướng has been to Huế three times for her heart condition, the first time for an operation to repair her heart valve, the other two times to see more specialists; however, the doctors are not hopeful there is much more that can be done. When she becomes sick, which is often, she must be taken to the nearest hospital in Tam Kỳ, the provincial capital, about 30 kilometers away. Another daughter, 21 years old, has some paralysis in her legs but is able to walk with the help of canes. She used to help her mother with the care of her brothers and sister but decided to go to Tam Kỳ for a vocational training program. Her father explains "she got tired of living at home, it was too difficult." On the days when Đồng does not need help, his son Hội travels 45 minutes each way by bicycle to the high school in the district capital. Hoi receives a scholarship from the government for his school fees. However, his school uniforms, supplies, lunches and extra classes take up a good percentage of the family's income. Travel costs to bring Kim Hương to the doctors take up another large percentage.[21]

Although Đồng and Thủy have more children with disabilities than most of the families I work with in Vietnam, their story is rather typical of the families that are believed to be affected by Agent Orange. The children have severe and/or multiple disabilities that require one caregiver, usually but not always the mother, to be home at all times. This leaves one wage-earner to meet the family's financial needs. Much of the income is utilized for medical costs and to send their other children to school or for vocational training. Many of the services they need for their children are located in the provincial capital or further away.

It is the situation of families like Đồng's that contributes toward many international and Vietnamese activists' anger at what they perceive as an insufficient humanitarian response by the US government to assist those believed to be affected by Agent Orange. However, the US government consistently states that there is not enough evidence to show whether or not the birth defects of children such as Đồng's children are related to Agent Orange and its dioxin contaminant (Marciel 2008: 19; Marciel 2009: 17; Palmer 2010: 26).

The United States to some extent is not wrong claiming that it is not possible to determine with scientific certainty who is affected by Agent Orange and who is not. Dioxin has been found to cause birth defects in animal studies in many different species including primates; however, there is disagreement about whether these studies can be extrapolated to humans (Birnbaum 2004). Therefore, one must rely on epidemiological studies to verify whether there is an association between dioxin and illnesses or abnormal birth outcomes. Most of the international epidemiological studies on dioxin have been conducted on populations that were environmentally exposed, such as US veterans, or those who were occupationally exposed, such as chemical factory workers (Institute of Medicine 2009). These studies do not mirror, however, the dioxin exposure that the Vietnamese population experienced, potentially over many years of spraying; but in the years immediately after the war, and for some, through present-day exposure at the dioxin hotspots.

Vietnamese scientists have been conducting epidemiological research on the impact of dioxin upon human health since the late 1960s. Studies of veterans who served in the south compared to those who did not have been found to have increased rates of cancer, and nerve, digestive, skin and respiratory disorders (Quang *et al.* 2007). Other than liver cancer, these are the same conditions that the US Department of Veterans Affairs (VA) has found to be associated with exposure to Agent Orange and/or dioxin and are on the list of conditions eligible for compensation (US Department of Veterans Affairs 2010). Vietnamese researchers have discovered in studies of both exposed males and females that there is an increased risk of abnormal birth outcomes, including infertility, miscarriages, still births, and birth defects, compared to those who were not exposed. Among the birth defects, spina bifida, hydrocephaly, malformations of the extremities, musculature issues, developmental disabilities, congenital heart defects and cleft-palate are found (Võ Minh Tuấn *et al.* 2002: 463). There are also higher rates of children with multiple disabilities among exposed populations. Vietnamese researchers have also come across in their research higher rates of birth defects among the grandchildren of exposed population compared to those who were not exposed. However, some western scientists may claim that these studies have not been peer reviewed or published in scientific journals and suffer from serious limitations and design flaws (Schecter and Constable 2006: 1231).

Nonetheless, the US Institute of Medicine, tasked by the US government to review all the studies on dioxin and the herbicides used in Vietnam, has found that there is "limited or suggestive evidence of an association between exposure to the herbicides and spina bifida in the offspring of exposed people" (Institute of Medicine 2009: 7). Children of US Vietnam veterans with spina bifida qualify for VA benefits. In addition, the VA provides compensation to children of female veterans who served in Vietnam if they have one of the 19 birth defects listed. However, the VA is clear to point out these birth defects may be connected to service in Vietnam and not specifically to exposure to the Agent Orange, dioxin or other herbicides used during the war.[22]

While the US Embassy in Vietnam has in the past accused the Vietnamese government of claiming that every child with a disability in Vietnam was a victim of Agent Orange, it is actually a more complex classification.[23] To be classified by the Vietnamese government as an "Agent Orange victim" in Vietnam, one must first have some connection to Agent Orange by one's own exposure, one's parent's or grandparent's exposure. In addition, there must be no other family history of the condition or some other known medical cause, such as birth injury or illness after birth. Serving or living south of the DMZ between 1961 and 1980 is sufficient evidence of potential exposure.[24]

Nonetheless, being labeled an Agent Orange victim is closer to a social classification than a scientific one. An Agent Orange victim is entitled to social benefits, for example, monthly stipends of about US$17 and occasional donations from Vietnam Association for Victims of Agent Orange/Dioxin (VAVA) or the Red Cross. However, according to VAVA and Red Cross officials who establish the list of beneficiaries, many families refuse to be classified as having an Agent Orange victim among their relatives. Although there has been an overwhelming level of solidarity for the Agent Orange victims in Vietnam, many children with disabilities still face stigma and discrimination in their communities (Lê Bạch Dương *et al.* 2007: 10). Many families do not want to take on that label of Agent Orange for fear that their DNA may be forever changed, bringing pain and suffering on future generations. They also worry that their healthy children may not find suitable mates if it becomes known that their family has been exposed to Agent Orange. Ministry of Labor, Invalids and Social Affairs (MOLISA) estimates that there are 1.2 million children with disabilities in Vietnam, while the Vietnam Red Cross estimates that 200,000 are affected by Agent Orange, so clearly the vast majority of the children with disabilities in Vietnam are not believed to be related to Agent Orange (UNICEF 2009: 11).[25]

Why Now?

Perhaps one reason why there has been such public support in Vietnam and internationally for "Agent Orange Victims" in the past few years is related to the lawsuit filed in US courts against the chemical companies on behalf of victims from Vietnam. The advocates for Agent Orange victims in Vietnam were successful in getting the Vietnamese government to provide small stipends for some former Northern Vietnamese soldiers, though civilians and veterans of the Army of the Republic of Vietnam (ARVN) who were also affected were left out. The advocates first tried a humanitarian appeal to get the American government to provide assistance to those affected by Agent Orange. After several years of little headway, some of the advocates decided that the only course of action was to file a lawsuit. They explained their decision in a "Letter to the American People."

> We, the Vietnamese people, ceaselessly thirsty for peace and friendship, have exerted great patience in demonstrating our preparedness for

cooperation with the US in solving the cruel war's consequences, especially those severe evils resulting from horrible chemical warfare. However, this has met no positive response ...

In face of this situation, the Vietnamese victims of Agent Orange feel it necessary to file a lawsuit against the US chemical corporations, the suppliers of this toxic substance used in the Vietnam War and who gained enormous profits from the sufferings of millions of people.[26]

The Vietnamese advocates first had to ensure that the lawsuit met the leadership's approval in Hanoi, many of whom were not pleased with such a direct confrontation with the United States during a sensitive time in the relationship between the two countries. By obtaining the support of one person that the Hanoi leadership could not ignore, General Võ Nguyên Giáp,[27] they received the blessing to go ahead with the lawsuit.[28]

The "David vs. Goliath battle" of Vietnamese Agent Orange victims against Dow, Monsanto, and the other producers of the dioxin-contaminated herbicides, quickly became international news. The Vietnamese press also began to write stories almost daily about Agent Orange. Many international peace activists, especially those who were active in the anti-war movement during the war in Vietnam, began to rally behind VAVA, raising their voices in solidarity with the Agent Orange victims in a call for "Justice."[29] While the suit was going on, more than 12 million Vietnamese signed a petition in support of the lawsuit (VietNamNetBridge 2008).

Many Vietnamese and many foreigners did not realize that the lawsuit was not against the US government, but the fact that the US government came out in support of the chemical companies did not help this perception (VAVA v. Dow Chemical *et al.* 2004).[30] The case was filed against the companies that supplied the toxic herbicides, alleging that the chemical companies had violated the Geneva Convention's prohibition on the use of chemicals in war. Much of the harsh rhetoric around Agent Orange and the defensiveness it provoked in the US government coincided with the progress of the lawsuit and the decision facing the US courts whether or not the herbicides were "chemical warfare." The lawsuit was dismissed by the US courts in 2005 and all subsequent appeals also failed to prove that the use of herbicides was a violation of international laws.

While the lawsuit played a major role in raising awareness about Agent Orange and its impacts on Vietnam and the Vietnamese people, it alone is not enough to explain why there still is a great deal of attention to Agent Orange victims in Vietnam. In fact, one could argue that the failure of the lawsuit has helped to increase support for those affected.

VAVA has morphed from an association representing the plaintiffs in the lawsuit to a mass organization with chapters throughout the country that conduct programs to provide services for families believed to be affected by Agent Orange. VAVA, the Vietnam Red Cross, *Tuổi Trẻ* ("*Youth*") Newspaper, and Vietnam Television all have raised millions of US dollars for Agent Orange victims. Perhaps the outpouring of donations is simply, as Trần Văn Thủy stated while introducing his film several years ago, because "we work first perhaps to ease our own conscience, work first for ourselves" and that these Agent Orange victims remind one of "how lucky I am that nothing happened to me, and that my two children are healthy" (Trần Văn Thủy 2004).

Whatever the reason, those affected by Agent Orange are now out of the shadows and showcased; they are often being portrayed by the press as "survivors," their triumphs and successes highlighted. They are slowly, although not completely, losing the moniker "victim" and are no longer simply seen as helpless individuals waiting for the courts in the United States to acknowledge their suffering and their rights for "justice."[31] In other words, bodies of some Agent Orange-affected individuals have themselves become sites of resistance and resilience.

A Breakthrough in the Stalemate

The dismissal of the lawsuit also ended much of the harsh rhetoric that many advocates and foreign and domestic media were using to define "Agent Orange." With the legal questions out of the way, what remained was a moral and humanitarian question of whether one could turn one's back on land that was so heavily contaminated and on a population so clearly in need. By removing the question of who was at "fault," it became possible for the US to contribute mitigating the impacts of Agent Orange simply for humanitarian reasons. The end of the lawsuit also coincided with a time of closer and stronger US-Vietnam relations on political, economic and security fronts. The US was now beginning to see Vietnam as a country and a powerhouse in Southeast Asia, strategically located next to China, and no longer as the war that had ended poorly and ushered in the "Vietnam syndrome."

The Hatfield research on dioxin contamination in Vietnam led not only to a greater understanding of the ongoing impacts of dioxin, but also helped lead to a breakthrough in the US-Vietnam dialogue and action on resolving this issue. Before the Hatfield studies, the Vietnamese government was hesitant to push the US government to address this issue in bi-lateral discussion, in part because of the fear that it would be perceived that the entire country, which was now becoming a major food exporter, was contaminated with dioxin. The Hatfield studies showed that dioxin contamination was limited to a few isolated areas, most of which were not agricultural lands. Tests conducted by Hatfield and other scientists also showed that the dioxin contamination of the fish and other animals was also isolated to those raised on hotspots (Schecter *et al.* 2003). At least, on the environmental contamination side, Agent Orange became a "manageable problem" (Dwernychuk 2006: 3).

One of the turning points to a more constructive dialogue on the Agent Orange issue was the joint statement made by President George W. Bush and Prime Minister Nguyễn Minh Triết in November 2006, where they agreed "that further joint efforts to address the environmental contamination near former dioxin storage sites would make a valuable contribution to the continued development of their bilateral relationship."[32] While not addressing the issue of disabilities related to Agent Orange, the statement publically acknowledged for the first time that dioxin contamination was a bilateral issue of concern to both nations. This joint statement paved the way for US Senator Patrick Leahy's office to request in the May 2007 Iraq Spending bill that $3 million be allocated for "remediation of dioxin hot spots in Vietnam and to support public health programs in the surrounding communities."[33] The US Congress has since increased these funds by nearly sevenfold from $3 million in 2009 to $20 million in 2012 (Leahy 2010: S7169).[34]

Putting the "One Significant Ghost" to Rest

Agent Orange is now described by the US Embassy in Hanoi as one of its three war-related humanitarian issues.[35] However, the United States continues to define the issue in terms of dioxin contamination at former US military bases, unlike the Vietnamese government, activists and the Vietnamese population in general who also define it in terms of dioxin's impacts on human health. When Secretary of State Hillary Clinton visited Hanoi in July 2010, she stated, "We've been working with Vietnam for about nine years to try to remedy the effects of Agent Orange. [...] I will work to increase our cooperation and make even greater progress together."[36] In a second visit to Hanoi in October 2010, Clinton clarified what this cooperation meant by announcing that the US government was committed to funding the clean-up the dioxin hotspot at the Đà Nẵng airport for a total estimated cost of $34 million (US Department of State 2010; Committee on Foreign Affairs 2010: 40). Not a word was raised about addressing the potential health impacts, though.

However, from my discussions with Vietnamese activists, those affected by Agent Orange, and ordinary Vietnamese people, it became clear that they are also looking for some acknowledgement that the Vietnamese have had their health impacted by Agent Orange, like the US Vietnam Veterans who are eligible for disability payments from the American government. This was evident in Dr. Nguyễn Thị Ngọc Phượng's testimony to the US Congress in July 2010.[37]

> The Vietnamese people, similar to the American Vietnam Veterans, are subject to all the diseases and birth defects recognized by American Veterans Administration, the Institutes of Medicine and the US Government ... More than that, in Vietnam, we have identified many additional health problems due to repeated exposure to dioxin at a greater scale and during a very long period of time. ... The US Veterans won a legislative victory for compensation for exposure to Agent Orange and received about $1.5 billion per year in benefits related to the use of this agent. ... I propose that Congress agree to provide resources for comprehensive medical services, chronic care, rehabilitation, and educational services and facilities for Agent Orange/Dioxin victims.

Dr. Phuong's testimony was followed by Ms. Trần Thị Hoan, a Vietnamese Agent Orange victim, who stated: "What do the victims need and want? We want those responsible for the terrible consequences of Agent Orange to hear our pain and then to respond as members of the human family. The chemical manufacturers and the US government who sprayed and dumped it in our country should respond to this human tragedy by doing the right thing" (Committee on Foreign Affairs 2010: 48).

The official position of the State Department on the health impact of Agent Orange in Vietnam according to the US Ambassador to ASEAN Scot Marciel is that "the United States does not recognize any legal liability for damages alleged to be related to Agent Orange. We continue to stress that the discussion of the effects of Agent Orange needs to be based on credible scientific research that meets international standards" (Marciel 2008: 10). The contrasting attitudes of one branch of the US government, the VA, providing monthly benefits totaling nearly $2 billion per year for more than 300,000 American veterans due to their exposure to Agent Orange, with another branch of the US government, the State Department, telling the Vietnamese that there is no causality between Agent Orange and illnesses and disabilities in Vietnam is not lost on the Vietnamese advocates.[38]

The US official position regarding humanitarian assistance is to "provide assistance to people with disabilities without asking for evidence of cause or origin of the disability" (Committee on Foreign Affairs 2010: 27). It is in essence the only policy that the US government can follow, as pitting one disabled person's needs against another's is not ethically or morally acceptable. However, it is hard to determine how much of the $49 million given by the United States for disabilities programs in Vietnam since 1996 has actually reached the population of people with disabilities that the Vietnamese believe are affected by Agent Orange. The target of most of US humanitarian aid for disabilities to date has been those whose conditions are not believed to be associated with dioxin exposure but by landmines/unexploded ordnance, and those with minor or moderate disabilities who are able to attend school or participate in job training programs.[39] They are all worthy recipients of humanitarian aid, but for the most part they are not those who are believed to be affected by Agent Orange and they are not those with severe, multiple and complex disabilities that the Vietnamese people and international activists are calling on the US government to assist.

Conclusion

It has been 50 years since the first spray plane dropped their load of herbicides over southern Vietnam. The violent past of the US' devastating air campaign manifests itself in various materializations today: ecologically degraded landscapes, toxic inhabited lands and, cruellest of all, people's bodies deformed through contamination with Agent Orange. One of the reasons why Agent Orange has captured the attention of so many in Vietnam and abroad may lie in the "victim," who is overwhelming perceived as an innocent person, someone who was born long after the war, whose birth was anticipated with such joy as any child is anticipated around the world, and future may be so bright in postwar Vietnam. But instead of thoughts of hope for the future, this child, believed to be affected by Agent Orange, brings back the dark past and is a daily remainder not only to the parents but to the neighbors and the nation of the pain and suffering, of the insecurity and the hopelessness of the decades of war. Almost four decades after the end of the conflict, through a belated and painful recognition, Agent Orange-infected people have become themselves terrible *lieux de mémoire* for the American-Vietnam War, eliciting and embodying at the same time memories and images of inhuman violence. But perhaps their physical presence also functions as a necessary vehicle that forces Americans and Vietnamese alike to work through the unresolved issues of the Vietnam War that will enable us to finally put the war behind us and truly "normalize relations."

Nonetheless, much more needs to be done. For decades, the "Agent Orange" issue came between the United States and Vietnam as neither country understood what the issue meant to the other. At first, Agent Orange hindered the ability of the two countries to develop trust but over the past several years, Agent Orange is slowly becoming an "irritant." However, it is now an irritant that, with continued cooperation, can be eliminated. The US commitment to cleaning up Đà Nẵng will eliminate one of these hotpots but that leaves one more significant hotspot and up to 25 others whose level of contamination has not yet been identified. The more complicated issue is how to address the human health impacts which will take huge resources that need to be allocated by the Vietnamese government to develop the medical, educational and social welfare infrastructure that takes into account the specific needs of people with disabilities in general and those believed to be affected by Agent Orange in particular. This effort will also require international donors, in particular from the US government who cannot escape its history with Vietnam, of which legacies, among others, have resulted in the ongoing problems of Agent Orange and dioxin. However, until the US expands its humanitarian assistance to Vietnam to encompass more of the population that is classified by the Vietnamese as an Agent Orange victim, this "last significant ghost" will not be put to rest. Agent Orange will continue to have an impact on the people on both sides of the Pacific for generations to come.

Notes

1.   There are no accurate numbers of the number of Agent Orange victims. However, the Vietnam Red Cross, using data from a Ministry of Labor, Invalids and Social Affairs survey, estimated that there were up to three million Vietnamese suffering from the effects of Agent Orange and at least 150,000 are children with disabilities associated with their parents' or grandparents' exposure. Hence, this is the number often quoted by the Red Cross, the Vietnam Association of Victims of Agent Orange, Vietnamese government officials, the media and activists, but there is no reliable source for this estimate at this time. See http://www.agentorangerecord.com/impact_on_vietnam/health/ [accessed 23 June 2012].

2.   The definition of an "Agent Orange victim" will be explained later in the chapter. In brief, "Agent Orange victims" refers to those who have an illness or disabilities believed to be associated with exposure to Agent Orange and/or dioxin. It is not a scientifically valid classification.

3.   *Associated Press* (AP), 3 Mar. 2002.

4.   Interview with US Public Affairs Officer, US Embassy, Hanoi, 19 Apr. 2005.

5.   *HDNet* — World Report, 2010, Video. Minute 40:18–40:26.

6.   US Embassy Unclassified Memo, Hanoi, 16 Feb. 2003.

7.   In a 1 Feb. 1973 letter to the then Prime Minister of the Democratic Republic of Vietnam, Phạm Văn Đồng, President Nixon indicated that the US would provide approximately $3.25 billion in grant aid for postwar reconstruction in Vietnam as part of Article 21 of the *Agreement on Ending the War and Restoring Peace in Vietnam* signed in Paris on 27 Jan. 1973 (US Department of State 1977). Article 21 states: "In pursuance of its traditional policy, the United States will contribute to healing the wounds of war and to postwar reconstruction of the Democratic Republic of Vietnam and throughout Indo-china" (US Department of State Bulletin 1973). This promise of "reparations" was frequently raised by the Vietnamese government during the postwar attempts to normalize relations. However, the US position was that because the 1973 Peace Accords failed, the "promise" had no legitimacy (Martini 2007: 28–30). The Vietnamese government dropped their demand for repara-tions during negotiations for normalization of relations under the Carter and later the Bush and Clinton administrations, and reparations became offi-cially off the table when US and Vietnam normalized their relations in 1995. Nonetheless, this promise of reparations in the Nixon letter is raised today by some of the international advocates calling for justice for victims of Agent Orange.

8.   Interview with Nguyễn Thị Ngọc Toàn, 24 Apr. 2011, Hanoi, Vietnam.

9.   This figure does not include those Vietnamese soldiers from both sides of the war who traveled through the sprayed regions during the war and those who were exposed on US military bases.

10.   A footnote in Lê Cao Đài's memoir notes that it is likely that Dai actually saw a C-123, not a C-130. The C-130 was a transport plane that looked very similar to a C-123. However, the C-123s were the planes used for spraying herbicides (Lê Cao Đài 2004: 150).

11.   Agent Orange Litigation (2006: 61–6). The amount of TCDD in the 2,4,5-T used in Vietnam ranged from less than 0.05 ppm to just less than 50 ppm (Zinke 1974: S-11).

12.   MACV (Military Assistance Command Vietnam). Translation of pamphlet panel to the left: Panel 5: "Because of the propaganda activities of the Việt Cộng, Mr. Nam also worried about the herbicides that the government was using. Mr. Nam: 'Hey! Friend, are these sprays harmful to people, our

animals, the soil or our drinking water?' Man Spraying: 'How are you Nam? The only effect of the spray is to wilt the trees and make their leaves fall off. It causes absolutely no harm to humans, or to animals, the soil or drinking water. Look at me; you can see how healthy I am. Every day, while performing my duties, I'll usually breathe in a lot of the spray. Look at me, do I appear sick to you?'"

13. Hatfield 1998 Introduction, paragraph 4, Section 4, p. 1.

14. Hatfield 1998 Introduction, paragraph 5, Section 4, p. 1.

15. Interviews with residents, A Lưới District, Đông Sơn Commune, 9 Oct. 2008.

16. Hatfield Consultants base in West Vancouver Canada is an environmental firm that measures and monitors contamination from persistent organic pollutants in the environment. Since 1994, they have been working in Vietnam to identify the level of residual dioxin and other contaminants at former US military bases as well as helping the Vietnamese to develop mitigation measures to prevent further exposure to the local population.

17. Hatfield (2000), Table 2.3. Typical background level of TCDD in the soil of industrialized nations is less than 10 pg/g. 1 pg/g is equal to 1 ppt.

18. Interview with residents, A Lưới District, Đông Sơn Commune, 18 Apr. 2011.

19. The National Steering Committee 33 under the Ministry of Natural Resources and the Environment is tasked to provide expert advice to the Vietnamese government on the activities related to overcoming the consequences of the herbicides and other chemicals used by the US military during the Vietnam War.

20. Recent films include: *Last Ghost of War* (Gardner 2008); *Agent Orange: Thirty Years Later* (Trinh 2009); and *Agent Orange: A Personal Requiem* (Sakata 2007). Documentary photography include: Philip Jones Griffiths (Griffiths 2003); Goro Nakamura (Nakamura 2001); James Nachtwey (Nachtwe 2006). News articles include: "Unfinished Business: Suffering and Sickness in the Wake of Agent Orange," *Cleveland Plain Dealer Series* (Shultz 2010); "Agent Orange: A Lethal Legacy," *Chicago Tribune* (Grotto and Jones 2009). Books include: *The Invention of Ecocide: Agent Orange, Vietnam, and the Scientists Who Changed the Way We Look at the Environment* (Zierler 2011) and *Agent Orange: History, Science, and the Politices of Uncertainty* (Martini 2012).

21. Interview with residents, Tiên Phước District, 24 Apr. 2011.

22. US Department of Veterans Affairs 2010. Other conditions may also be eligible for compensation if the veteran can prove that there was no family disorder, birth injury, or conditions with well-established causes.

23. *AP*, 1 July 2010.

24. The Vietnamese government does not have criteria to identify Agent Orange victims; however, according to conversations with VAVA and the Vietnam Red

Cross, these are the criteria used to add an individual to their respective lists of those eligible for assistance due to Agent Orange. Formal criteria for identifying Agent Orange victims is being developed by Committee 33 with input from the Ministries of Labor, Invalids and Social Affair and Health, VAVA and the Vietnam Veterans Association.

25. According to one of their brochures, the Vietnam Red Cross estimates that at least 200,000 children have disabilities believed to be associated with Agent Orange (Vietnam Red Cross, unknown date). However, they have also given this number as 150,000 so it is unclear how many children are considered Agent Orange victims. These estimates are expected to change as more surveys are done to identify "Agent Orange victims" using official criteria for classification.

26. Vietnam Association for Victims of Agent Orange (VAVA) 2004. Available at: http://www.ffrd.org/Lawsuit/VAVAletter.htm.

27. General Võ Nguyễn Giáp is considered the chief architect of the successful defeat of the French army, and therefore, a national hero. While long retired, Giap still has considerable influence within the ruling elite in Vietnam. However, his influence might be more symbolic than real.

28. Interview with Nguyễn Ngọc Toàn, 24 Apr. 2011, Hanoi, Vietnam.

29. Two international organizations supporting VAVA in their call for "justice" were the Britain — Vietnam Friendship Society that began an online petition calling for "Justice for Victims of Agent Orange" and the Vietnam Agent Orange Relief & Responsibility Campaign, a project of the US-based Veterans for Peace whose motto is "Justice for all Agent Orange Victims."

30. VAVA v. Dow Chemical *et al.* (2004). Due to sovereign immunity, one cannot sue the US government unless it agrees to be sued.

31. "AO Victim Tutors Children of Poor," *Vietnam News Service*, 17 May 2011; "Positive Attitude Vital in Life Without Arms Takes," *Vietnam News*, 18 Nov. 2010.

32. White House of President George W. Bush (2006).

33. US Senate Report 110-037. 22 Mar. 2007. Available at http://thomas.loc.gov/cgi-bin/cpquery/T?&report=sr037&dbname=110&. [accessed 5 Nov. 2012].

34. Department of State, Foreign Operations and Related programs Appropriations Bill 2011: 55. Note: an additional $3 million was appropriated for health activities for dioxin impacted communities as per personal correspondence between Senator Leahy's staff and Susan Hammond; Department of State, Foreign Operations and Related Programs Appropriations Bill Committee Report: 47.

35. As described by Ambassador Michael Michalak at a Jan. 2010 visit to the embassy in Hanoi. The other two issues are accounting for the Missing in Action and unexploded ordnance.

36. *AFP*, 26 July 2010.

37. Dr. Phuong has been researching the impact of dioxin on reproductive health in Vietnam for many decades at the Tu Du Maternity hospital in Ho Chi Minh City.

38. *Al Jazeera English*, 10 Sept. 2009, Minutes 6:10–12:20; *Voice of Vietnam News*, 5 May 2011.

39. There is no breakdown of where the funding from the US for disabilities has been allocated. Early on, the US funds were mostly for mobility-related needs of landmine and war victims; more recently funds have been used to support disability rights, inclusive education and job training programs (Management Systems International 2005).

CHAPTER 8

Aesthetic Forms of Post-Conflict Memory: Inspired Vessels of Memory in Northeast Cambodia

Krisna Uk

Introduction

In many highlander villages in northeast Cambodia, which have once been the theater of violent conflicts, villagers living in the northeast fringes of Cambodia have adjusted to the impacts of 30 years of conflicts that have destroyed their man-made and natural environment.[1] Indeed older and younger generations alike continue to find new "meanings" in the traumatic events, which featured the Americans' intense bombardment of the region from the mid-1960s to 1973 and the brutal Khmer Rouge regime in Cambodia from 1975 to 1979.[2] The aftermath of war often calls for processes of healing and memory. The work of remembrance and healing is left to the survivors who seek to maintain the continuity of life despite the discontinuity brought by the violence of the past.[3] Such traces of the past can be found in local aesthetic practices, which simultaneously crystallize, communicate and transmit individual and collective memory in tangible forms.

The objective of this chapter is less to add to the vast existing literature on memory established by Maurice Halbwachs, Paul Connerton, Maurice Bloch, and Paul Ricoeur, amongst others, than to look at alternative vessels of memory produced through the arts of sculpting, painting and weaving. Particular attention will be paid to the role of the craftsman from the old and youngest generations as a conscious, dedicated and skilful individual who does not simply create, but creates in a beautiful manner.[4] In reproducing work and seeking inspiration from earlier times, the technique of the craftsman becomes the means whereby memories of the past, perceptions of the present, and predictions of the future are given aesthetic and material form.[5]

The following ethnographic examples concern two Jorai villages and a Tampuon village where local craftsmanship reproduces objects which remain deeply imbued with the history of warfare in the region.[6] The purpose is to reflect on the ways the war-torn landscape — or its symbolic association with the destructive power of high technology warfare specifically — becomes a source of inspiration that culminates in object design. It thereby also seeks to examine how through this very process the craftsman and his recipients can treat the past as a project that is continually revisited.[7]

Barbara Mills argued that the term "memory-work" refers to the "many social practices that create memories, including recalling, reshaping, forgetting, inventing, coordinating, and transmitting."[8] By using his skills, emotions and experience (or lack thereof), the craftsman can attribute new meanings and functions to the inherited past as will be shown by the woodcarver who encapsulates personal and collective war memories in a plane replica, by the funerary painter who writes the past and foretells the future of the dead on a funerary monument, and by the fabric-weaver who manipulates threads of personal and vicarious experiences.

All the sites to which I had traveled were formerly a part of what the Americans called the "Ho Chi Minh Trail" — a complex and organic transportation corridor of immense military and political significance. Therefore the cases profiled feature the production of what has been termed "trench art," which can be defined as: "any item made by soldiers, prisoners of war and civilians, from war matériel directly, or any other material, as long as it and they are associated temporally and/or spatially with armed conflict or its consequences."[9] Although such memory-objects described in this chapter originate neither from parts nor from whole physical remnants of war, they can still be considered a meaningful manifestation of trench art. While all of them recall Aristotle's wax tablets in the way that they bear the visual prints of warfare episodes that have marked the lives of the inhabitants of this area, their intrinsic resonance also unveils how villagers respond to whispers from the past, voices of the present and echoes of the future simultaneously.

Leu Village: Sculpting and Carving Funeral Effigies

The village of Leu is home to some 300 souls, comprising 27 families of
the Jorai ethnic minority and three families of Khmers — the dominant
ethnic group in Cambodia. An Austronesian ethnic minority linguistically
akin to the Malays and the Chams, the Jorai of Leu speak a Chamic language which belongs to the Malayo-Polynesian language family.[10] The
Jorai villagers of Leu organize their social structures along matrilineal
lines and attach strong importance to kin and affine-based relationships.[11]
The livelihood of the Jorai inhabitants of Leu is based throughout the year
on a range of subsistence procurement activities. These include slash-and-
burn clearance to allow the cultivation of vegetable plots and orchards
(*hwa*), wet rice cultivation, hunting, fishing and the collection of non-
timber forest products. A few people find seasonal employment in plantations or large farms and occasionally participate in house-building in return
for a wage. James Scott and Jean Michaud argue that this kind of range of
livelihood activities is a key characteristic of acephalous societies, whereby
their relative autonomy enables them to remain beyond the state control.[12]

The Mnemonic Functions of Sculpting

Funerary statuary in the Jorai village of Leu encompasses a wide range
of old and relatively new forms of traditional sculptures, which include
animal and human effigies as well as war-related items. Village effigies
that belong to the pantheon of funerary sculptures such as the mourner
(a crouching male with his chin resting on the palms of his hands), the
peacock (the legendary surrogate mother of the Jorai and a symbol of
beauty), the elephant (an animal associated with power and prestige), and
the monkey (a popular dweller of the forest) now stand, however, alongside war-inspired carvings like the helicopter and bombing plane. In the
case of grave decorations, planes appear in both sculpted and drawn forms
and can be regarded as fulfilling aesthetic and symbolic functions. According to Siu, a talented woodcarver, the plane is a *damnang*, a substitute
(in Khmer) for the traditional mourner who looks after the dead until their
souls travel to the next world.

In the village of Leu, the association between the plane and the US
bombardment that devastated the region more than 30 years ago remains
strong, particularly amongst the adult segment of the population. In his
study of man-made objects derived and inspired by conflicts, Nicholas
Saunders noted that the Vietnam War generated a plethora of "Trench Art"
such as models of warfare equipments manufactured from war debris by

soldiers for whom the American Huey helicopter gunship became "the definitive icon of technological war during the conflict."[13] Furthermore, the fact that commercial air travel remains outside the experience of most Jorai people living in the district of Andong Meas and beyond maintains the innate relationship between planes, bombing, and death for which the plane itself has ultimately become the sign (what announces death) and the symbol (the conception of death, not death itself).

Indeed, for the older generation, a carved plane is also invested with personal experiential significance. Some of my informants view the presence of a sculpted plane on top of a particular grave as a way to remember the deceased as a former soldier or "a person who was very quick and efficient in gathering food and weapons." In the same way as the funerary sculpture of a man holding a machine gun identifies a former soldier, the plane effigy — beyond its aesthetic and symbolic role — acts as a semiotic device that often tells the past history of the dead.

Following the US bombardment from the end of the 1960s to the mid-1970s and the United Nations Transitional Authority in Cambodia (UNTAC) intervention to support Cambodia's reconstruction in 1992 (where military aircraft dominated Cambodia's skyscapes this time in the form of UN planes and helicopters), Leu villagers were keen on creating replicas of the planes they had seen for display in both their cemetery and their village. In the latter case, on the occasion of the buffalo sacrifice to propitiate spirits, the plane effigies featuring at the top of the sacrifice pole convey a particular memory of past perceptions and behavior;[14] according to a village elder: "The planes remind people about their foolishness ... now we laugh at the thought that we were once so scared of them and that we were all running to hide ... [the sculptures] tell our children about our experience of the past." However, most people who have survived the conflicts believe that because of its intrinsic power (*peutrang*), the plane can preside at the death of the animal while warding off evil spirits at the same time. As another village elder comments, "This is a bombing plane, the same as the ones that came to wage war on us! It is powerful, beautiful and it inspires fear!" An epitome of beauty and power, the plane has, since the aftermath of the wars, supplanted traditional icons like the ibis bird or the Jorai drinking at the rice wine jar.

Most village elders and middle-aged persons I worked with do not feel any sense of recrimination toward the Americans. Some feel they had no or very little power over the course of the conflicts, and that as time passes, any resentment has become irrelevant. Despite seeing the US bombardment as being particular harrowing, some village elders nonetheless say that they now view their past belief in the planes being "flying gods" as a rare comic element amidst otherwise traumatic memories of this long period of protracted conflicts.[15]

According to Paul Ricoeur, forgetting and forgiving are two crucial and interdependent components of the ethics of memory.[16] For the villagers living in Leu though, the presence of a sculpted plane during rituals often acts as a mirror, which triggers collective remembering as well as the contemplation of the self in the past. For the village elders, remembering and laughing at one's past mistake can also lead to forgiveness. In this particular context, the process of forgiving oneself and others relies more on the act of remembering than forgetting. For the same village elders, the fear that they felt when first seeing the bombing planes today makes way for an appreciation of the fascination that this same image inspires amongst the youngest inhabitants of the village. As one of them put it: "when the animal is killed at the foot of the sacrifice pole, the plane at its top shakes and moves to the great delight of the children." Each time a plane features in a village ritual, the flying sculpture comes to life, engendering a range of wide-ranging emotions amongst its inhabitants.

Most of the village's youngest inhabitants have never seen a real plane before while some I worked with told me that they have not seen a plane since the UNTAC period ended more than 15 years ago. This does not prevent them from carving, drawing or imagining planes, however. On the occasion of the funeral of a village elder, a cow and a buffalo were offered to the spirits at the sacrifice post which was decorated with a sculpted plane. For Wai who is 27 years old and a member of the post-conflict generation, the plane "[...] is something the sculptor has imagined. We imagine from what other people — old people — have told us. I don't know why we do that, but as far as I can remember I have always seen this. The plane is there because it looks like it is where it needs to be ... It has landed for the funeral!" In fact Wai's comment underlines the fact that the capacity to reproduce an object does not need to be sanctioned by empirical experience (seeing the object) but can be inspired by stories of village elders, local wooden sculptures as well as television, newspapers, toys, printed T-shirts and other sources of visual stimulation. For his maker who is 14 years old and who got inspired through such visual channels, the plane he created is simply "beautiful."

Carving a Better Plane

Siu, 35 years old, whose father taught him the secrets of wood carving, is regarded by his fellow villagers as one of the most skilful craftsmen in the area. Whether he is producing wood sculptures, handles for knives, or house parts, Siu is perceived to have a special connection with his material, which seems naturally to flow through the deft movements of his sculpting knives. Having spent several months working with him, my hours of observation led me to conclude that his ability equally to tame wood, bamboo and water reeds so as to coincide exactly with the shape of his imagined object is not only stimulated by his apparent passion to make but the passion to make beautifully. In many instances, this craftsman re-fashions objects started by others, drawing on his aptitude for turning the object into *the* object they had in mind.

Siu occasionally sculpts objects for people living outside the village. In the past, he and his relatives have sculpted men, women and animal effigies (elephants and monkeys) for the decoration of a hotel in Banlung, the provincial capital of Ratanakiri. For a full day or two of work, Siu is paid in cash. In December 2007, Siu completed the wooden effigy of a helicopter that I commissioned for the Cambridge Museum of Archeology and Anthropology. Because it had three propellers, a Khmer visitor commented that this effigy could not be the true representation of a real aircraft. Unperturbed, Siu replied with undisguised pride: "This plane is awesome, powerful, more so than the ones that flew here before." One of the most interesting issues raised by this comment is Siu's inference that there is more to sculpting that the mere illustrative reproduction of an object. In the eyes of the external beholder, the plane was not and could not possibly be real, given the incongruity in its engineering. For Siu, conversely, the plane was even more real because it illustrated perfectly his idea of what a plane should be.

When considering the sculpting of a plane, one can infer that the material used (wood) is a tactile medium that can shape the very idea of the plane. From this perspective, which emphasizes the relationship between the maker and the object, the actual material that is shaped is less the tangible, palpable and possibly destructible log than the virtual material (or *matière*) in which the idea of the plane itself is made. Borrowing Dorine Kondo's expression, the attentive sculpting of the effigy thus demonstrates how "crafting fine objects" can become synonymous with "crafting a better idea of the objects."[17]

Indeed, crafting the plane allows the individual to reconstruct the idea of a plane (what a plane should be, not what it was in the past or what it is today), thus gaining control over the object and its inherent powers. By harnessing such powers through craftsmanship, the woodcarver can attribute new meanings to the object. Encoded with renewed ideas and values, the plane can eventually be invested with a guardianship duty so as to care for the living and the dead or simply remain a symbol of power and beauty. All of this poses the interesting question of whether carving and adapting such images might be a means of taming the dangerous object so as to shift the status of the carver from one of victim (Siu's father died during the protracted conflicts) to that of master and controller.

Whether war-associated sculptures function as guardians or vessels of power, their local use is often a matter of doing or redoing, which according to Alfred Gell fits into this system of actions intended to change the world rather than being a mere representation of its phenomenological perception.[18] In furthering Gell's "action-centred approach to art," however, the appropriation, manipulation and display of the formidable objects are all forms of praxis that not only produce "meaning" but can also become meaningful actions as they are being performed by the artisan himself, who may find in sculpting a way to heal some of his war traumas (for instance, the anxiety caused by the bombing plane). In this sense, the crafting of warfare objects is also a creative psychological process that enables its maker to harness their intrinsic power for positive purposes, thus turning them into signs of life. The following vignette explores this idea further.

Peuho Village: Painting Individual and Collective Memories

Peuho is a Jorai village located southeast of Leu in the neighboring district of O You Dav. It is only a few miles from the Vietnamese border. Its inhabitants live a life of subsistence activities, notably farming and collecting bomb debris for sale across the border. A village elder told me that since the bombing event, people in Peuho and other Jorai villages along the border have been singing songs that narrate the history of the bombardment. Most of these songs are revived in the first few months of the year when the work in the *hwa* (fruit and vegetable orchard) is very limited and when various celebrations and rituals to the *yang* (spirits) take place. As an alternative to songs, the village funerary rituals offer, like in Leu, a rich system of inscription that gives another insight into the local hermeneutics of memories.

The Funerary Monument: A Distinctive "Lieu de Mémoire"

In the village cemetery, one cannot fail to notice a *posat atâo*, a tall funerary monument, with a roof shaped like a saddle, which although almost completely covered by the vegetation, still reveals colorful images illustrating everyday life underneath a large flying plane.[19] In the immediate aftermath of the death, the inhabitants of Peuho keep watch over the deceased for a few days and make a series of sacrifices involving buffaloes, pigs and chicken.

Keulagn Beuragn is the 70-year-old painter who decorated the *posat atâo*, following the death of a young boy a few years ago. He explains that nobody has ever taught him how to paint, as "one needs to see and naturally know how to do it." More than a skill that can be passed on through the generations, Beuragn regards his aptitude for painting as a gift from the *yang* (spirits). In his view, the craftsman who is dedicated to his work is an initiate who has been chosen by the spirits to fulfil specific duties. As a result, trying to teach someone how to paint would be *kanm* (taboo). In lieu of payment, the funerary painter receives a gift in exchange for his artistic work. Just as he sees his skill being a gift donated by the *yang*, his painting for other villagers is in turn considered a gift to them.

The making of the *posat atâo* marks the second burial of the dead. The *posat atâo* is a four-meter-high edifice with four sides; the largest sides being the ones on the front and on the back.[20] It takes two to three days to fully decorate it. During this time, the act of painting is guided by a series of taboos which isolate the individual in a variety of ways. As Beuragn explains, in the course of this decorating period, the painter is not allowed to return to the village as he is considered polluted by his proximity with death. He is thus compelled to live temporarily outside the village boundaries in a small hut where he sleeps and eats until the end of his work. This physical exclusion seems to reflect the fact that the painter is socially considered "dead." Only with the completion of what Beuragn describes as a "risky" work can he re-integrate with the social collectivity of the village.[21]

A further taboo is associated with naming the person who did the painting: "If some villagers returned from a day's work in the field, saw the decoration and asked who created it, it is *kanm* (taboo) to say the name of the person who painted it." For Beuragn, naming before the completion of the work can place the painter in a hazardous situation whereby he can be directly affected by the death (by becoming ill). In other words, preserving the anonymity of the painter is a way to guarantee his safety so that the potential evil *yang* would find it difficult to identify him and harm him. An additional proscription relates to the maturity of the painter who needs to be at least 60 years of age. According to Beuragn, it is traditionally taboo for anyone under 60 to try to decorate a *posat atâo*; children especially, since they are considered more vulnerable to the malevolent spirits. However, as will be shown later, taboos associated with painting the *posat atâo* have been frequently infringed.

Partly because of the costs and labor entailed, most people in Peuho believe that it is not necessary to build a *posat atâo* for a child. Indeed, villagers tend to ornament the grave of a child only at the point when the deceased would have reached the age of 15 and thus attained adulthood. As a villager commented: "in the past people used to build these funerary monuments all the time ... they were richly decorated with images of women winnowing, people using mortar and pestle ... but today fewer and fewer people can afford them." Yet in the above case where the bereaved family was relatively affluent and very fond of their child, the head of the household decided to build a *posat atâo* on top of his ten-year-old son's grave and asked Beuragn to decorate it. The latter explained that in this case, a child's grave should look identical to an adult's. In the words of the painter, the most important consideration is that "it needs to be as beautiful as a temple" so that the dead will like his new home.

Beuragn's typical *posat atâo* decoration combines motifs of flowers, items of everyday life, warfare objects and celestial beings. One fine example is shown in Plate 8.1. Beuragn comments that he always imagines the motifs that he wants to create first (his favorite motif being the stars) and draws them using a succession of horizontal rows. There is no specific order in terms of which motif should come first and the *posat atâo* painter is quite free to decorate it following his own designs and choice of colors.[22] The drawing takes a day to produce and shows the following:

On the top corners of the edifice are what the painter describes as "flowers with heavenly hands."
Rows 1 and 2: flowers (or Row 2 can also feature elephant trunks)
Row 3: hand grenades
Row 4: orchids growing on trees
Row 5: lighter sheaths (for a lighter composed of two stones to rub against one another)
Row 6: Water gourds
Row 7: Two fighting snakes, with one about to eat the other
At the bottom: A bombing plane over a house

This example of a *posat atâo* decoration shows an interesting mixture of flowers and objects. For the painter, the act of painting and knowing which images should come first, and in which color they should be depicted, is a spontaneous process. An important factor, though, is the relative

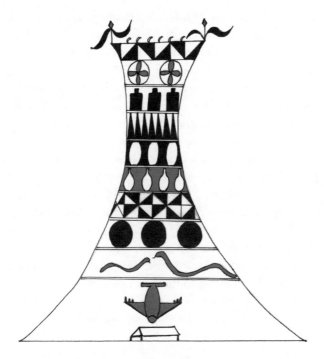

Plate 8.1 Reproduction of the artist's drawing of a *posat atâo*.

symmetry with which the objects are placed. In this example, the shapes in the row of hand grenades are reminiscent of the row of water gourds; similarly, the two flowers "with heavenly hands" at the top visually echo the fighting snakes. Flowers are recurrent and particularly praised *posat atâo* funerary motifs, while the man-made objects depicted include not only water gourds and lighter sheaths but also hand grenades. An intriguing feature is the last row depicting two snakes fighting each other, which in the words of the artist show the largest "about to eat the other." For the painter, the snakes act as a beautiful allegory of the war in which "one has to become the winner." In a sense, this bottom row announces the warfare theme, which as he commented, often fills in the entire bottom space.

The last image on the large panel at the base of the monument thus features a warfare scene, which depicts a bombing plane about to destroy a house. Beuragn does not clearly remember when he started to draw war-associated objects but he acknowledges that since the protracted conflicts in the region, grave decorators have progressively incorporated images of war that they remember. While drawing and coloring the plane at the bottom part of the virtual *posat atâo*, Beuragn recalls that bombings in the area started from 6–7.00 am and lasted until 4.00 pm. Each plane that flew over the village used to drop four bombs. Beuragn clarifies, however, that: "if the cause of death is natural then the *posat atâo* will not be decorated with much warfare imagery." Conversely if someone has died from the war or as a result of some other form of violence, the edifice will feature a lot of planes, knives, grenades and assault rifles because "it is for other people to know the cause of death."

In the case of the boy's grave described above, Beuragn recalls having painted both ordinary and warfare-related objects. As the boy died from a long illness following the UNTAC military presence in the northeast, the edifice was subsequently decorated with a few weapons mixed together with images of everyday life. The painter also claimed that the objects that are depicted are "not for the dead to take along into the afterlife" (like proffered objects placed on an ordinary Jorai grave would be) but only visual enhancements to turn the *posat atâo* into a beautiful edifice. For Beuragn, war-inspired themes like hand grenades or flying bombing planes have now become established aesthetic motifs.

If a pregnant villager who died during childbirth is often represented by a woman with a large womb, and a man carrying an assault rifle on his shoulder commonly identifies a soldier who died in combat, roof drawings can illustrate the former life of the dead in a similar manner. A lot of funerary sculptures and illustrations may also be used for their symbolic value, however, in the sense that images of weaponry will enable the dead to be well-protected, strong, brave and respected in his next life. Like bringing personal objects to the grave, sculpting, drawing and painting contribute in some way in the making or invention of someone's future identity. These good wishes for the dead either translate into three-dimensional representations such as sculptures, or two-dimensional drawings and paintings on traditional funerary monuments such as the *posat atâo* which enables the family to foretell a successful life in order to lead the dead toward a more fulfilling existence.

For the painter, narrating the past — whether it is someone's existence or excerpts of the village history — is entangled with narrating the present. In fact, objects that were commonly used during previous times of peace and conflicts (the old lighter and sheath or the hand grenade) have found their own space amongst objects of the present. Beyond transcending times, these warfare objects also stand amidst objects of peace to the extent that for the external observer, they have somehow lost their hostile

Plate 8.2　Example of a
posat atâo, O'Kop village,
Andong Meas District.

properties. As the row of hand grenades resembles the row of water gourds
in both shape and color, the painter seems to have captivated — or rendered more visible — an artistic dimension of the war-associated object.

The Collective Functions of the Posat Atâo

The large panel at the base is a distinctive space which enables the family
to tell the past story of the dead or an imaginary story of his future existence, which may become true in the afterlife. In this sense, war-associated
ornaments on a ten-year-old boy's grave, for example, do not necessarily
mean that the child was a soldier or had any connection with the war. It
only means that his parents hope that in the next world, the child will live
a longer and happier life by being strong, valiant and respected; qualities
which are suggested by the manipulation of symbols of warfare.[23]

When working in the village cemetery, therefore Beuragn often leaves
this particular space provisionally empty so that the bereaved family can

decide which motifs they want, although he says that he is often free to illustrate the entire *posat atâo* following his own inspiration. He comments, however, that these days not very many people want to have many planes and bombs since they prefer images that convey a sense of natural peace, especially if the deceased person has suffered for a long time before passing away. According to Beuragn, some people believe that commissioning an impression of beauty and peace is a way to conjure a future existence that may be free of violence. Indeed, even if telling an imaginary story for the dead is a well-established practice in most local Jorai and other ethnic minority cemeteries, the introduction of war-related effigies as characters, symbols or mere aesthetic illustrations can remain subject to taboos, since their fundamental association with death may be perceived as insuperable.[24] Painting the impression of tranquility on the wooden structure of the *posat atâo* is therefore comparable to writing the future of the dead soul. In this case, the painter acts as a scribe who not only records the memory of the past but also tells the memory of the future.

As the sound of his voice seems to indicate that some images are uninspiring, Beuragn admits that he never paints people celebrating and drinking at a rice wine jar. In cases in which the bereaved family places an order for this particular illustration, they will then need to ask someone else to complement Beuragn's work, and who is well able to paint a specific impression beautifully. In a sense, the collective agency fulfills the taboo mentioned earlier of not naming the painter as a result of the multiplicity of the participants. Death being a total social event, the painting of the *posat atâo* can also constitute a social endeavor in itself as it may involve several villagers to complete. When characterized by collective participation, the *posat atâo* thus illustrates Alfred Gell's remark that "decorative patterns attached to artefacts attach people to things, and to the social projects those things entail."[25]

Whether inspired from the family's wishes or sourced from the painter's own imagination (or both), the result is often an impressively rich piece of work based on a colorful "bricolage" of images, patterns, scriptures and geometrical forms.[26] Such a collective undertaking often highlights individual roles and duties and their good wishes for the dead. Acting as a space of creative painting and writings, the funerary monument becomes the site for other painters' investments where individual and collective thoughts, memories, and wishes are intrinsically bound together. In a sense, the experience serves to strengthen the community as a whole, hence contrasting with the previous image of the painter who is physically isolated.[27] Functioning as a large *loci memoriae* or *lieu de mémoire* to borrow Pierre Nora's expression, the *posat atâo* thus offers personal and collective visions of the past, the present, and the future simultaneously.[28]

The diversity of the ethnic groups living in the province of Ratanakiri opens up a multitude of lines of enquiry, as the notion of ethnicity is intimately connected to the sense of belonging and identity. However, in a place where provincial and international borders are being constantly renegotiated, spatial mobility and habits play a significant role in repositioning oneself vis-à-vis the "other." Inter-ethnic influences, I have been told, are most frequent when Jorai villages are located near Tampuon ones, thus giving birth to sources of inspiration that may affect customary laws, death rituals and aesthetic forms of memories.[29] Such rapprochement is made especially visible in the domain of the arts whereby geographical proximity, interrelations and reciprocal influences have to some extent united them. Siu, the woodcarver of Leu village, told me that the Tampuon also have a funerary tradition to erect a *posat atâo* on the grave of their dead. He commented that the Tampuon *posat atâo* are traditionally covered with a large piece of fabric that would be richly decorated with painted images, and are hence more beautiful than the Jorai ones. As he puts it: "[the Jorai and Tampuon] are the same, we live next to each other, we copy them and they copy us."

Having examined the Jorai use of war-related iconography in the crafting and decoration of funerary objects, the following examines the role of the tourism market in influencing the memory-landscape of a Tampuon village in the outskirts of the provincial capital.[30] This example will serve to show how the manufacture of local memory can become an exclusive income-generating activity as memory-makers provide for both memory-consumers in search of war memorabilia, as well as for themselves.

Laom Village: Weaving and Manufacturing Memories

Laom is a small Tampuon village located in the district of Yeak Laom, on the northern road leading to Andong Meas district. Large portions of the communal land have already been sold to Khmer land prospectors who often turn the fields into plantations; a trend which is increasingly widespread in Ratanakiri, often bringing with it disputes between ethnic minorities and Khmer investors. At times when unscrupulous village or district chiefs sell the land where the village cemetery has been preserved for generations, villagers often feel that the link to their ancestors and customary spirits — an important aspect of their social life — has been irremediably lost.

Owing to its proximity to the relatively large town of Banlung, Laom is substantially exposed to the nearby hustle and bustle of the provincial capital and there are signs that the attachment to customary practices still highly visible in other villages is weakening. One example is the abandonment of the practice of grave (*posat atâo*) -making and ornamentation, which Laom's inhabitants say is too costly and time-consuming to maintain. Besides, a large part of the forest that shelters the village cemetery has already been sold to Khmer investors who have turned the land into a cash crop field. This has in turn reinforced the idea that it may only be a matter a time before the entire cemetery disappears along with its traditional arts and rituals. A few women in the village have kept up the tradition of fabric-weaving, however. While this was previously a crucial means of commodity transactions between households and villages (for example, a large woven piece of fabric was exchangeable for a bag of rice), it is now primarily oriented toward the external market that caters for Khmer and especially foreign tourists.[31]

Being one of the most skilful fabric-weavers in Laom, Sing, like other women living in the outskirts of Banlung, has seen the changing economic landscape bring with it new opportunities to further the production of village handcrafts. A mature craftswoman, Sing teaches her seven daughters how to weave old traditional patterns together with images of high-technology weapons. She told me that her mother and grandmother used to weave and now it was her turn to transmit these skills to her own daughters. If in the previous cases, carving and decorating funerary objects is reserved to men, fabric-weaving in Laom is an exclusive female domain as it is passed on from mothers to daughters.

Integrating New Weaving Patterns

Sing's personal craftwork represents some of the richest and most colorful fabric designs produced in the village and the surrounding area. As she proudly points out, her next door neighbor, who is also a weaver, often ends up buying the fabric that she makes. In her view, "she doesn't know how to make beautiful ones!" According to Sing, her designs are also being sought out and copied in other villages.

She explains that she generally uses blue, red, and white threads, as they constitute the village's traditional fabric colors, but that she sometimes weaves with other tones such as pink, green, and black, so as to diversify her products or simply provide for a special order. The fabrics

Plate 8.3 Sing modeling some of her creations, Laom village, Banlung District.

are generally of two sizes and the larger ones, which are for use as skirts, vary in price between US$10 and US$25. The skirts are dominated by broad horizontal bands of colors interspersed with narrower ones in contrasting shades. Their most striking feature, however, is a third type of band that Sing incorporates. These are galleries of icon-like motifs which juxtapose everyday household objects with darker themes of war.

Sing describes that she makes her own fabric designs by using traditional motifs (taught by her mother) as well as new ones inspired by things she has seen (planes, for example). She adds that she also weaves images of war-related objects she has never seen but only heard of from her husband and fellow villagers. For instance, she explains that the hand grenade — one of her favorite motifs — is one of the many images that her husband once described to her and drew on paper so that she could reproduce them with her loom. Despite this being an object she has never set her eyes on, she says that she has heard a lot about it and even knows details of how the grenade functions.

Sing recalled that she got used to seeing planes, guns, and assault rifles in the past. If in doubt about their exact shapes, she usually asks her husband for advice. The latter claimed that these objects are deeply etched in his memory because explosive items were left lying on the ground during the US bombardment of the region. Today these warfare motifs form an intrinsic part of Sing's weaving style, alongside long-established Tampuon iconography like landscapes (hills and mountains), insects and animals (spiders, lizards, dogs), everyday objects (ladders), and ritual objects (urns, Tampuon *posat atâo*).

By means of remembrance, visual representation and association of ideas, Sing manages to weave large pieces of fabric into illustrated patterns, giving shape, color and texture to her and her husband's memories. Another factor in her choice of imagery is external demand, however, not least as Sing now supplies Khmer retailers in Banlung who market war-related souvenirs to foreign tourists. Sing claims that one of these vendors asked her to teach weavers from four or five other villages how to weave warfare images so as to increase overall local production. "[War designs] are very popular with tourists!" she notes, before asking me if I want to place an order and whether I can draw the warfare images I would like her to weave.

Looking at a series of fabrics completed by Sing, one cannot fail to notice that some warfare motifs are quite sketchy. She brushes this off lightheartedly: "It's quite new to me, so I am still learning!" Sing goes on to explain, however, that some of the less well-defined war icons are the product of her daughters' tentative efforts to help her meet the increased demand and simultaneously add new images to their own weaving portfolios. Interestingly, even a single piece of Sing's fabric reveals the various pairs of hands at work, with a spectrum in terms of levels of mastery of the warfare images.

Although Sing is quite keen on weaving motifs that resemble the shape of the original object, she also appears to enjoy working and re-working them as if they are malleable substances. On the one hand, objects such as planes and bombs are evoked using a minimum of lines, as though reduced to their elemental form. On the other hand, objects like the traditional Tampuon graves (*posat atâo*) are depicted to a more sophisticated level of detail. Sing comments that her motifs are spontaneously woven one after another, independent of any desire to produce a particular story-line (with a beginning, middle, and an end). Extracting images sourced from different times and domains and placing them side by side enables her to tell any tale. Her main objective is to turn the fabric into a fine, visual and discursive object that can lend itself to an infinite number of interpretations. With reference to the Jorai tradition of fabric-weaving,

Jacques Dournes once wrote: "[...] the weaving patterns are to be read in relation to the formulas of mythological narratives. Repetitions, redundancies, rhythm and symbolism come together and are explained by one another. As representations of mental space, existing this time outside all language, the fabric is also a text to be deciphered" (Dournes 1987: 168).[32]

Memory-Makers and Memory-Consumers

In light of this, the work of reproduction involved in weaving underlines its textual and recording functions. Well aware of foreigners' fascination with warfare imagery, Sing appears to have specialized in the production of conflict-associated motifs, although she claims that she started to weave weapons long before today's influx of tourists. However, the current market for war memorabilia (and especially for things related to the regional conflict of the 1970s) seems to have further stimulated her exploration of the domain of warfare iconography, which she likes to mix with traditional motifs, patterns, and colors.

Representations are essential to the process of memory, whether it is the personal work of an individual or the product of collective remembering. In this sense, passing on the experience of the war appears less relevant than passing on a particular narration of the war. In Laom, as well as in Leu and other villages, members of the post-conflict generation use their own understanding, imagination and means of representation to tell their version of the conflicts. As Aletta Biersack argues persuasively: "In the interpretive mode, re-narration requires coming to terms with the events *as narrated*; and understanding and explanation become alike windows on historical consciousness."[33] Yet as the inheritance of the past is handed on from generation to generation, the understanding of the event itself evolves through time as a dynamic entity.

What is worth noting here is that, more than transmitting the memory of the past, as it might have been transmitted from mother to daughter, Sing is willing to tell stories that are outside her own experience. In other words, by complying with the external demand for a particular set of illustrations, the craftswoman becomes a tool, albeit an essential one, in the fabrication of memory — or stories — which can be perceived as driven by the tourists' quest for war memorabilia. Within this fabrication process, the memory-makers (the craftswomen) may indeed fulfil the needs of memory-consumers (the tourists). This idea can be summarized as follows:

Local memory-object > foreign souvenir-object

However, memory-makers can sometimes become their own consumers, whether it is the craftsperson (who weaves or carves) or the buyer
(in search of a specific story).[34] Illustrative of Paul Connerton's distinction
between types of memory, Sing gives the impression that the informed
knowledge she has of the hand grenade (cognitive memory) is part of her
personal experience (personal memory).

> There is, first, a class of *personal* memory claims. These refer to those
> acts of remembering that take as their object one's life history. We
> speak of them as personal memories because they are located in and
> refer to a personal past [...] A second group of memory claims — cog-
> nitive memory claims — covers uses of 'remember' where we may be
> said to remember the meaning of words, or lines of verses [...] What
> this time of remembering requires, is not that the object of memory be
> something that is past, but that the person who remembers that thing
> must have met, experienced or learned of it in the past.[35]

Through the knowledge gained from the repetitive act of aesthetic
representation (copying), cognitive memory and personal memory have
eventually collapsed into each other, thus giving the craftswoman a firsthand, albeit virtual, experience of the object.

In asking me to draw images of weapons, it is clear that Sing is anti-
cipating including additional warfare icons to her portfolio. She may also
feel, however, that she could incorporate someone else's memories through
the repetitive and learning process of weaving, which would in turn allow
her to know — and to some extent experience — the object. In the same
way as medieval scholars read and memorize texts and illuminations, Mary
Carruthers draws attention to the fact that when engaged in the intellectual
exercise that renders things "familiar" they should make it "a part of [their]
own experience" — in other words, "making one's own."[36] One could thus
surmise that the act of weaving provides a continuum that enables makers
to digest transmitted knowledge in order to become consumers and vice
versa. As a result of the market dynamics of supply and demand, memory-
makers and memory-consumers thus become interchangeable.

Searching for Authenticity

The tourist industry in Ratanakiri has steadily been increasing for the past
decade and it is likely to develop further with the expansion of the infrastructure linking Cambodia, Lao PDR, and Vietnam. While commercial

flights between the capital city of Phnom Penh and the town of Banlung have been discontinued for more than ten years, road transportation systems are benefiting from aid-funded development projects, and more and more vehicles travel daily between the two towns, with the journey taking nine to 12 hours and sometimes more during the rainy season. Travel agencies advertise the two northeastern provinces of Ratanakiri and Mondulkiri as a destination for eco-tourism, marketing their national parks and ethnic minority villages as singular environmental and cultural attractions that remain relatively unscathed by mass tourism.[37]

Numerous young, ambitious and self-employed Khmer tourist guides are now based in the northeast. The touristic itineraries they devise include the "discovery" of local handicrafts as well as ethnic minority cemeteries beautifully decorated with war-inspired ornaments. Those people I met who showed a particular interest in going with Khmer guides to visit these places and acquiring war memorabilia included retired US soldiers who had previously worked in the region during the Vietnam War (often training Jorai special forces), unexploded ordnance and landmine experts, former military personnel deployed in the area at the time of the UNTAC,[38] and young backpackers in search of unusual souvenirs to take back home.

For each of these categories of memory-consumers, the objects in question mediate a different relationship between the individual and the illustrated episodes of the war.[39] In all cases, however, it is the memories, images, and the storylines conveyed, rather than the object or receptacle itself (be it a water gourd or a piece of fabric), that are the main source of attraction and hence the real object of commodification. In keeping with Igor Kopytoff and Arjun Appadurai's "social life of things," the illustrated memories of past and present craftswomen show that intangible things can also generate their own biography as they become someone else's possession.

The 1979 to 1989 Soviet occupation of Afghanistan prompted a similar incorporation of war-inspired motifs into the designs of the carpets woven by Afghan women. According to J. Lee: "the images of war often … evolved from traditional natural forms: helicopters from chickens, hand grenades from the floral *boteh* or Paisley motif" and these conflict-themed rugs became known as *qalin-e jangi* (fight-carpets) and *qalin-e jihad* (war carpets)" (Lee cited in Saunders 2003: 202) As their popularity increased, the rugs circulated (back) to the USSR through trade and personal purchases from Russian officers, with some eventually finding their way to European markets.[40] From this perspective, conflict rugs manufactured by

Afghan women in Afghanistan are categorized as being more "authentic" than those made by Afghan refugees in Iran for instance. For Lee, "Afghan War rugs ... provide a potent insight, both beautiful and terrifying, into one of the 20th century's great cultural and historical catastrophes" (ibid.).

Amidst this growing market for memory (or souvenir) consumption, the external buyer creates a specific demand for local war narratives, which eventually turns objects into overloaded vessels of war iconography. In items that may once have carried a fine and understated *mélange* of traditional patterns and warfare adornments, they can become oversized illustrations of war-associated themes. This resonates with Alfred Gell's concept of the art "spectator as agent" who is essentially a consumer: his "demand for art is the factor ultimately responsible for its existence, just as the existence of any commodity on the market is an index of consumer demand for it."[41]

Authenticity can be a puzzling concept, especially when some local crafts are being shaped by external demand. For foreign buyers, authenticity may reside in the fine balance between what they perceive as essentially traditional and the subtle hint of external influence and/or modernity. For others, authenticity means that which has been made by the persons living in the area where the depicted events have unfolded. For a local provider like Sing, the fabric-weaver from Laom village, authenticity may be an irrelevant concept, as it matters less to her than the need to satisfy demand and her ability to expand her knowledge and iconographic skills. Yet in providing objects for the wider war memorabilia market, the act of weaving enables her (and her daughters) to make or create authenticity for the foreigners (as well as for herself), as these images and their stories genuinely become her own. This point can be summarized as follows:

Local memory-object > foreign souvenir-object > localized foreign memory

The biographies of such memory-objects show that their prolonged journey through time, refashioning hands, buyers and consumers, indeed turns them into unusual objects that are continually in the making.

Conclusion

This chapter has examined the ways in which a traumatic event that has destroyed the man-made and natural environment of three ethnic minority villages has had an impact on people's artistic, social and economic practices. It has sought to demonstrate how 30 years of prolonged conflicts

— and the episode of intensive aerial bombardment in particular — have generated its own material culture that is the testimony of local resilience and creativity. Indeed objects derived from craftsmanship, as well as the act of crafting itself, can provide a new framework of analysis of the ways post-conflict villages in Ratanakiri in northeast Cambodia interact with the physical and spiritual landscapes affected by a violent past.

Since the end of the conflicts, people have reconstructed their livelihoods from the rubble, both in a literal and a metaphorical sense. Interacting with a familiar landscape — now rendered hazardous — through the re-collection of material, bodily and intangible remnants of war, can lead to financial and spiritual rewards, although not without courting considerable danger.

Although risk-coping mechanisms can be developed through recuperation of material debris, the symbolic appropriation of war-related objects by means of manufacturing, ritual utilization or commercial transaction provides us with a deeper insight into the array of local survival strategies. Subsequent to the passage of the foreign "other," the encounter with the dangerous object can be re-enacted through the reproduction of weaponry that enables people to reconcile themselves to their violent past. Through their incorporation into the local arts, war-associated objects have become an established feature of the post-conflict landscape.

There is a double narrative at work here whereby the material and psychological war debris can be given new shapes and meanings and new value. For Tim Ingold, "Art" disengages consciousness from current lived experience so as to treat that experience as an object of reflection."[42] Similarly, both individual and collective memories can be treated as malleable material, which skilful hands can refashion in the same way in order to give past experiences and narrative accounts new shapes and better meaning. In this regard, the role of the craftsman provides an interesting window into material culture in this physically and spiritually traumatized landscape. Indeed, the wide range of local artistic practices is illuminating in the way it shows a mosaic of memories from different times and places that are encapsulated in manufactured objects.

Some of these objects offer layers of narrative accounts, thus acting as *vistas* on the ways conflict survivors reflect on their past and the ways that the younger generation of villagers inherit this past and in turn reflect on it. In this sense, the inspired craftsman may claim that "the past is never dead. It's not even past" since memories of the present and future may be shaped out of their own material substance.[43] As they gaze into their future, members of the post-conflict generation also try to make sense of a violent past that they have inherited and carve their own historical space in a fast changing world. Today, new manifestations of power, this time in the guise of religious and material forms of consumption, give both the physical and memory landscape renewed contours.

Notes

1. Whilst the population of Cambodia is officially composed of 90% of Khmer and 10% of Chinese, Vietnamese, Lao, Cham and highland peoples (NGO Forum 2006), Ratanakiri province, which is bordered by Laos to the north and Vietnam to the east, is home to several ethnic groups such as the Jorai, Tampuon, Kreung, Brao, Lum, Kravet, and Kachok (Bourdier 2005).

2. The bombing campaign affected Vietnam, Lao PDR, and Cambodia with official data showing that the bombardment of Cambodia started in 1969 whilst unofficial records indicate that it started much earlier (Kiernan 1996; Shawcross 1979).

3. Scheper-Hugues and Bourgois (2004); Kwon (2006).

4. Sennett (2008).

5. Drawing on Aristotle's definition of memory as the ability of the mind to store and retrieve sensations, thoughts and knowledge of the past (Ricoeur 1984).

6. To preserve the anonymity of my informants, names of persons and places have been changed.

7. In Leu village, my informants found it difficult to conceptualize the Euro-American notion of "Art" (see Gell 1998). In a sense, each and every object that is produced by what we would consider artistic means (sculpting, carving, painting, drawing, weaving, etc.) has first and foremost a functional and practical purpose. This chapter uses the term "artistic" to refer to this set of practices but will try, whenever possible, to avoid using the word "art" on its own as its Euro-American definition has little relevance for my informants.

8. Mills and Walker (2008): 4.

9. Saunders (2003): 11.

10. Delvert (1961); Lap (2009).

11. Dournes (1972); Goy and Coué (2006).

12. Michaud (2006), Scott (2009).

13. Saunders (2003): 200.

14. The buffalo sacrifice is a significant ritual that broadly marks important social events amongst the Jorai as well as other highlanders in the Southeast Asian region (see Condominas 1957; Lafont 1963; Goy and Coué 2006).

15. This chapter uses the word "trauma" in light of the following definition: "Trauma means wound, rupture, discontinuity in a tissue, in a fabric of relationships or in a life pattern. It is a break, an incision. Originally a surgical concept it has become a useful metaphor for characterizing the *breaking point*

in the lives of people who continue to suffer from repetitive death fears and of severe constriction of the personality. Trauma can be described either as an *event, a response* or an inner *experience*" (Dasberg *et al.* 1987: 1).

16. Ricoeur (1984).
17. As Kondo wrote: "For a mature artisan is a man who, in crafting fine objects, crafts a finer self" (1990: 241).
18. Gell (1998).
19. The construction of a *posat atâo* marks the second burial of the dead when the deceased is expected to finally embark upon his/her journey into the afterworld. For further information on the subject, see Hertz (1960).
20. For a historical impression of a *posat atâo*, see Henri Maitre (1912): 226.
21. See Bloch and Parry (1982).
22. Beuragn uses a mixture of black, blue, and red dyes extracted from crushed stones and flowers.
23. In *posat atâo* villages, people think that only male graves will benefit from these types of illustrations as girls or women are believed not to need any of these particular human qualities.
24. Such depicted weaponry include: knives, spears, crossbows and, more recently, hand grenades, assault rifles, rocket launchers, bombs, and planes. Amongst 30 villages spread in four districts that were visited — with the majority of them Jorai — 90% have used plane and other war-associated representations for sacred and more profane purposes. Indeed, such beliefs are not shared by every village in the two communes, though, as some people insist that the graves should not bear any war-related effigies since this may tragically affect the dead in his/her next life, hence being a bad omen of a violent death.
25. Gell (1998): 74.
26. Some edifices feature sentences, names and birth and death dates.
27. Individual endeavor, such as keeping oneself safe in times of death, may also be an important source of motivation. In fact, other painters may only feel that they can further protect themselves from potential evil spirits by participating in the illustration of the funeral edifice.
28. For Nora, an object ranging from the most intellectually abstract to the most concrete is susceptible to qualify as a *lieu de mémoire* (see Ageron and Nora 1997).
29. For further details on such influences, see Dournes (1972): 265 and (1978): 136; Guérin *et al.* (2003): XVII–XVIII; and Bourdier (2006): 131.
30. The most numerous of ethnic minorities in Ratanakiri, the Tampuon, belong to the Mon-Khmer linguistic group (Bourdier 2006; Michaud 2006).
31. Like the *arpilleras* from Peru and Chile or the "story cloth" manufactured by the Hmong in Southeast Asia, textile-weaving featuring war themes is a key source of income generation, especially for refugees (Saunders 2003: 218–9).

32. Author's translation from French.

33. Biersack (1991): 20

34. For Wolf Kansteiner: "[...] we should conceptualize collective memory as the result of the interaction among three types of historical factors: the intellectual and cultural traditions that frame all our representations of the past, the memory-makers who selectively adopt and manipulate these traditions, and the memory-consumers who use, ignore, or transform such artifacts according to their own interests" (Kansteiner 2002: 2).

35. Connerton (1989): 22.

36. Carruthers (1990): 204–5.

37. Mass tourism which, for instance, targets world heritage sites like Angkor Wat in the northwest.

38. United Nations Transitional Authority in Cambodia from 1992–93.

39. See Saunders (2003).

40. Indeed, the object eventually returns to its place of origin albeit in another form and texture: "the Soviet war matériel such as AK-47 assault rifles, Hind M-24 helicopters, HIP-8 troop carrying helicopters, BMD-2 armoured personnel carriers and a miscellany of rockets, grenades, handguns and aeroplanes" (Saunders 2003: 202) find their way back as illustrated motifs on a locally-woven carpet.

41. Gell (1998): 34.

42. Ingold (2000): 111.

43. Quote from William Faulkner, *Requiem for a Nun* (1951): Act I Scene 3.

CHAPTER 9

Remembering Old Homelands: The Houay Ho Dam, the Resettlement of the Heuny (Nya Heun), Memory, and the Struggle for Places

Ian G. Baird

Introduction

Memory can be linked to landscapes in various ways. People have memories of places they visited as children, and memories of places where certain significant things in their lives occurred. People also have social or group memories (Fukushima 2002; Halbwachs 1992), including those that link particular landscapes with important events that occurred long ago, sometimes even before they were born, thus leading some, such as William Turkel, to characterize certain landscapes as constituting "archives of memory" (Turkel 2007). These latter memories are often generated through stories that people have heard and reheard, and read and reread. This fits well with Bill Cronon's ideas about "telling stories about stories" (Cronon 1992: 1375). People often use geographical features to symbolize particular memories; we can think of these landscapes as "discourse made material" (Dwyer 2004: 422). Indeed, there is considerable interplay between materiality and discourse, with each potentially influencing the other. Memories do significantly affect present-day ideas and actions. They are complex, and just as landscapes change over time, so do memories.

I use the word "places" above to refer to particular landscapes. In human geography, scholars have looked at the concept of place in various ways. The humanist Yi-Fu Tuan describes "places" as spaces that are endowed with particular meaning to people; as he put it, "'Space' is more abstract than 'place'. What begins as undifferentiated space becomes place as we come to know it better and endow it with value" (Tuan 1977: 6). Places, in this view, are spaces where significant experiences occurred. Similarly, Wolfgang Sachs (1992) considers places to be imbued with experiences, both present and past, while James Duncan defines places as "bounded settings in which social relations and identity are constituted" (Duncan 2000: 582). Places can be thought of as fundamentally constituted through history, and history, in turn, is affected by politics (Gordillo 2002, 2004), and is ultimately influenced by multiple forms of power; as John Allen argues, "[P]ower is *inherently* spatial, and conversely, spatiality is *imbued* with power" (emphasis in original) (Allen 2003: 3). Thus, memory, power, and places are closely linked. Recently, however, some theorists in geography, such as Doreen Massey (2005) and Sallie Marston (2000), have argued that all spaces — not just those we constitute as "places" — are produced through social processes. This view leads to the conclusion that there is no longer a place (or space) for the concept of "place." While I find this argument compelling, it remains possible to argue that the ways we apply meanings to the concepts of place and space — in common usage — are different, and that places are spaces connected with certain types of meanings that are particularly important to us, and are linked to experiences and intimate memories. While places and spaces are both socially constituted, we do not normally use the terms in the same ways.

We typically recognize memories to be particular recollections of events that occurred — and in their purest form, that is what they are. Memories are indeed founded on recollections of the past, but they are far from simple or neutral. In fact, even from the first moment that a memory is constituted, when a person remembers something that happened just moments before, such as having dinner with a friend, memories are always refracted through human thought processes, so that depending on who we are, what we are interested in, and the significance of certain aspects of an event to us, memories manifest themselves in very different and unique ways. While my memory of the dinner might revolve around a particular conversation that is relevant to me, yours could vary significantly, and possibly be focused on a totally different discussion, or it might simply be attentive to the quality of the meal. Therefore, one person's memory of a particular moment or period of time is never the same as someone else's, even if both people have physically experienced the event in seemingly identical ways. Each of us has our own different package of pasts and associated places, and we always construct memories within the context of other memories, and constitute places in relation to other places.[1] Memories never exist in isolation but are entwined with each other, always in different and frequently surprising ways.

Things become even more complex with the passage of time, as memories shift and morph and variously transform based on different factors. When we ponder something that occurred in the past, and try to remember what happened, it seems as if we are trying to find a particular page in a book, one written when the event first occurred. If only we can recall the page, it would seem possible to fully recreate the moment, in a pure way. The reality, however, is not so simple. Memories never remain untouched by one's disposition, nor are they immune from the influences of politics, including national, ethnic group, community, and even interpersonal politics between two people.[2] As I have argued elsewhere, our memories of the past are frequently political (Baird and Le Billon 2012). Moreover, Fentress and Wickham's perspective (1992) on the role of politics and struggle in the production of memories and histories makes sense; they indicate how important politics is for refracting visions of history.

Over time, memories become less about revealing the "true facts of what happened" and more about engaging particular performances, ones that are inevitably entangled with worldviews, politics, and a myriad of feelings and relationships. Paul Connerton (1989) thus argued that performance is crucial for sustaining and transforming social memory. Vatthana Pholsena, in recording the histories of ethnic minority revolutionary women in southeastern Laos, wrote, for example, "I am more interested in the witness of these revolutionary fighters for what their stories reveal about their own understanding of historical events" (Pholsena 2008: 460). This does not mean that memories are not useful for reconstructing particular "facts" of what happened, but if we are only looking to recreate the past, we are missing crucial aspects of what memories can offer. Memories, even if presented as being simply recollections of hard facts, can tell us much more. We need to see memories as experiences that are not simply recalled, but are rather produced and reproduced over time, and entwined with agency, so that in the end people are not simply recalling past acts, but are considering past productions and reproductions of the past. Thus, new recollections of the past can be seen as new constructs, as hybrids that combine "facts" with various social, cultural, and political influences that variously affect how we remember things, how we choose to organize our memories, and how we present them to others in varied ways, depending on our audiences. In addition, as Bill Cronon (1992) reminds us, producing memories is as much about forgetting, omitting and erasing than it is about remembering. Ultimately, as Paul Ricoeur (1986) and Elizabeth Tonkin (1992) astutely point out, narrative accounts of the past can reproduce memories as well as create them, sometimes to achieve new ends not previously conceived.

In addition, the ways people remember landscapes are greatly affected by their previous experiences with those landscapes. For example, if one's profession or livelihood is not greatly dependent on a particular landscape, being displaced from it is likely to foster different and potentially (but not necessarily) less traumatic reactions compared to if one's life was heavily dependent on the landscape that the person is displaced from, and if one's knowledge is tied up and only particularly relevant in the context of the landscape. In such cases, being displaced to a new landscape, and new livelihood circumstances, is likely to lead to more difficulties in adapting. Clearly, such results often lead to particular memories that are linked to landscapes.

So, when we study memories, we should not only do so in the hope of learning about the facts of particular events, but also to better understand the various factors that affect the ways memories are constructed. Certainly, how people typically remember landscapes depends on a whole array of factors. Memories of landscapes that people have left on their own terms are likely to be remembered differently from how landscapes that they have been forced to abandon are recollected. The circumstances of one's departure from a particular landscape, the ability to adapt, to reinvent oneself, to prosper by one's own standards in one's new surroundings, are all crucial for understanding what can be broadly considered to be the politics of memory. Understanding these memories and how they are produced and reproduced is not only useful for considering people's perceptions of the past, but also for recognizing why things are as they are now.[3]

In this chapter, I present a case study that deals with a particular "package" of memories, and a certain assemblage of conditions and influences, many of which are affected by geography. Because the people who I write about were forcibly dislodged from particular landscapes that they had inhabited for as long as they could remember (again, social memories are crucial for understanding the context), and because they have not been officially allowed to return to those landscapes on a permanent basis, a particular form of nostalgia for the "places" they left has become part of memory. But unlike the type of nostalgia that frequently affected refugees living across oceans from their original homelands, the landscapes that these people have been displaced from are within relatively close proximity of where they have been resettled. They are too far away to walk back and forth to on a daily basis, but they are close enough that those relocated are still frequently able to access those places. These landscapes are not only a part of a displaced person's memory, they also continue to be part of people's present-day experiences, but the relationship with the land has changed. While those displaced can still go there frequently, even for long periods, they cannot truly return and call the landscape their official home, at least not yet. They are positioned as "partially displaced" from the landscape, precariously situated with insecure and uncertain tenure over land and resources. These experiences ultimately create particular memories related to landscapes, ones that may be less abstract and more material than memories of more distant landscapes, and in this particular case, support particular struggles for the right to permanently return "home."

The Houay Ho Dam

Paksong District, located in Champasak Province, encompasses much of the Bolaven Plateau, a high mountainous area in the south of the Lao People's Democratic Republic (Lao PDR or Laos) that straddles the mainstream Mekong River to the west and the Xekong River to the east. Reaching up to over 2,000 meters above sea level, the climate of the plateau is unlike the rest of southern Laos. It receives much more rain (over 4,000 mm annually at some locations), and is subject to a relatively cool climate, with temperatures occasionally reaching below freezing (Phetsavanh 2004; Delang and Toro 2011). The plateau supports a wide variety of plants and wildlife, especially along its steep escarpment.[4] It is home to two Mon-Khmer language-speaking groups of indigenous peoples who call themselves the Heuny (Nya Heun) and the Jrou (Laven) (Phetsavanh 2004).

Situated 160 kilometers east of Pakse, the capital of Champasak Province, and 30 kilometers northwest of Attapeu town, in southern Laos, the Houay Ho Dam — a concrete-faced and rock-filled 76-meter-high structure with a 980-meter-long concrete-lined waterway that runs into a 104-meter vertical pressure shaft (Baird and Shoemaker 2008; Sparkes 2000; Delang and Toro 2011: 573) — was built at an estimated cost of US$220–250 million.[5] The dam's 32.5–37 km² reservoir is located on the Bolaven Plateau in Paksong District, while the powerhouse is situated at the bottom of the Bolaven Plateau, near the Xekong River, in Samakhixay

District, Attapeu Province (Baird and Shoemaker 2008). Houay Ho was the largest dam constructed in southern Laos in the 1990s (Nok 2008: 73; Delang and Toro 2011).

In 1993, the large Korean conglomerate and automobile maker, Daewoo Engineering Co. Ltd., began negotiating with the Government of Laos (GoL) regarding the Houay Ho Dam. A Memorandum of Understanding (MoU) to investigate the project was signed in March 1993, and in July, the Tasmanian firm, the Hydro-Electric Commission Enterprise Corporation (HECEC), began conducting a feasibility study (Wyatt 2004: 145; International Rivers Network 1999: 41; Hydro-Electric Commission Enterprise Corporation 1993). Just two months later, however, long before the study was completed, a 30-year concession agreement to proceed was signed (Baird and Shoemaker 2008: 349). In November 1994, construction began on the 150 Megawatt (MW) capacity hydropower dam, which was one of the first Build, Own, Operate, and Transfer (BOOT)[6] projects in Laos (Wyatt 2004; International Rivers Network 1999: 41; Delang and Toro 2011: 573). Daewoo held 60 percent of the shares in the Houay Ho Power Company (HHPC) — created specifically for the project — while Loxley Public Company Ltd., a leading Thai trading firm, and Électricité du Laos (EdL), Laos' state-owned electricity agency, held 20 percent each (International Rivers Network 1999: 41).

The project developed rapidly, even though Daewoo and Loxley had little experience building dams. As a GoL observer from the Ministry of Industry and Handicrafts told Andrew Wyatt years later, "It had a bad smell. We never got to see any studies for the project. I don't think any were done" (Wyatt 2004: 144; Delang and Toro 2011: 574). Apparently the investors were anxious to gain the rights to one of the most profitable hydropower projects in Laos, and the Deputy Prime Minister and Minister in charge of coordinating foreign investment at the time, Khamphouy Keoboualapha — who was said to have had close connections with Thai business interests, including Loxley — signed off on the project without much consultation with the Ministry of Industry and Handicrafts or EdL. Signing without legal representation resulted in the GoL getting an extremely poor deal,[7] and is rumored to have been part of the reason for Khamphouy Keoboualapha's fall from both the Politburo and Party's Central Committee, the regime's two most powerful political bodies, soon after. In October 1995, a power purchase agreement for selling electricity from the project to Thailand was signed by the Electricity Generating Authority of Thailand (EGAT).[8] On 1 September 1999, Thailand began purchasing electricity from the project (International Rivers Network 1999: 3). Electricity sales to Thailand have continued ever since.

A number of observers, including both critics of hydropower dams and some frequently sympathetic to the hydropower industry, have criticized the project (Delang and Toro 2011; Nok 2000, 2008; Baird and Shoemaker 2008; Wyatt 2004; Phetsavanh 2004; Sparkes 2000; International Rivers Network 1999; Halcrow 1998; Dennis 1997). An Environmental Impact Assessment (EIA) was conducted by the Swiss consulting firm Electrowatt, but construction began before the study was completed, and the EIA may never have been finalized as it was apparently seen as unnecessary by Daewoo once the concession agreement had been signed, which indicates the very low level of concern they had regarding the project's social and environmental impacts.[9] The project essentially proceeded without its potential returns, risks, or costs being known (Wyatt 2004). Furthermore, the project agreement did not stipulate any mitigation or compensation,[10] and as a result, Daewoo only made a single US$230,000 payment for all social and environmental impacts, and left the GoL to take responsibility for any additional impacts (Nok 2008: 73; Delang and Toro 2011: 573). Both the HECEC and Electrowatt studies were of poor quality. Most seriously, the various impacts of the project on the culture and livelihoods of the Heuny people, the main inhabitants of the project area, were largely discounted, overlooked or only superficially addressed (International Rivers Network 1999: 41).

Indicative of how poorly planned the Houay Ho Dam was, the developers built a road right to the edge of the 236-meter escarpment of the Plateau. The original plan was for the road to go down the escarpment to Attapeu town, but when the bulldozers reached the edge of a high cliff, they realized that they would have to abandon part of the road and double back in order to find a more moderately-sloped route down a valley. Daewoo widened 100 kilometers of road, and built at least 38 kilometers of new roads. In some cases, debris from the road-building was needlessly discarded into rivers, causing unnecessary environmental impacts (International Rivers Network 1999: 46). Some local cemeteries, which were located adjacent to the widened roads, were also carelessly bulldozed by road workers,[11] causing considerable resentment amongst communities (International Rivers Network 1999: 46–7). Due to poor planning, there have been problems with the tunnel cracking.[12] The reservoir has also been leaking, resulting in considerably less water being available for producing electricity (Baird and Shoemaker 2008: 355; *Khao San Pathet Lao*,

20 February 2002). This has led the owners to look for possible ways to divert more water into the reservoir.

Only one village (Nam Han) was located directly within the project area of the Houay Ho Dam, and another village (Thong Ngao) was situated downstream of the dam, where the river would dry up, thus eliminating fishing opportunities, and leading project planners to recommend its relocation. Latsaxin Village was also slated for resettlement, as it was located near the dirt extraction site for the dam (Baird and Shoemaker 2008: 351). In the end, 2,500 people living in 11 communities were resettled due to the Houay Ho Dam and in anticipation of the construction of the Xepian-Xenamnoy Dam, which was also expected at the time to proceed in the same general area (Nok 2008: 73; Delang and Toro 2011: 574). The idea was to prevent future erosion impacts on both projects (International Rivers Network 1999: 42). The resettlement areas were initially collectively designated as a government "focal site," which typically, in Lao development jargon, represents an area allocated for "developing" resettled ethnic minorities from the uplands (Baird and Shoemaker 2007: 874–5; Baird and Shoemaker 2008: 124–5). This designation was, however, revoked for this particular area in 2000. The villages of Thong Ngao, Nam Han, Nam Tieng and Latsaxin were the first to be relocated, followed by Keokhoun-muang, Nam Leng, Nam Kong and Xenamnoy, in 1996–97. Don Khong and Houay Soy were moved in 2000, and Tayeuk Seua in 2003. All of the relocated villages except for one (Don Khong, whose inhabitants are Jrou) were populated by Heuny people. The vast majority of the Heuny were resettled to a location known as "*Ban Chat San* Unit #8," which is near the ethnic Jrou villages of Nam Kong and Nam Tang.

In 1997, Daewoo and Loxley were forced to liquidate some of their assets as a result of the Asian financial crisis. Thus, in 2001, their 80 percent share in the Houay Ho Dam was sold to the Belgian company Tractebel S.A. and its Thai subsidiary MCL for US$140 million (Tractebel 2001; International Water Power & Dam Construction, 1 October 2001; Nok 2008: 73; Delang and Toro 2011: 575), with the support of Belgium-government-sponsored export credits (Baird 2005: 357). Tractebel has denied responsibility for the problems facing those relocated for the project (Nok 2008: 74), thus leaving a vacuum of accountability, and little recourse for those who have still not been appropriately compensated. Tractebel seems to have thought that they could buy the dam's assets without acquiring the dam's unfulfilled past responsibilities, and so far they have been able to get away with it! There is a strong argument for legal responsibility, as when a company is purchased, all its assets and liabilities, including unsettled compensation issues, typically come with it. At the very least, there would appear to be a moral obligation for them to carefully consider the resettled people.

Problems with the Resettlement of the Heuny (Nya Heun)

The ethnic Heuny people — commonly referred to as the Nya Heun — are only found on the east side of the Bolaven Plateau in what is presently designated as Paksong District.[13] They speak their own particular language, which is included within the Western Bahnaric linguistic branch of the Mon-Khmer family. In 2005, the national census indicated that the total Heuny population was just 6,785 (National Statistics Centre 2006: 15). Approximately 40 percent of the global Heuny population was resettled as a result of dam development in the late 1990s (International Rivers Network 1999: 43).[14] In the 1960s and early 1970s, much of the Heuny population aligned themselves with the Royal Lao Government and joined "Special Guerrilla Units" (SGUs) organized, paid for, and directed by the US Central Intelligence Agency (CIA). The primary job of the Heuny was to conduct covert operations for collecting intelligence about the Ho Chi Minh Trail to the east, and engaging in operations to disrupt the Trail.[15] Despite heavy fighting in the area during the Second Indochina War in Laos (1964–73), very few people fled their homelands, although some did move around on the eastern Bolaven Plateau (International Rivers Network 1999: 42). Prior to being resettled, the Heuny people largely subsisted on swidden agriculture combined with fishing, hunting and the collection of non-timber forest products (NTFPs). Some also had small coffee plantations. They could be characterized as living close to nature, with knowledge intricately linked with the land. As Barbara Wall showed in the only detailed ethnography of the Heuny so far conducted, these people were not nomadic "slash-and-burn cultivators" who damaged primary forest. Instead, they lived in largely fixed settlements near flowing water, where they conducted well-organized swidden agriculture (Wall 1975).

In 1995, when the Xepian-Xenamnoy Hydropower Project began being surveyed by the Korean company Dong Ah Co., consultants hired to investigate found that Heuny agricultural practices did not threaten sustainable forest management, as only one percent of the forest was under agricultural use each year. The population density was low, allowing for long well-over-20-year forest regrowth. The consultants found that with limited exceptions, most of the Heuny families were self-sufficient in rice and other foodstuffs.[16] While not everything was perfect, many Heuny now reflect on those days nostalgically. A woman from Houay Soy village was quoted as saying, "We want to return to our former village. Over there we have plenty of fruits. The water from the stream is cool and clean, and catching fish is very easy" (Phetsavanh 2004: 10).

The main problem with the resettlement was the lack of available agricultural land, as well as the dearth of forests and streams for fishing, hunting and collecting NTFPs. For example, prior to resettling, people from Xenamnoy Village reported that 60 percent of their animal protein originated from wild fish (Roberts and Baird 1995), but once they arrived in the resettlement area, fish consumption dropped dramatically, affecting nutrition levels (Baird and Shoemaker 2008: 352). Although it was agreed that those resettled would require a minimum of three hectares of agriculture land per household,[17] there was insufficient land, and much of the land allocated was not "empty," as claimed by GoL officials. Instead, most of the land provided to those resettled were the fallow agriculture fields of neighboring ethnic Jrou villages. Therefore, once the Heuny tried to cultivate it, they realized that their neighbors were unwilling to give it up. Soon, less than 20 percent of the allocated land remained available for those resettled to cultivate, thus resulting in chronic food security problems. There is even less land now. There are variations between different resettlements, with some villages having access to only four to five hectares of agricultural land nearby for whole communities.

There were also conflicts with the existing communities in the area over the use of nearby forests and streams, as the historical foraging rights of preexisting communities in the area came under pressure by the resettled people. Thus, resources were rapidly depleted locally due to the influx of so many people accustomed to living off the land in low population densities. The resettlement plan also depended on a strategy to rapidly convert subsistence swidden cultivators into market-oriented cash crop coffee growers. This would have been difficult even under the best of circumstances, but was made even less feasible because the people received inadequate land and training on how to cultivate coffee. Crucially, coffee prices declined rapidly right around the time the Heuny were resettled, reducing incentives for people to cultivate it (Nok 2008: 74).

One of the biggest concerns of the Heuny was territorial, as they had to move west of the Xenamnoy River. Historically, the Heuny had always lived east of the river while the Jrou lived to the west. There was a socially constructed (but not humanly marked) boundary between the two groups.[18] Since they had a history of violent conflict, the Heuny were initially quite anxious about the prospects of moving to Jrou territory.

Villagers bitterly complained about this issue when I visited Xenamnoy and Latsaxin villages in 1995 to conduct the fisheries EIA for the dam. The Heuny believed that the spirits would become angry due to displacement if they moved west of the Xenamnoy, and that this anger could cause serious illnesses or death to the people. This further added anxiety to the resettlement process.

Officials promised the resettled people three years of rice rations, for adapting to their new surroundings and circumstances. However, only a small amount was delivered, causing considerable resentment. According to John Dennis, who visited the resettlement area in September 1997, "[I]f our informant is accurate, this situation is a human rights emergency which requires immediate attention at a high level in Vientiane" (Dennis 1997: 14–5). But little was done, and by February 1998, the situation had deteriorated. Many complained of hunger and food shortages. Some were forced to borrow from moneylenders in the Paksong District center to buy rice (International Rivers Network 1999: 45). While the Daewoo project manager apparently expressed concern about too many people being resettled, no actions were taken by the company or government officials (Dennis 1997). The situation has worsened in recent years, as there is less land available for cultivation than ever, not only because the original inhabitants have taken land back, but also due to various economic land concessions for agriculture which have moved into the area. For example, there are various Vietnamese coffee concessions, and relatives of a senior Lao politician are investing in a cattle ranch.

Gaining access to good water sources is another serious problem. When reminiscing about their old villages, the Heuny quickly point out that they always had access to high-quality flowing stream-water. The resettlement villages are, however, located away from good water sources. Initially, some deep bore-hole wells were drilled in the resettlement villages, but the quality of water available from most was poor. In some cases, well water, when used to water vegetables, was found to kill the plants (I observed this in the late 1990s). Later, Tractebel installed new water systems after they were embarrassed in 2004 by a Belgian NGO, which challenged them regarding the continuing resettlement problems. The NGO argued that Tractebel should take responsibility for these problems, since they purchased the dam using Belgium export credits, and thus were responsible for following the environmental and social responsibility guidelines of the Overseas Economic Cooperation and Development Organization (OECD) (Baird 2005: 357; Baird and Shoemaker 2008: 356; Delang and Toro 2011: 575). Still, the wells constructed by Tractebel were of poor quality, and most have now broken down. According to a man from Tayeuk Seua Village, "When we lived in our former village, we never faced shortages of water because our village was located near a stream with clean water, and catching fish was very easy. In the resettlement village, we face many difficulties" (Phetsavanh 2004: 7). More recently, a man living in the resettlement area reported to me that, "Now we have to dig shallow wells at the edge of a natural pond in order to obtain water, and the water is not good quality."

Those who live in the resettlement areas have had to increasingly rely on selling their labor. It is now typical for some members of almost every family to work as day laborers picking coffee or cutting grass and weeding for non-Heuny people in neighboring villages or coffee plantation companies. The wages they receive are low and variable, often the equivalent of less than one dollar per day, depending on the work, season, and who is hiring, but it is necessary for them to take such work as in the resettlement areas they have so few independent options for making money or producing their own food. Still, there are sufficient day-labor opportunities to have prevented significant out-migration of Heuny people from Paksong District. Yet some are only able to generate enough income as wage-laborers to buy rice to subsist on a day-to-day basis, thus putting many in precarious situations.

The poverty that people in the resettlement areas have experienced appears to be the main reason why those resettled have reported an increase in petty crime in their communities since being moved (Phetsavanh 2004: 6). Delang and Toro (2011) have characterized the area as facing more poverty problems than anywhere else on the Bolaven Plateau. Poverty, in turn, has impacted on community solidarity, leading people to mentally construct the resettlement villages as "difficult places," as "places of poverty" (*bone thouk nyak* in Lao). In addition, the Heuny report that due to various factors, including increased poverty and the need to work as daily wage-laborers, as well as a general fragmenting of communities, there are less traditional rituals in the resettlement area than there were before the people were resettled (Phetsavanh 2004). This is largely because people cannot afford to buy the items (pigs, chickens, rice, rice beer, etc.) required for rituals, and also because they have to go to work as wage laborers more frequently, thus leaving them with less time to prepare for and conduct rituals. For the Heuny, who are explicitly Animist (they believe that illnesses and bad fortune are frequently caused by spirits), this symbolizes community disintegration, as the main times when community members gather in large groups are when rituals are organized. This change is something that the Heuny generally lament.

One of the most disappointing aspects of the resettlement of the Heuny is that despite being resettled as a result of hydropower development for export, well over a decade after the dam started exporting electricity to Thailand, the people living in the resettlement areas still do not have access to electricity. Many Heuny feel abandoned by the State. For example, in February 2003, an old Heuny man from Tayeuk Seua Village was quoted as saying, "I'd rather return to my former village because here nothing has improved. The officials have never visited us. They treat us like people who do not have any relatives" (Phetsavanh 2004: 8). Echoing the above comment, another resettled Heuny woman told Phetsavanh, that, "I miss my former village and I want to return to it because I used to live there for a long time. I've left behind the trees that I used to collect fruits from every year. I miss them a lot. Whenever I think of them I cry a great deal. Here in the resettlement village, we cannot eat any fruits because they are stolen before they are ripe" (Phetsavanh 2004: 6). One can see how people are becoming nostalgic for certain places and the trees that mark them; places that are materially significant for their livelihoods.

Abandoning Resettlement Areas

My relatives and I don't want to live in the resettlement village but we were forced to and we could not protest. We miss our native lands where we used to live for hundreds of years, our crops, vegetables and our happy lives.

— A villager from Thong Ngao village[19]

As a result of the serious land and resource problems facing the resettled Heuny, many have become nostalgic for their old homelands, located just over a day's walk from the resettlement sites (actually, about 17–19 hours' walking, or six to seven hours by bicycle). Soon after being resettled, many began looking for ways to leave the resettlement areas and return to their old villages, but the GoL refused to allow them to move. As time passed, and conditions continued to deteriorate, more and more families began subverting government rules to return to their homelands. The first excuse used was that they wanted to return to their old swidden fallows or small coffee plantations to obtain stockpiles of rice that had been stored in barns. They also argued that they needed to return to collect vegetables and coffee beans still growing in their old fields. These people frequently requested permission from authorities to make the trip, but often would not return for two or three months, after which time they would stay for a few days before going to their former homes again, claiming that they had eaten all the rice they had brought with them and needed to return for more. Over time, once people realized that they had fewer and fewer options in the resettlement areas, and that they could subvert official directives for them to remain in the resettlement areas by claiming to return to their old fields on a temporary basis, more and more people left, and those who left spent less and less time in the resettlement areas. After a few years, some families had in reality abandoned the resettlement sites, although they were still officially residents there. One only had to walk through the resettlement areas to see that many of the houses were deteriorating, and had not been inhabited for a long time. As Phetsavanh reported, "[t]he people do not listen to government authorities anymore. They were told that in the resettlement villages they would be provided with all the facilities needed, but so far nothing has happened, which has made the people unhappy" (Phetsavanh 2004: 11). There are certainly some differences between what older and younger people want, with the latter desiring modernity more than the former, but these differences may be less pronounced than in some other cases when indigenous peoples have been resettled, as younger people are still interacting with the old village spaces on a regular basis, and thus have more chances to generate new memories through engaging in real work characteristic of the ways things were done in the distant past, such as conducting swidden agriculture near their old villages. It is not just about the older people remembering these more traditional activities, while the younger people have not seen them in practice, as is the case for some Brao people living outside Virachey National Park in northeastern Cambodia (Baird 2009a).

The Heuny have also left the resettlement villages in order to avoid conflicts with neighboring communities and their own people over the small amount of land available for agriculture. As one man told me, "We never had any land shortages when we lived in our old territories. There were never any land shortages. Only since we have come to the resettlement villages have we had to deal with land disputes." According to Phetsavanh, there are now more disputes over land belonging to the neighboring villages, because there are no clear boundaries like there were in the Heuny's previous village areas (Phetsavanh 2004 : 10). In 2003, about 50 percent of the people in the main resettlement were spending significant amounts of time near their original villages (Phetsavanh 2004: 6). Then, in

2006, it was estimated that 70 percent of the resettled families were living away from the resettlement areas, and in 2010 approximately 80 percent of the population had essentially returned to their old areas.[20] In 2011, a Heuny man living in one of the resettlement villages told me that if the government allowed people to live where they wanted, virtually nobody would remain, mainly because of the lack of agricultural and foraging land, but also due to the poor quality of water sources.

While the villagers have managed to partially subvert government plans, in ways reminiscent of the type of indirect resistance that James Scott describes in his well-known book, *Weapons of the Weak* (1985), this has not been under ideal circumstances, and has frequently come at a heavy cost. For example, many children have moved from the resettlement area with their parents and are now unable to attend school. Moreover, not all children living away from the resettlement sites are being vaccinated. Families have also sometimes been split up, with some staying in the resettlement areas and others returning to their old homelands. Conducting communal village business has become difficult as most of the official residents of the villages are not in residence in reality.

After a number of years of living precariously, spending most of their time near their old villages, but still officially living in resettlement villages, in 2008 a group of over 50 Heuny families submitted a document to the subdistrict government asking for permission to establish an official village near their former communities. The subdistrict chief, despite himself being Heuny, did not respond favorably. Instead, he prepared a document that fully rejected the request. He strongly told those proposing the "new village" that they should never consider this option again. When local people pointed out that there was insufficient land near the resettlement communities for them to make a living there, the subdistrict chief was unable to suggest any solutions. Still, the people had to be particularly careful in voicing their objections, as many were previously CIA SGU soldiers, making them vulnerable to accusations of being "against government policy," a label with potentially serious repercussions in the Lao context. Even if government officials did not mention the previous affiliations of many of the Heuny, recognition of past affiliations held by many Heuny were enough to significantly reduce their confidence. Indeed, very few Heuny were allied with the Pathet Lao. People still have memories of the years immediately following the communist take-over of the country, when former soldiers were sent for "reeducation," or "*samana*" in Lao. People feared accusations of being aligned with anti-government insurgent groups, or of at least providing them with food. Although past political alliances are not spoken of as much now as they were earlier, people are still aware of what side of the conflict others were on, and these "political memories" continue to influence development outcomes (Baird and Le Billon 2012).

The Return of the Xepian-Xenamnoy Hydropower Project

The Xepian-Xenamnoy Hydropower Project, which the Korean company Dong Ah started hastily developing in the 1990s after a MoU for constructing the project was signed with the GoL in February 1994 (International Rivers Network 1999), was discontinued entirely once the Asian financial crisis hit, and before substantial construction on the dam had begun.[21] However, the project is now being revived by new investors, including the Korean companies, SK Engineering and Construction and Korea Western Power, and the Thai company, Ratchaburi. The Project Development Agreement for the 390 MW capacity dam was completed in 2008, at which time it was expected to be producing power by 2015 (Nok 2008: 75). In particular, Xepian-Xenamnoy is seen as being potentially useful for supplying some of the massive amount of electricity that would be required for a planned large-scale bauxite mine and aluminum smelter project, which is being touted by the Australian mining company Ord River Resources and its Chinese partner, China Nonferrous Metals. They claim that the project has the potential to be developed into a "world class aluminum industry" (Vaughn 2006; Riseborough 2006), even though the aluminum industry is well-known for causing serious negative environmental and social impacts (International Rivers Network 2005). This particular development would cause many environmental and livelihood problems in the Paksong area and the Xekong River Basin more generally (Nok 2008; Baird and Shoemaker 2008; Delang and Toro 2011).

There is, however, more to the development of the bauxite mine than meets the eye. Here we see how memories of landscapes are important. When the Heuny were initially resettled from their homelands in the late 1990s, government officials told them that their relocation had been justified on environmental grounds. The plan was to designate their homelands as a protected area. This fit with new protected areas on the Bolaven Plateau proposed by the US-based Wildlife Conservation Society (Wildlife Conservation Society 1995). The Heuny are not only upset about being moved, but are annoyed that the government has added insult to injury by lying to them (at least that is how many perceive it). Rather than turning the area into a protected area, the Heuny noticed changes in the landscape.

They started finding large craters in the ground, at different locations. These craters were dug as part of the mine-surveying process; they are test holes. These scars on the landscape have been troubling for many Heuny, especially the elders, who do not like the idea that their homelands are being dug up without their knowledge, let alone their permission. They feel doubly betrayed by the government, as they now realize that their former territories are slated to become the center of a large open-pit bauxite mining operation that would cover a wide area and alter the landscape in ways that would make the test holes seem insignificant in comparison (Nok 2008: 75).

In addition, Houay Chote and Nong Phanouane — the two villages in the area that managed to avoid resettlement in the late 1990s through continually arguing that they were already doing well where they were, that they had contributed strongly to the revolution, and that there was not enough space or resources for those who have already been resettled, let alone them as well — would need to be resettled for the project, along with another two villages previously not slated for relocation. They have all been told that each family will receive US$5,500 in compensation for losses (Nok 2008: 75), but the people remain disappointed, as they believed that they had finally succeeded in avoiding resettlement after resisting for over a decade. They were particularly happy when, in May 2005, GoL officials informed them that they would not be resettled after all (Baird and Shoemaker 2008: 361), since at the time plans to build the Xepian-Xenamnoy Dam remained uncertain. Now it seems likely that they will have to move after all.

Continuing Attachments to the Land

The Heuny have indicated particular interest in the landscapes that were previously theirs. For example, there is a sacred forest near the Champasak-Attapeu provincial border in Paksong District where people from the Heuny ethnic group conduct important community Animist rituals each year.[22] While only covering four hectares, this place is located at the base of a mountain, near a waterfall. Even though the Heuny have been resettled from their original lands, they have not abandoned this sacred place. Therefore, when rumors started emerging about how the forest in the area might be damaged if the government proceeded with a plan to develop a large irrigation project in the area, elders expressed concern, at least to the sub-district chief. It is unclear, however, when and if the project will actually materialize, and since nothing has occurred so far, serious protests have yet to erupt. But even the initial concern shown indicates the continued attachment many Heuny have to their old homelands.

One of the most powerful indicators that the Heuny are still strongly attached to their old landscapes is that people from the various resettled villages, which have all maintained their village names from before they were resettled — itself a significant indicator of their attitude to resettlement — are not just returning anywhere east of the Xenamnoy River. They are almost all going back to the same village territories where they previously resided. For example, the people from Xenamnoy Village are returning to their old territory, as are those from Nam Kong, and so on. Even though nobody officially has rights to their old lands, the different communities continue to informally recognize village territories and associated boundaries that existed prior to their resettlement. It is also significant that former village cemeteries, which each community maintained in their old village territories before resettlement, are still being looked after despite the villages having been dismantled years ago. As one man told me in 2011, "If people are in their old villages when they die, they are buried in their old cemeteries, which are maintained as in the past."

Since there is little land for developing coffee in the resettlement areas, and much of the land available is not particularly good for coffee cultivation anyway, many Heuny have planted coffee in their old homelands. While some Heuny had small coffee gardens before being resettled, these plantations have been expanded, and many have started new ones. Often they plant rice together with coffee seedlings in the first year, and then allow the coffee to dominate in subsequent years, with rice no longer being cultivated. Therefore, apart from cultivating swidden fields with subsistence crops, the investment in long-term perennial crops clearly indicates that many Heuny believe that they will continue to have access to their old homelands long into the future, even if the GoL does not allow them to officially live there "permanently." In addition, people's knowledge of the soil conditions of their old lands continues to influence their agricultural decisions. People are not just cultivating swiddens and coffee randomly. For example, one man from Xenamnoy Village informed me, in 2011, that, "The land in our area is generally suitable for swidden agriculture, so that is what people from my village mainly do there. There is only a small amount of land suitable for coffee. However, the land of Houay Soy and Nam Leng is very good for coffee, so they grow more. People from Xenamnoy also move toward these territories to plant new coffee."

The Heuny have built small houses on their previous homelands. More permanent and slightly larger houses have been constructed near more permanent coffee plantations, while temporary houses, designed for people to live in only during single rainy seasons, are built on swidden fields. There are no villages left in the old homeland of the Heuny, but there are various houses distributed throughout the landscape, with most people locating themselves according to former patterns, and on their own community territories. The coffee plantations have, in recent years, been quite profitable, as coffee prices are much higher now than they were in the late 1990s. Thus, many Heuny families have generated significant income from coffee, which has further contributed to people becoming attached to their old homelands. This income has also allowed for the purchase of motorcycles. In the late 1990s, the Heuny had very few motorcycles, but now they have many. Part of the reason is an influx of relatively cheap Chinese motorcycles, which have made it feasible for even poor families to pool money to purchase them. Crucially, changes in modes of transportation have significantly reduced the travel time and effort required to move between the resettlement villages and the old homelands, since the Heuny can now travel the more-than-40-kilometer journey in only about three hours in the dry season and about four hours during the rainy season. In essence, the purchasing of motorcycles and improvements of roads in the area have resulted in what David Harvey (1989) has called time-space compression.[23] This has effectively made the resettlement villages closer to the old villages, and actually encouraged Heuny people to return to their old homelands, as it is no longer as arduous a journey as in the past.

Subdistrict government officials living in the resettlement area have also become increasingly concerned about the number of people going back to their old lands. They clearly fear that district and provincial officials may become angry with them for not being able to keep the people from leaving the resettlement areas, and causing the district and province to acknowledge that the resettlement program, which was once the flagship focal site of the province, has been an utter failure. Furthermore, they are losing control of the population as more and more people refuse to stay in the resettlement areas. This is threatening the authority that has been put in them by the State. As a response, since 2009, these officials have begun trying to reinvigorate their faltering control over the people and space by insisting that every villager be present in their official villages on the 15th day of each month, at which time a sort of "roll call" is performed as a way of both reminding the Heuny in their political jurisdiction that these officials are still able to wield some power, and also to protect themselves from criticism from government officials higher up. At least they can claim that they are trying to keep the people in the resettlement villages, as they can say that everyone is present in the resettlement villages at least once a month, although they are certainly aware that the whole exercise has more symbolic value than actually serving to keep people in the resettlement villages, or increase their attachment to them. While this is an attempt to control the Heuny population, the fact that the people are still able to return to their old villages demonstrates a certain level of compromise that allows both the interests of the government and the people to be partially met. Officials can do little more, as they have little to offer them in the resettlement sites.

Therefore, people drive their bicycles and motorcycles, or sometimes their tractors (*lot toke toke* in Lao) so that they are present on the 15th of each month, and then soon after they return to their old territories until the next month. They cannot stay in the resettlement villages for long, as the original houses built for them when they were first resettled have largely deteriorated. Termites have eaten much of them, and most are no longer habitable, even if the people wanted to live in them.

While not exactly the same as during the French colonial period, the GoL is nonetheless continuing to administer the Heuny primarily through using Heuny local officials, as the French did through the *Nai Kong* system, when *Nai Kong* were selected by the French to be leaders of particular ethnic groups or groups of villages, especially with regard to acting as their representatives when dealing with the French administration. But Heuny officials, as part of the government, are also involved in influencing and interpreting government policies. This has resulted in Heuny villagers frequently engaging in verbal disputes with local officials from their own ethnic group, rather than government officials from other ethnic backgrounds. Thus, much of the jostling going on is actually between Heuny and other Heuny, with people from other ethnic groups higher up in government hearing little if anything about what is happening.

Conclusion

Ultimately, this chapter has been about what Porteous and Smith call "domicide," or the destruction of home (Porteous and Smith 2001). In this case, it is the landscapes that are particularly important, rather than the houses themselves. As with Porteous and Smith, I have examined "how and why powerful people destroy the homes of the less powerful, which happen to be in the way of corporate, political, or bureaucratic projects" (Porteous and Smith 2001: ix). I concur that there has been insufficient attention paid to the impacts of destroying homes, or removing people from landscapes endowed with meaning. My emphasis, however, has not only been on the destruction of homelands, but also on the human agency of a particular social group of people who have become the victims of what can appropriately be called "attempted domicide." It has only been attempted because those targeted have used memory as one tool for remaining attached to their homelands, and ultimately subverting state efforts to commit domicide against them.

In the case of the Heuny, the strategy for doing this has focused on removing people from their homelands by physically resettling them, and dismantling their previous houses and villages, and subsequently trying to prohibit them from returning to their homelands. Certainly officials who desire change recognize that memory is a significant obstacle for them in successfully reorganizing the people. This is one of the reasons that positive memories about the pre-1975 period, such as those related to interactions between Heuny and American aid workers, or being able to conduct swidden agriculture without as many constrictions, are discouraged, so as to eventually lead to those experiences being forgotten and memories being replaced with new ones of positive aspects of the post-1975 political system. For example, the people are now said to be "independent," whereas they are characterized as having been under American imperialism (a point that some would dispute) prior to 1975.

In any case, the Heuny have managed to maintain close links to their homelands through reproducing memories of the past, as well as deepening their material connections to the landscape through various practices, including conducting swidden agriculture, developing coffee plantations, maintaining cemeteries, and continuing to recognize sacred places and previously defined village territorial boundaries. As Halbwachs (1992) has indicated, maintaining physical relations with landscapes is crucial for the ways we construct and reconstruct landscape memories, or what can be called "memoryscapes." Even if their original houses and villages are no longer intact, Heuny connections to their homelands have remained strong, and have seemingly strengthened over time, despite government efforts to prevent this from happening. These present-day material links to the landscape and the agency acquired through memory are both important for understanding these particular attachments to places.

Memories are crucial, as their maintenance through the production and reproduction of particular discourses have allowed the Heuny to compare the past with the present, and to see their old homelands as places of relative prosperity, as places without land conflicts and disputes, as places where people are free to do as they please, and as places where the Heuny can look at landscapes and call them their own. Memories are helping to empower the Heuny with visions for the future that link them to particular places viewed as homelands. The GoL has made sure that the original houses and villages of the Heuny have been destroyed, but they have been unable, at least so far, to destroy the memoryscapes that constitute the true "homes" of the people.

Acknowledgements

Although the identities of my informants must remain anonymous in order to protect them, I would like to thank all the Heuny people who have, over the years, helped me understand their circumstances. Any deficiencies in this chapter are entirely my responsibility. I would like to thank Oliver Tappe and Vatthana Pholsena for providing useful comments on an earlier version of this chapter. Thanks, also, for the comments of two anonymous reviewers. I take full responsibility for any deficiencies that remain.

Notes

1. See Baird (2009b).
2. For examples related to Laos, see Baird (2007); Pholsena (2003, 2004, 2006, 2008); and Evans (1998).
3. See, for example, Pholsena (2008).
4. Wildlife Conservation Society (1995).
5. US$50 million was financed through equity and the rest of the financing came from a variety of international banks and financial institutions (Sparkes 2000).
6. BOOT projects involve private investment in infrastructure, in this case a hydropower dam. The investor has the ability to sell electricity for a specified period, maybe 25 or 30 years. The infrastructure is then handed over to the government. These types of projects are also sometimes referred to as Built Operate and Transfer (BOT) projects.
7. The concession agreement was not transparent, and as already mentioned above, the contract was not favorable to the GoL, since few taxes and royalties were required, even though the GoL had to make US$1.8 million annual payments in interest beginning in 2000 when it took out a US$10 million

equity loan for the project from Daewoo, at nine percent interest (Nok 2008). The GoL was also not scheduled to receive any benefits from the project for 10–12 years, until the foreign investors had recovered their entire investment (International Rivers Network 1999).

8. The Thai government agreed to buy 126 MW of power from Houay Ho at a price of 4.22 cents/KWh.

9. It was not until 1999 that the GoL passed its Environment Law, making EIAs for large dams compulsory (Baird and Shoemaker 2008: 350).

10. At the time, legislation had not yet been passed that would require that all large dams be subjected to detailed social and environment impact assessments.

11. Unlike the lowland Lao, the Heuny and the Jrou bury their dead in cemeteries.

12. "Tractebel Moves into Southeast Asian Hydro," *International Water Power & Dam Construction*, 1 Oct. 2001.

13. In the 1960s and early 1970s, part of their territory was included in Sayasila District in Attapeu Province; see Sage (1970).

14. Other Heuny villages in Paksong are also presently scheduled for resettlement, as well as other impacts, as a result of the development of the Xekatam Dam (Lawrence 2008).

15. See Conboy (1995) and Briggs (2009) for a general overview of the role of road-watchers.

16. Gary Oughton, personal communication, Apr. 1995.

17. Ibid.

18. For a similar example of village-to-village borders among a Western-Bahnaric language-speaking group, see Baird (2008), in relation to the ethnic Brao of southern Laos and northeastern Cambodia.

19. Quoted by Phetsavanh (2004: 5).

20. Dot La-ounmuang, personal communication, Feb. 2006 and Mar. 2010.

21. However, Dong Ah Co. built a number of new roads, and upgraded others, in preparation for full-scale construction before the project was cancelled.

22. Animist rituals involve sacrificing chickens, pigs or buffaloes to malevolent spirits that are believed to cause illness or misfortunate to people if they are not appeased through sacrifices.

23. That is, space has shrunk because it has become possible to pass through it with much less effort, and over much shorter periods of time.

BIBLIOGRAPHY

110th Congress US Senate. "Making Emergency Supplemental Appropriations for the Fiscal Year End September 30, 2007 and For Other Purposes." *Senate Conference Report*. Washington, DC: General Printing Office, 2007.

Agence France-Presse. "Clinton Vows to Increase Cooperation on Agent Orange," 26 July 2010.

Ageron, Charles Robert, and Pierre Nora. *Les Lieux de Mémoire*, tome 1. Paris: Gallimard, Collection Quarto, 1997.

Al Jazeera English. "101 East — Vietnam After Agent Orange, Part 2," 10 Sept. 2009. Available at http://www.youtube.com/watch?v=AaWRNEy1ukw&feature =share&list=PLBA9A8330B893A804 [accessed 16 May 2011].

Allen, John. *Lost Geographies of Power*. Oxford: Blackwell, 2003.

Allerton, Catherine. "Landscape, Power and Agency in Eastern Indonesia." In *Southeast Asian Perspectives on Power*, ed. Liana Chua *et al.* London: Routledge, 2012, pp. 67–80.

Alleton, Isabel. "Les Hmong aux confins de la Chine et du Viêtnam: La révolte du 'Fou' (1918–1922)." In *Histoire de l'Asie du Sud-Est. Révoltes, réformes, révolutions*, ed. Pierre Brocheux. Lille: Presses Universitaires de Lille, 1981, pp. 31–46.

Alneng, Victor. "What the Fuck is a Vietnam? Touristic Phantasms and Popcolonization of (the) Vietnam (War)." *Critique of Anthropology* 22, 4 (2002): 461–89.

Ang Cheng Guan. *The Vietnam War from the Other Side: The Vietnamese Communists' Perspective*. London: RoutledgeCurzon, 2002.

Appadurai, Arjun. "Introduction: Commodities and the Politics of Value." In *The Social Life of Things: Commodities in Cultural Perspective*, ed. Arjun Appadurai. Cambridge: Cambridge University Press, 1986, pp. 3–63.

————, ed. *The Social Life of Things: Commodities in Cultural Perspective*. Cambridge: Cambridge University Press, 1986.

Argenti, Nicolas, and Katharina Schramm. "Introduction: Remembering Violence." In *Remembering Violence: Anthropological Perspectives on Intergenerational Transmission*, ed. Nicolas Argenti and Katharina Schramm. Oxford: Berghahn, 2009, pp. 1–40.

Assmann, Jan. *Das kulturelle Gedächtnis: Schrift, Erinnerung und politische Identität in frühen Hochkulturen*. Munich: Beck, 1992.

_____. *Moses the Egyptian: The Memory of Egypt in Western Monotheism*. Cambridge: Harvard University Press, 1997.

Associated Press. "USATODAY.com — Conference Tackles 'Ghost' of Vietnam War," 3 Mar. 2002. Available at http://www.usatoday.com/news/world/2002/03/03/orange.htm [accessed 16 May 2011].

_____. *Decades On, Agent Orange Still Stalks Vietnam* [video], 1 July 2010.

Augé, Marc. *Non-Spaces*. London: Verso, 1995.

Baird, Ian G. "Laos." In *The Indigenous World 2005*. Copenhagen: International Work Group for Indigenous Affairs (IWGIA), 2005.

_____. "Contested History, Ethnicity and Remembering the Past: The Case of the Ay Sa Rebellion in Southern Laos." *Crossroads* 18, 2 (2007): 119–59.

_____. "Controlling the Margins: Nature Conservation and State Power in Northeastern Cambodia." In *Development and Dominion: Indigenous Peoples of Cambodia, Vietnam and Laos*, ed. Frédéric Bourdier. Bangkok: White Lotus Press, 2009a.

_____. "Spatial (Re)Organization and Places of the Brao in Southern Laos and Northeastern Cambodia." *Singapore Journal of Tropical Geography* 30 (2009b): 299–312.

Baird, Ian G., and Bruce Shoemaker. "Unsettling Experiences: Internal Resettlement and International Aid Agencies in Laos." *Development and Change* 38, 5 (2007): 865–88.

_____. *People, Livelihoods and Development in the Xekong River Basin of Laos*. Bangkok: White Lotus Press, 2008.

Baird, Ian G., and Philippe Le Billon. "Landscapes of Political Memories: War Legacies and Land Negotiations in Laos." *Political Geography* 31 (2012): 290–300.

Basu, Paul. "Palimpsest Memoryscapes: Materializing and Mediating War and Peace in Sierra Leone." In *Reclaiming Heritage: Alternative Imaginaries of Memory in West Africa*, ed. Ferdinand de Jong and Michael Rowlands. Walnut Creek: Left Coast Press, 2007, pp. 231–59.

Baughman, Robert, and Matthew Meselson. "An Analytical Method for Detecting TCDD (Dioxin): Levels of TCDD in Samples from Vietnam." *Environmental Health Perspectives* 5 (1973): 27–35.

Beck, Ulrich. *Risk Society: Towards a New Modernity*. London: Sage Publications, 1992.

Bender, Barbara. *Landscape: Politics and Perspectives*. London: Berg, 1993.

Beng Hong Socheat Khmero. "Phnom Penh and Its Lost Battle for Preservation of Historic Buildings from the 1970's." *Siksacakr* 2 (2000): 10–3.

Bensinger, Gail. "Shadows of Agent Orange, Third Generation of Vietnam Victims." *San Francisco Chronicle*, 24 Mar. 2003, p. A1.

Bensoussan, Georges. *Génocides: Lieux (et non-lieux) de mémoire*. Paris: Centre de documentation juive contemporaine, 2004.

Bertrand, Didier. *Children Affected by UXO Accidents in Lao PDR: A Psychological Study of Impacts of UXO Accident on Children and Their Families*. Vientiane: Handicap International, 2004.

Biersack, Aletta, ed. *Clio in Oceania*. Washington, DC: Smithsonian Institution Press, 1991.

Birnbaum, Linda. *What is Dioxin?* [video], S. Lewis, Interviewer, 19 Apr. 2004.

Bloch, Maurice, and Jonathan Parry. *Death and the Regeneration of Life*. Cambridge: Cambridge University Press, 1982.

Boholm, Asa. "The Cultural Nature of Risk: Can There be an Anthropology of Uncertainty?" *Ethnos* 68, 2 (2001): 159–78.

Boltanski, Luc. *Distant Suffering: Morality, Media and Politics*. Cambridge: Cambridge University Press, 1999.

BOMICEN (Technology Centre for Bomb and Mine Disposal) and VVAF (Vietnam Veterans of America Foundation). *Report on Vietnam Unexploded Ordnance and Landmine Impact Assessment and Rapid Technical Response in Six Provinces of Nghe An, Ha Tinh, Quang Binh, Quang Tri, Thua Thien Hue and Quang Ngai*. Hanoi, 2009.

Bounsang Khamkeo. *I Little Slave: A Prison Memoir from Communist Laos*. Washington, DC: Eastern Washington University Press, 2006.

Bourdier, Frédéric. *Management of Indigenous Minorities Land and Natural Resources in Cambodia*. Phnom Penh: Institut de Recherche et de Développement (IRD), 2005.

_____. *The Mountain of Precious Stones Ratanakiri, Cambodia: Essays in Social Anthropology*. Cambodia: Center for Khmer Studies, 2006.

Branfman, Fred. "Air War in Laos." Statement in *US Congressional Record*. Washington, DC: US Government Printing Office, 14 Oct. 1971.

_____. *Voices from the Plain of Jars: Life under an Air War*. Vientiane: Cluster Munition Coalition, 2010 (orig. publ.: New York: Harper and Row, 1972).

Briggs, Thomas L. *Cash on Delivery: CIA Operations during the Secret War in Laos*. Rockville, MD: Rosebank Press, 2009.

Caplan, Pat, ed. *Risk Revisted*. London: Pluto Press, 2000.

Carruthers, Mary. *The Book of Memory: A Study of Memory in Medieval Culture*. Cambridge: Cambridge University Press, 1990.

Casey, Edward. *The Fate of Place: A Philosophical History*. Berkeley, CA: University of California Press, 1998.

Central Intelligence Agency. *World Factbook, Laos*. Est. pop., July 2012. Available at https://www.cia.gov/library/publications/the-world-factbook/geos/la.html [accessed 19 Oct. 2012].

Chandler, David. *Voices from S-21: Terror and History in Pol Pot's Secret Prison*. Berkeley, CA: University of California Press, 1999.

_____. *A History of Cambodia*, 4th edition. Boulder, CO: Westview, 2008a.

_____. "Cambodia Deals with Its Past: Collective Memory, Demonisation and Induced Amnesia." *Totalitarian Movements and Political Religions* 9, 2–3 (2008b): 355–69.

Chanh Cong Phan. "The Vietnamese Concept of Human Souls and the Rituals of Birth and Death." *Southeast Asian Journal of Social Science* 21, 2 (1993): 159–98.

Chanthi Deuansavan. *Senthang haeng sivit* [*The Way of Life*]. Vientiane: Lao Writers Association, 2007.

Ciorcari, John D. *The Khmer Rouge Tribunal*. Phnom Penh: Documentation Center of Cambodia, 2006.

Cohen, Stanley. "State Crimes of Previous Regimes: Knowledge, Accountability, and the Policing of the Past." *Law & Social Inquiry* 20, 1 (1995): 7–50.

_____. *States of Denial. Knowing about Atrocities and Suffering*. Cambridge: Polity Press, 2001.

Cole, Jennifer. *Forget Colonialism? Memory and the Art of Sacrifice in Madagascar*. Berkeley and Los Angeles, CA: University of California Press, 2001.

Colombijn, Freek. "Introduction. On the road." *Bijdragen tot de Taal-, Land- en Volkenkunde* 158, 4 (2002): 595–617.

Conboy, Kenneth (with James Morrison). *Shadow War: The CIA's Secret War in Laos*. Boulder, CO: Paladin Press, 1995.

Condominas, Georges. *Nous Avons Mangé la Forêt de la Pierre-Génie Gôo*. Paris: Mercure de France, 1957.

Confino, Alon. "Traveling as a Culture of Remembrance: Traces of National Socialism in West Germany, 1945–1960." *History & Memory* 12, 2 (2000): 92–121.

_____. "Review Article. Telling about Germany: Narratives of Memory and Culture." *The Journal of Modern History* 76 (2004): 389–416.

Connerton, Paul. *How Societies Remember*. Cambridge: Cambridge University Press, 1989.

Cotterill, Colin. *Disco for the Departed*. Vientiane: Lao-Insight Books, 2006.

Courtney, K.D., D.W. Gaylor, M.D. Hogan, H.L. Falk, R.R. Bates, and L. Michell. "Teratogenic Evaluation of 2,4,5-T." *Science* 168, 933 (1970): 864–6.

Cronon, William. "A Place for Stories: Nature, History, and Narrative." *The Journal of American History* 78, 4 (1992): 1347–76.

Culas, Christian, and Jean Michaud. "A Contribution to the Study of Hmong (Miao) Migrations and History." *Bijdragen tot de Taal-, Land- en Volkenkunde* 153 (1997): 211–43.

Cupet, Pierre-Paul. *Travels in Laos and Among the Tribes of Southeast Indochina. The Pavie Mission Indochina Papers, Vol. 6*. Bangkok: White Lotus, 2000 [orig. publ. 1900].

Daniel, E. Valentine. *Charred Lullabies: Chapters in an Anthropography of Violence*. Princeton, NJ: Princeton University Press, 1996.

Dasberg, H., S. Davidson, G.L. Durlacher, B.C. Filet, and E. de Wind. *Society and Trauma of War*. Sinai Papers, Van Gorcum, Assen Maastricht, The Netherlands, 1987.

Del Testa, David Willson. "Paint the Trains Red: Labour, Nationalism and the Railroads in French Colonial Indochina, 1898–1945." Unpublished PhD thesis, University of California, Davis, 2001.

Delang, Claudio O., and Matthew Toro. "Hydropower-Induced Displacement and Resettlement in the Lao PDR." *South East Asia Research* 19 (2011): 567–94.

Delvert, Jean. "Le Paysan Cambodgien." Unpublished PhD thesis, École Pratique des Hautes Études, Paris, 1961.

Dennis, John. *Field Visit to the Se Kong Basin, September 1997: Summary of Sociological Findings, for the Se Kong-Se San and Nam Theun River Basins Hydropower Study*. Vientiane, Lao PDR, 9 Oct. 1997.

DiGregorio, Michael. *Recycling in Hanoi*. Southeast Asia Discussion List, 5 Feb. 1995. Available at http://www.hartford-hwp.com/archives/25b/003.html [accessed 10 June 2011].

————. "Things Held in Common: Memory, Space and the Reconstitution of Community Life." *Journal of Southeast Asian Studies* 38, 3 (2007): 441–65.

Doray, Bernard, and Concepcion de la Garza. "Conventional War and Chemical Warfare in A Luoi from a Psychological Angle." *Proceedings from the International Scientific Conference: Victims of Agent Orange/Dioxin in Vietnam — The Expectations*. Hanoi: Center for Genter, Family, Environment and Development, 2006.

Douglas, Mary. *Purity and Danger: An Analysis of the Concepts of Pollution and Taboo*. New York: Routledge, 1966.

————. "Risk as a Forensic Resource." *Daedalus* 119, 4 (1990): 1–16.

————. *Risk and Blame: Essays in Cultural Theory*. London: Routledge, 1992.

Douglas, Mary, and Aaron Wildavsky. *Risk and Culture*. Berkeley, CA: University of California Press, 1983.

Dournes, Jacques. "Coordonnées — Structures jörai familiales et sociales." *Travaux et Mémoires de l'Institut d'ethnologie*, tome LXXVII, Musée de l'Homme, Paris, 1972.

————. *Forêt, Femme, Folie. Une traversée de l'imaginaire jörai*. Paris: Aubier-Montaigne, 1978.

————. *Florilège Jörai*. Paris: Sud Est Asie, 1987.

Duncan, James. "Place." In *The Dictionary of Human Geography*, 4th edition, ed. Ron J. Johnston, Derek Gregory, Geraldine Pratt, and Michael Watts. Oxford and Malden, MA: Blackwell, 2000.

Dương Vương Lợi. "80 công ty tìm hiểu đầu tư vào khu kinh tế Lao Bảo" [80 Companies Survey Investment in the Lao Bảo Economic Zone], *VietnamPlus*, 10 Mar. 2010. Available at http://www.vietnamplus.vn/Home/80-cong-ty-tim-hieu-dau-tu-vao-khu-kinh-te-Lao Bao/20113/81053.vnplus [accessed 10 June 2011].

Dwernychuk, Wayne. "The Agent Orange Problem in Vietnam: A Manageble Problem." Paper presented at the 26th International Symposium on Halogenated Persistent Organic Pollutants — DIOXIN2006, Oslo, 2006.

——————. "What is Dioxin?" Available at http://www.agentorangerecord.com [accessed 25 Aug. 2010].

Dwyer, Owen. "Symbolic Accretion and Commemoration." *Social and Cultural Geography* 5, 3 (2004): 419–35.

Dy Kamboly. *A History of Democratic Kampuchea (1975–79)*. Phnom Penh: Documentation Center of Cambodia, 2007.

Dyrchs, Susanne. *Das hybride Khmer Rouge Tribunal. Entstehung, Entwicklung und rechtliche Grundlagen.* Frankfurt: Peter Lang, 2008.

Emde, Sina. "Please Compose Yourself. Testimony, Memory and Emotion at the Extraordinary Chambers in the Courts of Cambodia." In *Trauma, Memory and Transformation in South East Asia*, ed. Sharon A. Bong and Andrew Ng Hock-soon (in preparation).

Endres, Kirsten. *Ritual, Fest und Politik in Nordvietnam: Zwischen Ideologie und Tradition.* Münster: Lit, 2003.

——————. "Engaging the Spirits of the Dead: Soul-Calling Rituals and the Performative Construction of Efficacy." *Journal of the Royal Anthropological Institute* 14, 4 (2008): 755–73.

Engelbert, Thomas, and Christopher E. Goscha. *Falling Out of Touch: A History of Vietnamese Cambodian Relations, 1930–1975.* Melbourne: Monash University Monographs Series, 1995.

Erll, Astrid. "Cultural Memory Studies: An Introduction." In *Cultural Memory Studies: An International and Interdisciplinary Handbook*, ed. Astrid Erll and Ansgar Nünning. Berlin and New York: de Gruyter, 2008, pp. 1–15.

Evans, Grant. *The Politics of Ritual and Remembrance: Laos since 1975.* Honolulu, HI: University of Hawai'i Press, 1998.

——————. *A Short History of Laos: The Land in Between.* Crow's Nest, Australia: Allen & Unwin, 2002.

——————. "Book Review: Lao Gulags." *Bangkok Post*, 13 Sept. 2003.

——————. *The Last Century of Lao Royalty: A Documentary History.* Chiang Mai: Silkworm, 2009.

Fawthrop, Tom, and Helen Jarvis. *Getting Away with Genocide? Elusive Justice and the Khmer Rouge Tribunal.* London: Pluto, 2004.

Feldman, Allen. "The Actuarial Gaze: From 9/11 to Abu Ghraib." *Cultural Studies* 19, 2 (2005): 203–26.

Fentress, James, and Chris Wickham. *Social Memory: New Perspectives on the Past.* Oxford: Blackwell Publishers, 1992.

Flower, John M. "A Road is Made: Roads, Temples, and Historical Memory in Ya'an County, Sichuan." *The Journal of Asian Studies* 63, 3 (2004): 649–85.

Form, Wolfgang. "Justice Thirty Years Later? The Cambodian Special Tribunal for the Punishment of Crimes against Humanity by the Khmer Rouge." *Nationalities Papers* 37, 6 (2009): 889–923.

Foropon, Jean. "La province des Hua-Phan (Laos)." *Extrême-Asie* 14 (1927): 93–106.

Fox, Diane. "'One Significant Ghost': Agent Orange Narratives of Trauma, Survival and Responsibility." Unpublished PhD thesis, University of Washington, 2007.

François, Étienne. *Lieux de mémoire: D'un modèle français à un projet allemand.* Berlin: Centre Marc Bloch, 1996.

Fukushima, Masato. "Social Memory Reconsidered." In *Cultural Crisis and Social Memory: Modernity and Identity in Thailand and Laos*, ed. Shigeharu Tanabe and Charles F. Keyes. New York and London: RoutledgeCurzon, 2002, pp. 287–99.

Galbraith, Kenneth. *The Anatomy of Power.* Boston: Houghton Mifflin, 1983.

Gardner, Janet (Director). *Last Ghost of War* [motion picture], 2008.

Garnier, Francis. *Voyage d'exploration en Indochine.* Paris: Editions La Découverte, 1985 (1873).

Gay, Bernard. "La frontière Vietnamo-Lao de 1893 à nos jours." In *Les Frontières du Vietnam: Histoire des frontières de la péninsule indochinoise*, ed. Pierre B. Lafont. Paris: l'Harmattan, 1999, pp. 204–32.

Gell, Alfred. *Art and Agency: An Anthropological Theory.* Oxford: Clarendon Press, 1998.

Geneva International Center for Humanitarian Demining. *A Study of Scrap Metal Collection in Lao PDR.* Geneva, Switzerland, 2005.

Giddens, Anthony. *Modernity and Self-Identity: Self and Society in the Late Modern Age.* Palo Alto, CA: Stanford University Press, 1991.

Gordillo, Gastón R. "The Dialectics of Estrangement: Memory and the Production of Places of Wealth and Poverty in the Argentinean Chaco." *Cultural Anthropology* 17, 1 (2002): 3–31.

————. *Landscapes of Devils: Tensions of Place and Memory in the Argeninean Chaco.* Durham, NC and London: Duke University Press, 2004.

————. "Ships Stranded in the Forest." *Current Anthropology* 52, 2 (2011): 141–67.

Goscha, Christopher E. "Une guerre pour l'Indochine? Le Laos et le Cambodge dans le conflit franco-vietnamien (1948–1954)." *Guerres mondiales et conflits contemporains* 3, 211 (2003): 29–58.

————. "Vietnam and the World Outside: The Case of Vietnamese Communist Advisors in Laos (1948–1962)." *South East Asia Research* 12, 2 (2004): 141–86.

————. "The Revolutionary Laos of the Democratic Republic of Vietnam: The Making of a Transnational 'Pathet Lao Solution' (1954–1957)." In *L'échec de la paix? L'Indochine entre les deux accords de Genève (1954–1963)*, ed. Christopher E. Goscha and Karine Laplante. Paris: Les Indes savantes, 2010, pp. 61–84.

————. *Going Indochinese: Contesting Concepts of Space and Place in French Indochina.* Copenhagen: Nordic Institute of Asian Studies, NIAS Classics series, no. 3, 2012.

Gottesman, Evan. *Cambodia after the Khmer Rouge: Inside the Politics of Nation Building*. New Haven, CT: Yale University Press, 2003.

Government of the Lao PDR. "Laos Pursues Goals of Cluster Munitions Convention." Vientiane, 2012a. Available at http://www.laopdr.gov.la/ePortal/news/detail.action;jsessionid=JsT8QWhLyJFmh3Dhg31KsGf24rrnWQBpVcGtKlQGt22VxKyCP7gG!257450768?id=33470&from=ePortal_NewsDetail_FromHome [accessed 1 Nov. 2012].

_____. *National Strategic Plan for the UXO Sector in the Lao People's Democratic Republic 2011–2020, "The Safe Path Forward II."* Vientiane, Lao PDR, 22 June 2012b. Available at http://www.nra.gov.la/resources/UXO%20Sector%20Strategy/SPFII%20%20Eng.pdf [accessed 9 Oct. 2012].

_____. *Statement of the Delegation of LAO PDR on Victim Assistance: Third Meeting of the States Parties to the Convention on Cluster Munitions*. Oslo, Norway, Sept. 2012a. Available at http://www.clusterconvention.org/files/2012/09/Victim-Assistance-Lao.pdf [accessed 28 Oct. 2012].

_____. *Statement of the Delegation of LAO PDR on Victim Assistance: Third Meeting of the States Parties to the Convention on Cluster Munitions*. Oslo, Norway. Sept. 2012b. Available at http://www.clusterconvention.org/files/2012/09/Victim-Assistance-Lao.pdf [accessed 15 Oct. 2012].

Goy, Bertrand, and Jean-Yves Coué. *Jaraï. Art de guerre et de mort chez les montagnards d'Indochine*. Paris: Mémoires françaises, Les Indes savantes, 2006.

Grabowsky, Volker, and Oliver Tappe. "'Important Kings of Laos': Translation and Analysis of a Lao Cartoon Pamphlet." *Journal of Lao Studies* 2, 1 (2011): 1–44.

Greene, Sandra E. *Sacred Sites and the Colonial Encounter: A History of Meaning and Memory in Ghana*. Bloomington, IN: Indiana University Press, 2002.

Griffiths, Philip Jones. *Agent Orange Collateral Damage*. London: Trolley Books, 2003.

Grotto, Jason, and Tim Jones. "Agent Orange's Lethal Legacy: For US, A Record of Neglect." *Chicago Tribune*, 4 Dec. 2009. Available at http://www.chicagotribune.com/health/agentorange/chi-agent-orange1-dec04,0,1766354.story [accessed 16 May 2011].

Guérin, Matthieu, Andrew Hardy, Nguyen Van Chinh, and Stan B.H. Tan. *Des montagnards aux minorités ethniques. Quelle intégration nationale pour les habitants des hautes terres du Viêt Nam et du Cambodge?* Bangkok-Paris: L'Harmattan-IRASEC, 2003.

Gustafsson, Mai Lan. *War and Shadows: The Haunting of Vietnam*. Ithaca, NY: Cornell University Press, 2009.

Halbwachs, Maurice. *La mémoire collective*. Paris: Université de France Press, 1950.

_____. *On Collective Memory*. Chicago, IL: The University of Chicago Press, 1992. Translated from: *Les cadres sociaux de la mémoire*. Paris: Presses Universitaires de France, 1952.

Halcrow, Sir William, and Partners. *Se Kong-Se San and Nam Theun River Basins Hydropower Study — Initial Environmental Examination.* Manila: Asian Development Bank, 1998.

Handicap International. *Living with UXO: Final Report on the National Survey on the Socio-Economic Impact of UXO in Lao PDR.* Brussels: Handicap International Belgium, 1997.

_____. *Circle of Impact: Report on the Fatal Impact of Cluster Munitions.* Brussels: Handicap International Belgium, 2007. Available at http://www. handicap-international.be/publicaties/%E2%80%9Ccircle-of-impact%E2%80% 9D-rapport-over-de-fatale-impact-van-clustermunitie [accessed 14 June 2011].

Haney, Walt. "A Survey of Civilian War Casualties Among Refugees from the Plain of Jars." *1971 Senate Hearing before the Subcommittee to Investigate Problems Connected with Refugees and Escapees*: US Senate 22 July 1971. Washington, DC: USGPO, 1971, pp. 65–106. Available at http://legaciesofwar. org/resources/walt-haney-papers/ [accessed 7 July 2011].

_____. "A Survey of Civilian Fatalities among Refugees from Zieng Khouang Province, Laos." *Subcommittee to Investigate Problems Connected with Refugees and Escapees. United States Senate 9 May 1972.* Washington, DC: USGPO, 1972, pp. 53–66. Available at http://legaciesofwar.org/resources/walt-haney-papers/ [accessed 7 July 2011].

_____. "The Pentagon Papers and the United States involvement in Laos." In *The Pentagon Papers, Gravel edition: Critical essays, Vol. 5*, ed. Noam Chomsky and Howard Zinn. Boston, MA: Beacon Press, 1972. Available at http://legaciesofwar.org/resources/walt-haney-papers/ [accessed 7 July 2011].

Harris, Ian. *Cambodian Buddhism: History and Practice.* Honolulu, HI: University of Hawai'i Press, 2005.

Harvey, David. *The Condition of Postmodernity.* Oxford: Basil Blackwell, 1989.

Hatfield Consultants. *Preliminary Assessment of Environmental Impacts Related to Spraying of Agent Orange Herbicides during the Vietnam War.* Vancouver, Canada: Hatfield Consultants, 1998.

_____. "Summary of the Dioxin Contamination at the Đà Nẵng, Phù Cát and Biên Hòa Airbases." Washington, DC: Powerpoint Presentation, June 2009.

Hatfield Consultants & Committee 33. *Assessment of Dioxin Contamination in the Environment and Human Population in the Vicinity of Đà Nẵng Airbase, Việt Nam.* West Vancouver, Canada: Hatfield Consultants, 2007.

_____. *Comprehensive Assessment of Dioxin Contamination in Đà Nẵng Airport, Vietnam: Environmental Levels, Human Exposure and Options for Mitigating Impacts.* West Vancouver, Canada: Hatfield Consultants, Ltd, 2009.

Hatfield Consultants, 10-80 Committee. *Development of Impact Mitigation Strategies Related to the use of Agent Orange Herbicide in the A Luoi Valley, Vietnam.* West Vancouver, Canada: Hatfield Consultants Ltd, 2000.

HDNET World Report. *Vietnam's Lingering Ghost: Facing the Legacy of Agent Orange* [video], 2010.

Heidegger, Martin. *Being and Time*. New York: Harper & Row, 1962 (orig. publ. Tübingen: Niemeyer, 1927).

Henig, David. "Iron in the Soil: Living with Military Waste in Bosnia-Herzegovina." *Anthropology Today* 28, 1 (2012): 21–3.

Hertz, Robert. *Death and the Right Hand*, trans. Rodney and Claudia Needham. London: Cohen and West, 1960.

Herzfeld, Michael. *A Place in History: Social and Monumental Time in a Cretan Town*. Princeton, NJ: Princeton University Press, 1991.

_____. *Cultural Intimacy — Social Poetics in the Nation State*. London: Taylor & Francis, 1996.

Heuveline, Patrick. "Between One and Three Million: Towards a Demographic Reconstruction of a Decade of Cambodian History (1970–1979)." *Population Studies* 52 (1998): 49–65.

High, Holly. "Violent Landscape: Global Explosions and Lao Life-Worlds." *Global Environment* 1, 1 (2007): 56–79.

Hinton, Alexander. *Why Did They Kill? Cambodia in the Shadow of Genocide*. Berkeley, CA: University of California Press, 2005.

_____. "Truth, Representation and the Politics of Memory after Genocide." In *People of Virtue: Reconfiguring Religion, Power and Moral Order in Cambodia Today*, ed. Alexandra Kent and David Chandler. Washington, DC: NIAS Press, 2008, pp. 62–81.

Hirsch, Eric, and Michael O'Hanlon, eds. *The Anthropology of Landscape: Perspectives on Place and Space*. Oxford: Clarendon Press, 1995.

_____. "Introduction: Between Place and Space." In *The Anthropology of Landscape*, ed. Eric Hirsch and Michael O'Hanlon. Oxford: Clarendon Press, 1995, pp. 1–30.

Hizney, Mark. "Operational and Technical Aspects of Cluster Munitions." *United Nations Institute for Disarmament Research Forum 2006*, pp. 15–25. Available at http://www.unidir.ch/pdf/articles/pdf-art2530.pdf [accessed 28 Oct. 2012].

Holt, John C. "Caring for the Dead Ritually in Cambodia." *Southeast Asian Studies* 1, 1 (2012): 3–75

Hughes, Rachel. "Nationalism and Memory at the Tuol Sleng Museum of Genocidal Crimes." In *Contested Pasts: The Politics of Memory*, ed. Katharine Hodgkin and Susannah Radstone. London: Routledge, 2003, pp. 175–92.

_____. "Memory and Sovereignty in Post-1979 Cambodia: Choeung Ek and Local Genocide Memorials." In *Genocide in Cambodia and Rwanda: New Perspectives*, ed. Susan Cook. New Brunswick, NJ: Transaction Publishers, 2005, pp. 257–79.

_____. "Fielding Genocide: Post-1979 Cambodia and the Geopolitics of Memory." PhD diss., The University of Melbourne, University of Melbourne Digital Repository, 2006.

_____. "Dutiful Tourism — Encountering the Cambodian Genocide." *Asia-Pacific Viewpoint* 49, 3 (2008): 318–30.

Husserl, Edmund. *The Crisis of European Sciences and Transcendental Philosophy.* Evanston, IL: Northwestern University Press, 1970 (orig. publ. 1936).

Huy Vannak. *Bou Meng: A Survivor from Khmer Rouge Prison S-21.* Phnom Penh: Documentation Center of Cambodia, 2010.

Huyssen, Andreas. *Present Pasts: Urban Palimpsests and the Politics of Memory.* Palo Alto, CA: Stanford University Press, 2003.

Hydro-Electric Commission Enterprise Corporation. *Interim Report on Feasibility Study of Houay Ho Hydropower Project*, Volume 1, Australia, 1993.

Ingold, Tim. "The Temporality of the Landscape." *World Archaeology* 25, 2 (1993): 152–74.

————. *The Perception of the Environment: Essays in Livelihood, Dwelling and Skill.* London: Routledge, 2000.

Institute of Medicine. *Veterans and Agent Orange: Update 2008.* Washington, DC: Institute of Medicine of the National Academies, 2009.

International Rivers Network. *Power Struggle: The Impacts of Hydro-Development in Laos.* Berkeley, CA, 1999.

————. *Foiling the Aluminum Industry: A Toolkit for Communities, Activists, Consumers and Workers.* Berkeley, CA, 2005.

International Water Power & Dam Construction. "Tractebel Moves into Southeast Asian Hydro." 1 Oct. 2001.

IRIN Humanitarian News and Analysis, United Nations Office for the Coordination of Humanitarian Affairs. "LAOS: UXO Casualties Down but Challenges Remain." Available at http://www.irinnews.org/report.aspx?reportid=93154 [accessed 6 July 2011].

Jellema, Kate. "Everywhere Incense Burning: Remembering Ancestors in *Doi Moi* Vietnam." *Journal of Southeast Asian Studies* 38, 3 (2007): 467–92.

Jeong, Yeonsik. "The Rise of State Corporatism in Vietnam." *Contemporary Southeast Asia* 19 (1997): 152–71.

Kansteiner, Wulf. "Finding Meaning in Memory: A Methodological Critique of Collective Memory Studies." *History and Theory* 41, 2 (2002): 179–97.

Karnow, Stanley. *Vietnam: A History.* New York: Penguin, 1983.

Keane, Webb. *Signs of Recognition: Powers and Hazards of Representation in an Indonesian Society.* Berkeley and Los Angeles, CA: University of California Press, 1997.

Kent, Alexandra. "Reconfiguring Security: Buddhism and Moral Legitimacy in Cambodia." *Security Dialogue* 37 (2006): 343–61.

————. "Peace, Power and Pagodas in Present-Day Cambodia." *Contemporary Buddhism* 9, 1 (2008): 77–97.

————. "A Buddhist Bouncer: Reflections on Violence and the Control of Desire in a Cambodian Buddhist Monastery." *Journal of Contemporary Religion* 24, 3 (2009): 291–303.

————. "Sheltered by Dhamma: Reflecting on Gender, Security and Religion in Cambodia." *Journal of Southeast Asian Studies* 42, 2 (2011): 193–20.

Kent, Alexandra and David Chandler, eds. *People of Virtue: Reconfiguring Religion, Power and Moral Order in Cambodia Today*. Copenhagen: NIAS Press, 2008.

Keo, Dacil. "Fact Sheet on 'S-21' Tuol Sleng Prison." *Searching for the Truth December 2010*. Phnom Penh: Documentation Center of Cambodia, 2010. Available at http://www.dccam.org/Archives/Documents/Confessions/pdf/Fact_Sheet_on_S-21_Tuol_Sleng_Prison.pdf [accessed 7 Mar. 2011].

Khambay Nyundalath. "The Pluriethnical People's Affection and Confidence for President Souphanouvong." In *Autobiography of Prince Souphanouvong*, ed. Sisana Sisane. Vientiane: Committee of Social Sciences, 1989, pp. 133–8.

Khamphanh Thammakhanty. *Get to the Trunk, Destroy the Roots: The Fall from Monarchy to Socialism*. Portland, 2004, self-published.

Khamvongsa, Channapha and Elaine Russell. "Legacies of War," *Critical Asian Studies* 41, 2 (2009): 281–306.

Khao San Pathet Lao [KPL]. "Houay Ho Hydropower Station Runs into Problems." *Pathet Lao Daily Newspaper*, Vientiane, Lao PDR, 20 Feb. 2002.

Khu di tích lịch sử địa đạo Củ Chi (Cu Chi Tunnels Historical Remains). *The Documentary Album of Cu Chi 1960–1975, Album no. 2*. Ho Chi Minh City: Mũi Cà Mau, 2002.

Kiernan, Ben. *How Pol Pot Came to Power: Colonialism, Nationalism, and Communism in Cambodia, 1930–1975*. London: Verso, 1985.

_____. *The Pol Pot Regime: Race, Power and Genocide in Cambodia under the Khmer Rouge, 1975–1979*. New Haven, CT: Yale University Press, 1996 (1985).

_____. "The Demography of Genocide in South East Asia. The Death Tolls in Cambodia, 1975–1979, and East Timor, 1975–1980." *Critical Asian Studies* 35, 4 (2003): 585–97.

_____. "External and Indigenous Sources of the Khmer Rouge Ideology." In *The Third Indochina War: Conflict between China, Vietnam and Cambodia, 1972–79*, ed. Odd Arne Westad and Sophie Quinn-Judge. New York: Routledge, 2006, pp. 187–206.

Kiều Oanh. "300 năm nữa, Việt Nam mới sạch bom, mìn?" [Only After Another 300 Years will Vietnam be Clean of Bombs and Mines?]. *Tiền phong* [*Vanguard*], 1 Aug. 2009, pp. 1, 15.

Kleinman, Arthur, and Joan Kleinman. "The Appeal of Experience; The Dismay of Images: Cultural Appropriations of Suffering in Our Times." In *Social Suffering*, ed. Arthur Kleinman, Veena Das, and Margaret Lock. Los Angeles and Berkeley, CA: University of California Press, 1997, pp. 1–23.

Kleinen, John. *Facing the Future, Reviving the Past: A Study of Social Change in a Northern Vietnamese Village*. Singapore: Institute of Southeast Asian Studies, 1999.

Kondo, Dorinne K. *Crafting Selves, Power, Gender and Discourses of Identity in a Japanese Workplace*. Chicago, IL: University of Chicago Press, 1990.

Kopytoff, Igor. "The Cultural Biography of Things: Commoditization as Process." In *The Social Life of Things: Commodities in Cultural Perspective*, ed. Arjun Appadurai. Cambridge: Cambridge University Press, 1986.

Kristeva, Julia. *Powers of Horror: An Essay on Abjection*, trans. Leon Roudiez. New York: Columbia University Press, 1982.

Kuhn, Philip. *Rebellion and Its Enemies in Late Imperial China; Militarization and Social Structure, 1796–1864*. Cambridge: Harvard University Press, 1970.

Kwon, Heonik. *After the Massacre: Commemoration and Consolation in Hà Mỹ and Mỹ Lai*. Berkeley, CA: University of California Press, 2006.

————. *Ghosts of War in Vietnam*. Cambridge: Cambridge University Press, 2008.

Ladwig, Patrice. "Prediger der Revolution: Der buddhistische Mönchsorden in Laos und seine Verbindungen zur Kommunistischen Bewegung (1957–1975)." *Jahrbuch für Historische Kommunismusforschung* (2009): 181–97.

Lafont, Pierre-Bernard. "Prières Jarai." Collection de textes et documents sur l'Indochine. Paris: École Française d'Extrême Orient, 1963.

Lagrou, Pieter. *The Legacy of Nazi Occupation. Patriotic Memory and National Recovery in Western Europe, 1945–1965*. Cambridge: Cambridge University Press, 2000.

Lamb, David. "In Khe Sanh, Serenity Belies a Bloody Past." *Los Angeles Times*, 30 Jan. 1999, p. 2.

Lambek, Michael. *The Weight of the Past: Living with History in Mahajanga, Madagascar*. New York: Palgrave Macmillan, 2002.

Langer, Lawrence L. *Holocaust Testimonies: The Ruins of Memory*. New Haven, CT: Yale University Press, 1991.

Lao National Tourism Authority. *Voices of Viengxay — Stories from the 'Hidden City' from Interviews with People who Lived under Bombardment in North-eastern Laos from 1964 to 1973*. Vientiane: LNTA, 2010.

————. *Botlaingan sathiti kanthòngthiaew khòng s.p.p. lao pacham pi 2010* [*Statistical Report on Tourism in Lao PDR, Year 2010*]. Vientiane: LNTA, 2011.

Lap, Siu M. "Developing the First Preliminary Dictionary of North American Jarai." Unpublished Masters thesis in Anthropology, Texas Tech University, 2009.

Lary, Diana. *The Chinese People at War: Human Suffering and Social Transformation, 1937–1945*. Cambridge: Cambridge University Press, 2010.

Lary, Diana, and Stephen MacKinnon, eds. *The Scars of War: The Impact of Warfare on Modern China*. Vancouver: UBC Press, 2001.

Lash, Scott. "Risk Culture." In *The Risk Society and Beyond*, ed. Barbara Adam, Ulrich Beck, and Jost van Loon. London: Sage, 2000, pp. 47–62.

Latour, Bruno. *Pandora's Hope*. Cambridge, MA: Harvard University Press, 1996.

Lawrence, Mark Atwood. *The Vietnam War: A Concise International History*. Oxford: Oxford University Press, 2008.

Lawrence, Shannon, ed. *Power Surge: The Impacts of Rapid Dam Development in Laos*. Berkeley, CA: International Rivers, 2008.

Lê Bạch Dương, Khuất Thu Hồng and Nguyễn Đức Vinh. *People with Disabilities in Vietnam: Findings from a Social Survey at Dong Nai, Quang Nam, Da Nang and Thai Binh*. Hanoi: Institute for Social Development Studies, 2007.

Lê Cao Đài. *Agent Orange in the Vietnam War: History and Consequences*. Hanoi: Vietnam Red Cross Society, 2000.

_____. *The Central Highlands*. Hanoi: The Gioi Publishers, 2004.

Le Pichon, Jean. "Les chasseurs de sang." *Bulletin des Amis du Vieux Hué* 4 (Oct.–Dec. 1938): 353–409.

Lê Quý Đôn. *Phủ Biên Tạp Lục* [*A Compilation of the Miscellaneous Records when the Southern Border was Pacified*]. Hà Nội: Nhà Xuất Bản Văn Hóa – Thông tin, 2007.

Leahy, Senator Patrick. *Congressional Record*, 16 Sept. 2010, Washington, DC.

Ledgerwood, Judy. "The Cambodian Tuol Sleng Museum of Genocidal Crimes: National Narrative." *Museum Anthropology* 21, 1 (1997): 82–98.

_____. "Buddhist Practices in Rural Kandal Province, 1996 and 2003. An Essay in Honor of May Ebihara." In *People of Virtue. Reconfiguring Religion, Power and Moral Order in Cambodia Today*, ed. Alexandra Kent and David Chandler. Copenhagen: NIAS Press, 2008, pp. 147–68.

Lefebvre, Henri. *La production de l'espace*. Paris: Gallimard, 1974.

Legacies of War. *A Peaceful Legacy Now: Briefing & Discussion on Cluster Bomb Removal and Assistance in Laos: 5 Nov. 2009 Conference Report*. Washington, DC, 2009. Available at http://legaciesofwar.org/files/peaceful-legacy now/A_Peaceful_Legacy_Now_Report.pdf [accessed 28 Oct. 2012].

Lemire, Charles. *Le Laos Annamite. Régions des Tiêm (Ailao), des Moïs et des Pou-Euns (Cam-Môn et Tran-Ninh) restituées en 1893*. Paris: Augustin Challamel, 1894.

LeVine, Peg. *Love and Dread in Cambodia: Weddings, Births and Ritual Harm under the Khmer Rouge*. Singapore: NUS Press, 2010.

Li Tana. *Nguyễn Cochinchina: Southern Vietnam in the Seventeenth and Eighteenth Centuries*. Ithaca, NY: Southeast Asia Program Publications, Southeast Asia Program, Cornell University, 2002.

Locard, Henri. "The Khmer Rouge on Trial: The Court of Law as an Instrument of Understanding and Reconciliation?" Paper presented at the Free University of Berlin, 12 May 2011. Unpublished manuscript.

Lockhart, Bruce. "Pavatsat Lao: Constructing a National History." *South East Asia Research* 14, 3 (2006): 361–86.

Low, Setha. *The Anthropology of Space and Place: Locating Culture*. Malden, MA: Blackwell, 2003.

Lowenthal, David. *The Past is a Foreign Country*. Cambridge: Cambridge University Press, 1985.

Luong, Hy V. *Discursive Practices and Linguistic Meanings: The Vietnamese System of Person Reference*. Amsterdam: John Benjamins, 1990.

_____. *Revolution in the Village: Tradition and Transformation in North Vietnam, 1925–1988*. Honolulu, HI: University of Hawai'i Press, 1992.

Lyttleton, Chris, and Alison Allcock. *Tourism as a Tool for Development*. Vientiane: LNTA, 2002. Available at http://www.mekongtourism.org/site-t3/uploads/media/Lyttleton_Allcock.pdf

Maitre, Henri. *Les Jungles Moï. Mission Henri Maitre (1909–1911) Indochine Sud-Centrale*. Paris: Emile Larose, 1912.

Maitre, Jacques. *The Painful Highlands. Victims of Agent Orange/Dioxin in Vietnam — The Expectations*. Hanoi: Center for Gender, Family, Environment and Development, 2006.

Malarney, Shaun. "The Limits of 'State Functionalism' and the Reconstruction of Funerary Ritual in Contemporary Northern Vietnam." *American Ethnologist* 23, 3 (1996): 540–60.

_____. "'The Fatherland Remembers Your Sacrifice': Commemorating War Dead in North Vietnam." In *The Country of Memory: Remaking the Past in Late Socialist Vietnam*, ed. Hue-Tam Ho Tai. Berkeley, CA: University of California Press, 2001, pp. 46–76.

_____. *Culture, Ritual and Revolution in Vietnam*. London: RoutledgeCurzon, 2002.

_____. "Festivals and the Dynamics of the Exceptional Dead in Northern Vietnam." *Journal of Southeast Asian Studies* 38, 3 (2007): 515–40.

Management Systems International. *Vietnam Disability Situation Assessment and Program Review*. Washington, DC: US Agency for Internatioanal Development, 2005.

Marciel, Scott. "Testimony to the House Committee on Asia Pacific and Global Environment." Washington, DC, May 2008.

_____. "Testimony to the House Committee on Asia Pacific and Global Environment." Washington, DC, May 2009.

Margara, Andreas. *Der Amerikanische Krieg: Erinnerungskultur in Vietnam*. Berlin: regiospectra, 2012.

Margolin, Jean-Louis. "L'Histoire brouillée. Musées et mémoriaux du génocide cambodgien." *Gradhiva* 5 (2007): 84–95.

Marston, Sallie A. "The Social Construction of Scale." *Progress in Human Geography* 24, 2 (2000): 219–42.

Martini, Edwin. *Invisible Enemies: The American War on Vietnam 1975–2000*. Amherst, MA: Univerity of Massachusetts Press, 2007.

_____. *Agent Orange: History, Science, and the Politics of Uncertainty*. Amherst, MA: Univerity of Massachusetts Press, 2012.

Massey, Doreen. *For Space*. London: Sage, 2005.

Merleau-Ponty, Maurice. *Phenomenology of Perception*. London: Routledge, 1962 (orig. publ. Paris: Gallimard, 1945).

Mertz, Elizabeth, and Richard Parmentier, eds. *Semiotic Mediation: Sociocultural and Psychological Perspectives*. Orlando: Academic Press, 1985.

Meskell, Lynn. *Object Worlds in Ancient Egypt: Material Biographies Past and Present*. Oxford and New York: Berg, 2004.

Messerli, Peter *et al.*, eds. *Socio-Economic Atlas of the Lao PDR: An Analysis based on the 2005 Population and Housing Census*. Bern and Vientiane: Swiss National Centre of Competence in Research (NCCR) North-South, University of Bern, 2008.

Michaud, Jean. *Historical Dictionary of the Peoples of the Southeast Asian Massif*. Lanham, MD: The Scarecrow Press, 2006.

Military Assistance Command Vietnam (MACV) Herbicide Operations. "Brother Nam Has Questions About Defoliant Chemicals." National Archives and Records Administration, RG 472/270, Box 6, Folder #20-59, n.d.

Military History Institute of Vietnam. *Victory in Vietnam: The Official History of the People's Army of Vietnam, 1954–1975*. Lawrence, KS: University Press of Kansas, 2002 (orig. publ. 1988).

Miller, Daniel. *Materiality*. Durham, NC: Duke University Press, 2006.

Miller, Edward, and Tuong Vu. "The Vietnam War as a Vietnamese War: Agency and Society in the Study of the Second Indochina War." *Journal of Vietnamese Studies* 4, 3 (2009): 1–16.

Mills, Barbara J., and William H. Walker. *Memory Work: Archeologies of Material Practices*. Santa Fe, NM: SAR Press, 2008.

Mines Advisory Group. "Laos: All Female Clearance Team." Available at http://www.maginternational.org/news/laos-all-female-clearance team/?keywords=xieng+khouang+province [accessed 14 Mar. 2011a].

————. "Laos: Community Liaison at Work." Available at http://www.maginternational.org/news/laos-community-liaison-at-work/ [accessed 14 Mar. 2011b].

Ministry of Information and Culture. *Pavatsat Lao* [*History of Laos*]. Vientiane: State Printing Office, 2000.

Mithouna. *La Route N° 9. Témoignage sur le goulag laotien*. Paris: L'Harmattan, 2001 (in collaboration with André Rosset).

Moyes, Richard. *Tampering: Deliberate Handling and Use of Live Ordnance in Cambodia*. Report prepared for Handicap International, Belgium, Mines Advisory Group (MAG) and Norwegian People's Aid, 2004.

Munn, Nancy. *The Fame of Gawa: A Symbolic Study of Value Transformation in a Massim (Papua New Guinea) Society*. Durham, NC: Duke University Press, 1992.

Nachtwey, James. "The Agent Orange Syndrome." *Vanity Fair*, 24 July 2006, pp. 106–11.

Nakamura, Goro. *Agent Orange in the Vietnam War*. Tokyo: Iwanami Publishers, 2001.

Nakhonkham Bouphanouvong. *Sixteen Years in the Land of Death: Revolution and Reeducation in Laos*. Bangkok: White Lotus, 2003.

Nalty, Bernard C. *The War against Trucks: Aerial Interdiction in Southern Laos, 1968–1972*. Washington, DC: Air Force History and Museums Program United States Air Force, 2005.

National Regulatory Authority for UXO/Mine Action in the Lao PDR. *National Survey of UXO Victims and Accidents Phase 1*. Vientiane, Lao PDR, 2009. Available at http://www.nra.gov.la/resources/Reports%20and%20Studies/NRA %20Phase%201%20VA%20Report%20FINAL.pdf [accessed 18 Oct. 2012].

————. *The Unexploded Ordnance (UXO) Problem and Operational Progress in the Lao PDR, Official Figures*. Vientiane, Lao PDR, 2 June 2010a. Available at http://www.nra.gov.la/resources/Official%20UXO%20Statistic/UXO% 20Sector%20Official%20Statistics%20-%20signed.pdf [accessed 1 Nov. 2012].

————. *Vision into Action, UXO/Mine Action in the Lao PDR and the Convention on Cluster Munitions*. Vientiane, Lao PDR, Nov. 2010b. Unpublished report.

————. *UXO Sector Annual Report 2011*. Vientiane, Lao PDR, 2011a. Available at http://www.nra.gov.la/resources/Annual%20Reports/UXO%20Annual%20 Report%202011_ENG_final.pdf [accessed 19 Oct. 2012].

————. *10-Year-Plan Concept Paper for the CCM Implementation*. Vientiane, Lao PDR, Version 13 June 2011b. Unpublished report.

————. "The Safe Path Forward II." *National Strategic Plan for the UXO Sector in the Lao People's Democratic Republic 2011–2020*. Vientiane, 2012. Available at http://www.nra.gov.la/resources/UXO%20Sector%20Strategy/ SPFII%20%20Eng.pdf [accessed 5 Nov. 2012].

National Statistical Centre. *Results from the Population and Housing Census 2005*. Steering Committee for Census of Population and Housing, Vientiane, 2006.

Navaro-Yashin, Yael. "Affective Spaces, Melancholic Objects: Ruination and the Production of Anthropological Knowledge." *Journal of Royal Anthropological Institute* 15, 1 (2009): 1–18.

Neudorfer, Corinne. *Meet the Akha — Help the Akha? Minderheiten, Entwicklung und Tourismus in Laos*. Bielefeld: Transcript, 2007.

Ngo Anh D., Richard Taylor, Christine L. Roberts, and Nguyễn V. Tuấn. "Association between Agent Orange and Birth Defects: Systemic Review and Meta-Analysis." *International Journal of Epidemiology* 35, 5 (2006): 1220–30.

NGO Forum on Cambodia. "Indigenous Peoples in Cambodia." Phnom Penh: NGO Forum on Cambodia, 2006.

Ngo Xuan Hien. "Scrap Metal Collector Seriously Injured by Explosion." *Mine Action Alert*, Project Renew, 26 June 2010.

Nguyễn Đôn Tự (Major General). "Victims of Agent Orange." *Quân đội Nhân dân*, 2 Feb. 1997.

Nishizaki, Yoshinori. "Suphanburi in the Fast Lane: Roads, Prestige, and Domination in Provincial Thailand." *The Journal of Asian Studies* 67, 2 (2008): 433–67.

Nivat Vongsingh. "Thinking of Xamneua the Land of Heroes." *Muong Lao* 29 (2006): 42–9.

Nok Khamin. "Case Study Nine: Houay Ho Hydropower Project." In *Power Surge: The Impacts of Rapid Dam Development in Laos*, ed. Shannon Lawrence. Berkeley, CA: International Rivers, 2008.

Nok Khamin. "More Trouble for the Nya Heun." *Indigenous Affairs* 4 (2000): 22–9.

Nora, Pierre. *Les lieux de mémoire*, 3 vols. Paris: Gallimard, 1984–1992.

————. "Between Memory and History: Les Lieux de Mémoire." *Representations* 26 (1989): 7–25.

————. *Realms of Memory*, vol. 3. New York: University of Columbia Press, 1998.

Norwegian People's Aid and Project RENEW. *Study on Scrap Metal Collectors/ Dealers: Quang Tri, Quang Binh and Thua Thien Hue. Final Report*. Huế: Center for Social Sciences and Humanities, 2008.

Olick, Jeffrey. "The Ciphered Transits of Collective Memory: Neo-Freudian Impressions." *Social Research* 75, 1 (2008): 1–22.

Osborne, Milton. *River Road to China: The Mekong River Expedition, 1866–73*. Sydney: Allen & Unwin, 2000 (1975).

Palmer, Matthew. *Testimony to the House Committee on Asia Pacific and Global Environment*. Washington, DC, 15 July 2010.

Parmentier, Richard. *The Sacred Remains: Myth, History and Polity in Belau*. Chicago, IL: University of Chicago Press, 1987.

Parsch, Andreas. *Equipment Listing*. Available at http://www.designation-systems. net/usmilav/asetds/u-c.html#_CBU [accessed 7 July 2011].

————. "US Military Aviation Designation Systems, CAU to CXU." 2012. Available at http://www.designation-systems.net/usmilav/asetds/u-c.html#_CBU [accessed 1 Nov. 2012].

Pathet Lao Daily. "50 pi. Phakpasasonpativatlao. 22 mina 1955–1975." Vientiane, 2005.

Patt, Douglas. "Hobby Deminers in Quang Tri Province: Notes from the Field." *Journal of Mine Action* 4, 2 (2000). Available at http://maic.jmu.edu/journal/ 4.2/Notes/hobby.htm [accessed 10 June 2011].

Pelley, Patricia. *Postcolonial Vietnam: New Histories of the National Past*. Durham, NC: Duke University Press, 2002.

Pham Quynh Phuong. *Hero and Deity: Tran Hung Dao and the Resurgence of Popular Religion in Vietnam*. Bangkok: Mekong Press, 2009.

Phetsavanh Sayboualaven. "Hydroelectric Dams and the Forgotten People of the Bolaven Plateau." Unpublished paper, 2004.

Pholsena, Vatthana. "Narrative, Memory and History: Multiple Interpretations of the Lao Past." *Asia Research Institute Working Paper Series* 4, Singapore, 2003.

Bibliography

————. "The Changing Historiographies of Laos: A Focus on the Early Period." *Journal of Southeast Asia Studies* 35, 2 (2004): 235–59.

————. *Post-War Laos: The Politics of Culture, History, and Identity*. Ithaca, NY: Cornell University Press, 2006.

————. "Highlanders on the Ho Chi Minh Trail." *Critical Asian Studies* 40, 3 (2008): 445–74.

————. "Life under Bombing in Southeastern Laos (1964–1973) through the Accounts of Survivors in Sepon." *European Journal of East Asian Studies* 9, 2 (2010): 267–90.

Phong Xuân. "Positive Attitude Vital in Life without Arms Takes." *Vietnam News*, 18 Oct. 2010.

Phoumi Vongvichit. *Khuam songcham khòng sivit hao nai khabuan vivat haeng pavatsat khòng pathet lao [Memory of My Life in the Movement of the History of Laos]*. Vientiane: State Printing Office, 1987.

Phraxayavong, Viliam. *History of Aid to Laos: Motivations and Impacts*. Chiang Mai: Mekong Press, 2009.

Porteous, Douglas J., and Sandra E. Smith. *Domicide: The Global Destruction of Home*. Montreal and Kingston: McGill Queen's University Press, 2001.

Prados, John. *The Blood Road. The Ho Chi Minh Trail and the Vietnam War*. New York: John Wiley & Sons, Inc., 1998.

Project Renew, with Department of Foreign Affairs and Department of Health, Quảng Trị Province. "A Study of Situation of Victims of Land Mines/ Unexploded Ordnance and Knowledge — Attitudes — Practices — Beliefs of People in Quảng Trị Province." Quảng Trị, Việt Nam, 2006.

Prokosch, Eric. *The Technology of Killing*. London: Zed Books, 1995.

Provincial Tourism Office Houaphan. *Tourism Development Strategy 2007–2020*. Sam Neua: PTO Houaohan, 2007.

Quang LB, Hậu DH, Lương HV. "Study on Diseases Related to Herbicide/Dioxin on Vietnamese Veterans." *Human and Environmental Impacts of Herbicides/ Dioxin in Vietnam*. Hanoi: Office 33 — Vietnam Ministry of National Resources and Environment, 2007.

Ricoeur, Paul. *Time and Narrative*, vol. I. Chicago, IL: University of Chicago Press, 1984.

————. "Dialogues with Paul Ricoeur." In *Dialogues with Contemporary Continental Thinkers*, ed. Richard Kearney. Manchester: Manchester University Press, 1986.

————. *Time and Narrative*, vol. III. Chicago, IL: University of Chicago Press, 1990.

————. *Memory, History, Forgetting*. Chicago, IL: University of Chicago Press, 2004.

Rigg, Jonathan. *Living with Transition in Laos: Market Integration in Southeast Asia*. London: Routledge, 2005.

Riseborough, J. "Ord River Flags Lao Bauxite Project Potential." *Mining News*, 16 Nov. 2006.

Roberts, Tyson R., and Ian G. Baird. "Rapid Assessment of Fish and Fisheries for the Xenamnoi Xepian Hydroscheme in Southern Lao PDR." Unpublished report for the Wildlife Conservation Society, Vientiane, Laos, 1995.

Rogers, Paul. *The Secret War in Viengxay.* 2005. Available at http://www.laoscave project.de/Reports/The_Secret_War_Viengxay.pdf [accessed 11 Sept. 2011].

Rose, Nikolas. *Powers of Freedom: Reframing Political Thought.* Cambridge: Cambridge University Press, 1999.

Rose, Sven-Erik. *Ambivalent Sites of Memory in Postwar Germany.* Durham, NC: Duke University Press, 2010.

Roseman, Sharon R. "'How We Built the Road': The Politics of Memory in Rural Galicia." *American Ethnologist* 23, 4 (1996): 83660.

Rust, William J. *Before the Quagmire: American Intervention in Laos, 1954–1961.* Lexington, KY: University of Kentucky Press, 2012.

Sachs, Wolfgang. "One World." In *The Development Dictionary. A Guide to Knowledge as Power,* ed. Wolfgang Sachs. New York and London: Zed Books, 1992.

Sage, Bill. *Reference Paper — Education — Muong Sayasila.* CDA/USAID, Ban Houei Kong, Attopeu, Laos, 1970.

Sakata, Masako (Director). *Agent Orange: A Personal Requiem* [motion picture], 2007.

Sakti, Victoria Kumala. "'Thinking Too Much' — Tracing Local Patterns of Emotional Distress after Mass Violence in Timor-Leste." *The Asia Pacific Journal of Anthropology* (forthcoming).

Saunders, Nicholas J. "Bodies of Metal, Shells of Memory: 'Trench Art' and the Great War Re-Cycled." In *The Material Culture Reader,* ed. Victor Buchli. Oxford and New York: Berg, 2002, pp. 181–206.

_____. *Trench Art: Materialities and Memories of War.* New York: Berg, 2003.

Schecter, Arnold, and John Constable. "Commentary: Agent Orange and Birth Defects in Vietnam." *International Journal of Epidemiology* 35, 5 (2006): 1230–2.

Schecter, Arnold, Marian Pavuk, Rainer Malisch, and John Jake Ryan. "Are Vietnamese Food Exports Contaminated with Dioxin from Agent Orange?" *Journal of Toxicology and Environmental Health* 66, 16 & 19 (2003): 1391–404.

Scheper-Hughes, Nancy, and Philippe Bourgois. *Violence in War and Peace: An Anthology.* Oxford: Blackwell Publishing, 2004.

Schlecker, Markus. "Going Back a Long Way: 'Home Place', Thrift, and Temporal Orientations in Northern Vietnam." *Journal of the Royal Anthropological Institute* 11 (2005): 509–26.

_____. *Bones and the Emergent Welfare State in Late Socialist Vietnam* [provisional title]. Unpublished monograph, currently under review.

Schofield, John, William Gray Johnson, and Colleen M. Beck, eds. *Matériel Culture: The Archaeology of Twentieth-Century Conflict.* London and New York: Routledge, 2002.

Schramm, Katharina. "Landscapes of Violence: Memory and Sacred Space." *History and Memory* 23, 1 (2011): 5–22.

Schwenkel, Christina. "Recombinant History: Transnational Practices of Memory and Knowledge Production in Contemporary Vietnam." *Cultural Anthropology* 21, 1 (2006): 3–30.

————. *The American War in Contemporary Vietnam: Transnational Remembrance and Representation*. Bloomington, IN: Indiana University Press, 2009.

Scott, James C. *Weapons of the Weak: Everyday Forms of Peasant Resistance*. New Haven: Yale University Press, 1985.

————. *The Art of Not Being Governed: An Anarchist History of Upland Southeast Asia*. New Haven, CT: Yale University Press, 2009.

Sennett Richard. *The Craftsman*. London: Penguin Books, 2008.

Shaw, Rosalind. *Memories of the Slave Trade: Ritual and the Historical Imagination in Sierra Leone*. Chicago, IL: University of Chicago Press, 2002.

Shawcross, William. *Sideshow: Nixon, Kissinger and the Destruction of Cambodia*. New York: Simon and Schuster, 1979.

Shultz, Connie. *Unfinished Business: Suffering and Sickness in the Endless Wake of Agent Orange*, 30 Jan. 2010. Available at http://www.cleveland.com/agentorange/index.ssf/2011/01/unfinished_business_suffering.html [accessed 16 May 2011].

Sion, Brigitte. "Conflicting Sites of Memory in Post-Genocide Cambodia." *Humanity* 2, 1 (2011): 1–21.

Sonh, C.H. Boehringer. "Re: Chlorine Acnt. Illustration of Trichlorphenol." *Letter to Dow Chemical, Midland MI*, 2 Nov. 1957.

Sontag, Susan. *Regarding the Pain of Others*. New York: Farrar Straus & Giroux, 2003.

Sparkes, Stephen. *TA for Capacity-Building for Environment and Social Management in Energy and Transport. Case Study 2: Houay Ho Hydropower Project (TAR Lao 3501)*. Vientiane: Asian Development Bank, 2000.

Sperfeldt, Christoph. "Cambodian Civil Society and the Khmer Rouge Tribunal." *The International Journal of Transitional Justice* 6 (2012): 149–60.

Steinberg, Michael K., and Matthew J. Taylor. "Public Memory and Political Power in Guatemala's Postconflict Landscape." *Geographical Review* 93, 4 (2003): 449–68.

Stellman, Jeanne Mager *et al.* "The Extent and Patterns of Usage of Agent Orange and Other Herbicides in Vietnam." *Nature* 422 (2003): 686–7.

Stewart, Pamela J., and Andrew Strathern, eds. *Landscape, Memory and History*. London: Pluto, 2003.

Stewart, Susan. *On Longing: Narratives of the Miniature, the Gigantic, the Souvenir, the Collection*. Durham, NC: Duke University Press, 1993.

Stoler, Ann Laura. "Imperial Debris: Reflections on Ruins and Ruination." *Cultural Anthropology* 23, 2 (2008): 191–219.

Strathern, Marylin. *Property, Substance and Effect: Anthropological Essays on Persons and Things*. London: Athlone Press, 1999.

Stuart-Fox, Martin. *A History of Laos*. Cambridge: Cambridge University Press, 1997.

Tappe, Oliver. *Geschichte, Nationsbildung und Legitimationspolitik in Laos*. Berlin: Lit, 2008.

————. "The Escape from Phonkheng Prison — Revolutionary Historiography in the Lao PDR." In *Multidisciplinary Perspectives on Lao Studies*, ed. Karen L. Adams and Thomas J. Hudak. Tempe, AZ: Southeast Asia Council, Arizona State University, 2010, pp. 237–54.

————. "From Revolutionary Heroism to Cultural Heritage: Museums, Memory and Representation in Laos." *Nations and Nationalism* 17, 3 (2011a): 604–26.

————. "Memory, Tourism, and Development: Changing Sociocultural Configurations and Upland-Lowland Relations in Houaphan Province, Lao PDR." *SOJOURN: Journal of Social Issues in Southeast Asia* 26, 2 (2011b): 174–95.

Tatum, James. "Memorials of the America War in Vietnam." *Critical Inquiry* 22, 4 (1996): 634–78.

Taylor, Philip. *Goddess on the Rise: Pilgrimage and Popular Religion in Vietnam*. Honolulu, HI: University of Hawai'i Press, 2004.

Terdiman, Richard. *Present Past: Modernity and the Memory Crisis*. Ithaca, NY: Cornell University Press, 1993.

Thomas, Philip. "The River, the Road, and the Rural-Urban Divide: A Postcolonial Moral Geography from Southeast Madagascar." *American Ethnologist* 29, 2 (2002): 366–91.

Till, Karen E. "Places of Memory." In *A Companion to Political Geography*, ed. John Agnew, Katharyne Mitchell, and Gerard Toal. Oxford and Malden, MA: Blackwell, 2003, pp. 289–301.

Todorov, Tzvetan. "Communist Camps and their Aftermath." *Representations* 49 (1995): 120–32.

Tonkin, Elizabeth. *Narrating the Past. The Construction of Oral History*. Cambridge: Cambridge University Press, 1992.

Tractebel. "Tractebel Buys into Laos Hydro Project." Tractebel Press Release, Brussels, 13 Sept. 2001.

Tran Duc Sang. "The Trading Road between the Katu and the Kinh (Case Study in Thuong Long Commune, Nam Dong District, Thua Thien Hué)." *Social Sciences* 6 (2004): 71–87.

Tran Hong Chi. "Clear Path International Beneficiaries in Vietnam Become Deminers Thanks to Mines Advisory Group." Blog post, 26 Feb. 2009. Available at http://clearpathinternational.org/cpiblog/archives/000983.php [accessed 10 June 2011].

Trần Văn Thủy. *Letter to American Friends*, 9 Nov. 2004. Available at http://www.ffrd.org/AO/Thuy%27s%20letter%20to%20benefit.htm [accessed 1 Feb. 2013].

Trapp, W.B. *Subject: Trichlorophenol Research*. Midland, MI, USA, *Letter to L.C. Chamberlain, Dow Chemical, Midland MI*, 26 Jan. 1965.

Tréglodé (de), Benoît. *Héros et révolution au Viêt Nam, 1948–1964*. Paris: L'Harmattan, 2001.

Trinh, John (Director). *Agent Orange: Thirty Years Later* [motion picture], 2009.

Truong Huyen Chi. "Changing Processes of Social Reproduction in the Northern Vietnamese Countryside: An Ethnographic Study of Dong Vang Village." PhD thesis, University of Toronto, 2001.

Tuan, Yi-Fu. *Space and Place: The Perspective of Experience*. Minneapolis, MN: University of Minnesota Press, 1977.

Tunbridge, John E., and Gregory J. Ashworth. *Dissonant Heritage: The Management of the Past as a Resource in Conflict*. Chichester: Wiley, 1996.

Tuong Vu. "From Cheering to Volunteering: Vietnamese Communists and the Arrival of the Cold War 1940–1951." In *Connecting Histories: The Cold War and Decolonization in Asia (1945–1962)*, ed. Christopher Goscha and Christian Ostermann. Stanford, CA: Stanford University Press, 2009, pp. 172–204.

Turkel, William J. *The Archive of Place: Unearthing the Pasts of the Chilcotin Plateau*. Vancouver: UBC Press, 2007.

Ty, Kanara. "Cambodian Americans: Religion." In *Encyclopedia of Asian American Folklore and Folklife*, ed. Jonathan X. Lee and Kathleen M. Nadeuau. Santa Barbara, Denver and Oxford: ABC Clio, 2011, pp. 209–14.

Tyner, James A. *Military Legacies: A World Made by War*. New York: Routledge, 2010.

Ullberg, Susann. "Disaster Memoryscapes. How Social Relations Shape Community Remembering of Catastrophe." *Anthropology News*, Oct. 2010. Available at http://www.aaanet.org/publications/upload/51-7-Susann-Ullberg-In-Focus.pdf [accessed 10 Apr. 2011].

UNDP. *Crisis Prevention and Recovery: Examples of the Impact of Cluster Munitions on Civilians*, 28 Nov. 2007. Available at http://www.undp.org/cpr/whats_new/cluster_munitions_civilians.shtml [accessed 6 June 2011].

————. *Human Development Index 2011*. Available at http://hdr.undp.org/en/media/HDR_2011_EN_Table1.pdf [accessed 14 Sept. 2012].

UNESCO. *Lao Unesco Programme for "Safeguarding the Plain of Jars."* Bangkok, 1998. Available at http://www.unescobkk.org/culture/heritage/world-heritage-and-immovable-heritage/the-plain-of-jars-important-but-imperiled/ [accessed 16 Mar. 2011].

UNICEF. *Research Report on Children with Disabiltiies and their Families in Đà Nẵng*. Hanoi: UNICEF, 2009.

United States Department of State, Office of Weapons Removal and Abatement, *To Walk the Earth in Safety*. Washington, DC, July 2010. Available at http://www.state.gov/documents/organization/145116.pdf [accessed 28 Oct. 2012].

United States Department of State, US Embassy Laos. *Fact Sheet: Saving Lives in Laos*. Vientiane, Lao PDR, 9 Nov. 2010. Available at http://www.state.gov/r/pa/prs/ps/2010/11/150696.htm [accessed 28 Oct. 2012].

United States Senate Congressional Record. Washington, DC: US Government Printing Office, 14 May 1975, p. 14266.

US Department of State. "Former President Nixon's Message to Prime Minister Pham Van Dong." *Department Of State Bulletin*, 27 June 1977.

————. *Remarks by Secretary Clinton, Vietnam Foreign Minister Khiem*, 30 Oct. 2010. Available at http://www.america.gov/st/texttrans-english/2010/October/20101031105353su0.604421.html&distid=ucs#ixzz1413KqPVs [accessed 16 May 2011].

US Department of State Bulletin. "Agreement on Ending the War and Restoring Peace in Vietnam (Paris, 27 Jan. 1973)." Volume LCVIII (2 Feb. 1973): 169–88.

US Department of Veterans Affairs. *Agent Orange: Diseases Associated with Agent Orange Exposure*, 4 Nov. 2010. Available at http://www.publichealth.va.gov/exposures/agentorange/diseases.asp [accessed 16 May 2011].

————. *Agent Orange: Birth Defects in Children of Women Vietnam Veterans*, 12 Nov. 2010. Available at http://www.publichealth.va.gov/exposures/agentorange/conditions/birth_defects.asp [accessed 16 May 2011].

US Embassy, Hanoi. "Agent Orange: Will US Compensate Victims," 10 June 1997. Hanoi, Vietnam: Declassified memo obtained via FOAI request of 15 Apr. 2009 ID 200805769.

————. "Joint Research on Health/Environmental Effects of Agent Orange/Dioxin — An Assessment of Vietnamese Attitudes." Unclassified memo, 16 Feb. 2003.

US House of Representatives Committee on Foreign Affairs. *Agent Orange in Vietnam: Recent Developments in Remediation*. Washington, DC: US Government Printing Office, 15 July 2010.

US Senate Appropriations Committee. Making Emergency Supplemental Appropriations for the Fiscal Year Ending Sept. 30, 2007, and for Other Purposes, 22 Mar. 2007. Report 110-037. Available at http://www.gpo.gov/fdsys/pkg/CRPT-110srpt37/pdf/CRPT-110srpt37.pdf.

————. Department of State, Foreign Operations and Related programs Appropriations Bill 2011, 29 July 2010. Report 111-237. Available at http://www.gpo.gov/fdsys/pkg/CRPT-111srpt237/pdf/CRPT-111srpt237.pdf.

————. Department of State, Foreign Operations and Related programs Appropriations Bill 2012, 22 Sept. 2011. Report 112-85. Available at http://www.gpo.gov/fdsys/pkg/CRPT-112srpt85/pdf/CRPT-112srpt85.pdf.

US State Court of Appeals. "Agent Orange Product Liability Litigation," 05-1760-cv, 17 Apr. 2006.

UXO Lao. *National Unexploded Ordnance Programme 2009 Annual Report*. Vientiane, Lao PDR, 2010. Available at http://www.uxolao.org/Download%20files/2009%20UXO%20LAO%20Annual%20Report%20-%2024Aug10.pdf [accessed 29 Oct. 2012].

Van de Put, Willem A.C.M, and Maurice Eisenbruch. "The Cambodian Experience." In *Trauma, War and Violence: Public Mental Health in Socio-Cultural Context*, ed. De Jong, Joop. New York: Kluwer, 2002, pp. 93–156.

Van Staaveren, Jacob. *Interdiction in Southern Laos: 1960–1968*. Washington, DC: Center for Air Force History, 1993.

Vann Nath. *A Cambodian Prison Portrait: One Year in the Khmer Rouge's S-21*. Bangkok: White Lotus, 1998.

Vannak, Huy, *Bou Meng. A Survivor from Khmer Rouge Prison S-21. Justice for the Future Not Just for the Victims*. Phnom Penh: Documentation Center of Cambodia, 2010.

Vaughn, Michael. "Ord River Awash with Lao Bauxite." *Mining News*, 28 Feb. 2006.

Verdery, Katherine. *The Political Lives of Dead Bodies: Reburial and Postsocialist Change*. New York: University of Columbia Press, 1999.

Vickery, Michael. *Cambodia 1975–1982*. Boston: South End Press, 1984.

Vietnam Association of Victims of Agent Orange/Dioxin. *To the American People*. Hanoi, Aug. 2004. Available at http://www.ffrd.org/Lawsuit/VAVAletter.htm

Vietnam Association for Victims of Agent Orange/Dioxin *et al.* v. Dow Chemical *et al.*, 04 CV 400, US District Court for the Eastern District of New York, 2004.

Vietnam Museum of Ethnology. *Highway no. 9: Opportunities and Challenges*. Hanoi: Vietnam Museum of Ethnology, 2009.

Vietnam News Service. "AO Victim Tutors Children of Poor." *Vietnam News*, 17 May 2011.

VietNamNetBridge. *12.5 Million Signatures for AO/Dioxin Victims*, 27 Nov. 2008. Available at http://www.vietnamnews.biz/125-million-signatures-for-AOdioxin-victims_832.html [accessed 16 May 2011].

Vietnam Red Cross. *Agent Orange Victims Fund*. Hanoi: Vietnam Red Cross, n.d.

Võ Minh Tuấn, Huỳnh Thị Thu Thuỷ, Nguyễn Thị Ngọc Phượng. "The Association between Exposure of AO/Dioxin and Situation of Congenital Deformities." Vietnam-United States Scientific Conference on Human Health and the Environmental Effects of Agent Orange/Dioxin, Hanoi, 3–6 Mar. 2002.

Voice of Vietnam News. "More Evidence for Dioxin Victims' Lawsuit against US," 5 May 2011. Available at http://english.vietnamnet.vn/en/society/7923/more-evidence-for-dioxin-victims—lawsuit-against-us.html [accessed 19 May 2011].

Wall, Barbara. *Les Nya Non, Etude Ethnographique d'une Population du Plateau des Bolovens (Sud-Laos)*. Vientiane: Editions Vithagna, 1975.

Wantanee Suntikul, Thomas Bauer, and Haiyan Song. "Pro-Poor Tourism Development in Viengxay, Laos: Current State and Future Prospects." *Asia Pacific Journal of Tourism Research* 14, 2 (2009): 153–68.

Waugh, Charles., and Huy Liên. *Family of Fallen Leaves: Stories of Agent Orange by Vietnamese Writers*. Athens, GA: The University of Georgia Press, 2010.

Weber, Eugen. *Peasants into Frenchmen. The Modernization of Rural France, 1870–1914*. Stanford, CA: Stanford University Press, 1976.

Weldon, Charles. *Tragedy in Paradise*. Bangkok: Asia Books, 1999.

Westing, Arthur H. *Herbicides in War: The Long-Term Ecological and Human Consequencecs*. London and Philadelphia: Taylor and Francis, 1984.

_____. "Assault on the Environment." In *Long Term Consequences of the Vietnam War: Ecosytems*. Stockholm: Foreningen Levande Framtid, 2002, pp. 2–4.

White, Geoffrey. "Emotional Remembering: The Pragmatics of National Memory." *Ethos* 27, 4 (2000): 505–29.

_____. "National Subjects: September 11 and Pearl Harbor." *American Ethnologist* 31, 3 (2004): 293–310.

_____. "Memory Moments." *Ethos* 34, 2 (2006): 325–41.

White House of President George W. Bush. *Bush Statement*, 17 Nov. 2006. Available at http://www.warlegacies.org: http://www.warlegacies.org/Bush.pdf [accessed 16 May 2011].

Wildlife Conservation Society. *Results of a Survey of Terrestrial Wildlife in the Area to be Affected by the Proposed Xe Nam Noy-Xe Pian Hydroelectric Project*. Vientiane, 1995.

Williams, Paul. "Witnessing Genocide, Vigilance and Remembrance at Tuol Sleng and Choeung Ek." *Holocaust and Genocide Studies* 18, 2 (2004): 234–54.

Williams, Raymond. *The Country and the City*. London: Chatto and Windus, 1985.

Winter, Jay M. "Thinking about Silence." In *Shadows of War: A Social History of Silence in the Twentieth Century*, ed. Efrat Ben-Ze'ev, Ruth Ginio, and Jay Winter. Cambridge: Cambridge University Press, 2010, pp. 3–31.

Winter, Jay M. *Sites of Memory, Sites of Mourning: The Great War in European Cultural History*. Cambridge: Cambridge University Press, 2003.

World Food Program. *Country Overview of Laos*. Available at http://www.wfp.org/countries/lao-pdr/overview [accessed 30 Oct. 2011].

Wyatt, Andrew B. "Infrastructure Development and BOOT in Laos and Vietnam: A Case Study of Collective Action and Risk in Transitional Developing Economies." PhD thesis, Division of Geography, School of Geosciences, University of Sydney, Sydney, 2004.

Young, Alvin L. *The History, Use, Disposition and Environmental Fate of Agent Orange*. New York: Springer, 2009.

Young, James E. *The Texture of Memory: Holocaust Memorials and Meaning*. New Haven, CT: Yale University Press, 1993.

Young, Marilyn B., John J. Fitzgerald, and A. Tom Grunfeld, eds. *The Vietnam War: A History in Documents*. New York: Oxford University Press, 2002.

Young, Marilyn B. *The Vietnam Wars 1945–1990*. New York: HarperPerennial, 1991.

Zaloom, Caitlin. "The Productive Life of Risk." *Cultural Anthropology* 19, 3 (2004): 365–91.

Zierler, David. *The Invention of Ecocide*. Athens, GA: Univerity of Georgia Press, 2011.

Zinke, Paul. *The Effects of Herbicides in South Vietnam*. Washington: National Academy of Sciences, 1974.

Zucker, Eve. "Transcending Time and Terror: The Re-Emergence of Bon Dalien after Pol Pot and Thirty Years of Civil War." *Journal of Southeast Asian Studies* 37, 3 (2006): 527–46.

CONTRIBUTORS

Ian G. Baird is an assistant professor in the Department of Geography, at the University of Wisconsin-Madison. A Canadian presently residing in Madison, he lived, worked and conducted research in Laos, Thailand and Cambodia for most of the time between 1986 and 2010. He is the author of various articles, book chapters and monographs related to upland peoples (and their relations with lowlanders) in mainland Southeast Asia.

Sina Emde holds a PhD in anthropology from the Australian National University and is currently a research fellow at the Cluster of Excellence "Languages of Emotion" and the Institute for Cultural and Social Anthropology at the Free University Berlin. Her research project focuses on emotion, memory, and violence in Cambodia.

Susan Hammond is the Founder and Executive Director of the War Legacies Project, a non-governmental organization based in Vermont that focuses on the long-term impacts of war to develop a fuller understanding of the costs of war, foster public dialogue about the impacts of war and conduct programs that help mitigate the impacts of war at home and abroad. Prior to founding the War Legacies Project, Susan worked as Deputy Director for the Fund for Reconciliation and Development for nine years where she lived and worked in Cambodia, Laos, Vietnam, and New York. She received her MA in International Education from New York University.

Vatthana Pholsena (editor) is a research fellow at the French National Center for Scientific Research (CNRS). Currently based in Singapore, she is also the representative for the Institute of Research on Contemporary Southeast Asia (IRASEC), and affiliated with the Department of Southeast Asian Studies at the National University of Singapore. She is the author of *Post-War Laos: The Politics of Culture, History and Identity* (ISEAS and Cornell University Press, 2006) and *Laos: Un pays en mutation* (Éditions Belin-La documentation Française, 2011).

Elaine Russell graduated with a BA in history from the University of California Davis and obtained an MA in economics at California State

University Sacramento. She worked as an environmental and energy consultant for many years before turning to writing full-time. She is an advisor to and former board member of Legacies of War, a US-based, non-profit which advocates for greater funding to clear unexploded ordnance in Laos. With Legacies of War Executive Director, Channapha Khamvongsa, she co-authored "Legacies of War: Cluster Bombs in Laos" published in *Critical Asian Studies* (June 2009). She is also the author of several novels, such as *Across the Mekong River*, and the Martin McMillan middle-grade adventure series.

Markus Schlecker is an affiliated researcher at the Max Planck Institute for Social Anthropology, Halle, Germany. He has written on Vietnamese imaginations of the social, paranormal experience, and the role of context in the Human Sciences. He is currently completing a monograph on burial practices in contemporary Vietnam.

Christina Schwenkel is an associate professor of anthropology at the University of California, Riverside, USA. She is the author of *The American War in Contemporary Vietnam: Transnational Remembrance and Representation* (Indiana University Press, 2009). Her work on social suffering and the transnational politics of memory in Vietnamese museums, media, and sites of trauma tourism has appeared in *Cultural Anthropology*, *Journal of Vietnamese Studies*, and *American Anthropologist*. Her current research examines urban aesthetics and socialist humanitarian ideologies underlying postwar reconstruction of Vietnamese cities.

Oliver Tappe (editor) is a research fellow at the Max Planck Institute for Social Anthropology in Halle, Germany. He published his PhD thesis, *"Geschichte, Nationsbildung und Legitimationspolitik in Laos"* [History, Nation-Building and Politics of Legitimacy in Laos], on Lao historiography and iconography in 2008. Parts of this research have appeared in the journals *Nations and Nationalism*, *Asian Studies Review*, and *Journal of Lao Studies*. His current research interests include the history of the upland frontier region of Laos and Vietnam, interethnic dynamics, and (colonial) state-minorities relations.

Krisna Uk is the Director of the Center for Khmer Studies in Cambodia. She received her PhD in social anthropology at Cambridge University. Her current research interests focus on the survival strategies of post-conflict communities in anti-personnel landmine and unexploded ordnance affected regions, the material culture derived from war, the economics of bomb salvaging, and the concept of risk.

INDEX